The State Must Be Our Master of Fire

The State Must Be Our Master of Fire

*How Peasants Craft
Culturally Sustainable
Development in Senegal*

DENNIS C. GALVAN

University of California Press

BERKELEY   LOS ANGELES   LONDON

University of California Press
Berkeley and Los Angeles, California
University of California Press, Ltd.

London, England

Library of Congress Cataloging-in-Publication Data

Galvan, Dennis Charles.

The state must be our master of fire : how peasants craft culturally
sustainable development in Senegal / Dennis C. Galvan.

    p. cm.

Includes bibliographical references and index.

   ISBN 0-520-22778-6 (cloth : alk. paper)—ISBN 0-520-23591-6
(pbk. : alk. paper)

   1. Land tenure—Senegal—Sine-Saloum—History.   2. Serer
(African people)—Government relations.   3. Sine-Saloum
(Senegal)—Social conditions.   4. Sine-Saloum (Senegal)—
Economic conditions.   5. Acculturation—Senegal—Case studies.
I. Title.

HD1019.Z8 S55   2004

333.3'089'96321—dc21   2003011739

Manufactured in the United States of America

13   12   11   10   09   08   07   06   05

10 9 8 7 6 5 4 3 2 1

The paper used in this publication meets the minimum requirements
of ANSI/NISO Z39.48-1992 (R 1997) *(Permanence of Paper).* ∞

To
Kirst, Ben, and Sam
and
O Pog Mafan

Contents

Illustrations

Tables

Acknowledgments

This project would not have been possible without the cooperation and support of colleagues, institutions, and friends, both in Senegal and the United States, to whom I express my sincere thanks. Generous grants from the National Science Foundation, the Social Science Research Council, and the Andrew and Mary Rocca Foundation of the Institute for International Studies at the University of California, Berkeley, supported me before, during and after my fieldwork in Senegal. I am grateful for their support.

I am deeply appreciative of Robert Price, David Leonard, and Ira Lapidus, who saw me through the initial iteration of this project with a combination of keen insight, gentle encouragement, flexibility when I reached a crossroads, and unwavering support when I made wrong turns. I benefited enormously from their guidance, and I hope that this text reflects some of the inspiration and ideas they have shared with me over the years. I also thank Robert Kagan, Giuseppe Di Palma, Ruth Collier, and Pierre Ostiguy for careful reading and insightful comments as this project unfolded. While in Senegal, I drew tremendous benefit from the advice and guidance of Charles Becker, Saliou Mbaye, André Lericollais, and Jean-Marc Gastellu, whose insightful suggestions helped me rework my project to make the most of what my research showed.

While inspiration for this project grew from a variety of sources, I am particularly indebted to Richard Roberts and Larry Diamond, at whose encouragement I first made my way to Africa, and whose advice and insights continue to shape my work. I also express my appreciation for the late Carl Rosberg, who took me under his wing when I first came to Berkeley and shared his extraordinary perspective, marvelous wit, and gentle hospitality through every step of my graduate work.

In the course of reworking and revising my manuscript, I was indeed fortunate to find myself in the interlocking intellectual communities of the University of Florida's African Studies Center and Political Science Department. That nourishing environment helped me broaden my sense of the meaning and significance of my findings. I am especially grateful to Goran Hyden, Michael Chege, Philip Williams, Larry Dodd, and Leslie Paul Thiele for their support, advice, and inspiration. In the final days of preparing this volume, I benefited enormously from the insights and reactions of new colleagues at the University of Oregon's International Studies Program and Political Science Department.

I owe a tremendous debt of gratitude to those whose cooperation, hospitality, and goodwill were absolutely indispensable for this project and to whom it is in part dedicated, the people of Njafaj, in the Siin region of Senegal. They graciously welcomed me into their homes, housed me, fed me, looked after me, and endured my endless, sometimes entirely too prying, questions. I again offer them my sincere thanks for their unbounded *teranga*, and express my apologies for questions and research distractions which may, on the surface, have seemed disconnected from the immediacy of their daily life struggles. I hope that the pages which follow accurately represent their opinions and beliefs and may prove useful as they chart their own course for the development of their communities.

In the Njafaj region, I am especially grateful to the people of the village of Tukar, my home on several occasions since 1988. The Association des Paysans de Tukar smoothed my many arrivals, facilitated my work, and integrated me in the community. Jean-Baptiste Faye, Saliou Diouf, Samba Ndour, Ousmane Thiao, Al-Hassan Thiao, Gnilane Ndiaye, Omar Sene, Matar Gning, Sengane Gueye, Sombel Diouf, and so many others made me a part of their families and brought me much closer to what I was trying to study than I realized at the time. I add a very special and profound thanks to three sons of Tukar in particular: Wagaan Faay, Saliou Diouf, and Samba Ndour, whose tireless efforts as research assistants made my project actually work, and whose support as friends has so often and so thoroughly sustained me.

Finally, I must express personal thanks to Silvia Galvan for teaching me to fear neither creativity nor limits; to Ramon Galvan for modeling the intellectual for me and for sitting beside me around a bowl of *ceb u jen;* to Jean-Baptiste Faye for friendship and for wisdom about the culture of the Siin, about Senegal, the West, and me, and for the mixing of them all; to Ernie and Bob for that combination of intellectual camaraderie, cajoling, rescuing, and strategic distracting you can only expect from brothers and close friends; and most of all to Kirst, anchor, rudder, sextant, and shipmate all at once, for essential acts of ingenuity, patience, steadfastness, and joy; and of course, to Ben and Sam, who offer daily seminars in self-awareness, balance, and sustainable inspiration.

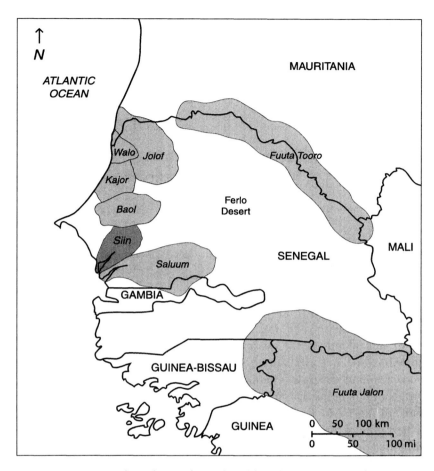

Map 1. Approximate boundaries of precolonial kingdoms of Senegambia.

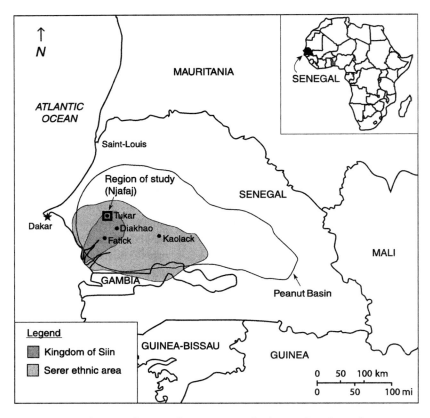

Map 2. Area of Serer ethnic predominance, in the former kingdom of Siin.

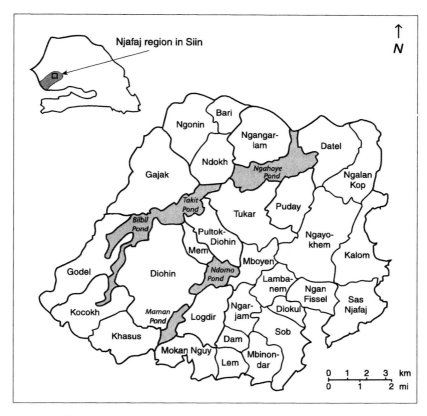

Map 3. Villages of the Njafaj subzone.

1 · "Buying Rope Is a Young Man's Job"

Transformations of Culture and Institutions

In the Siin region of Senegal, it's sometimes said that "buying rope is a young man's job." The logic of the free market, by contrast, tells us that anyone, male or female, sixteen or sixty years old, should be able to go and buy rope. After all, standardization—particularly standardization of people in all their uniqueness into consumers, workers, homogeneous interchangeable units—is a basic element of marketization and modernization. Yet to many Serer (the people of the Siin), it isn't right for just *anybody* to go buy rope, because rope has long been something that a young man should be able to *make*. The ability to weave baobab bark into cord was once a sign that a young man was mature enough to marry and assume responsibility as head of a household. The need to arrive at such a sense of dignity remains, but thanks to readily available cheap manufactured rope, the material basis, the practices and forms of production associated with that sense of dignity, no longer exist. As a result, an ordinary, everyday economic task has been invested with an odd solemnity. A residual meaning has worked its way into a generic economic activity, distorting the "normal" functioning of market exchange. Market exchange has become a syncretic, or blended, institution: buying rope is now a young man's job.

Knowing who is supposed to buy rope in a few Sahelian villages may not contribute much to our understanding of social change and development in sub-Saharan Africa. But figuring out the patterns of transformation in this simple story—the ongoing process by which subordinate people unexpectedly inscribe local meanings onto imposed institutions—will prove to be of considerable consequence, revealing much about the functioning of state, market, and other vectors of modernity in post-colonial Africa.

The logic of "buying rope" is the underlying logic of syncretic response to marketization, development, and "modernity" in the corners of rural Senegal of interest here. Consider another more political and visual example. In the village of Tukar, where much of the research for this project took place, a fertility celebration called Raan occurs every year, just before planting, eight days after the new moon in April. During Raan, members of the family of the master of fire, former custodians of fields, forests, and soil fertility, assemble the community and confront the powers that rule the Siin. In the old days, before independence, Raan let the master of fire and his companions engage in ritual acts of role reversal designed to humiliate the Mandé-descended kings of Siin. Today, representatives of the modern postcolonial state sit where the Mandé kings once did, and they receive, as in the cover photo, admonitions, complaints, and sometimes ridicule at the hands of customary elites associated with the old masters of fire (some of whom are depicted during the 1993 Raan). This is a moment to make the "king," and now the state, listen, to vent frustration at its alien rules and arbitrary behavior. Now that masters of fire are powerless, replaced by state agencies, Raan is a time to remind government to get serious about respecting and upholding "traditional" land tenure and resource management systems. This is the moment to repeat a plaintive but not entirely hopeless local formula for institutional syncretism: "The state must be our master of fire."

Especially in an era of increasing disenchantment with democratic retrenchment, market irregularities, and weak civil societies, such processes of rereading new institutions in terms of local meaning become particularly important. They allow us to rethink development failure and institutional breakdown as processes by which ordinary people reappropriate both the subjectively meaningful content of "traditional society" and the objectively imperative structures of Western-brand modernity.

This book is a case study in local adaptation of imposed political and economic institutions. It focuses on the making of syncretic institutions, institutions that result from a deliberate and coherent recombination of administrative forms, rules, habits, or norms from more than one sociocultural origin. Syncretic institutions can make development, and modernity itself, culturally sustainable. Syncretic institutions render the organizational and behavioral vectors of modernity—private property, market exchange, the legal order, bureaucracy, democracy—familiar, locally meaningful, even legitimate. The absence of syncretism, by contrast, creates debilitating disjuncture: elites promote various developmental versions of progressive change that ordinary people reject as alien, arbitrary, coercive impositions. This book considers institutional syncretism in the Siin region of west-central Senegal, where ordinary farmers have responded ingeniously to the imposition of new economic and political institutions that manage land, the most important form of capital in this agricultural society. It follows the Serer of Siin as they reconfigure three externally imposed institutions in terms of their idealized memories of precolonial institutions, culture, and social relations.[1]

First, in response to new models of property and exchange associated with commodification and Islamicization in the 1930s, Serer farmers did not create a market in land, as colonial officials hoped. Instead they developed an innovative, syncretic kind of land-pawning system that permitted the exchange of fields for cash but also guaranteed the customary inalienability of land. Second, most Serer rejected an idealistic 1960s land reform policy designed to "restore" African socialist egalitarianism, in part because the reform ignored the products of decades of Serer institutional syncretism. The well-intentioned land reform widened the gap between state and society, producing a chaotic, agriculturally unproductive, and environmentally destructive dualistic tenure system.

Finally, in the 1970s, Serer farmers initially embraced a promise of syncretism offered by new, democratically elected rural councils. Following the logic of syncretic adaptation, local people, as elected rural councilors, tried to recombine the new national land-tenure regime with remembered practices of legitimate resource management (the state must and might indeed be the master of fire). But state officials, wary of democratic decentralization, subordinated the rural councils to the centralized administration. As a result, most Serer came to think of the rural councils as new manifestations of a much despised, alien, and arbitrary preindependence local monarchy (the state is decidedly not the master of fire). Voluntary compliance with the councils' judgments is now laughable, no one legitimately manages land and natural resources, soil has eroded, yields have plummeted, and the rural exodus has accelerated.

Together, these accounts of syncretism direct attention to popular memories of "traditional" institutions and culture as subordinate peoples in postcolonial settings avoid, circumvent, and ultimately transform the organizations and practices behind civilizing missions, modernization campaigns, and development schemes.[2] Peoples like the Serer of Siin adapt the institutions of Western liberal-capitalist modernity so that they make sense in terms of idealized yet changing memories of precolonial society and culture. As a result, these institutions turn out rather like the rope stall in the village marketplace, a bit like state officials at *Raan*: although we might expect them to function according to standard "universal" principles, instead we find they have been subtly adapted to conform to other systems of meaning.

Although colonialism (and in the Sahel, the simultaneous expansion of Islam) wiped out, radically altered, or destabilized many local institutions, the shards of these institutions lie about everywhere. They are still useful in discrete contexts for organizing social relations and resource allocation. Likewise, the institutions that have been used to promote various notions of "progressive" modernity—the bureaucratic state, legal order, representative democracy, the free market—have been only partially established in many postcolonial settings. They too are like broken pieces, shards of modernity, usable in fragmentary ways to mobilize political groups, pattern relations, organize power, and inspire sacrifice.

Local actors in the rural postcolonial world may lack the means to systemically craft national-scale institutions from these fragments. But they have the means to fashion discrete, ingenious recombinations of institutional elements that offer a sense of continuity with a historic past, as well as a tool for addressing the practical demands of making a living in a liberal capitalist order. Institutional syncretism is the work of these *bricoleurs*, who gather the detritus of locally embedded and exogenously derived social orders to fashion creative recombinations. These innovative fusions are themselves *essais*—drafts, sketches of an alternative, and probably more sustainable, local modernity in the making.

The fragments of "traditional" society, although situated in a specific historical context, are nevertheless subject to ongoing contestation and reinvention. As the analysis of survey data in chapter 3 suggests, historical memories of authentic tradition vary along class, gender, caste, religious, and other lines. Syncretism thus amounts to a process of investing new institutional forms with local meaning while simultaneously struggling to claim the semantic high ground of "traditional culture." When a particular segment or group in society (elder male Muslims, for example) determines hegemonic definitions of authentic culture, it also sets terms for adapting new institutions, thereby positioning itself to benefit from new arrangements for accumulating wealth and acquiring prestige.

This understanding of the residue of "tradition" points not to the primordial, unchanging, modernity-subverting "tribalism" often evoked by references to precolonial African culture. Rather, it suggests something generic to cultures everywhere: the ongoing creative redeployment of locally embedded informal rules, values, and systems of meaning to help people respond to rapid changes in how they make a living, deal with authority, and organize their communities. Notions of local political and economic culture, genealogically linked to precolonial society but by no means frozen in time, are crucial factors in local response to developmental change.

Over time, this process of making sense and recrafting may lead people to adapt, perhaps only partially, a new institution to fit a worldview that has more to do with idealized memories of local rules, practices, and values than with the sociocultural framework in which the institution was originally concocted. Put simply, buying rope may mean more than just the anonymous acquisition of a generic commodity by a standardized consumer. In a subtle, probably unintended, possibly somewhat ludicrous way, it may stand in for an assertion of dignity or adulthood.

In this chapter, I set the stage for an exploration of Serer institutional syncretism by piecing together crucial shards of the political culture and institutionalist and development literatures. Institutional syncretism helps us escape the cul-de-sac of African development by rethinking the invidious culture-institutions dichotomy. That dichotomy, rooted in limiting state-society and tradition-modernity distinctions, has been an obstacle to creative reassessment of the social forces behind development stagnation, sluggish state consolidation, and the precariousness of democracy in Africa. Institutional syncretism helps us reinterpret culture and institutions in a way that gives us new tools to see the dynamism and spontaneity of African institutional life. Recognizing this dynamism is a crucial first step in alleviating the crisis of underdevelopment in Africa and similar postcolonial regions.

RECONCEPTUALIZATION AND THE
POSTCOLONIAL AFRICAN CRISIS

More than four decades after the unbridled optimism of formal decolonization, Africa seems to many observers hopelessly mired in a numbing repetition of economic stagnation, state incapacity, and national disintegration. Each vision of a new dawn for Africa, from the first five-year development plans to the promise of structural adjustment, seems to sink into a familiar morass of internal breakdown and despair, external misunderstanding and abandonment. Despite lofty expectations, the first decades of African independence yielded a bitter harvest of parasitic prebendal elites, unproductive, sometimes destructive agricultural policies, unrealistic modernization schemes and bloated, inefficient states grounded on fanciful notions of national political community.[3] Structural adjustment then consciously dismantled the African state, amputating institutions that had, despite ledger-book inefficiency, at least sometimes maintained social peace through political cooptation and the projection of state authority outside urban coastal enclaves. By the late 1980s, observers like Thomas Callaghy called attention to the fact that African states were increasingly characterized by "diminishing control, repression and extraction, resilience of traditional authorities, corrupt and inefficient administration, enormous waste, poor policy performance, debt and infrastructure crises, curtailment of capacities, endemic political instability, and societal resistance and withdrawal."[4]

A few years later, seemingly by conspiracy, events well beyond the continent dealt a hammer blow. When the end of the cold war pushed Africa off the geopolitical map, the West lost interest in maintaining the military aid, currency stabilization, and budgetary bailouts that had financed so many of the continent's patronage regimes. Wracked by economic crisis and interelite struggles over shrinking sinecures, the weakest of the pseudostates—Liberia, Somalia, Zaire, Sierra Leone, not to mention former "economic miracles" like Côte d'Ivoire—have come almost irreparably unglued.

The so-called winds of change, the fresh air of post–cold war political liberalization and general unshackling of the human spirit, never seem to blow quite strong enough on the almost-forgotten continent. Each democratic breakthrough seems to give way to authoritarian takeover. In spite of high-minded schemes like the New Economic Plan for African Development (much promoted by Presidents Thabo Mbeki of South Africa and Abdoulaye Wade of Senegal), the greatly anticipated African economic renaissance lurks ever more timidly around some proverbial but unreachable corner.[5]

In Africa, global liberal triumphalism has forced even the more coherent states into retrenchment and dismantling, into a kind of externally induced autophagy in which urban elites who now call themselves "democrats" or "civics" jockey for the best position from which to milk privatization and to safeguard their piece of a shrinking pie. As developmental elites, military guardians of civil order, and would-be pluralists eat what is left of the state, they abandon the rural areas to negotiate their own terms with the international donor community, withdraw into subsistence, or spin off in centripetal separatism.[6] At the same time, growing numbers of young, disenchanted urban aspirants have been left hanging around outside the locked doors of the state banquet, gradually realizing to their dismay that very, very few of them will ever gain the coveted seat at the table they have come to consider an entitlement of independence, education, and modernization.

The continent's chronic and multiple crises suggest the need for a fundamental reconceptualization of development and social change in postcolonial Africa. At the heart of the matter, we find the disjuncture between the forces of nonstate social mobilization and the institutional formalities of public life, the state, the bureaucracy, the market, and democracy. Africa, unlike other developing regions of the world, stands out for the stark division, the almost hermetic seal, that separates Peter Ekeh's *primordial* and *civic publics*.[7] The former is an unofficial realm of trust, volunteerism, powerful bonds of association and self-sacrifice for the community. It is where we find Robert Putnam's "bonding" social capital: forms of association and trust rooted in shared, usually ascriptive forms of identity, like kinship, ethnicity race, or exclusionary forms of religion.[8] The primordial public helps constitute its idealized antithesis, the civic public, an official realm utterly lacking in popular legitimacy, ruled by an ethos of individual utility maximization, venality, and unbridled personal gain. African civic publics were set up under imperialism and, after independence, remain tainted with the living legacy of the hypertrophic, disproportionate, coercive, alien, authoritarian state.[9] In the primordial public, strong and viable social ethics and institutions constrain and channel self-interested behavior in a way utterly unheard of in the civic public's free-for-all of personal gain. The civic public is where Putnam expects to find "bridging" forms of social capital, a willingness to trust, associate with, and volunteer with others not like ourselves because we share a common interest of some kind.[10] Ekeh and postcolonialism show Putnam the future he fears for the United States: a civic realm so devoid of shared interest and legitimacy that we find, instead of bridging forms of social capital, a free-for-all of unrestrained personal utility maximization run amuck.

This disjuncture between the primordial and the civic knows many names apart from the one that Ekeh gives it. Goran Hyden situates it in a framework that fuses political economy and political culture, emphasizing the economy of affection of the peasant mode of production in contrast to the economic rationality of the capitalist or urban mode.[11] The democratization literature of Larry Diamond, Naomi Chazan, and others sees it in the need to build some meaningful link between formal electoral regimes and nascent but exceptionally weak civic culture.[12] Richard Sklar's notion of developmental democracy builds on this frame, suggesting a regime blueprint that might overcome Ekeh's dichotomy.[13] Achille Mbembe and

Jean-François Bayart see it as a discursive division pitting *commandement* against an implicit, if undeveloped, notion of local community.[14]

But at the end (and the beginning) of the day, Africa's debilitating bifurcation—its incapacity to harness the deep reservoirs of nonstate, unofficial social organizational energy, trust, and self-sacrifice for the sake of development of a public sphere and an official economy—cannot be understood without surmounting false dichotomies of tradition versus modernity, backwardness versus advancement, indeed culture versus institutions. This *episteme* of evolutionary dichotomy is deeply rooted in the study of social change in Africa and other postcolonial regions. In spite of the nearly complete excoriation of Talcott Parsons's "pattern variable" dichotomies between "traditional" and "modern" cultures, belief in systemic syndromes of sociocultural, economic, technological, and political transformation dies hard.[15] The presumed inevitability and irreducibility of the project of modernization—be it capital-intensive infrastructure development, the rational planning of a command economy, the magical-realist logic of the decentralized free market, or the universal expansion of human rights and electoral democracy—have, in Africa, meant that most scholars and activists turn unquestioningly from the "traditional" past, toward a progressive, transformative, and transcendent "modernization."

This work is by no means the first to argue that this tradition-modernity dichotomy is false and that the dichotomy itself represents a key obstacle to progressive change.[16] However, this project seeks to reconceptualize the relationship between two crucial tools of social science analysis—culture and institutions—in terms of a critique of the false tradition-modernity dichotomy. My reconceptualization privileges local agency in the incremental, ongoing, dynamic reconstitution of cultural and institutional structures in all settings. It recognizes the instrumentality of choice and the socially embedded and historically derived constraints on behavior. It refocuses efforts to make sense of development on the point of articulation where ordinary actors innovatively reconcile ways of life, habits, and values suggested to them by their sense of the past with practices and organizations that emanate from beyond the locality. This reconciliation leads to endless, spontaneous *essais* at recombination, at grafting together pieces of the wreckage of the old order with fragments of the incomplete new order. This refocus leads us to recognize the multiplicity of local, adapted forms of modernity. It calls for us to "try development" only after we understand the local terrain of grassroots institutional change, the innumerable local processes of making sense and rebuilding.

SYNCRETISM FROM THE SHARDS OF POLITICAL CULTURE

The cases of institutional syncretism explored in this book underscore how historical memory, notions of tradition, and a local culture perceived to be authentic constitute a cognitive and moral framework for responding to and adapting "modern" state and market institutions. My rural Senegalese illustrations concern questions of political and economic culture at the same time they require us to transcend and reframe these concepts.

Roots of Political Culture

While the causal and explanatory framework of modernization theory lies long discredited, post–cold war studies of neoliberalism and democratization have inadvertently inherited, or deliberately rehabilitated, a good deal of modernization's conceptual apparatus, particularly with regard to political culture. Especially since Gabriel Almond and Sydney Verba, political culture has been conceptualized to highlight the specific orientations and values thought to support Western democracy. As Almond and Verba make plain in their very first sentence, "this is a study of the political culture of democracy and of the social structures and processes that sustain it."[17]

The seemingly incomplete and conflicting operationalizations of political culture woven into modernization theory make sense when understood as heuristic devices for elaborating the various facets of *civic culture*, the form of political culture presumed essential for democracy.[18] As Lucian Pye himself said, the question is, "above all, to what extent is it possible to accelerate and direct political change, and how can traditional societies be transformed into democratic polities?"[19]

Thus, in the modernization theory tradition, the study of political culture per se has been short-circuited. Culture—as a variable in comparative analysis, as a realm of socially significant action, and as an arena in which to identify and track causally significant independent variables—has been truncated in the postwar analysis of social change and development because we do not really need to know about culture as such, since we already know which culture we are looking for and what functions we expect it to perform.

Moreover, as the modernization school refined the concept, it became more clearly rooted in the aggregation of the psychological orientations of individuals. For example, the 1968 *International Encyclopedia of the Social Sciences*, the most significant text of modernization theory, calls political culture "the set of attitudes, beliefs, and sentiments which give order and meaning to a political process and which provide the underlying assumptions and rules that govern behavior in the political system. . . .

Political culture is thus the manifestation in aggregate form of the psychological and subjective dimensions of politics."[20] In this Parsonian framing, relational or historical aspects of culture (its function in social networks and in repeated habits of group action, as well as its link to a perceived traditional past as an inherited structure subject to ongoing contestation and redefinition) sink into obscurity as we focus clearly on this amassing of individual value-orientations.

Thinking about culture in this liberal, sociologically atomic way flows as much from methodology as from ideology or ontology. In 1963, when Almond and Verba's pathbreaking *The Civic Culture* appeared, new tools for analyzing mass opinion survey data were the rage in the social sciences. The tool drove the conceptualization. Social scientists had never been so able to reconcile deep knowledge of individual beliefs with broad observations of patterns of belief across societies. This was a new kind of insight, and it helped ensure that culture would be construed as an aggregation of individual orientations.

As George Lakoff's insights on metaphor and concept formation suggest, this individualistic approach to culture also reflects the core metaphor of modernization, "society is a person" or "society is an organism."[21] Individual organisms traverse clear, recognizable, and universal developmental paths, often oversimplified in terms of dichotomous poles: child-adult, dependence-independence, curiosity-wisdom, freedom-responsibility, impulses–self-control, play-work, and so on. Scaling this kind of metaphor of developmental dichotomies up from the individual to the society, modernization theorists conceived of economic development and social change as necessarily linear, teleological processes of evolutionary growth.

Political culture, embedded in this theory of linear, dichotomous developmental progress, became an indicator of progress along this developmental path (or perhaps a vector for change; modernization theory never quite worked out the causality). Modernization saw change as a kind of irreversible and systematic syndrome (change in one arena or system [e.g., mass use of radios] would yield change in all other areas or systems [e.g., radios will spread individuation, civicness, democracy, capitalism]).[22] Thus, particular configurations of political culture that did not support democracy would naturally and inevitably give way to ones that do support democracy.[23]

Mechanistically functionalist, reductionist in its analytic agenda, and narrowly focused on the individual as the unit of analysis, political culture became one of the chief targets as the modernization school itself was discredited. Indeed, critiques of the inner details of political culture went hand in hand with a wider rejection of the functionalist logic undergirding political development and modernization, as well as with a shift in explanatory emphasis toward structuralist-institutionalist approaches.[24] By the mid-1980s, even Robert Putnam, a leader a decade later of a political culture revival, admitted that the role of culture in political analysis seemed all but dead.[25]

Reviving and Overcoming Political Culture

In spite of the absence of a comprehensive reconceptualization of culture as sociopolitical variable on the scale of Almond and Verba's political culture, two successive developments in the late 1980s and 1990s precipitated a gradual, fragmentary "return to culture." The "bringing the state back in" literature, along with the normative concern for democracy, launched a trajectory of analytic rediscovery: concern for the state as an institutional actor and for democracy as a regime type led scholars like Larry Diamond, Joel Migdal, and Philippe Schmitter to explore the social bases for particular regime configurations (strong versus weak states, consolidated versus crumbling democracies).[26] This led to an analytic rediscovery of "civil society."[27] Emphasis on associational life and extrastate centers of power and accumulation of wealth naturally led to comparative exploration of the roots of civil societies (as opposed to the many forms of un-civil ones), thus drawing our attention back to culture, specifically political culture conceptualized within the framework of Almond and Verba's civic culture.

Now, this trajectory (from state back to democratization in Southern Europe and Latin America to civil society to political culture) already had considerable momentum by 1989. The collapse of the wall in Berlin and the subsequent disintegration of the Soviet Union greatly enhanced the renewed importance of culture in at least two ways. First, the end of the Soviet empire solidified the importance of neoliberalism both as an analytic framework and as a development policy for the new independent states of the 1990s in eastern Europe and Central Asia. Like the old independent states of the 1960s in Africa and South Asia, today's versions of the Central African Republic and Bangladesh have been instructed to establish parliamentary multiparty democracy, liberal market economies, and supporting legal infrastructure, social networks, and normative frameworks. Success is promised to those fortunate few (Hungary, Poland, and the new Czech Republic, for example) where institutions of civil society flourish and where political culture supports civicness (read: where one finds Almond and Verba's civic culture). Failure comes in dramatic and tragic fashion to those new states where culture is somehow fundamentally not civic. The states that arose from the former Yugoslavia best exemplify (so far) this construction of the purported dangers of exclusivist, intolerant, ethnically based political culture for which the old African pejorative *tribalism* is simply too tempting a label not to apply.[28]

Contemporary approaches to culture set in the basic framework of Almond and Verba's civic culture concepts are useful in addressing a distinct set of analytic questions. It's just that, especially with regard to the *general* relationship between culture and institutions that is so central to the problematic of development and social change in the postcolonial world and in this book, the approach ignores crucial questions.

Putnam, for example, accounts for the difference in effectiveness, strength, and representativeness of local democratic institutions in the north and south of Italy in terms of the differential prevalence of "civic community," an adaptation of Almond and Verba's civic culture.[29] Ultimately, we have the fact that the north is culturally more civic and blessed with a rich associational heritage, and therefore it enjoys healthier democratic regional government.[30] The south, on the other hand, has little or no experience with independent associational life and minimal civic institutions. Its experience of regional democracy ends up having more to do with patronage networks, corruption, and nepotism—the familiar cesspool of amoral familism.[31]

Democracy fares poorly where civic and participatory norms—rooted in what Putnam in a later work calls "bridging" social capital[32]—are lacking. The south of Italy is thus especially interesting from a comparative point of view: we know that it does not have the "right" cultural fit for good governance and successful local democracy, but, as in many sub-Saharan African societies, that is nearly *all* we know about the relationship between culture and institutions there.

Rather than dismiss the southern Italys of the world (Sicily as much as Senegal) as pathological bastions of the "wrong" culture, we should pull back our analytic lens. Both the south and the north of Italy exhibit a kind of articulation between new governmental institutions and local norms regarding social interaction and authority. It just so happens that in the north this articulation leads to a functional, positive outcome from the point of view of good governance and liberal democracy. Not coincidentally, in the north local culture and social relations are very much like the original soil of representative democracy as it developed in various places in western Europe (including, in fact, the city-states of northern Italy).

But in the south, rather than seeing only dysfunction and pathology, it is possible to see simply another articulation between institutions and local culture. The articulation at work in the south yields very different results than in the north, but it does yield results. Representative institutions may be coopted into patron-client networks and familial structures of authority and legitimacy. This is a kind of articulation between culture and institutions—indeed, an adaptation of institutions to fit certain local, historically rooted patterns. It just happens to produce a result that proponents of Weberian legal-rational bureaucracy and parliamentary liberal democracy do not like.

This distinction—southern Italy as pathological breakdown, as absence of appropriate cultural roots for representative democracy versus southern Italy as one instance of a wider phenomenon but still a case of a general, comparable process—is crucial when we consider what to do about the southern Italys of the world. Development practitioners either "foster a civic culture" by some unknown means (especially given that Putnam demonstrates the historical rootedness of civic traditions in Italy) and hope that after some time (decades? generations?) it takes root, or they find a way to work with the particular articulation between local culture and political institutions evident in the literal south of Italy and the metaphorical southern Italys of the world.

The south of Italy brings us back to the crises of postcolonial Africa and the need for a reconceptualization. From the analytic perspective of the modernization theory and civic culture tradition, the dilemma for sub-Saharan Africa is the same as the dilemma for southern Italy: what can be done, given cultural-historical limitations, apart from simply writing off the poor backward "amoral familists?"[33] This nonanalysis leaves those who sense that systems of meaning, culture, consciousness, and values are somehow salient to wider questions about the performance of political and economic institutions with an unsatisfying theoretical dead end.

We can begin to imagine new ways of seeing the relationship between institutional change and cultural change by unlearning the rigid, almost teleological link between modernization theory concepts of culture (as either civic or not) and modernist developmental outcomes (the promotion of liberal democracy, successful establishment of liberal market economies, emergence of strong civil societies, and growth of an individualistic politics of identity-group tolerance). To do this requires thinking more openly and broadly about the conceptual link between culture and institutions themselves.

SYNCRETISM FROM THE FRAGMENTS OF INSTITUTIONS

Like the shards of the late-twentieth-century political-culture concept, fragments of recent scholarship on institutions are essential in constructing an approach to syncretic institutional change. Before gathering together these fragments, metallurgy, an unexpected source of analogy, suggests how to begin to combine cultural and institutionalist approaches.

Iron Smelting and Institutional Syncretism

> Bloom smelting is a difficult process to execute because specific chemical and physical conditions must be met if metallic iron is to be made . . . [yet] the necessary conditions can be attained through many alternative furnace designs and smelting procedures. Examination of the methods of bloom smelting used by different peoples can reveal aspects of the smelting technology that were determined by cultural preference rather than technical requirements.
>
> Robert Gordon and David Killick, "Adaptation
> of Technology to Culture and Environment"

In their comparison of bloomery iron smelting in nineteenth-century Appalachia and late-twentieth-century Malawi, the geologist Robert Gordon and the anthropologist David Killick explore how a metallurgical technology limited by clear (indeed, universal) chemical and physical constraints in fact assumes very different forms in distinct cultural settings. The gendered and supernaturally charged social meaning of metalworking in Malawi yields techniques for melting iron ore different from those that emerged in a society where production was organized around maximization of socially alienable profit and the autonomous, secular individual as wage laborer.

Iron smelting is far removed from land tenure regimes and the wider framework of imposed markets and bureaucracies, not to mention the place of culture and institutions in comparative political analysis. Yet to the extent that we might think of institutions (land tenure regimes, elected local councils, or state and market structures) as technologies, Gordon and Killick's graphic analysis of the culture of iron smelting offers intriguing heuristic insights. At first glance, the technologies might seem to be limited by immutable universal constraints: to melt iron ore requires temperatures of 1,200°C and constraining the air flow to maintain a "reducing atmosphere" in which ore becomes slag; to maximize the developmental use of capital such as land requires clear individual title and the right to sell land in a free market. But it is possible to meet the universal criteria in many different ways. The choice of technique depends on social and individual goals, which may, to a great extent, be a function of wider social preferences or predominant historical patterns, often expressed by the shorthand notion "culture."

As in the case of bloomery smelting, the importance of cultural factors cannot be reduced to whether the degree to which a specific cultural pattern—say, civic associationalism—exists or not. In Gordon and Killick's framework, this would amount to arguing that a society can develop the technology to melt iron ore only if (a) its culture highlights sacred male labor or the dangers of witchcraft, or (b) its culture emphasizes individualism and capital accumulation as the basis for yield maximization and labor efficiency. Rather, cultural factors matter to the extent that they are at work in processes of adapting institutions, always culturally embedded, to meet the demands of local experience, organizational legacies, and systems of meaning.

Institutional Superstructure and Infrastructure

To understand the adaptation of institutional technologies along the lines of Gordon and Killick's culturally rooted adaptation of metalworking technology requires a brief ordering of the cluster of concepts that come together under the headings "institutions" and "institutional analysis" across methodological and epistemological divides.

From a choice theoretic or econometric perspective, institutions are typically seen as the rule structures, formal and informal, that self-interested, utility-maximizing individuals create to facilitate social interaction, ensure predictability and order, and overcome collective action problems.[34] Much of the original work on institutions in the contemporary social sciences reflected an unproblematized borrowing from economics, in which values were almost indistinguishable from Benthamite self-interest, utility preferences, and material maximization. Especially in later elaborations such as the "analytic narratives" branch of game theory, however, the "utilities" that rational actors maximize are not limited to material gain or some measure of simple economic well-being. Rather, rational choices and the institutions generated by rational choice are said to emanate from distinctive utility functions and preferences rooted in local particularities of ideology, history, context, and culture.[35]

This turn to local context, history, and culture in the analytic narratives approach, in behavioral economics, and in other later variations of rational choice or econometric institutionalism helps reconcile a universal idea of (rational) behavior with the sometimes rather distinct, seemingly path-dependent and context-driven local calculations that yield distinctive institutional arrangements. In effect, when Douglass North alludes to the "supply problem of institutions" and Robert Bates calls for a "return to the behavioralists," they acknowledge the need for *extraeconometric, nonutilitarian* understandings of the values and value structures in which preferences, and therefore choice and choice-derived institutions, are rooted.[36] The idea that institutions may be rooted in culture, history, and context, or perhaps partially shaped by them, begins to emerge from the mist.

Partly in response to this movement away from the strict models and equations of the economists and back to the messy, contextually embedded observations of the anthropologists, historical, ideational, and organizational approaches to institutions explore the independent ways in which values, cultural legacies, and ideologies constrain the operation of social institutions. Kathryn Sikkink shows how statist-developmental institutional arrangements, when put into actual practice in Latin America, were read by Argentine and Brazilian political elites through specific cultural and historical legacies, resulting in considerable variation in the actual functioning of state-led development in these new contexts.[37] Peter Hall goes further to argue that actors and the institutions they create must be situated within broad processes of social learning mediated by ideological frameworks (akin to Kuhnian paradigms or Foucauldian *épistèmes*), which help implicitly and explicitly define assumptions, categorizations, notions of the possible, and rational actions.[38] Organization theorists like James March and Johan Olsen have long argued for an eclectic approach of this sort, treating worldview, ideas, and the culture of bureaucratic organizations as largely independent factors in the shaping of institutional forms.[39] Institutions appear to be not simply linked to culture and values but positively embedded in, if not enveloped by, them.

At the end of the day, both the econometric and the noneconometric approaches to institutions help disaggregate the layers that make up any institutional structure. Administrative structures (the officialdom, organizational charts, and hierarchies, offices, and physical spaces associated with parliaments, bureaucracies, political parties, interest associations, unions, and even bowling leagues), with their functionally specific tasks, explicit organizational structures, and standardized office-holding, always incorporate or depend upon formal, codified, officially promulgated rules. Together, administrative structures and formal rules constitute two key subcomponents of what are usually referred to as institutions, even though for precise analytic purposes we should disaggregate them and think of formal rules as supportive and constitutive of, but distinct from, formal organizations.[40] We can thus think of administrative structures and formal rules as the two upper layers of a more general institutional arrangement (see figure 1).

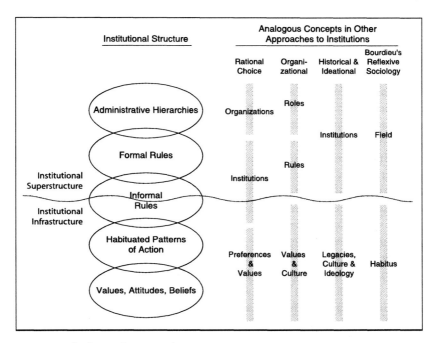

Figure 1. The layered nature of institutions.

But as we attempt to fully understand the operation and normative under-pinnings of institutions and institutional change (especially in the aftermath of the transfer or imposition so common in the developing world), these two layers only help us scratch the surface. In the same sense that administrative structures and formal rules are not reducible to one another but are in fact layered one on top of the other, so too are formal rules closely associated with and supported by sets of informal rules that govern social behavior in an implicit, noncodified but enforceable and prescriptive fashion.[41]

As figure 1 suggests, these informal rules in turn are analogously related to habituated patterns of regularized, taken-for-granted, widely repeated behavior that are roughly analogous to what Pierre Bourdieu calls habitus.[42] Informal rules depend for their implicit, "everyone knows this is the way it's done here" quality on the fact that they translate into rule form behaviors and patterns of action that are given meaning through normatively endorsed repetition. This in turn suggests that underneath habituated patterns of action lie individual and social values, attitudes, and beliefs that provide the normative support and legitimation not simply for habituated patterns of action but also for the informal rules that emanate from the habituated patterns, and for the formal rules and administrative structures that build, in cumulative fashion, on this base.

Thus, institutions and institutionalized practices do not exist simply as rules and rule arrangements (whether formally codified or not), nor are they reducible to administrative entities. They draw support from, are embedded in, and are in part constituted by their embeddedness in culture, understood as values, habituated patterns of action, and informal rules. As the mapping of major approaches to institutions in figure 1 suggests, most of the literature on institutions focuses primarily on their formal, "above the waterline," superstructural elements, treating what I refer to as the infrastructure as a kind of black box of preferences, ideology, or culture.

The diagram helps me suggest that institutions (be they institutional organizations (primarily superstructural) or institutional practices (primarily infrastructural) should be understood as ordered regimes of coordination up and down this schema of institutional elements. Figure 2 offers illustrations of an institutional organization (Western liberal democracy) and institutional practices (racism in the United States prior to the Civil Rights era) mapped onto the schematic of figure 1.

Institutional organizations constrain and pattern social behavior largely through administrative hierarchies and formal rules. But in spite of their superstructural primacy, institutional organizations garner compliance through a meaningful correspondence with informal rules, habits, and values. This correspondence not only supports the formal rules and administrative structures but also establishes a moral-ethical or practical-instrumental shared logic between the administrative hierarchies and formal rules and the informal rules, habits, and values.

Institutional practices constrain and pattern social behavior largely through the operation of informal rules, habituated patterns of action, and shared values. But they usually operate with increased scope and effectiveness to the extent that they correspond with and are promulgated by administrative structures deploying formal rules. Again, this correspondence does not simply suggest that formal administrative structures and rules enforce or promote the values, habits, and informal rules of institutional practices. It means that, in situations of maximum institutionalization, a moral-ethical or practical-instrumental logic links institutional practices and associated administrative structures and formal rules.[43]

Indeed, the great flaw in teleological schemes for developmental modernization (of the Parsonian-liberal or Marxian-radical variety) lies, in James Scott's language, in their tendency toward "high modernist simplification" (not always by the state, not always authoritarian).[44] This involves

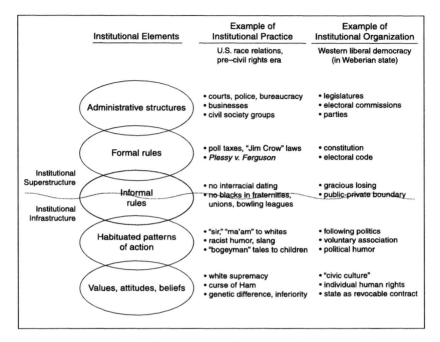

Figure 2. Examples of the layered nature of institutional practices and institutional organizations.

an assumption, in terms of figure 1, that a deliberate, planned reformulation of formal organizations and rules that is designed to achieve "progressive" or "desirable" goals (from the point of view of the planner) can and will entail a natural and corresponding adjustment of the informal infrastructural or, below the waterline, elements of institutional practice.[45] The U.S. civil rights movement and the end of apartheid in South Africa eliminated formal rules and organizations behind state-sanctioned racism, but racist practices still exist in a different yet still *institutionalized* form (as informal rules and habituated patterns of action, not to mention values) in both societies. Likewise, the sometimes mechanical exportation of democratic electoral regimes to the Togos of the 1960s or Tajikistans of the 1990s has not, in spite of extensive elite socialization and reworked incentive structures, resulted in necessary and ubiquitous supportive change in values, habits, and informal rules (the emergence of a strong civil society and a civic culture). The challenge in "making democracy work," or in progressive social reform of any kind, is to find ways to make desirable transformations at the level of administrative structures and formal rules correspond with and draw genuine support from transformation in the informal rules, habits, and values that immediately undergird the formal realm.

Figure 1—like the work of Bertrand Badie and Pierre Birnbaum on the historical and cultural origins of the nation-state, and the recent contributions of Peter Evans on state-society developmental relationships—underscores the cultural embeddedness of formal organizations in general.[46] The embeddedness insight, however, should not be limited to a search for congruence, a search for the degree to which formal organizations and rules match or draw support from informal rules, values, and habits.[47] Putnam has done this exceptionally well for northern and southern Italy, but we still need a sequel to his work: what happens to imported institutions in the southern Italys of the world?

SYNCRETISM AND THE ONGOING RECONSTITUTION OF INSTITUTIONS

Embeddedness, examined over time and with a sensitivity to agency and structural change, gives us syncretism. To get to this point, we must consider figure 1 in dynamic terms, rather than as a static system in which essential, primordial community values give rise to stereotypical "traditional" norms and ways of doing things that, in turn, effectively support only customary formal rules and customary organizations. Anthony Giddens's basic "duality of structure" helps us break out of this trap by recognizing the ongoing, everyday reconstitution of all elements of the figure 1 institutional schematic: "Structure is both medium and outcome of the reproduction of practices. [It] enters simultaneously into the constitution of . . . social practices and 'exists' in the generating moments of this constitution. . . . Structures must be conceptualized as not simply placing constraints upon human agency, but as enabling."[48]

Not only administrative hierarchies and formal rules but also the cultural underbelly of institutions are structures in this "duality of structure" sense, as Giddens's own notion of the virtual quality of structures suggests. On the one hand, they function as constraints, as normative frameworks for action, for assigning significance to social behavior, and for setting priorities (defining "preferences" in choice theoretic language).[49] But informal rules, habits, and especially values do not come out of thin air, nor are they passed along from generation to generation like some unalterable, sacred artifact. Rather, social actors constantly struggle to refashion cultural principles to suit their interests in particular socioeconomic circumstances. Culture is thus also an "outcome of the reproduction of practices," in Giddens's language.

To the extent, then, that we can think of syncretism not as a peculiarity of the interaction between the "local" and the "alien" but as an ongoing process *within* societies, it is useful precisely because it conveys this sense of process and *creativity*. Since societies are never truly isolated, processes of integration of new values, habits, rules, and administrative hierarchies are going on all the time. Instances of contact, or conquest, may provide more pronounced illustrations of the introduction and incorporation of such new elements, but the processes of incorporating new elements to reconfigure culture and institutions are ordinary and ongoing.

We deepen our conceptualization of the incremental, everyday reconstitution of institutions and culture across the figure 1 schematic by moving beyond Giddens to consider Bourdieu on the ongoing reconstitution of habitus. For Bourdieu, the habitus refers to "a system of dispositions," an underlying framework of values and orientations that both patterns social action and is itself gradually reshaped (not necessarily consciously) as a consequence of social action. Among his many elaborations of the concept, he refers to habitus as "a system of lasting, transposable dispositions which, integrating past experiences, functions at every moment as a *matrix of perceptions, appreciations and actions,* and makes possible the achievement of infinitely diversified tasks, thanks to analogical transfers of schemes permitting the solution of similarly shaped problems."[50] Habitus is an underlying orienting logic that coordinates social behavior. It functions like an implicit code: "The homogeneity of *habitus* is what . . . causes practices and works to be immediately intelligible and foreseeable, and hence taken for granted. This practical comprehension [dispenses], for the ordinary occasions of life, with close analysis of the nuances of another's practice and tacit or explicit inquiry ('What do you *mean?*')."[51] Those who share the same habitus share a common body of implicit, taken-for-granted references and common assumptions, which together form an orientation that makes interaction, communication, and life in general relatively predictable.

The habitus functions in Giddens's *constraining* sense of structure because it embodies "present and past positions in the social structure that biological individuals carry with them, at all times and in all places, in the form of dispositions."[52] It operates in tandem with and helps constitute the field, the objective social structures (law, government, the market, religion, and so on) that bound and constrain social behavior.

Yet the habitus also provides a dynamic, constantly changing model of culture and its effects on institutions. Just as Giddens sees structures in general as the product of ongoing acts of construction on the part of self-interested agents, so Bourdieu links the habitus to the "objective circumstances of its production." This is where we encounter the seemingly self-reflexive, paradoxical, indeed playful language that unfortunately renders Bourdieu relatively inaccessible to those who have not been initiated to his discursive style. The habitus thus appears as a series of "structured structures predisposed to function as structuring structures . . . [that are] collectively orchestrated without being the product of the orchestrating action of a conductor."[53]

Although reflective of changing socioeconomic conditions (changes in Bourdieu's field) familiar to any structural materialist, it would be a serious mistake to dismiss habitus as an epiphenomenal piece of cultural or psychological superstructure that simply responds, in a reflexive, deterministic manner, to underlying changes in "material conditions." This is precisely the point of Giddens's "duality of structure," which Bourdieu frames, in his usual self-reflexive syntax, as "coordination of practices and practices of coordination." Social or instrumental action (and consequently socioeconomic material relations) are themselves framed in terms of the generally meaningful, commonsensical categorizations and valorizations summed up in Bourdieu's concept of a habitus. Structure is the object of intentional action and raw material for reconfiguration, but as such, it is also a constraint on the manner, type, and content of social action.

The infrastructural elements of an institutional structure (figure 1), like habitus, are subject to processes of reconstruction that are *not necessarily* self-conscious or instrumentally oriented. Rather, like Giddensian structures constantly reshaped by acts of human agency, institutional elements, like habitus, change—slowly or suddenly, depending on circumstances—in response to social action. Especially for Bourdieu, these changes take place in response to social action that moves a community into new economic circumstances, systems of production, or configurations of social relations.

Cultural frameworks, values, habituated patterns of action, and informal rules thus may lag behind the instrumental, self-interested acts of agency that help create and reshape them. It takes time to rework a Giddensian structure. Thus, habitus does not respond automatically or mechanically to changes in individual preferences or interests. Rather, habitus and institutional infrastructure have an enmeshing effect, holding their adherents to the comprehensive, holistic precepts of a structurally sticky moral framework that may violate an individual's immediate, concrete, utility-maximizing interests and may contradict formal rules. As we will see in chapter 3, syncretic adaptation of imposed institutions takes place in part because enmeshing and holistic worldviews have changed more slowly in rural Senegal than have material conditions or institutional superstructure.

Reconstitution after Imposition

This ongoing social reconstitution of institutions and culture becomes a much more complex process, requiring a thorough conceptualization of institutional syncretism, when we consider the systematic imposition (or transfer) of administrative structures, rules, habits, or values from one society to another. Colonialism, capitalist incorporation, the worldwide standardization of Weberian legal-rational bureaucracy, missionary evangelism, the "development discourse," and of course the globalization of liberal democracy and capitalism, all can be understood as such institutional transfer or imposition, as syncretisms waiting to happen.[54]

In this vein, it is useful to note that James Scott situates institutional imposition squarely within the operative logic of states themselves. States inherently simplify human and natural realities for the purpose of administrative management, resource extraction, and the provision of services. They impose a new grid, a new state-defined ontological framework, onto land tenure, city planning, and forests—a universe of human and natural configurations that may have been, prior to "simplification," organized according to quite different and heterogeneous logics.[55] This simplification can efface close-to-the-ground, locally specific, long-adapted forms of practical, or *mētis*, knowledge embedded in cultural values, habits, and informal rules.[56] When states embrace a high-modernist faith in centrally planned rationality and make use of political authoritarianism to administer their goals, this natural pursuit of simplification becomes a relentless imposition of a presumed superior institutional form at the expense of local knowledge and practices.

Colonialism is the quintessence of authoritarian, high-modernist state simplification. Colonial commodification of property relations imposed formal rules and administrative structures that effaced local values, habits, and practices. The postcolonial state, Crawford Young's Bula Matari, inherited the high-modernist and authoritarian tendencies of its colonial ancestor.[57] Even under a democratic socialist regime like Senegal's, land reform and establishment of new, elected local government bodies followed the structural logic of Bula Matari, illustrating the crushing effects of Scott's authoritarian high-modernist simplification. Yet in this work, I show not simply the persistence of Scott's *mētis* knowledge but also the ingeniously creative efforts of actors who reformulate their own memories of their *mētis* ways and new institutional elements to solve practical problems of land use, governance, and the maintenance of meaning.

Michael Watts takes us one step beyond Scott's authoritarian high-modernist state simplification with his notion of reworking modernity. He argues that the global diffusion of what he sees as the central institutional forms of Western modernity—capitalist relations of production—does not result in worldwide homogenization based on universal patterns of relations to the means of production and class stratification. It instead yields disparate, multiple, and complex processes of articulation between capitalist economic structures and particular features of local communities (distinct local systems of production, institutions of domination, systems of meaning, and forms of consciousness): "Globality and locality are inextricably linked[;] but through complex mediations and reconfigurations of 'traditional' society . . . [a] working class is made; yet through its own use of cultural and symbolic resources, it makes itself. In our language, a working and reworking of modernity."[58]

In this inversion of modernism, Watts goes beyond simply highlighting the existence or functional superiority of some form of small-scale, community-level distinctive practices, institutions, and relations. Rather, he shows that these forms of local knowledge are precisely relevant to the extent that they form the raw material for the articulation with and eventual transformation of institutions imposed in the process of modernization. In Watts's lexicon, "the realm of 'tradition' or 'custom' provides much of the symbolic raw material around which local communities, interest groups and classes rework and refashion the modernizations of capitalist transformation."[59] Local responses to state simplification entail a reworking of the formal structures of modernity in the context of pre- or extramodern values, relations, and institutions. The result, Watts tells us, is the proliferation of multiple "modernities" across geographical and cultural sites.[60]

Watts's notion of reworking modernity (or more specifically, reworking modern capitalism), when linked to Scott's ideas on *mētis* knowledge, offers a direct and theoretically rich framework for the notion of syncretism at the heart of this project. Like Watts's Malay semiconductor assemblers or devotees of the Maitatsine Islamic movement in northern Nigeria, Serer peasants draw upon what they perceive as their own "authentic tradition" and "true history" (themselves reworked, new constructs) to respond to the dramatic dislocations and upheavals associated with being dragged first into imperial commodity production, and later into the extension of direct central state authority after independence.[61] "Response," as we shall see, and as Watts is keen to emphasize, is not simply a spasmodic reassertion of some local tradition but a true articulation, in which both the content of local culture and social relations, as well as newly imposed political and economic institutions, are recrafted.[62] The result is syncretic new institutions, cultures, and identities.

Syncretism and Evangelism

I deliberately borrow this language of syncretism from the anthropology of religion to convey Watts's creative local response to Scott's notion of authoritarian high-modernist state simplification. Charles Stewart and Rosalind Shaw define syncretism as "the synthesis of different religious forms." They underscore the controversies surrounding the term, which, for some, denotes contamination of universalistic systems of belief by local impurities, but which for others (like me) conveys a privileging of local agency in cultural change.[63]

In a context in which we find Scott's authoritarian high-modernist state simplification, particularly a context of what James Ferguson calls "developmentalism," the literal language of religious syncretism offers a perfectly accurate image. These efforts at modernization and development, like civilizing missions before them, have been embedded in the telos of the uninterrupted march out of backward, stifling tradition into a future of steady, relentless progress. We find here an unproblematic acceptance bordering on religious faith that technology, science, and rational planning will provide enough energy, food, housing, work, equality, rights, leisure, and meaning to steadily raise overall human standards of living.

This modernist faith—such a driving assumption behind contemporary efforts at third world development—amounts to a kind of institutional evangelism, a process by which external actors and local collaborators work together to replicate systems of production, exchange, domination, and belief borrowed from supposedly more advanced locales. This process becomes evangelistic when animated by a conviction that "progress" requires close, at times dogmatic, reproduction of original institutions in new settings. This is especially true for those parts of the world deemed politically or economically "pathological." In these contexts we find an evangelistic certainty that institutions characteristic of Western liberal capitalist modernity—parliamentary multiparty democracy, individualized human rights, legal-rational bureaucracy, market economic systems, and freehold property—*must* be transferred to "less developed" societies.

Thomas Basset identifies this quasi-religious, proselytizing quality in contemporary economic development prescriptions focusing on land tenure relations in rural Africa: "Given the World Bank's renewed interest in tenure issues[,] . . . there is a need to transcend its technocratic and theological approaches that posit a direct link between freehold tenure and productivity. . . . Such calls for sweeping tenure change are misconceived."[64] In the sense that this project is specifically concerned with the local responses to such efforts at institutional evangelism, the language of syncretism applies in a very nearly literal sense. People subject to such impositions, like the Serer of Senegal, respond to the quasi-dogmatic transfer and promulgation of "modern" social relations and institutions by working with and subtly adapting these new structures to fit with their own institutional forms, local systems of production, domination, and meaning (which are simultaneously vestigial and undergoing a process of recrafting). In doing so, they may produce new versions of imposed institutions, innovative structures and relations—in short, syncretic institutions. The case studies at the heart of this project (see chapters 4 through 6) show particular forms and developmental consequences of such syncretism, providing the empirical foundation for a typology of forms and consequences of institutional syncretism (see chapter 7).

Syncretism and Symbolic Contestation

Administrative structures and formal rules (figure 1)—especially those newly introduced or imposed in developing countries—are received, recognized, reinterpreted, and perhaps reworked within a framework of local informal rules, habituated patterns of action, and values, which are themselves also being reconstituted. Indeed, the struggle for or against particular formal rules and administrative structures may also take the form of a struggle over the underlying institutional infrastructure (since the superstructure is largely ineffective without corresponding roots in the infrastructure). Thus *ideational*, cultural, symbolic contestation, the contestation within the domain of the habitus that Bourdieu refers to, is not simply some ethereal, aesthetic, or semiotic struggle for artists, intellectuals, literati, and other superfluous effetes. It is the essence of real political struggle, as Latin American social movement theory recognizes.[65] Those who control and shape dominant values, habituated patterns of action, and informal rules also set the terms for acceptance of, rejection of, cooperation with, or sabotage against formal rules and formal organizations.

In this regard, David Laitin draws on Antonio Gramsci to remind us that culture is manufactured to suit the instrumental interests of certain individuals or social groups. These dominant actors use their control over systems of symbolic production to propagate their own constructions of culture as the taken-for-granted way of viewing the world that their subordinates will, in a successful construction of hegemonic power, imbibe and adopt as their own.[66]

Pushing the search for patterns of cultural hegemony down from the colonial or postcolonial state as hegemon, this work examines intracommunity contestation over cultural meaning and the emergence of dominant versions of culture and local memories of institutions. Senegal's Siin region has different, sometimes competing versions of exactly what constitutes historical memory of local institutions and culture (different origin myths, narratives of community founding, bases for the authority of customary elites, and constructions of moral economic and social relations; see chap. 3). To some extent, we can extrapolate from these cleavages and trace contestation over the meaning of authentic local culture and the emergence of hegemonic cultural narratives, whereby one social group's version of "true history" and "authentic tradition" emerges as dominant and gradually becomes the taken-for-granted, orienting framework for society as a whole during a given period of time. Once such a hegemonic meaning framework has been established, newly imposed institutions will be read (through a process of syncretic reworking) in terms of that dominant framework.

Those whose versions of tradition become dominant or even hegemonic are well positioned to take advantage of new opportunities for accumulating wealth and acquiring prestige offered by the new institutions that accompany rapid social change. Since these versions of tradition play a crucial role in responding to new institutions, in "reworking modernity" in Watts's language, then those whose versions of authentic tradition and true history become taken for granted via the process of building hegemony thus position themselves to reap significant instrumental benefit.

Significantly, those who are actually engaged in this type of cultural contestation do *not* generally perceive their actions in terms of this kind of "struggle over meaning." They do not engage in elaborate instrumental calculations that reflect a self-conscious appreciation of the significance of cultural-meaning frameworks in adapting new institutions. Research for this book shows that, in the eyes of local actors, struggle over meaning represents an end in itself, rather than a deliberate mechanism for taking advantage of new opportunities posed by modernization. Such cultural contestation, however, takes place *alongside* much more explicitly instrumental efforts to use new institutional opportunities to one's personal (or group) advantage.

Neither the importance of taken-for-granted meaning frameworks nor the link between the material and symbolic realms of contestation is self-evident to individual actors, because the process of adaptation is gradual, is usually incremental, and depends on the aggregation of many individual propagations of versions of culture and uses of imposed institutions. Put another way, the time horizon of (a) the process of building syncretic institutions is much longer than that of either (b) contestation over culture or (c) the instrumental use of new institutional opportunities. As a result the way in which (a) links (b) to (c) remains relatively obscure to those who actually spend their lives participating in these processes, unable to step outside the struggles and gain perspective on what they are doing.

Syncretism versus Grafting

Institutional syncretism, then, is the intentional recombination of institutional elements of diverse sociocultural, geographical, or temporal origin in a coherent manner that yields correspondence and supportive articulation between institutional superstructure and infrastructure (see figure 1).

With this is mind, it is important to differentiate genuine syncretism from the mechanical "sticking together" of modern superstructure with premodern infrastructure (for purposes of hegemonic control, this is precisely how authoritarian regimes from the Mobutu regime to the Suharto regime, and many in between, have used institutional syncretism). This *pseudosyncretic grafting* might combine *extant, unchanged* Western or modern administrative structures and formal rules with *reified, unalterable* idealizations of traditional informal rules, habits, or values. Some late modernization theory work on the role of tradition in social change explored the implications of these sorts of static recombinations.[67] This type of institutional grafting can be developmentally useful as a mechanism of legitimation, although it easily shades into a device to build authoritarian hegemony.

In contrast, syncretism involves an ongoing, incremental, creative transformation of *all* elements of institutional structure (super- and infrastructure), drawing on the full range of "modern" and "premodern" institutional elements as raw material for the creation of institutional structures that are new and blended *at all levels* of superstructure and infrastructure. In a process of syncretism, new administrative structures, formal rules, informal rules, habits, and values are themselves redefined and refashioned. Genuine syncretism shows no respect for "traditional" culture as a historic and unchangeable given or for "modernity" as a desirable and unalterable progressive form. Syncretism destabilizes tradition and modernity, using them both as the raw materials in new efforts at creative recombination. In its creative process, dynamic syncretism draws inspiration, models, and raw materials from local-traditional and imposed-modern institutional orders. But, at all levels of the figure 1 diagram, syncretism is a process of new transformation. It is the work of Claude Lévi-Strauss's *bricoleur*, who cobbles together meaning, culture, and in this case, new institutional arrangements, like the collage artist pieces together found scraps of preexisting graphical representations to generate an entirely new, innovative, and recombinatory work.[68] Fred Riggs's work on prismatic societies points in this direction.[69] Lloyd and Susan Rudolph's exploration of the fundamentally modern political redeployment of caste identity and customary law in postcolonial India provides a direct example of the dynamics and functionality of this type of holistic reworking.[70]

The Serer of Siin have experienced both grafting and syncretism. Their creation of a novel mechanism of land pawning in the interwar years illustrates genuine syncretism and its grassroots legitimating and mobilizational effects. Both the National Domain Law (a land reform law) and the Rural Council Law (as implemented) represented imposed formal rules and administrative structures, dressed up in a neotraditional patina of Serer informal rules, habits, and values. With regard to both the land and local government reforms, pseudosyncretic grafting was too obviously a tool for authoritarian control. By blocking the deeper process of syncretic transformation, especially in response to the rural councils, the state actually intensified the problem of an illegitimate, distant state "floating above" idealized, yet partially dismantled, local culture and institutions.

A CLOSING HERSKOVITS/CARTER CAVEAT

I do not claim, in the vein of Melville Herskovits or Gwendolyn Carter, that new political institutions like states, parties, unions, land laws, or local governments will unproblematically take on the style and structure of "traditional," precolonial political systems.[71] There was a genuine danger in this early generation of work on cultures and institutions to treat tradition and modernity as unchanging and mutually distinct, such that the influence of the traditional on the modern could be understood as a kind of blending of blue and yellow to make green. As I have argued, neither blue nor yellow is especially pure, nor are the cans that hold them especially well sealed from outside contamination. The syncretism described in this book draws not on extant and pure, but on already changing and continually hybridized, "pools" of culture and institutions. Pushing the metaphor, the Serer and Western institutional-cultural matrices out of which syncretism may emerge are like old, open cans of paint left about in a spot where all sorts of other colors and types of paint have dribbled into the cans over time. Syncretism is a much more complex process than it appeared to be to Herskovits and Carter (or beyond Africa, Harry Eckstein, Fred Riggs, Reinhard Bendix, or later, Giuseppe Di Palma or Ernst Haas) because it involves the intentional, incremental extracting of preferred dribs, drabs, and beads of paint from each can to create a new, decidedly motley but useful, hue. In the Sahel, it really is Jackson Pollock meets the politics of postcolonial development.

However, once we have accepted all the necessary caveats regarding the earlier work on "blending tradition and modernity" (caveats having to do with the dangers of essentialism and of lack of sufficient sensitivity to the heterogeneity of culture and its social constructedness and the way it changes over time), there is much to be said for the *impulse* behind this kind of work in the 1960s. As later analysts like Jean-François Bayart point out (in language so different—even when translated into English—that the parallel is almost unrecognizable), Herskovits and Carter were on the right track in their concern for historical continuities between the pre- and postcolonial periods, in their rejection of the notion that independence and the tilt-up construction of new political arrangements would unproblematically sweep away vestiges of traditional politics. However, apart from the sometimes overly facile correspondences that they constructed, analysts like Herskovits and Carter ran into trouble when the link between the past and the present in sub-Saharan Africa became not the grounding of new republics on customary democracy but the relationship between personal rule, military coups, one-party regimes, and prebendalism on the one hand and the ugly, arbitrary, inegalitarian, patriarchal, authoritarian side of "traditional" political life on the other.

The real danger thus became, especially for analysts on the left (both liberals and radicals), the possibility that a concern for historical and cultural continuities was somehow tantamount to claiming that contemporary politics was a politics of "primitivism" or "tribalism." The great tribalism stigma raised its head because the logic of Herskovits and Carter's argument regarding democratic antecedents in Africa suggested that contemporary *undemocratic* politics might somehow be linked to, or even *caused by*, precolonial culture. Rather than accept or confront this stigma head-on, liberals and radicals concerned about African politics retreated to "hope" for the emergence of liberation movements and class revolution—a kind of transposing of a Latin American political dynamic and sensibility on very different peasant societies in which such class structures, alliances, and politics were simply not possible.

Yes, "traditional" cultures have normatively "desirable" and "undesirable" components (consensus decision-making and patriarchy, respectively) from the point of view of contemporary liberal democracy or democratic socialism. But this is not the point. It is a Parsonian waste of time to sort out the modernity-supporting features from the tribalist-traditionalist features of precolonial African culture. Tribalism (and the tradition-modernity dichotomy of which it is simply an emblem) was and remains a distraction, a label that is at best an excuse for a lack of real analysis, because African cultures and institutions are like cultures and institutions everywhere—subject to ongoing, syncretic processes of change, innovation, blending, and reformulation. Moreover, the problematic of postcolonialism is not *which* values, practices, or rules will be dredged extant from the primordial African past into postcolonial modernity ("good" village democracy or "bad" caste inequality), but what is the nature of the ongoing redefinition of both the "traditional" and the "modern," by whom, and to what end?

In a way then, this book cautiously picks up the thread of this earlier awareness that "things traditional" in developing postcolonial societies are not so easily shunted to the dustbin of history and will not simply fade away according to the schemes of social engineers and development planners. Instead, to make deep sense of the contemporary crisis of African development, we must make sense of how and to what end the versions of "traditional" ways of life and institutions resurface in new and sometimes unexpected ways. With regard to productive economic arrangements, the effectiveness of the state, and the possibility of local self-government, precisely how "things traditional" resurface and interact with progressive new institutional designs and social orders matters a great deal.

There is a deliberateness and intentionality to this resurfacing. This is the ongoing work of the *bricoleur*. Colonialism and postcolonialism have rushed new institutional structures, new administrative forms and rules, new elements, onto the palette of the *bricoleur*. For reasons of historical legitimation, the *bricoleurs* persistently return to the detritus heap of old culture and institutions, sifting for crucial raw materials in their work. The farmers of the Serer of Siin are these *bricoleurs*. Their art forms are sometimes only *essais*, sketches, drafts for recombination. Sometimes, out of the many trials and sketches, they arrive at genuinely new institutional structures whose recombination of Western-imposed and locally remembered elements helps them manage their integration into liberal-capitalist modernity.

The central chapters of this book tell the story of three such processes of bricolage combining remembered values, rules, and ways of life with new state and market institutions. Chapter 4 examines the emergence of land pawning as the Serer of Senegal's Siin region respond to new models of property and exchange associated with commodification and Islamicization in the 1930s. Chapter 5 brings the narrative into the era of the postcolonial state, exploring how Serer responses to an idealistic African socialist land reform project of the 1960s have generated an organizationally schizophrenic, developmentally dysfunctional dual land tenure system. Chapter 6 shows how a new system of democratically elected local government bodies promised the Serer a way to bring their particular vision of legitimate authority into the structure of the state and the direction of governance. When these elected councils were rebuked for their attempts to behave syncretically and reminded of their status as administrative agents of the state, the Serer interpreted and vilified the local government system as a decrepit version of the hated precolonial monarchy in the Siin.

But first, chapter 2 lays out the historical, ethnographic, and sociopolitical background on Senegal, the Siin region, and the Serer, which is needed to make sense of their responses to the institutional imposition accompanying colonialism, independence, and development. Chapter 3 explores the social topography of cultural contestation, noting how historical memories vary according to social structural factors, and how historical memory and cultural meaning frameworks appear to have independent predictive power of their own. Finally, chapter 7 canvasses the forms and implications of syncretism resulting from the institutional creativity of the Serer of Siin. It uses these examples to develop a typology of syncretism, arguing that this form of innovative adaptation holds the key to making development and modernity culturally sustainable.

2 · The Serer of Siin

"Le type même du paysan africain"

The stories of institutional syncretism at the heart of this book are set in a cluster of thirty villages, in a region historically known as Njafaj, the heartland of the precolonial Serer kingdom of Siin. The Siin, situated in the south-central part of Senegal's old Peanut Basin, is a densely populated area only a half day's drive from the capital, yet it has long been considered the home of some of the most "traditional peasants" in the old French African empire.

As in any case study, we are confronted early on with a number of fundamental questions. Who are these Serer? What is this Siin? Why explore institutional syncretism in *this* corner of rural Senegal and not somewhere else? This chapter answers these and related questions about case selection and provides historical and ethnographic background on the people at the center of this project, the Serer of the Siin region of west-central Senegal. Before we can appreciate how Serer villagers have transformed market and state institutions to conform to local cultural memories, we must understand what those cultural memories are and where they come from. To that end, this chapter describes the diversity of the peoples called Serer and explains in some detail the social, religious, economic, and political practices and institutions of the Serer of the kingdom of Siin.

Serer peasants draw on several centuries worth of historical memories as they respond to and adapt the imposed institutions of liberal capitalist modernity. The oral historical record in this region reaches back at least to the fourteenth century. Even as oral history filters, distorts, and reinterprets, it has kept alive memories of sacred land custodians, "priests" of the shrines of ancestrally allied spirits, the Mandé matrilineal clan that conquered the Serer in the fourteenth century, castes free and unfree, and the gradually expanding brotherhoods of the Sufi Islamic marabouts. These and other archetypal, stylized characters figure prominently as people in today's Siin region idealize and vilify the past to make sense of and sometimes refashion the organizations, rules, habits, and values of the modern state and market. There are two layers of struggle and contestation here: Historical memory serves as a template to build a meaningful critique—or praise-song—for modern development schemes. At the same time, the oral historical process of producing narrative, memory, and authoritative information is itself a living process fraught with contestation and political struggle. This chapter provides a review of what is known about Serer history, as well as cultural and institutional change in this region, so we can make sense of the processes of contestation examined in the following chapter and grasp the narratives, allusions, imagery, and characters evoked when we explore specific processes of institutional syncretism in chapters 4 through 6.

This chapter builds on an already extensive literature (largely francophone) in anthropology, geography, history, and agricultural economics on the Serer and on Senegal's Peanut Basin as a whole.[1] In situating my own research with regard to that rich body of work, I am guided in part by David Laitin's remarks on the relationship between his *Hegemony and Culture* and Yoruba studies:

> As a contribution to Yoruba studies, already a rich and well-documented field, this book can provide some new ideas and data. . . . But since my primary audience is the social scientist and not the student of Yoruba society, I have tried to make Yoruba politics accessible to the generalist. This means that I had to drive over turf well known to the area specialists, and to finesse many issues that remain unsettled among experts. I cannot in any way hope to have probed the depths of Yoruba culture, which is far too extensive for me to have explored. I hope that my summaries of the secondary literature do no disservice to the field.[2]

Likewise, I see my project building upon a solid foundation of historical, ethnographic, and economic research already undertaken among the Serer and surrounding communities. My contribution is a new way of looking at a certain class of phenomena, a contribution that does cast some light on the Serer and rural Africa, but that more directly illuminates the relationship between culture and institutions in processes of change broadly lumped under the term *development*. I argue that, by looking closely at the Serer experience over a long period of time, we can learn something of widespread applicability in postcolonial societies in general: how culture, especially shifting, competing historical memories of culture, affect the performance and transformation of important economic and political institutions.

While we must of course understand Serer ethnography and history, my aim in this chapter is not to establish the *representativeness* of the Siin as a case. I do not argue that the exact sociostructural dynamic in the Siin (a certain level of inequality, a certain legacy of centralized state institutions, a certain dynamic of class formation), or the exact trajectory of sociostructural change in the region in response to commodification in the 1920s or the land reform in the 1960s, make this case distinctive or interesting or worth exploring. Rather, I argue that what is interesting and noteworthy is a process, set against this particular Serer background, by which nonelites draw on their historical memories to respond to and eventually adapt new institutions. It really does not matter if the actual institutional and historical background or even the trajectory of rural socioeconomic change in the Siin is particular to that place or if it is representative of Senegal or the Sahel or rural Africa as a whole. What is generic here is not necessarily the nature of land tenure relations or rural class structure but a specific kind of transformation that I explore in the chapters which follow: reification of the seemingly authentic and traditional, followed by adaptation of new institutions "in the idiom of" the reified traditional, a process that may ultimately produce a coherent synthesis between the imposed institutions and reconstituted tradition. The local history and ethnography presented in this chapter are essential as background to exploring this syncretic blending of "modern" institutions and "traditional" culture, a blending of considerable, and underexplored, theoretical significance.

CASE SELECTION

Why Senegal?

For a study of institutional syncretism, Senegal is at once an ideal and an unexceptional choice of case. Squaring the circle of this apparent contradiction reminds us of the fundamentally generic nature of the syncretic blending of "modern" and "traditional" institutions and culture.

Simply by virtue of the *historical duration* of its experience with institutional imposition, Senegal represents an ideal venue in which to explore culturally informed local responses to new state and market structures. This is clearly true with regard to democracy in the Four Communes (urban centers of early colonial settlement, which served as coastal laboratories of French assimilation policy) but also applies to the penetration of market economic relations in peasant communities of the interior.[3] Through both the politics of assimilation and incorporation into imperial commodity production, urban and rural Senegal has had generations in which to work out compromises between new institutions and local beliefs, expectations, and social relations.

Assimilation in the coastal enclaves, it is important to note, skimmed the cream off the top of Senegal's educated elite and sent them to the metropole to complete their *formation,* at which time they encountered firsthand the deep streak of racism lurking just beneath the rhetoric of the rights of man and universal culture. Young elites from Africa, the Caribbean, and other colonial regions saw, in spite of what they had been taught about France and the Enlightenment, that their African origins still mattered, still limited how they were treated, still denied them social, economic, and political access. The generation of Aimé Césaire and Léopold Senghor realized that assimilation was motivated less by a genuine belief in universal human equality and potential, and more by a desire to *prove* through a quasi experiment that things French were indeed human universals. If the culture, language, philosophy, and ideology of post-Enlightenment, postrevolutionary France could be taught to the "near-apes" or at best "subhumans" of Africa, this would demonstrate that French civilization was indeed a human universal achievement, although it would not change the character of the population of subhumans from whom the *evolués* had been drawn.

As a result of this crisis in the self-image of the *assimilé* elite, Senghor, Césaire, and others developed the philosophy of *négritude,* a relativistic redefinition of culture and civilization that at once restored value to and reified African cultures and social forms effaced by assimilation.[4] Since the socialization of *evolués* of the coast (like Senghor) had been a process of distilling *out* traces of Africanness, elites had to "rediscover" some memory of African culture and society.[5] *Négritude* was thus rooted in a neotraditional reappropriation of African tradition by partially Westernized elites, lending a certain romanticism to its conceptualization of colonialism as Euro-African cultural exchange and mutual transformation.

While elites in the coastal enclaves were realizing that they *needed* at some psychological or moral level to think of themselves and their society *as if it were somehow syncretic* (the essence and purpose of *négritude*),[6] the irony is that, hidden out in the "remote" countryside, their own rural cousins, routinely dismissed as the rhetorical equivalent of bumpkins, were themselves actually doing the real work of blending new, European-derived institutions with local African systems of value and social organization. Especially in places like the Siin, where political and social structures had not been completely displaced (as in the Wolof kingdoms to the north), long exposure to new market institutions provided time to both adapt to them and adapt them.[7] Land pawning (discussed in chapter 4) offers a clear illustration in which Serer peasants drew on their own ideas about property and tenure to modify increasingly dominant models of individualized title and alienability, producing a new property regime.

Decades later, when the ideology of *négritude* syncretism had become official postcolonial dogma, the coastal *evolué* elites were still so absorbed in their aesthetic imperative and neotraditional romanticizations about Africa that they failed to notice the creative, syncretic institutional products that had helped their country relatives manage, sidestep, slow down, and sometimes redirect the steamrollers of commodification and state simplification. African socialist land reform and rural democracy were institutional syncretisms that might have existed but were truncated by the conflict between the state and Serer peasants' divergent notions of blending modernity and tradition.

Distortions of neotraditionalism aside, *négritude* underscores Senegal's richness as a site for the study of syncretisms of all kinds. Senegal's unique assimilation legacy has been deep enough for the cultural and institutional encounter to move into a new, more sophisticated phase, a self-conscious recognition, indeed a celebration, of the fact that *blendedness* itself is the distinctive feature of long-colonized societies. In its politics, culture, religion, music, and art, Senegal seems the very caricature of *metissage*, or blending and hybridity. This is the land of Senghor, the simple Serer peasant who became the first African member of the Académie Française; of Youssou Ndour, country griot and international pop star, chief international symbol of world music, and inventor of the *mbalaax* fusion of Sahelian rhythms and Western acoustical technology; and of the Mourides, an Islamic Sufi brotherhood built in part out of the fragments of Wolof occupational castes.[8]

So, on the one hand, Senegal stands out for its rich legacy of institutional imposition and its varied history of adaptive response. Yet on the other hand, one could argue that this long history is helpful, but not decisive, in the choice of Senegal as case study. As the theoretical approach outlined in chapter 1 suggests, processes of syncretism (not always successful in outcome) take place *everywhere*, especially in contexts where we find institutional imposition across cultural boundaries. In this sense, Senegal's long history of contact with European institutions provides only a more layered and complex version of the same processes traceable among Native Americans under U.S. domination, Tajiks in the old Soviet Empire, and Tibetans living under the political control of Beijing. The comparative significance of this case study, then, does not lie in the sui generis qualities of Senegal.

However, in terms of practical research logistics, Senegal clearly offers advantages. This historical crossroads of African, Arab-Muslim, and European civilizations provides a rich vein of syncretism. In coastal enclaves and rural villages alike, culturally informed responses to externally induced structural change have been taking place over many decades and in many sectors of society. In such a setting, single issue areas, such as land tenure relations, become prismatic. They refract a variety of contrasting notions of "traditional" culture and competing invocations of an authentic past in responding to new political and economic realities. The "social density" of syncretic processes greatly facilitates research of the kind conducted for this project. Senegal stands out for the sheer abundance of illustrations one can accumulate while working with limited time in a finite space.

Who Are the Serer, and Why Study Them?

Like so many other ethnic designations of the former colonial world, the term *Serer* masks a colonial-era lumping together of heterogeneous populations more than it designates a deeply rooted, extant, and self-conscious ethnolinguistic group (let alone a "tribe").[9] As it has been employed since the colonial period, *Serer* actually describes a broad umbrella category that encompasses seven major subgroups. It includes the inhabitants of the two historically centralized kingdoms of Siin and Saluum, as well as a number of more decentralized, small-scale societies to the west and south of these states (Niominka, Dieghem, None, Safen, Ndut).[10] Together these various Serers occupy a rough quadrangle bounded on the northeast by the Wolof kingdoms of Baol and Jolof, the south by the river Gambia, the east by the Ferlo Desert, and the west by the Atlantic Ocean (see map 1).

Physically, this "Serer country" is dominated by the estuaries of two now moribund rivers, the Siin and the Saluum, both of which flowed with freshwater before their headwaters, lying to the north of the Serer zone, were denuded by peanut production. The two erstwhile rivers meet in a brackish, swampy delta dotted with innumerable islands and byzantine canals. This delta is home to the Serer-Niominka, also known as the Serer of the Sea, usually described as a "fishing people."[11] The Serer zone in general is flat, with the highest elevations (about fifty meters) found in a large plateau that dominates the northwestern corner of the region. These uplands, relatively more forested than surrounding areas, provided shelter in the nineteenth century for reclusive Serer-None and Serer-Ndut bands, familiar to the early colonial administration for their frequent raids on colonial outposts and equally sudden retreats into the forest.[12]

To the east and south of the plateau, the land settles into gently rolling hills and flatlands punctuated by the shallow valleys of the two rivers. The landscape is dotted with a variety of trees adapted to the dry climate, most prominent of which are the baobab and the *Acacia albida*. Soils in this area are sandy and generally poor. Situated in a classic Sahelian isohyet, rainfall totals between 450 and 600 millimeters per year in the Serer zone and is concentrated in three summer months, roughly from late June to late September.[13]

In spite of important historical and regional variations, as well as dramatic change in recent decades, Serer peoples are still renowned for their system of three-year crop rotation and fallowing, in which their large herds add nutrients to otherwise marginal soils every third year. They are also highly praised in the literature for their knowledge of nitrogen-fixing and other nutritive trees. Their maintenance of trees like the *Acacia albida* (a robust nitrogen fixer) and other natural resources led French agronomists to describe Serer country as a carefully managed "park."[14] These generalizations about Serer agriculture helped define colonial and contemporary ideas about the Serer as a group but mask a good deal of heterogeneity within the category "Serer."

Although the various Serer subgroups appear to share common origins in the Senegal River valley, through their multiple waves of migration, divergent settlement patterns, and perhaps most important, distinct experiences of state formation they have become mutually distinguishable in terms of language, cultural practices, social institutions, collective historical experience, agricultural systems, and political structures. The seven subgroups can be grouped into three major categories: the Serer of the centralized state of Saluum, those of the centralized state of Siin, and five much smaller Serer communities characterized by highly decentralized, small-scale, and nonhierarchical political structures (None, Safen, Niominka, Dieghem, and Ndut).

Even limiting ourselves to the three broad groupings noted above, when we look at a series of important characteristics (table 1), we find complex patterns of overlap and divergence among the heterogeneous Serer groups. Politically, the people of Siin and Saluum share a common heritage: both regions were conquered during the late fourteenth and early fifteenth centuries by a Manding matrilineal band known as the Gelwaar, who installed themselves as an aristocratic ruling elite and established centralized state institutions. In contrast, the communities to the west avoided conquest by the Gelwaar and remained less hierarchical, smaller scale, and much more decentralized.[15]

TABLE 1. Variation in Key Social and Ethnographic Characteristics across Major Serer Subcategories

Characteristics	Serer-Siin	Serer-Saluum	Western, Small-Scale Serers
Language	Generally intelligible with Saluum	Generally intelligible with Siin	Not intelligible with Siin or Saluum; generally mutually unintelligible
Political structure	Centralized state	Centralized state	Decentralized
Caste system	Hierarchical, complex, and endogamous	Hierarchical, complex, and endogamous	Simplified, flexible, or nonexistent
Religion	Limited and recent Islamization; widespread animism; considerable Christian missionary activity	Long experience with Islam and deeper conversion; weak animism; limited Christian missionary activity	Limited and recent Islamization; widespread animism; considerable Christian missionary activity
Land tenure system pre–1964 reform	Strong "traditional" local institutions (*lamanic* system)	Weak "traditional" institutions; some Sufi *daara* plantations	Strong "traditional" local institutions (*lamanic* system)
Agricultural practice	Widespread agropastoral, rotation, and resource management practices	Vast pasture areas; limited crop rotation, fallow, and resource management	Wide variation depending on terrain (forest, rocky plateau, delta)
Dominant inheritance pattern	Bilineal	Patrilineal	Bilineal or matrilineal
Dominant residence pattern	Patrilocal	Patrilocal	Some matrilocal

Linguistically, the two kingdoms also cluster together: despite some-times significant local variation (adjacent villages may employ different grammatical structures, not to mention vocabulary), the language of the two states is generally mutually intelligible. This is very much not the case with regard to the less centralized communities. The None, Ndut, and Safen, geographically isolated for many centuries in the forested plateau at the base of the Cap Vert peninsula, speak languages that are fully unin-telligible to the people of Siin and Saluum. The language of the Dieghem and Niominka represents a middle category: not the same Serer as that of Siin and Saluum, but not as distinct as that of the None, Ndut, or Safen.[16]

The pattern repeats with regard to caste: the centralized states developed rather rigid endogamous caste systems, akin to those of the Wolof king-doms to the north, with the Gelwaar ruling matrilineage evolving into an aristocratic dominant caste. A variety of quasi-noble court retainers (valets, grooms, stable keepers, and domestics of various kinds) constituted a series of high status occupational castes. The vast majority of the Serer population of the two kingdoms belonged to an ambiguous "free farmer" category, sometimes understood as "those without caste." Below the free farmers were a variety of semiservile occupational castes, including blacksmiths, weavers, potters, woodworkers, and the oral historians–bards known most widely by the French term *griot*.[17] Slaves occupied the lowest position in the caste hierarchy. In contrast, in the decentralized western Serer commu-nities, we find very simple caste structures with limited social salience. These societies lacked aristocratic elite castes and the attendant high-status court retainer occupational castes. Although they included griot and a num-ber of other low-status occupational castes, these groups were considerably more autonomous and socially integrated in the decentralized western communities than in Siin or Saluum.[18]

Yet in terms of religion, inheritance patterns, and agricultural systems, Siin and the decentralized western societies have more in common than do Siin and Saluum. Despite the common Gelwaar heritage of the two realms, Saluum was influenced more by the powerful, more Muslim Wolof states to the north, which occasionally controlled succession in that kingdom. Wolof influence in Saluum meant that, even prior to the Islamic jihads of the mid–nineteenth century, the elite of Saluum, if not the mass of the pop-ulation, were decidedly more Islamicized than the inhabitants of the Siin.[19]

In contrast, Siin and the decentralized west remained vociferously anti-Islamic and anti-Wolof well into the twentieth century. The basic tenets of Serer animism remain widely understood and respected even among many who call themselves Muslims, Catholics, or Protestants in the Siin and in the decentralized west. In general, these basic elements include some notion of a distant creator force; great emphasis on ancestral spirits and lineage spiritual companions (known as *pangool*) as the primary agents of supernatural guidance, support, judgment, and torment in human affairs; centrality of a wide variety of libations (offerings to *pangool* and other spiritual beings) as a means to direct the forces of nature and to secure benevolent intervention in this world; and belief in a shifting panoply of other unseen spiritual forces.[20]

The farther east we go in the Serer zone, the more Islamic patrilinealism and patriarchy eclipse the varied and complex pre-Islamic Serer patterns of familial and social relations. The decentralized Serers of the west, arguably the least influenced by Islam, follow a variety of inheritance and residence patterns, with a historic emphasis on matrilinealism and matrilocality. The people of the Siin have long occupied a middle position characterized by bilineal inheritance and dominant patrilocality.[21]

In terms of agricultural practices and land tenure systems, Saluum was again the outlier. In the decentralized west, the *lamans,* or "masters of fire"—elders of the lineage of a village founder who served as part resource manager, part rain priest, part land custodian, and part allocative and adjudicatory authority (discussed in greater detail below)—managed land tenure relations and supervised agricultural practices. In the Siin, conquest by the Gelwaar was eased by incorporation of this local land management aristocracy into the state structure. In contrast, the *lamans* of Saluum were marginalized from the early days of Gelwaar state formation and particularly after colonial contact, as that kingdom broke up into a series of quasi-feudal tributary principalities in which royal relatives and vassals competed with *lamans* for tenure control. Like their counterparts in the Wolof states to the north, *lamans* of Saluum were completely displaced in the late nineteenth and early twentieth centuries by the peanut plantations of the Islamic Sufi marabouts.[22]

Along with common *lamanic* institutions, the decentralized west and Siin shared agricultural practices that had disappeared in Saluum. The Serer of Siin and the decentralized states combined farming and herding in an intensive agricultural system that included complex fallow, rotation, and resource management systems. Directed by the *lamanic* elite, this intensive agricultural system produced, especially in the Siin, some of the highest population densities in West Africa. Population densities were somewhat lower in the decentralized west, where soils were rockier, and were significantly lower in Saluum, a geographically vast area where the *lamanic* land management system had been collapsing since the 1500s.[23]

The legacy of state formation plays an important role in understanding the trajectories of the various Serers (thus the commonalties between Siin and Saluum), but it is not the only factor at work in the historical variation among these peoples (thus the linkages between Siin and the western Serers). My choice of the Serer of Siin as the focus of this study reflects, in part, the fact that they are the least outlying, the most central, Serer subgroup.

From the perspective of Saint-Louis or Dakar, however, this complex array of sometimes quite distinct, sometimes related peoples was all Serer. In the colonial perspective, any feature that differentiated one of the Serer groups from their Wolof, Jola, or Mandé neighbors became general characteristics of the Serer as a whole. Thus, *Serer* came to mean the non-Muslim people south of the Muslim Wolof states but north of the Mandé peoples of the Gambia River basin and the Jola even farther south. The Serer were thus pagan and fiercely independent, especially with regard to Islam (even though this generalization failed to apply very well to Saluum). The Serer were also good, indeed ideal, peasants in that their religion and culture made them especially attached to the land and especially disposed to "husband" natural resources (even though this really only came close to being true in the Siin). The Serer were classic egalitarian peasant traditionalists with strong circuits of reciprocity and gift exchange to even out potential imbalances in wealth (even though both centralized states were rigidly stratified in caste terms). The rise of Islamic (primarily Mouride) peanut plantations made the Serer an even more compelling Other for the French. The category "Serer"—an agglomeration of a number of distinct peoples—thus tells us much more about colonial interests and anxieties in the late nineteenth and early twentieth centuries than it does about the politics, religion, culture, agricultural practices, or even language of the people who lived in the area that came to be known as the Serer country (see map 2).

Given the heterogeneity of the umbrella ethnic category "Serer," choosing the nouns and adjectives to describe the people and place under study in this project is somewhat problematic. In this book, I use the everyday language designations of self (Serer) and place (Siin) most common in the zone of this study. I do not mean to imply that my findings necessarily characterize all communities and peoples lumped under the umbrella label *Serer*. The rough sketch of social heterogeneity among the Serers above indicates that certain generalizations drawn from the Siin capture to some degree the social reality of Serer country as a whole, whereas others do not. I thus use the term *Serer* to refer to the people, language, history, and customs of the Serer of the former kingdom of Siin, as exemplified by the experience of one Serer-Siin subgroup, the communities of the subregion known as Njafaj.

The Subzone: About Njafaj

I conducted the majority of my dispute analyses, ethnographic observations, oral history interviews, and conversations with state and customary officials in a group of thirty villages in the region of Njafaj, the northwestern province of the old kingdom of Siin (see map 3). I focused my research for this project on the Njafaj area for both substantive analytic and logistical reasons.

First, the thirty or so villages of Njafaj together represent a wide range of Serer historical and cultural experience. Njafaj includes some of the oldest (and for many observers, the most "traditional") Serer settlements in the Siin. Indeed, communities such as Sob and Diokul seem to have been among the first locales where Serer migrants from the north settled, predating by several centuries the conquest by the Gelwaar in the late 1300s. Njafaj also includes communities established during the Gelwaar period that bear the stamp of a centralized state and, when contrasted with pre-Gelwaar communities, offer insight into how the imposition of state authority articulated with, transformed, and was itself altered by interaction with pre-Gelwaar Serer institutions and culture.[24] Because Njafaj lies at the frontier between the Serer kingdom of Siin and the Wolof kingdom of Baol to the north (bitter rivals during the century leading up to French conquest), it also includes new "frontier settlements" that themselves tell part of the story of social and political change in response to colonialism.[25] This range of village types provides a rich setting in which to explore divergent responses to commodification and the consolidation of postcolonial state power.

Second, as discussed above, when we consider the agglomeration of traits listed under the umbrella category "Serer" (animism and anti-Islamic sentiment, a tendency toward xenophobia, *lamanic* land tenure heritage, complex inheritance structures, an elaborate agropastoral system, a system of crop rotation and fallowing, high population densities, and a reluctance to relocate), the people of Njafaj exhibit more of these characteristics more clearly than do the people of most areas of the Siin, let alone Saluum to the east or the decentralized peoples to the west. The "traditionalist" image of the Njafaj region is accentuated by the fact that, despite its high population density, it has been poorly represented, indeed flatly ignored, in colonial and postcolonial patronage politics. The

Dakar-Niger railroad was routed to service the Wolof-Mouride heartland just to the north and the open, higher-rainfall zones of eastern Saluum, bypassing the center of the "traditional" Serer areas.[26] Likewise, a major national highway to the north follows the old railroad route, and the newer Dakar-Mbour-Fatick-Kaolack highway cuts to the south of Njafaj, linking contemporary administrative centers rather than "backward" villages. Moreover, the degree of positioning and patronage that Serer from the Siin have enjoyed in the administration has been of little help to those in the Njafaj region. This was especially true during the long reign of Senghor's (and later Abdou Diouf's) Parti Socialiste. When the Gelwaar elite of the Siin moved into low- and middle-level bureaucratic posts in the 1960s, they brought laterite and eventually asphalt roads, rural electrification, deepwater wells, telephones, and other projects to the region around Diakhao, the capital of the Siin, and to villages along the highways that were becoming new trading centers. But they tended to ignore "provinces" like Njafaj.

On the surface, then, Njafaj seems the very embodiment of the isolated, traditional, conservative African peasant community. But the thatched roofs and the baobabs belie the region's connections to the major changes of the twentieth century in the western Sahel. Once the peasants of Siin were coerced by the head tax into extensive peanut planting (in the early twentieth century), Njafaj became a major production area, with the Siin estuary providing a convenient marketing outlet for the crop.[27] While Islamic practice in Njafaj tends to be strikingly syncretic (prayer *together with* moonshine historically have been twin pillars of Serer-Muslim identity in this region), Islam has been a powerful vector for social change in Njafaj, contributing to the rise of patrilineal inheritance and the "liberation" of casted groups.

Njafaj is not an isolated rural zone untouched by major economic, religious, social, and political transformations of the colonial and post-colonial periods. Rather, it is a slightly marginalized pocket located an afternoon's bus ride from the national capital, a long day's walk from nascent urban administrative centers, in the heart of the original zone of commodity crop production (the old Peanut Basin) flanked not far to the north by the Mouride holy city of Touba. As a result, Njafaj offers a distinctive blend of the apparent vestiges of traditional Serer society and culture, long confronted by the most powerful forces of social change in twentieth-century West Africa: economic commodification, the partial and incomplete penetration of the state, and the spread of syncretic popular Islam.

Methods Used in and around Njafaj

At a logistical level, Njafaj also makes an excellent choice of focus because, for the past thirty years, the French government research agency Office de la Recherche Scientifique et Technique d'Outre-mer (ORSTOM) has conducted an extensive public health research project in the thirty villages of the area.[28] In addition to a wide range of epidemiological and experimental vaccine data, ORSTOM has accumulated a rich data set of basic demographic information for the region's thirty-five thousand inhabitants.[29] The data have been collected and refined over some thirty years by French research directors and Serer survey workers recruited from the Njafaj area. Nearly all the surveyors and staff assistants on the project were born in the area and speak the Serer of Siin as their native language.[30] They thus have unusual access to a population that has otherwise shown considerable mistrust of outsiders, especially outsiders who present themselves with pen, paper, clipboard, and intrusive questions about family size and economic activities. (As in many other formerly colonial areas, these instruments of survey research suggest tax collection for most people in the Siin.)

Building on the empirical base established by ORSTOM's extensive demographic survey data (complemented by my own survey, discussed below), I adopted a sixfold methodological strategy, centered on close analysis of disputes over land brought to the attention of the state's rural councils. I tracked the outbreak, adjudication, and aftermath of thirty-one land disputes, conducting semistructured interviews with 109 litigants and adjudicatory officials in these conflicts. Disputes arose most often from contracts over land pawns, crises in the authority of a household, conflicts between the interests of cultivators and herders, inheritance claims, and boundary ambiguities.

These disputes served as an arena in which I witnessed more than just the conflict over who should inherit this field, or whether those boundary rocks should line up on the near or the far side of that baobab tree. In asserting claims and discussing the meaning of their conflicts, litigants led me into deeper discussion of underlying notions of legitimate ownership, authoritative resource management, and rightful forms of exchange.

My five other methodological strategies placed this core analysis of disputes over land in cultural, social structural, and historical context. First, I followed classic techniques of participant observation as I lived and sometimes worked alongside Serer agriculturalists in the Njafaj region. I had been conducting research and building relationships in the central village of the Njafaj region, Tukar, since 1988, when I was first assigned to that community as an intern on a rural development project. My field research beginning in the early 1990s thus extended long-developing relationships, deepening my access as a participant-observer. The majority of my conversations and interviews took place in a combination of French and Wolof, with Serer-Siin used on occasion. Regardless of my linguistic need for a translator (helpful when an interviewee spoke only Serer-Siin, in which I have facility but not fluency), I always conducted interviews with a local companion or partner from Tukar or one of the surrounding villages. I found that the presence of a local person situated me socially and rendered my questions and the interview process less alien and less potentially threatening.[31]

Second, to systematically embed land disputes in wider Serer systems of meaning, I conducted interviews based on hypothetical scenarios of dispute over property inheritance and exchange. I conducted these scenario interviews with the entire pool of individuals interviewed regarding land disputes, along with another 100 randomly selected individuals (for a total of 209 interviews). These interviews began by my recounting a brief vignette regarding the outbreak and resolution of a hypothetical property-related dispute. I then asked respondents how they might react if they were the protagonist in the scenario and why they felt certain authoritative interventions were appropriate or not, moral or immoral, legitimate or illegitimate.

Third, to more fully explore competing historical memories of Serer culture and precolonial social institutions, I conducted a series of open-ended interviews with individuals identified as knowledgeable leaders on subjects of "tradition" and control of land. In order to draw out interpretations unique to particular individuals, I conducted these interviews, unlike others, using a tape recorder. Prior experience suggested that the presence of the recorder would cause respondents to embellish their accounts, to describe their version of the ideal local political and cultural heritage rather than give the exact factual details of a stereotypical historical account. The machine generally produced the effect I anticipated. Respondents oriented themselves toward the tape recorder, producing rather self-conscious, stylized narrative-performances regarding their own subjective versions of "authentic" cultural history.

Fourth, working through the existing ORSTOM network of weekly demographic and epidemiological surveys, I implemented a 784-person survey that correlated attitudes about authority (contemporary and historical) against six social structural positioning variables (gender, class, caste, religion, family position, and degree of contact with the commoditized economy), as well as against a series of cultural-ideological factors. Chapter 3 presents the details, results, and meanings of this survey in greater detail.

Finally, I traced the roots of contemporary land tenure issues, as well as the wider encounter between the state and local culture, into the colonial period by exploring archival materials including colonial legal records, administrative reports, and correspondence between French colonial officials and local elites. My archival research focused on colonial legal records for cases dealing with land tenure and disputes over land found in both the Archives Nationales du Sénégal in Dakar and in unclassified collections at the Tribunal Régional in the regional capitals of Kaolack and Fatick. I also searched the archives for correspondence and reports illustrative of the process by which colonial officials self-consciously harnessed local political legitimacy to promote "principles of French civilization," central among which were free trade and the sometimes forced introduction of peanut production into local agricultural rotations. Together these materials amount to elements of a genealogy of Serer political institutions and political culture. They reveal the agency not only of French administrators, who functioned for a time as veritable cultural engineers, but also of Serer people who collaborated with, resisted, and sometimes subtly redirected the colonial project. The documents testify to the plasticity of institutions and traditions in the heyday of imperialism and provide the necessary backdrop for understanding uses of the "traditional" in our own time.

The Serer of Siin: A Defining Initial Exemplar?

As discussed above, the precise representativeness of Serer institutions and culture is less important for this study than Serer efforts at syncretic adaptation. Ironically, however, the Serer of Siin may be of considerable importance to our understanding of rural Africa because they are *suspiciously* illustrative of the so-called classical African peasant. The Serer of Siin may seem so characteristic of the "ideal African peasant" because of a possible prototype effect.[32] The Serer may represent a defining initial exemplar of rural African societies, the people with whom, by historical and geographical accident, the French had the earliest, most extensive, and most positive interaction. As a result the image of the Serer may exert a disproportionate influence in defining the wider generic conceptual category ("African peasants") of which they are a part.[33]

The earliest extensive French colonial contact with rural Africa occurred on the western coast, just south of the Sahara, in what is now Senegal.[34] The French worked closely with and came to know well the Wolof of Kajor (around their capital at Saint-Louis) and the Lebu fishermen of the Cap Vert peninsula (off the coast of which lay the French slave entrepôt, Gorée Island, on the shore of which Dakar would arise). The Wolof and Lebu were rural societies, to be sure. But, for a variety of reasons, neither occupied the place of "typical African peasant" in the French colonial *imaginaire*. Before their demographic and social collapse in the face of territorial pressure, the Lebu appeared in colonial accounts as a coastal fishing folk. The Wolof, who rapidly assumed important posts in the colonial administration and in the urban economy of the coastal enclaves, appeared partly as potential collaborators in colonial rule, partly as warriors and rivals to French expansion, and partly as sub-Saharan proto-Muslims.[35]

It was not until the traffic in slaves, and more important, commodity colonialism, drove the French toward the interior, that they encountered a people who struck them as quintessentially agrarian, as peasant folk. As they moved just inland from the Wolof and Lebu areas, they "discovered" the Serer, who most fully evoked nostalgic descriptions of the *bon paysan de Provence*, an idealized peasant clearly "industrious, respectful of the environment and social hierarchies, attached to his land and his religion and his customs."[36] To the limited extent that such observations reflect an awareness of variation among the Serer subgroups, the idealized-peasant label applied most frequently and fully to the Serer of Siin, and to lesser degrees to the Serer of Saluum and to the "acephalous" Serers of None, Dieghem, Safen, and Niominka. Idealization of the Serer deepened as a result of the specific position they held in the early spread of commodity crop production in Africa.

By the second decade of the twentieth century, Sufi brotherhoods, especially the Mourides, were quickly transforming their rural religious camps, or *daaras*, into plantations, the dominant mode of peanut production.[37] The French both loved and hated the *daara* plantation system. It was of course enormously successful in expanding peanut production. But it enhanced the power of Islamic leaders who enjoyed unparalleled popular legitimacy and with whom the French had fought, sometimes bitterly, to gain control of the Sahel.[38]

But just to the south of the Mouride heartland, the French had discovered a completely different mode of agricultural production in which "classical" peasants were religiously (literally) wedded to crop rotation, fallow, soil improvement, and the maintenance of nitrogen-fixing trees. "Ideal" Serer peasants seemed quite a bit more ideal in contrast to their Sufi-*daara* counterparts to the north. Although the French and the marabouts were settling into mutually beneficial relations of collaboration centered on peanut production, they remained wary of one another. In the early decades of the twentieth century, the colonial regime was keen to establish an alternative and counterweight to a Sufi elite that threatened to monopolize production of one of the more profitable cash crops in French West Africa.[39]

We should thus keep a few facts in mind while delving into this case study of one of the primary (and certainly most romanticized) Serer subgroups. First, colonial contact with the Serer began very early, probably earlier than with any other African group whom the French came to think of as "peasants." Second, beginning in the nineteenth century with the end of the slave trade and the rise of commodity colonialism, the Serer stood out in the French colonial imagination as an idealized, true African peasantry. Idealization of the Serer deepened in the twentieth century in the search for an alternative to the *daara* mode of production. The Serer were ideal African peasants not because of any representativeness as such but because their agricultural system and religion appealed to French notions about agrarian pasts and to French economic and political interests.

Generalizations about rural Africa in the colonial *mise en valeur* (putting to use) literature (and in its descendants, the modernization, development, and neoliberal approaches) correspond to a striking degree to the institutions and practices of the Serer, especially that "most Serer" subgroup, the Serer of Siin. Quasi-religious attachment to soil, careful husbanding of resources, mixed pasture and farming, lack of individual title, lineage–rain priest management of communal tenure systems, centrality of ancestral spirits in rain and fertility cults, reluctance to abandon subsistence for cash crops, tight circuits of reciprocity, antiaccumulative ethic, and complex lineage systems—these and other "truisms" regarding African peasants are especially applicable to the Serer.[40] They are so thoroughly applicable that—given the heterogeneity of rural Africa, early French contact with the Serer, and their special role as idealized peasants in the French colonial imagination—one must question whether the Serer are a classic illustration of the African peasant "type," or whether the concept "African peasant" is itself an overwrought generalization grounded in a prototype effect. If the latter is so, a strong case can be made for further research into the possibility that the Serer were the defining initial exemplar of the category "African peasant," distorting that supposedly generic category such that sui generis features of this one people have been raised to the level of "true generalizations" about African peasantries as a whole.

SERER AND GELWAAR BEFORE COLONIALISM

The precolonial history of the Serer of Siin spans at least five centuries of detailed oral historical accounts. Major episodes from competing oral historical accounts—versions of tales of migration and village founding, accounts of conquest by the Gelwaar matrilineage, and renditions of relations between the emerging Gelwaar state and historic Serer local authorities—provide the raw material for present-day contests over the politics of memory. For ease of presentation, the historical narrative in this chapter is a simplified account of dominant versions of historical memory. Later in the book, I unpack these dominant versions and suggest the complex politics of defining "authentic" local history and real "tradition," a politics that sets the stage for the syncretic adaptation of new developmental institutions in more recent times.

Serer Communities before Conquest by the Gelwaar

The oral historical record, written accounts by early Arab and European explorers, and physical anthropological evidence suggest that the various Serer peoples migrated south from the Fuuta Tooro region (Senegal River valley) beginning around the eleventh century, when Islam first came across the Sahara.[41] Although our knowledge of the pre-Islamic Fuuta Tooro remains rather sketchy, two points of note have emerged relatively clearly in recent historical and ethnographic work on this region.[42] First, the Senegal River valley was an important population, agricultural, and technological center of its day, and served as the common homeland for several of contemporary Senegal's major ethnic groups (Serer, the Pulaar-speaking Halpulaar, and Tukolor). Second, although the exact details of the cleavage remain obscure, it seems that, whether for religious-ideological or economic-material reasons, a fraction of Fuuta Tooro society resisted conversion to Islam. Following a classic pattern of response to social tension in low population density, land-abundant Africa, those who resisted Islam chose to migrate rather than convert. Thus began a journey south and westward through the nascent Wolof kingdoms of Jolof, Kajor, and Baol, and eventually beyond, into the then-sparsely populated valleys of the Siin and Saluum Rivers.[43]

The very etymology of the composite term *Serer* reflects this pattern of cleavage and migration. The term *Serer* is most probably a derivative of the Pulaar term *sererabe,* meaning to separate or to divorce.[44] Given the centrality of family and familial metaphors in structuring social, economic, and political relations in this region, it is perhaps no coincidence that *sererabe* connotes not simply cleavage in a physical sense but more precisely a *familial* cleavage.

A slow, multigenerational migration across Wolof territories and into the valleys of the Siin and Saluum Rivers allowed for considerable contact between Serer refugees and their Wolof hosts, accounting for the not inconsiderable linguistic overlap between Wolof and Serer, as well as a number of similarities in agricultural practices and land management institutions. Indeed, the Serer and Wolof share enough terminology, institutions, political structures, and practices that we are left uncertain about the origins of shared institutions: did the Serer, who would later develop sophisticated farming systems, teach the Wolof about fallow, rotation, and custodianship on their way south, or did the Serer, who may have been Pulaar-speaking herders when they left the Fuuta, learn their intensive farming system from the Wolof with whom they mingled in exile?[45]

In Serer-Siin oral histories, the account of the last stage of the journey from Fuuta Tooro usually depicts a heroic, itinerant founding ancestor making his way into the wild, forested valleys of the Siin and Saluum Rivers. There, most accounts depict the hero-migrant settling on a desirable parcel of bush, striking up a rude habitation of some sort, and setting fire to the surrounding brush and forest.[46] The ensuing wildfire cleared a vast estate, making space for farming, settlement, and civilization. Indeed, the fire establishes a fundamental ontological boundary—the division between the wild realm of uncontrolled, dark, threatening nature (the *o kop ale,* or "wilderness," in the language of the Serer of Siin) and the realm of human activity, community, and civilization—as an Arendtian act of human will to create a public space (in Serer-Siin, the *pind ke* or "group of compounds").[47]

This original fire set the terms for claims to use and control land. The burnt space came to represent the fire estate controlled by the founder-migrant's lineage. Eventually, control over this estate became an inheritable office, passing to eldest male in the lineage of the founder.[48] This office has many names in the Siin, from the evocative "master of fire" *(yal naay)* or "master of his little piece" *(yal ndaak)* to the now widely circulated title *laman.*[49] By the late twentieth century, these masters of fire, or *lamans,* will have become icons for the lost forms of trustworthy, culturally legitimate governance of land, people, and natural resources.

"Ownership" of these fire estates operated on a number of levels of meaning. *Lamans* and their descendants were not simply considered the creators of the land, nor did they simply "possess" land in a negative sense (one cannot use the fields of the fire estate without permission of the *laman.*) The *laman's* lineage was responsible not just for the use and disposal of the fire estate but also for its well-being. Both the land and its custodians possessed material and spiritual dimensions. Without a complete grasp of this concept of ownership as "holistic custodianship," we cannot make sense of the predominant Serer idea of property.

At a material level, the *laman* coordinated an elaborate system of land management and soil preservation through crop rotation, forest maintenance, and integration of herding with farming. For generations prior to commodification, this system ensured the fertility of rather poor, sandy soils and enabled the Serer to achieve one of the highest population densities anywhere in the Sahel.[50] By controlling the annual allocation of fields, *lamans* coordinated a three-year rotation of *pod* (large millet), *maac* (small millet), and *tos* (fallow). The *laman* ensured that members of the community pastured their livestock on the land during the fallow year, adding vital nutrients to the soil in the form of manure. He also safeguarded the remarkable *sas*, or *Acacia albida* trees, which not only fix nitrogen but also sprout new leaves toward the end of the dry season, providing food for livestock at a time of year when feed supplies and grazing lands have been exhausted.[51]

However, members of the *laman's* lineage were not custodians of the land only in this material sense. The *laman* and his lineage "owned" the fire estate in the sense that their ancestrally allied spiritual beings *(pangool)* inhabited and ensured the well-being of the *lamanic* estate itself. Serer religion places considerable emphasis on these ancestral spirits, sets of which are associated with each lineage. In the case of a *laman*, we usually find that a group of *pangool* accompanied the village founder on his journey, helping to make his extraordinary exploits possible. The first *laman* established a shrine to these *pangool*, becoming the priest-custodian of the shrine, "the intermediary among the land, the peasants, and the *pangool*."[52] *Pangool* associated with the founding of a village take particular interest in the well-being of the fire estate and the success of agriculture.[53] Climate and other forces beyond human control—rainfall, soil fertility, plagues, yield, and so on—are viewed as especially sensitive to the intervention of these *pangool*.

Thus, custodianship of the fire estate itself was a concern not just of the living members of the *laman's* lineage but of the dead and the unseen as well. In the dominant system of meaning in the Siin, a family along with its allied ancestral spirits held and watched over land. Those spirits played a role in removing the land from the chaos of the forest, and they continued to ensure its fertility and productivity in their capacity as allies of a *lamanic* family. Understanding this conception of ownership requires not exactly an acceptance of, but at least a sensitivity to, a distinct ontological perspective with regard to land—the kind of ontology long since hounded out of Western materialist-empiricist understanding of what is "real" in matters of, for example, real property (see chapter 4).

Gelwaar Conquest: Norman-Style Blending
and a Federal Compromise

Sometime in the late 1300s, a Mandé matriclan known as the Gelwaar arrived near the mouth of the Siin estuary.[54] Although we do not know the exact details of their experience, the Gelwaar appear to have worked their way westward after a conflict within their own society, usually placed somewhere in the old empire of Mali. The Gelwaar cooperated with the *lamanic* authorities they encountered on the coast, establishing their first capital at or near the village of Mbissel, heart of an ancient *lamanic* estate. Through intermarriage they made alliances with major *lamanic* lineages in the Siin. In a century-long process of military domination and dynasty building, the exact narrative of which remains sketchy, they established suzerainty over the entire region. As they conquered or coopted *lamanic* estates throughout the valley of the Siin, they gradually moved their capital upriver, settling finally at the village of Diakhao, near the geographical center of this densely populated Serer area.[55]

Within the first few generations of Gelwaar rule in the kingdom of Siin, foundations were also laid for a twin kingdom, Saluum. Gelwaar rivals of the *maad* (precolonial king) and pretenders to the throne were regularly shipped eastward, toward the Serer communities along the Saluum River. They eventually established a second kingdom that would rival Siin in importance and follow its own distinct historical trajectory.[56]

Although the Gelwaar conquered the Serer of Siin and Saluum and imposed a centralized state modeled on the Mandé empire of Mali, like the Normans in England they intermarried with their subjects. As a result, the Gelwaar became increasingly Serer in terms of language, culture, ritual practices, cuisine, style of dress, and to a great extent, religion. Early travelers' accounts, for example, suggest that—although the Gelwaar usually retained Islamic Sufi marabouts in their court (primarily for their command of useful communications technology: that is, they could read and write)—they were clearly adherents to the animist, ancestor worshipping religion of the ordinary Serer.[57]

Matrilineality made it possible for the Gelwaar to intermarry and assimilate culturally, without compromising their distinctiveness as a castelike ruling elite. Gelwaar noble status and succession to the throne of the *maad* passed from a particular male ruler to his sister's son.[58] A child was a Gelwaar noble if that child's mother was a Gelwaar. The social status of the father was of no significance for succession or for determining the nobility of offspring. Gelwaar princesses were thus free to have children with Serer men, cementing alliances with the preconquest ruling class without diluting royal bloodlines. This strict matrilineal descent system permitted the Gelwaar to avoid the dilemma of the Norman elite who conquered England. In the Gelwaar case, intermarriage did not threaten to dissolve the distinction between victorious aristocrats and subjugated population. Rather, intermarriage helped solidify alliances with local, subjugated notables.

Somewhat accidentally, Gelwaar matrilinealism also generated increasing numbers of seminoble offspring who would fill the ranks of a variety of retainer castes, occupational groups that tended to the needs of the *maad* and the noble entourage. In the strict logic of matrilineal inheritance, men would normally not think of their own offspring as heirs or successors but would instead devote such attention to their sisters' children. Yet the Gelwaar matrilineal system did not exist in a vacuum: the Serer region as a whole exhibited both matrilineal and patrilineal inheritance patterns, not to mention the constant encroachment of Islamic patrilineal standards. Men married to Gelwaar women (themselves often from *lamanic* families) *did* concern themselves not just with the well-being of their sister's children but also with the future of their own children. These children did not descend into the undifferentiated mass of commoners (Serer free farmers), but instead remained near the royal court and fulfilled royal-retainer occupational roles: royal valets, royal stable keepers, royal cooks, royal chamber maids, and so on.[59]

In addition to intermarrying with the *lamanic* elite, the Gelwaar studiously avoided undermining the bases for *lamanic* authority. They made no effort to reorganize land tenure relations or impose an agricultural levy or other means of resource extraction rooted in agricultural production.[60] When it came to land use, rotation, fallow, land allocation, and adjudication of land-related conflicts, they interfered only on exceptional occasions with *lamanic* control, effectively incorporating the old Serer elite as local authorities in a federal arrangement. This federal division of powers was central to the bloodless conquest of the Siin and the maintenance of a rather stable political system for almost four and a half centuries.

Centralization, Caste, and Gelwaar Constitutionalism

At their own, upper level of the federal state system, the Gelwaar established a number of centralized institutions. They divided their realm into quasi-feudal provinces over which they appointed agents, usually allies of the court or the more noteworthy among the husbands of the Gelwaar princesses. These agents, known most commonly as *jarafs*, oversaw and taxed trade, especially exchanges involving outsiders;[61] managed military affairs, especially recruitment; conducted border raids; captured slaves; and generally served as the eyes and ears of the royal court. While they did not impose an institutionalized system of taxation or resource extraction, they nevertheless used their power to arbitrarily seize livestock, grain alcohol, slaves, people of low caste, the young, or women when it suited their interests. Such extraction was generally limited to times of war and other community emergency, or was used as a form of punishment against those who offended or otherwise blocked the interests of the royal court.

Warfare and the economy of predation, important to the Gelwaar regime in general, were the special purview of its centralized military institution, the *ceddo* warrior-slave caste. As in many states in the western Sahel, in the kingdom of Siin the military was composed of a distinct, low-status occupational caste, whose members were largely drawn from those captured in battle. The *ceddo* caste was mainly endogamous, marrying occasionally with other low-status occupational caste members (griots, blacksmiths, weavers, potters, leatherworkers, and so on). As a military caste, the *ceddo* did not farm or receive provisions from the court, living instead from what they could plunder from enemies of the regime, when possible, or from the Serer population of Siin, when necessary.[62]

The *ceddo's* low social status reveals much about the political logic of the caste system among the Serer and other peoples of the western Sahel. As table 2 suggests, like the *ceddo*, both blacksmiths and griots produced goods and services that have considerable significance for the short-term stability of a political regime. One caste holds the secret to manipulating metal to produce weapons and other valuable tools. The other holds the secrets of the past, of genealogy, origins, and naming, and as such constructs and maintains the crucial ideological infrastructure of legitimacy for the regime.

The caste system of the Serer and Wolof states effectively blocks any group that provides a good or service of great significance for the short-term regime stability from enjoying high status. It is striking that free farmers have much higher social status than the politically significant warrior caste, who in fact are treated as slaves. But this makes sense given that, in the short term, farmers have less power, less potential to destabilize the regime than warriors. This caste structure thus relegates potentially threatening occupational groups—warriors, metal smiths, and information smiths—to the very lowest status. This particular caste hierarchy may have emerged—whether by intentional design or not is entirely unclear—as a way for demographically small noble lineages like the Gelwaar of Siin and Saluum to maintain political control and stability by ensuring the structural subordination of those best positioned to emerge as political rivals: that is, groups which controlled crucial instruments of immediate power such as warfare, weaponry, propaganda, and historical memory.[63]

TABLE 2. Social Status and Political Importance of Non-noble Occupational Castes

		Importance of Caste's Product or Service to Short-Term Political Stability of Regime	
		HIGH	LOW
Social Status and Autonomy	HIGH	Gelwaar and customary aristocrat	Free farmers
	LOW	Blacksmiths, griots, *ceddo* warriors	Weavers, potters, woodsmiths

In the Gelwaar regime, the *maad* was not an absolute monarch but rather a king-in-council. Major policy decisions, military matters, and perhaps most important, succession to the position of *maad* required the consent of a shifting array of relatives and close advisers of the *maad* as well as the holders of three high offices: *linguere* (royal sister), *grand farba* (head of the *ceddo*), and *grand jaraf* (de facto representative of the free farmers).[64] In the matrilineal descent system of the Gelwaar, the *linguere*, eldest sister of the monarch, held a pivotal position in succession, since her eldest son (the matrilineal nephew of the king) usually emerged as a natural, though not the automatic, heir to the throne (younger brothers of the *maad*, and junior, especially dynamic or aggressive matrilineal nephews, were the most common pretenders to the office).[65]

The *grand farba* played a decisive role in matters of war and in external relations and could, depending on his relationship with the *maad*, effectively direct the kingdom's military affairs.[66] Finally, the *grand jaraf* represented the free farmer group, the majority of the Serer population, who were neither of low-status nonagricultural occupational castes nor of the noble matrilineage (nor of any of the quasi-noble retainer castes that had developed around the court). This *grand jaraf*, who functioned as a kind of prime minister, served as leader of the royal council, managed deliberations over royal succession, and exerted considerable influence in the day-to-day affairs of the kingdom.[67] *Grand jarafs* do not appear to have been selected from among the *lamans*, although this may have been the initial arrangement, given the fragility of the early Gelwaar regime. Eventually, as the state became more consolidated, local-level officials appointed by the *maad (jarafs)* became more powerful and themselves emerged as the most likely candidates to become *grand jarafs*. Oral histories do refer, however, to instances where local leaders (such as *lamans*) rejected particular candidates for *grand jaraf*.[68]

The office of *grand jaraf* highlights the federal nature of the constitutional structure of the Gelwaar state, the degree to which the regime's stability depended on granting local autonomy to the conquered population. But it would be a stretch to call this a protodemocracy or a kind of constitutional monarchy in the making. If anything, the Serer constitutional order bears more resemblance to the "estates society" of early modern Europe,[69] wherein central, monarchical authority was checked by a quasi-corporatist system that granted voice to major status groups (nobles, church, burghers). This arrangement clearly reflects how, in the process of state building, the Gelwaar migrants developed innovative institutions to incorporate and coopt the populations they had conquered.

Gelwaar and Laman: Supernatural Dependence

Although the *lamans* were not formally incorporated into the *grand jaraf* mechanism for "popular influence" on the state, Serer accounts depict them as having considerable sway over affairs of the kingdom on an entirely different plane. As discussed above, after a few generations, the Gelwaar had adopted not just Serer language and cultural practices but also the Serer brand of animist religion. As a consequence, Serer accounts suggest, they accepted the supernatural importance of *lamanic* lineages.

Lamans could be useful to the Gelwaar leaders because of their special relationship with the *pangool* that had accompanied the village-founding ancestor and that still resided in and looked after *lamanic* fire estates.[70] The lineage of an important *laman* also included a secondary official of unusual supernatural vision, a *saltigué*. *Saltigués* were said to have the ability to predict the future, especially the rainy season and harvest, and the power to intervene to alter some future outcomes. The basis of a *saltigué*'s power was the fact that he was, by some accounts, a *naq*, a soul eater (also translated as witch or vampire), a supernatural being who appeared ordinary, but who was driven to slowly consume the souls of friends, neighbors, or loved ones.[71] Though considered to be *naqs*, these *saltigués* were thought to resist the temptation to use their power to "eat souls," instead turning their abilities to the identification and suppression of these creatures, as well as to divination for the benefit of the community.[72]

Serer accounts suggest that *lamans* and *saltigués* became important allies for the Gelwaar lineage once they had come to think of themselves as Serer and had come to accept Serer animism, with its attendant fear of being on bad terms with the *pangool* or having their souls "eaten." In villages with important *lamanic* traditions, oral histories tell of the regular visits of the *maad* and members of his court to secure the supernatural intercession of the *laman* or *saltigué,* or both, in order to ensure the longevity of a particular reign, to foretell the result of a particular policy initiative, to neutralize a specific rival in court, or to secure victory in an upcoming battle.[73] These visits ranged from regular attendance at annual community fertility rites (see the discussion of one such ritual in chapter 6) to secret journeys by leaders whose fear of court intrigue compelled them to visit the hut of a *saltigué* in the dead of night.

If we take the Serer oral histories at face value, the Gelwaar became so assimilated into Serer culture and religion that they depended on the *lamanic* elite for supernatural services that they could not obtain in any other way. This may of course be a kind of retrospective rationalization on the part of a subordinated people, a carving out of *some realm* of autonomy, and control by a people completely subjugated by an outside conqueror. Indeed, following this line of interpretation, this dependence on the *lamanic* elite illustrates the "ascent into the supernatural" as a means of making sense of and coping with material subjugation.[74]

Even if we consider Gelwaar dependence on the *lamanic* elite for supernatural services an inventive reworking of history to make the Serer *feel* less subjugated, it is a telling one in that it reiterates the basic theme of federalism at the heart of the political system. The Serer do not argue that they secretly controlled the state or sabotaged it by casting spells, poisoning leaders, or eating their souls. Rather, this version of historical memory places the accent on mutual dependence. The Gelwaar, with their *ceddo,* enjoy a monopoly of political power and control over the means of violence. But the Gelwaar are presented as *needing* the Serer elite for something. Whether historically accurate or not, this account casts the Gelwaar and the *laman* as partners in governance, an interpretation that reflects popular acceptance of a federal arrangement as a natural, taken-for-granted political structure.

ENCOUNTER WITH COLONIALISM

From its earliest encounters with Portuguese explorers to its incorporation as a loyal vassal state in the French African empire, the regime of the Siin found ways to benefit from new relations of exchange and new systems of domination that accompanied European expansion. Gelwaar and Serer adaptation to centuries of contact with European explorers, slave traders, commodity colonialists, and imperialists transformed the institutions, social structure, and what we have to come to know as the "ancestral tradition" of the Serer in important ways.

Early Colonialism, Slave Trade, and
Political-Economic Roots of the Regime

As the slave trade expanded down the West African coast, Dutch, Portuguese, French, and British traders established semipermanent outposts in the vicinity of the Serer state of Siin, including outposts at the coastal villages of Joal, Fadiouth, and Palmarin, as well as the slave trade emporium for this part of West Africa, the island of Gorée. Like other elites in the region, the Gelwaar took advantage of the new export economy in slaves in two primary ways. First, the European outposts on the Siin coast, and more important, the larger community at Gorée, needed regular supplies of wood, grain, cattle, and other provisions. Even in the late 1400s, the kingdom of the "Barbesin" figured prominently in supplying these trading outposts.[75] The elite of the Siin engaged in profitable exchanges of millet, meat, wood, and other raw materials for weaponry, horses, cloth, manufactures, new kinds of alcohol, and other European goods.

At the same time, the Gelwaar were able to redirect their domestic institution of slavery to provide a new kind of exportable commodity. Of course, as Philip Curtin and others have established, this represented both a major transformation in the institution of African slavery (captives had never been treated as salable commodities for export out of the community, except in limited numbers supplied to the Arab North African market) and a basis for significant sociopolitical transformation within communities like the Siin itself.

The distinctly collaborative, indirect rule relationship that began to develop in this period between the French colonial administration and the Gelwaar regime of the Siin may be rooted in part in geographical accident: peoples and communities closer to the European coastal presence at Saint-Louis and Gorée bore the brunt of socioeconomic transformation and political conflict, whereas "anterior" communities and peoples, like the Serer of the Siin, enjoyed the time and the distance necessary to "reposition" themselves to benefit from new economic and political relationships. Seeing the example of their Wolof and Lebu neighbors, the Serer recognized that part of this repositioning meant avoiding futile opposition to colonial expansion, and seeking out amicable and profitable relations of trade that preserved as much local autonomy as possible.[76]

There is reason to suspect that both the provisioning trade and the slave trade preserved the federal compromise at the heart of the Gelwaar regime. By the time the Gelwaar elite had consolidated their control over the Serer territories, the first Portuguese caravels were appearing off the coast of the Siin (in the mid-1400s). For this reason, the Gelwaar and the *ceddo* did not need to displace the *lamans* as a local economic elite that controlled agricultural capital and surplus, because they dominated the provisioning and slave trades and thereby enjoyed their own independent economic base. The slave and provisioning trades made possible a political system—with a king in council dominated by the *grand jaraf*—which provided for relative, institutional balance among the three key groups that enjoyed independent bases for economic survival (the free farmers, the *lamanic* elite, and the *ceddo*). The very persistence of "old" Serer cultural traditions centered on the *lamanic* elite is, then, a peculiar artifact of a centralized state powerful enough to protect the Serer from regional threats to the north—the Wolof states—yet sufficiently autonomous, thanks to the slave and provisioning trades, to leave the Serer peasants to themselves for some four hundred years.

By the 1830s, however, the political-economic arrangement that had balanced Gelwaar, *ceddo,* and peasant interests and thereby preserved the peculiar Gelwaar regime started to unravel. The slave trade, which had been waning for a century or so as the bulk of the traffic moved down the West African coast, well beyond Senegal, was coming to a close. In the remaining decades of the nineteenth century, colonies, and by extension, vassal states within colonies like the regime of the Siin, would be reevaluated for their usefulness in the new colonial raison d'être, commodity production.

Instability during the Search for a New Colonial Rationale: The Jihad Period

As the chief French administrative center on the African coast, the closest sub-Saharan colony to the metropole, and the site of an ongoing experiment in the transformative power of "universalistic" French civilization (the assimilation project in the Four Communes), Senegal enjoyed a favored position in the search for a new colonial raison d'être. Missionaries and enterprising administrators in the mid-1800s set up experimental farms in the Senegalese interior. They dabbled in cotton plantations. They planted orchards and vast expanses of tobacco, coffee, cocoa, palm oil trees, potatoes, tomatoes, corn, and a variety of other would-be commercial crops.[77] International competition, weak export markets, unreliable labor inputs, and a host of other unexpected obstacles frustrated many attempts to justify a costly presence in an arid region with poor, sandy soils, limited infrastructure, tropical diseases, and a recalcitrant population that, it was felt, could be redeemed from savagery only with great effort.

Peanuts and peanut oil—useful for lubricating the engines of industrialization and making soap to clean up the increasingly self-conscious unwashed masses of Europe—put Senegal squarely on the map of plausibly profitable colonial enterprise in the mid-1800s. It would nevertheless take several decades of persuading peasants that they *needed* to grow this new item for cash before the colony became a profitable exporter. In the Siin, the unusual reluctance of the Serer peasants to disturb their carefully managed agropastoral system added a few more decades to the delay.

The interim between the decline of the slave trade (in the 1830s) and the widespread cultivation of peanuts as cash crop for export (in the 1890s in the Wolof area of northern Senegal and a decade or two later in the Siin) was a period of considerable destabilization not just for the Serer peoples but also for the entire region. Following a pattern familiar in other nodes of European expansion in the Sahel, North Africa, and the Middle East, Islam became a major idiom of resistance to colonial expansion.[78] By the middle of the nineteenth century in the western Sahel, revitalized Islam took the form of jihad movements. Clerics responded to the midcentury period of crisis and destabilization by declaring twin holy wars: against the Wolof and Serer pagan states and against the invading Christian infidel. In this view, the drunkenness and moral laxity of the pagan elites (the *ceddo* were a favorite target) had made the African states easy prey to the beguiling Christians on the coast. The jihad movements fought to sweep away the pagan elites, force subject populations beneath them to convert to Islam, and unify fragmented ethnic groups and petty states under the banner of the prophet in order to block further European infidel expansion.

From the 1850s until the consolidation of continental imperial domination in the 1890s, a series of military-religious movements inspired large numbers of devout followers to destroy or completely transform most of the precolonial states. Whole villages were forced to choose between the razor or the sword: shave your head (a physical indication of the acceptance of the prophet) or face death as an infidel. Most chose the former; in some cases, entire communities suffered the latter.[79]

The kingdom of Siin faced the razor/sword ultimatum early and met with an unusual outcome—survival as a non-Islamic society—that would set its distinctive course (collaboration in a relationship of indirect rule that left it a reasonably intact colonial vassal state) for the remainder of the colonial period. Ma Ba Diakhou, born in the southern Saluum tributary state of Niumi, led one of the earliest jihads in the region. In 1862, he overthrew the regime of Saluum, converted or destroyed the *ceddo* of that state, and consolidated a theocratic regime. His next target: the pagans of the Siin.

Throughout the jihad period, colonial rulers in Saint-Louis were of two minds regarding the spreading theocratic movements. On the one hand,

French officials, like the Islamic cleric-generals, considered the Gelwaar and the *ceddo* belligerent drunkards, too lazy and uncontrollable to "civilize," too unpredictable to rely on as collaborators. In part because a number of key officials (like Governor Louis Faidherbe) had served in Algeria, the administration tended to see Islam as a civilizing force, bringing not just literacy but also labor discipline to "semisavage" Africans.[80] In this view (so characteristic of the origins of anthropology), Islam, although repugnant, at least represented an interim, partial step toward civilization, something halfway between European ideals (Christianity or Enlightenment, depending on your politics) and a "tribal" state of nature.[81]

On the other hand, as the jihad regimes spread and became more powerful, the French quickly recognized that these new states, rooted in an increasingly legitimate popular ideology, were less pliant than the pagan kingdoms and could pose a real threat to imperial domination. Colonial officials thus pursued careful, ad hoc policies designed to maximize rivalry and conflict among African groups, effectively using Islamic jihad leaders to sweep away or weaken the troublesome *ceddo*, but intervening when necessary to check the growing power and ambition of the cleric-generals.[82]

This is where the Siin came into the picture. As correspondence between Governor Faidherbe and Ma Ba Diakhou reveals, the colonial administration encouraged the Muslim leader in his struggle against the various tributary states of Saluum,[83] and eventually, in taking the entire kingdom in 1862. But as Ma Ba set his sights on Siin and worked out alliances with leaders of Wolof states to the north, the French accelerated their efforts to find a way to destroy the Islamic leader.[84]

Relations between Saint-Louis and Diakhao (the capital of the Siin) had remained steady for some time, despite occasional disagreements.[85] An alliance between the French and the Gelwaar regime of the Siin against the massing armies of Ma Ba Diakhou was thus being arranged in the mid-1860s. Saint-Louis would guarantee certain quantities of weapons and horses. The kingdom of Siin would strike no separate deal with the marabout. The French were not especially sanguine about their ally: they expected the Gelwaar and the *ceddo* of the Siin to be outmanned (which they were), undisciplined, and probably drunk when they faced an army of new converts eager for a battlefield death that would surely smooth their journey to paradise. The limited French garrison would remain in Saint-Louis and Gorée. They saw no sense in committing European blood to an uncertain and dubious cause: in any case, the French realized that victory by the marabout would diminish the clutter of obstreperous pagan dependencies and shift the ultimate destruction of his jihad to a point farther north somewhat later.

At the first encounter between the forces of the *maad* and the holy warriors of Ma Ba Diakhou, French caution proved prescient. The *maad*, much of the court, and the *ceddo* were encamped at the village of Jilass, where the *maad* had just taken a new young wife (his fifth, by most accounts). Ma Ba Diakhou caught the Gelwaar unawares and in midrevelry. The marabout condemned the marriage as unholy and kidnapped the young bride. The *maad* fled, barely escaping with his life, his entourage disorganized and scattered. However, Ma Ba Diakhou made the strategic error of not marching on Diakhao then and there. Confident that he could lay waste to the undisciplined pagans at whatever time and place he chose, Ma Ba withdrew to Saluum to consolidate his forces.[86]

This gave the Gelwaar time to regroup and prepare for the next encounter, some months later. Although *lamans* and *saltigués* across the Siin take credit for ensuring the victory, an influx of French weaponry may also have contributed to success at the battle of Somb. The Gelwaar received crucial intelligence just before the encounter in the southeast of the Siin, learning when and where the maraboutic army encamped the night before the final march on Diakhao. Among historians sympathetic to the Serer, this demonstrates that the distinct community solidarity of the Serer kingdom proved a vital, intangible military resource.[87] In this view, the legitimate federal regime enjoyed enough popular support that, in the face of imminent military threat, the whole population was mobilized, down to the old woman gathering fuelwood outside the village of Somb who saw the marabout's camp and dispatched a young nephew to Diakhao to warn the *maad*.

This time the *maad* caught the marabout by surprise, before the sun had risen and his army had decamped. The devastation was apparently swift and total. The marabout, unlike his rival, did not even have the chance to cut and run but was struck down as he prayed, surrounded by a circle of his most loyal followers.

Siin after the Jihad: Political Vassal, Sociocultural Island

The victory over Ma Ba Diakhou's jihad army was a crucial, defining moment, a critical juncture, in the history of the Serer kingdom of Siin for three main reasons. First, it marked a fork in the history of this already somewhat anomalous community. A victory for Ma Ba Diakhou would have taken the Siin down the path that its twin, Saluum, had followed. By the 1860s, Saluum had already become a series of principalities that were sometimes more, sometimes less Muslim, in which the distinctive compromise between central state and generally autonomous

Serer peasantry had largely disintegrated. Ma Ba's victory in Saluum simply accelerated the final collapse of the old arrangement, consolidating Islamic religious institutions and Islamic theocratic rule. A conquered Siin would have followed the same path of theocratic political domination and lack of tolerance for pagan institutions and practices (such as the Serer *lamanic* agroreligious system). As a result of the victory at Somb, the Serer of Siin would continue along their distinctive path, remaining a small, densely populated island not only of ethnographically unusual pre-Islamic beliefs but also of unusual economic and political institutions.

Second, the 1867 victory over Ma Ba helped solidify elements of the Serer-Siin sense of community, culture, and self that persist to the present day. Oral historical lore in the Siin glorifies the victory over Ma Ba as not simply a defining moment for the Siin but as a defining expression of Serer-Siin identity. An external conqueror, usually depicted as an ethnic Wolof or Tukolor, wanted to put an end to the *pangool* and to the drinking of alcohol, in the popular version of the story.[88] The *pangool* of Siin were too strong. Through the intervention of an especially visionary *saltigué,* they aided the *maad* in bringing down a fog that blanketed Somb and facilitated the surprise attack.

Third, victory at the battle at Somb consolidated full colonial collaboration as a new political-economic basis for the state, the court, and the *ceddo* military. After the surprising Gelwaar victory, the colonial regime did seem to appreciate this small but apparently thorny anti-Islamic knot that they had discovered in the Siin.[89] Surrounded by hostile forces (Muslim and Wolof), the regime of the Siin posed no real expansive threat and might continue to serve as a divide-and-rule counterweight to the dominant players that remained in the region, all of which were historically anti-Siin. In a series of treaties, colonial administrators drew the regime into ever tighter relations of economic, political, and social dependency.[90] The court consolidated its supply of arms, horses, luxury goods, and even education from Saint-Louis.[91] The French generally fulfilled the *maad's* "needs" but withheld aid when the regime threatened commerce, refused to turn over accused criminals, was lax in rounding up corvée (forced labor) gangs, or otherwise blocked colonial interests.

A pliant, collaborative regime in the Siin proved quite useful in the early decades of imperial rule. After the French destroyed the Wolof states and neutralized the resistance of Islamic jihad movements, the regime took on the role of counterweight to the new powers in northern Senegal: reformulated Sufi brotherhoods that came to dominate the peanut economy.

Siin in the Economy of the Peanut

In the decades of consolidation after the conquest (beginning in the 1890s, interrupted by World War I, and starting again in the 1920s), the paramount concern of the colonial regime was to make Senegal profitable by increasing peanut production. Ironically, the very same type of Sufi Islamic brotherhoods that had resisted French expansion in the jihad period (1850s–1890s) became essential collaborators in this new agricultural initiative.

Once militarily defeated, Sufi Islam in Senegal transformed itself and entered into new relationships with the colonial state. New Sufi leaders brought an end to anticolonial resistance and militancy, developed their own, new, modern cosmological and moral order (in contrast to the French-assimilationist model), and consolidated new rural social control within the institution of the religious brotherhood, or *tariqa*. The most successful proponent of this new Sufism was Cheikh Amadou Bamba, who, as Donal Cruise O'Brien describes in considerable detail, succeeded in part because his *tariqa* incorporated the social detritus of the conquered Wolof kingdoms.[92] The destruction of Kajor, Jolof, and Baol had precipitated dramatic upheaval: in particular, the social function of the *ceddo* warrior caste disappeared virtually overnight. A good portion of the former warriors followed one of their more charismatic leaders, Ibrahima Fall, into the nascent Mouride brotherhood of Amadou Bamba.

Fall became the confidant and alter ego of the cerebral, ascetic Bamba. He and his followers (the Baye Fall) wrestled into existence a completely new theological basis for Sufi spirituality that transformed Bamba's small, insignificant sect into the most important Sufi movement in the Sahel.[93] The Baye Fall Mourides, in diametrical opposition not just to orthodox Islam but even to mainstream Sufism, ignore injunctions to pray, fast, make alms, memorize the Koran, or behave in any manner that smacks of passivity or monasticism. Instead, Baye Fall spirituality is based on utter devotion and self-sacrifice to the personalistic leader, expressed in one simple manifestation: slavish, unquestioned, backbreaking hard work. In a loose recreation of Calvin in the Sahel, the harder one toiled for the marabout, the better one's chances of making it to paradise.

Within a few years, peanut farming emerged as the most readily available hard work, the preferred means to express devotion to one's marabout. As peanut production spread, marabouts issued *ndigels* (religious edicts) to farm the new crop. Indeed, they began to establish their own quasi plantations. These *daaras*, originally founded as remote rural Koranic schools, rapidly took on the new task of producing peanuts as a cash crop for the marabout. As the brotherhoods grew and the marabouts consolidated control, they expanded eastward, establishing new *daaras* in the Ferlo Desert that stretched to the east of Baol and Saluum, and then farther south and east into the relatively unpopulated new lands of the southeastern corner of Senegal.

What might be considered a "new" *daara* mode of production was based on extensive, shifting slash-and-burn cultivation. To maximize peanut production, *daaras* were completely cleared of trees and shrubs; a few harvests of nutrient-hungry peanuts left denuded, spent soils. *Daaras* never featured crop rotation, fallow, or soil conservation. On the one hand, they were capitalist enterprises par excellence: they efficiently allocated labor and resources in a way that expanded peanut production far more quickly than colonial administrators themselves could induce. They contributed to capital accumulation in the hands of an elite class. On the other hand, their constant demand for new lands and their unsustainable farming techniques left in their wake denuded forests and severely depleted soils.

In this context, the Serer of Siin emerged in the eyes of French officials as the ideal counterweight to Mouride domination of peanut production. If they could be counted on to apply their by-now famous agricultural diligence and love of the land to the peanut, instead of to their cattle and innumerable millet varieties, the French could become less dependent on the Mouride plantation system for the cash crop.[94] The Serer of the Siin had been growing peanuts on and off, in varying quantities, at least since the search for a commodity alternative to the slave trade in the 1840s. It took several decades of enforcing the head tax and some locally produced syncretic property institutions to convert the Serer, by the 1930s, into reliable commodity farmers.

French colonial interest in increasing Serer peanut production only embellished the widely held image of the Serer as ideal African agriculturalists, the very icon of the hardworking, conservative, reliable peasant. As the Mouride plantation system spread into the new lands beyond the old kingdom of Saluum, colonial officials concocted a scheme to encourage migration of Serer from the Siin to these territories to counterbalance the marabouts and their *daara* mode of production. The scheme recruited young Serer families during the mid-1930s, with the colonial government financing their transportation and resettlement in communities like Kaffrine and Tambacounda. But the project was abandoned after just four years because of low levels of recruitment and because very few who did relocate stayed for more than one or two growing seasons. Having earned some cash to "establish themselves" (this usually meant that a young, unmarried man earned enough to pay the bride price to a young woman and her father, mother, and maternal uncle), Serer migrants saw no reason to stay in the eastern Saluum. Frustrated French officials attributed the failure to the semimystical bonds that tied nostalgic Serer peasants to their ancestral territory in the Siin.[95]

COMMODIFICATION, ISLAMIFICATION, AND SOCIAL CHANGE: OVERVIEW

Despite French colonial stereotypes of the Serer of Siin as the archetypal, rooted, conservative African peasant, the Siin was undergoing processes of especially significant social and economic change, particularly during and after the period of peanut expansion (post–World War I). Although I take up these more recent dynamics in chapters 4, 5, and 6, a brief overview is in order to conclude this chapter's introduction of the Serer of Siin.

The same irony by which Sufi Islam, once the arch rival of colonial political expansion, had emerged as the economic handmaiden of imperialism was at play in the Siin. Despite the celebrated history of victory over Ma Ba Diakhou's jihad movement, Islam began making inroads in the Siin in the interwar years and has continued to expand to the point that, by the early 1990s, 59.7 percent of the Serer of Siin identified themselves as Muslim.[96]

The more pacifist and commercially oriented Sufism of Amadou Bamba's Mourides spread in the Siin not by violence or razor/sword ultimatums but rather by providing new economic opportunities and new linkages to emerging commercial activities and urban centers.[97] Islam has proven most appealing to those at the bottom of the traditional Serer social structure—especially those of low caste like griots, *ceddo,* and traditional artisans (see the discussion of dual stratification in chapter 4). It is also important to note that, in stark contrast to the razor/sword ultimatum of the jihad era, the kind of Islam that has gradually crept across the Siin in the twentieth century is highly flexible and has been subjected to considerable syncretism. Islam as it is practiced by all but a few very of the extremely orthodox does not preclude the adoration of the *pangool,* wearing gris-gris and other amulets for protection against evil spirits, consultation of healers and shamans in times of crisis, strong belief in the spiritual foundations of the *lamanic* land management system, or for many, the drinking of alcohol.

Interestingly, the vast majority of those who are recognized as marabouts in the community are in fact traditional healers and shamans (*o pan* in Serer-Siin). The appellation *marabout* has been syncretically appropriated by traditional healers as a kind of honorific, connoting special supernatural grace or power. In this same vein, shamans and healers have long incorporated the accoutrements of Islam into their rituals and services.[98] We do find the occasional exception, a marabout who has received more formal training outside the Siin among the established brotherhoods. These individuals generally serve as the imams of the sparsely scattered mosques in the Siin, only a few of which actually consist of more than a well-swept clearing or a few bricks designating the outline of a religious edifice "under construction."

It is striking to note how the Serer of Siin reconcile the cultural importance of the defeat of the jihad leader Ma Ba Diakhou with the fact that many Serer venerate Amadou Bamba. Informants generally agree that this is in no way a contradiction because Ma Ba was "like a *ceddo*," whereas Amadou Bamba was *o kiin Roog*, a person of God. Assigning Ma Ba to the reviled warrior-slave caste makes sense because he wanted to conquer the Siin and impose Islam by force, whereas Bamba was a person understood to follow the ways of God because he sought to convert the Serer more peacefully, slowly, and without violence. Of course, the term used here is *Roog*, the Serer designation for the creator and overarching deity, not *Allah*. It is not simply that Islamization became acceptable when it abandoned the sword. Islam became acceptable in the Siin when it was propagated by an *o kiin Roog*, a person who conducted himself in accordance with the ways of the *Serer* god.

Islamization went hand in hand with other processes of social change beginning in the interwar years. New demands for cash drew the Serer of Siin into processes of urbanization and labor migration that were transforming not just Senegal but French West Africa as a whole. For a small fraction of the Serer population, this translated into access to high levels of formal education (beyond a few years of primary school), opening the door to new economic opportunities and permanent relocation in the cities. Even in recent decades, this kind of social advancement has been limited to a very small stratum of Serer-Siin society.

For most of the last century, large numbers of Serer peasants have participated in complex networks of temporary labor migration, of which the organized relocation scheme to eastern Saluum in the 1930s was only an unusually institutionalized illustration. In the early decades of this century, young men from the densely populated Siin migrated to other regions of the Peanut Basin, especially the more sparsely populated northern reaches, to work as what the Serer of Siin call *surga* agricultural wage laborers.[99] The *surga* migrant agrees to work during some portion of the growing season (usually the weeding period or harvesttime) in exchange for a percentage of the total harvest. Laborers usually return to their home village or look for dry season work after the harvest, and might seek similar work in another region the following year.

While *surga* agricultural labor migration continues in the present day, in the decades since World War II new avenues for less temporary and seasonal labor migration have developed. Most young men in the Siin, and a considerable fraction of young women as well, spend some of their teens or twenties looking for quick money in the region of Dakar or in the rapidly growing secondary towns near the Siin (Thiès, Kaolack, Fatick, Bambey, and Diourbel).

As a result, significant Serer urban ethnic enclaves have developed, especially in Dakar, Kaolack, and Fatick.[100] These enclaves represent the initial landing point for new arrivals from the countryside and provide networks of support and mediation for those looking for jobs, housing, access to government services, and so on. While some migrants have settled more or less permanently in these ethnic enclaves, ties to rural communities remain strong. It is quite common, even expected, that semipermanent urban dwellers will send at least some members of their family, especially the young, to spend the growing season in their home village, where they can lend a hand at the busiest period of the agricultural cycle. But semipermanent residents are far outnumbered by temporary migrants, mostly young people who intend to return to their home in the Siin once some short-term economic objectives have been met or, in the words of many who describe this period of their lives, after they have "finished their adventures."

Beginning after World War I, the Siin also experienced rapid and intensive processes of commodification. The head tax and peanut production greatly increased the use of cash in exchanges of goods and services. Syrio-Lebanese merchants settled around the villages designated as *escales*, points where peanuts were weighed and purchased. They brought with them a variety of manufactured items, demand for which further increased the circulation of cash in the economy. In a familiar story retold throughout the colonial world, by the 1950s the local production of a number of handicraft items—cloth woven from locally grown cotton, pottery, baskets, wooden implements, and of course, rope—was declining rapidly as relatively cheap manufactures flooded the region. A generation or so later, such local handicraft manufacturing had almost completely disappeared. With the full incorporation of the peanut into the rotation system in the 1920 and 1930s, it became very difficult for many households to meet their subsistence food needs. Rice imports grew rapidly, and by the 1980s, rice had eclipsed millet as the preferred staple food among all but self-conscious traditionalists and the very poor.

The two world wars themselves precipitated highly significant social transformations in Siin, as in other parts of Africa and the developing worlds. Young men who were recruited to serve as Senegalese *tirailleurs* (colonial riflemen) and who eventually fought in Europe and North Africa to defeat fascism had undergone unusual, transformative experiences. They learned a good deal more French than anyone would learn in the Siin for a generation or two. And through their military experience, they became much more conversant with the functioning of large bureaucratic organizations than most of their fellow Serer-Siin.

So, in spite of the widely held stereotypical view of the Serer, and the Serer of Siin in particular, as *le type même du paysan africain,* the expansion of peanut production, ensuing commodification, the spread of a highly syncretic version of Islam, labor migration, and colonial military service represent only the most apparent and major processes of social transformation to which this rural people have been subjected over much of the last century.[101] The Serer of the Siin have certainly been buffeted and transformed by these essentially global forces of structural change. But they have in no sense been powerless and passive in the face of such transformations. In part because of a distinct legacy of local autonomy (in the Gelwaar federal system and, to an even greater degree, as a collaborative vassal state in the colonial administration), the Serer have had enough distance and time to respond gradually, incrementally, and in accordance with their own cultural logic (itself changing) to the new institutions with which they have been confronted.

Moreover, although this chapter has distilled the most reliable historical and ethnographic findings into a seemingly "authoritative" narrative of Serer culture and institutional history, contestation over historical memory, over the nature and meaning of historical institutions, is the very foundation of institutional syncretism in this society. This is why we need a detailed background on the centuries-long experience of Serer-Siin social change. The next chapter explores key patterns of social contestation over the meaning of tradition in the Siin. The ensuing chapters demonstrate how this contestation over historical memory set the terms for how the Serer have not only *adapted to* freehold property relations, state land reform, and legal-rational bureaucracy but also have subtly *adapted* many of the universalistic institutions that were to have been the vectors of modernizing, developing, and civilizing these "typical African peasants," the Serer of the Siin.

3 · "Tradition" in the Siin

Contested and Enmeshing

Notions of "tradition" matter because they shape responses to contemporary land tenure arrangements and elected local government bodies. In this chapter, I use survey data to explore the importance of historical memories of "traditional" institutions in three ways. First, I establish that "tradition" in so-called backward or developing societies is neither static nor uniform nor divorced from material conditions but is in fact malleable and contested. Notions of traditional culture and institutions vary according to ordinary indicators of social structural positioning including age, gender, wealth, education, degree of extralocal engagement, caste, authority within the household, and type and degree of religious affiliation. Indeed, instead of one, unitary idealization of Serer culture and Serer history, we in fact find evidence of divergent, competing historical memories of a moral social order.

Second, cultural values and associated historical memories are not simply epiphenomenal facades that wrap crude material interests in polite, euphemistic imagery. While historical memories cannot be divorced from real material interests, they also cannot be reduced to mere expressions of either class position or individual rational calculation. Attitudes about key development institutions and policies do not, as we might expect, vary according to socioeconomic positioning but rather seem to depend on what cultural values and historical memories of tradition one holds.

This might seem to suggest that culture and historical memory form a classic and simple intermediate variable, but the truth is more complex. Individuals may initially choose to adopt particular cultural values and historical memories for instrumental reasons closely associated with social structural positioning. While they are partially shaped and predicted by socioeconomic status, historical memories and notions of culture seem to enmesh respondents in internally coherent and comprehensive world-views. Once so enmeshed, respondents behave in ways that do not corre-late well—and sometimes do not correlate at all—with their material interests or socioeconomic status, but instead seem to flow from the com-prehensive, all-encompassing logic of an internally consistent worldview. What at first may seem like a mechanical intermediate variable turns out to hold independent predictive power owing to the peculiarity of value ori-entations enmeshed in comprehensive and demanding worldviews.

SURVEY OVERVIEW AND THE SOCIOLOGY OF NJAFAJ

The data presented in this chapter stem from a forty-question survey posed to a sample group of 784 adults selected through randomized, mul-tistage sampling from among the approximately 35,000 inhabitants of the Njafaj province of Siin. The survey was conducted with the assistance of researchers associated with the French government research organization ORSTOM, which has conducted public health research in a zone of thirty villages in Njafaj since the early 1970s.[1]

A team of five surveyors on the regular staff of the ORSTOM Njafaj public health research project implemented the questionnaire.[2] The survey work began in late September 1993, a few weeks after the end of the sea-son of extremely intensive agricultural activity, and was largely completed over the course of six weeks, by early November 1993. Deaths, migrations, and other causes of nonresponse reduced the original target sample from 784 to 727 respondents, for an overall nonresponse rate of 7.3 percent.[3]

Raw data from this survey extend the depiction of the Serer of Siin begun in chapter 2 by giving us a close look at basic demographic and socioeconomic indicators. Table 3 summarizes variables and findings for a series of social-structural positioning variables useful for exploring variations in both notions of tradition and political behavior and atti-tudes. As indicated in the table, some of these social-structural position-ing variables present raw data; others are indices constructed from a series of responses.

Before I use these variables to explore patterns of historical memory and political behavior, a few comments are in order regarding some of the findings. Given the importance of agricultural production in the wealth index, I should note that the 1993 harvest season was marked by average rain early in the season, followed by unusually heavy rain in September and early October. Late rains can damage the nearly ripe millet crop, breaking the fragile young cobs just as they begin to appear from their

TABLE 3. Overview of Social-Structural Positioning Variables

Variable	Type	Description	Results
Age	Continuous (z^1)	—	Mean = 47.6 years Standard deviation (SD) = 17.1 years
Gender	Categorical 0–1	Female = 0, male = 1	Men = 50.5% Women = 49.5%
Household head	Categorical 0–1	Not head of household = 0; head of household = 1	Head of household = 12.5% Other household members = 87.5%
Wealth	Index 1–100 (z)	Index based on the following indicators: 1. Kilos of peanuts sold in 1992 2. Will 1992 millet crop last until 1993? 3. Value of jewelry owned 4. Value of cotton cloth owned 5. Number of cows owned 6. Number of sheep owned 7. Number of fields controlled	Mean = 17.3 SD = 13.3
Extralocalism	Index 1–100 (z)	Index of extralocalism based on the following indicators: 1. Fluency in Wolof 2. Language spoken with own children 3. Dry-season economic activity ranked according to extralocality of work 4. Years since last purchase of chemical fertilizer	Mean = 31.4 SD = 11.7

TABLE 3. *(continued)*

Variable	Type	Description	Results
Education	Index 1–100 (z)	Index of level of educational experience, incorporating years in official state school system, in alternative educational institutions such as Koranic school, or in literacy training programs sponsored by nongovernmental organizations	Mean = 2.9 SD = 10.4
Caste category	Categorical	Groups castes into four categories: Gelwaar aristocrats = 20 Serer customary aristocrats *(lamans, saltigués,* and *yal bakhs)* = 40 Serer free farmer majority = 60 Stigmatized, endogamous castes (griots, blacksmiths, *ceddo* warriors, weavers, slaves, etc.) = 80	Gelwaar: 28.5% Serer aristocrats: 10.7% Free farmers: 45.4% Stigmatized castes: 15.4%
Religious affiliation	Categorical	Groups religions into four categories Animist (Serer traditional religion, or *pangoolism)* = 20 Muslim Mouride = 40 Muslim, non-Mouride = 60 Catholic or Protestant = 80	Animist: 5.8% Mouride: 43.3% Other Muslim: 16.4% Christian: 34.5%

TABLE 3. *(continued)*

Variable	Type	Description	Results
Religious orthodoxy	Index 1–100 (z)	Index of orthodoxy (vs. syncretism) in religious practice and belief based on the following indicators: 1. Religious payment of a Muslim *asaka* or *addiya*[2] or a Christian tithe 2. To whom tithe is paid (marabout, priest, "directly to poor") 3. Is ancestral spirit worship acceptable for Muslims and Christians? 4. Rankings of religious leaders when asked about most important factors for improvement of village	Mean = 41.6 SD = 18.4

1. A "(z)" appears next to variables standardized to a z-score for the purposes of multiple regression analysis.

2. Many Serer-Siin Muslims pay an annual *asaka* (financial or material gift), while a few Muslims make more occasional and informal payments to the Sufi leaders known as *addiya*.

husks and dry out in the fall sun. These same late rains, however, sometimes help the peanut crop. Sixty-five percent of respondents reported that their millet crop would not see them through to the next year.[4] While this was not a disastrous year for peanuts, it was no bumper crop, and the yield varied widely. The mean value for the peanut harvest was 36.5 kilos, with a standard deviation of 48.5 kilos, underscoring the inequalities in peanut production even in a moderate year. Indeed, the median value for peanut commercialization was zero, indicating that at least half the respondents sold no peanuts at all.

The wealth index includes somewhat sensitive questions to which respondents may have answered with less than total candor. As in many rural African societies, cattle represent a crucial form of capital and status, about which people are reluctant to speak freely, especially to outsiders. This is partly why I used a wealth index, rather than relying on any one datum to measure material well-being. Given the near-universality of underreporting on cattle, it may be reasonable to assume that reported data are at least somewhat proportionate to actual figures, and that, at the very least, irregularities are smoothed out by the breadth of the wealth index.

The extralocalism index measures the degree to which respondents' economic and social relations link them to the world beyond the Siin or, conversely, isolate them in their rural village and its environs. Commodification (producing cash crops for market, and engagement in other paid artisanal work or wage labor) plays an important role here. My qualitative findings suggest that integration with commodity production and wage labor of one kind or another is rather widespread (although there are meaningful questions of degree and type of commodification), but that mere commodification fails to capture a more profound cultural and behavioral cleavage between those whose work life and social networks remain largely confined to their extended kin and their village market contacts within the Siin and those who have made linkages to the towns and cities outside the region. Mastery of Wolof, the de facto national language of Senegal, thus offers insight on degree of extralocalism. Adopting Wolof, rather than Serer, as the language spoken at home with one's children is thus an important indicator of a high level of extralocal engagement.

With regard to the caste data, underreporting of low-caste status is likely, given the tendency to avoid open discussion (or completely deny the existence) of low-caste status in polite conversation in Serer and Wolof communities. At the other extreme, the Gelwaar figure is probably somewhat inflated by the fact that members of both the customary aristocratic and free farmer groups tend to seize upon Gelwaar status at the slightest hint of a connection to the royal family.

Under religious affiliation, the non-Mouride Muslim group consists largely of members of Senegal's second largest brotherhood, the Tijanes, who constitute 13.8 percent of the total population of the zone of study. The remaining 2.6 percent consists of two individuals who identify themselves as members of an especially fervent subsect of Mouridism, the Baye Fall; fourteen members of the Khadir brotherhood; and three respondents who indicate that they are Muslim without a brotherhood. For reasons discussed in greater detail below, it makes sense to lump all these groups together in one non-Mouride category, because they are quite distinct from their Mouride coreligionists in terms of fervor and style of religious belief and practice.

Religious self-identification is an even less reliable indicator of beliefs and practices than is the slightly distorted caste data. Only 5.8 percent of respondents call themselves animists in a society in which nearly every household head offers libations to family totems. Moreover, 65.8 percent of the self-reported Mourides and 57.8 percent of the non-Mouride Muslims insist that it is quite acceptable for a good, practicing Muslim to offer libations to ancestral spirits. Only 32.4 percent of self-reported Catholics held the analogous view.

It thus makes sense to consider not just religious *affiliation* by self-report but also the degree to which a respondent exhibits religiously orthodox or syncretic behavior and attitudes. Within the religious orthodoxy index, respondents were asked if they made any regular payment to a religious leader, and if so, which of a series of religious authorities received their payment (regular payment contributes to a higher score on the religious orthodoxy index).

We would expect the most orthodox Mourides, for example, to make their payments directly to a Mouride marabout, as 43.1 percent of them indicate they do (see table 4). Less orthodox (more syncretic) Mourides pay other recipients ("directly to the poor" is a very popular response, at 49 percent). In the analysis of social contestation over notions of culture, tradition, and historical memory in the next section, religious orthodoxy, or lack of syncretic outlook, emerges as a statistically and theoretically significant hallmark of sociocultural cleavage in the contemporary Siin.

SOCIAL CONTESTATION OVER "TRADITION" AND HISTORICAL MEMORY

Historical memories of informal institutions and culture are not unitary, nor do they float in the clouds of cosmology or ethnic mythology, unmoored to concrete social and economic realities. Rather, as the data gathered for this project suggest, they vary in part according to concrete differences in economic well-being and position in the structures of Serer society. To explore this variation, this section focuses on three sets of cultural beliefs and attitudes, each of which illustrates the dynamics of social contestation in the Siin and lays the groundwork for analysis of specific processes of institutional adaptation. I discuss first the salience of a centralized state authority in memories of traditional political institutions; second, idealizations about particular traditional institutions of authority; and finally, the tendency to blend diverse institutional legacies in notions of what constitutes historic Serer political traditions.

TABLE 4. Patterns of Religious Payment by Religious Group
(in percentages)

Paid To	Animist	Mouride	Other Muslim	Christian	Entire Sample
Mouride marabout	0.00	43.14	10.34	0.78	20.68
Tijane marabout	7.69	5.24	36.22	0.78	8.78
Khadir marabout	0.00	0.65	10.34	0.00	1.98
Catholic priest	15.39	1.96	0.00	62.79	24.36
Protestant pastor	0.00	0.00	0.00	5.42	1.98
Directly to the poor	76.92	49.02	43.10	30.23	42.22
Total	100	100	100	100	100
N	13	153	58	129	353

Statists versus Localists

The discussion of the Gelwaar state in the previous chapter makes clear that the Serer of Siin have a dual political institutional heritage. On the one hand, they are a people who for generations prior to independence lived under a centralized state and knew the demands and exigencies of centralized authority—taxation, predation, forced labor, and conscription in a very limited form. Yet at the same time, they lived under a decidedly federal state structure, in which customary Serer elites, especially those associated with land tenure and religion, enjoyed considerable local autonomy.

Despite the apparent reality of institutional duality, some versions of Serer history make it sound like the Gelwaar state never existed: "In the time before the National Domain Law, it was only the *lamans* that ruled. The *lamans* with their *saltigués* and their *pans* [shamans], they were the ones who decided important things here in this village."[5] Proponents of this kind of historical memory essentially recall a golden age when the traditional Serer authorities enjoyed great freedom and sovereignty, in contrast with the present day when the postcolonial state's National Domain Law, rural councils, and other reforms have displaced these local Serer authorities.

On the other hand, some respondents, when asked about the preindependence era, tell a story that highlights, to the point of idealizing, the centrality, power, and legitimacy of the Gelwaar state. Such accounts emphasize the economy of predation, the fear in which ordinary peasants lived, and the extractive power of the Gelwaar state. They tend to suggest that Serer customary elites like the *lamans* and *yal bakhs* were limited in their freedom of action by the machinery of the Gelwaar state, which could rein in the subordinate Serer authorities as needed.

This more centrist version of historical memory can even encompass nuances of difference in important community myths, like tales of village founding. Whereas, for example, most accounts of the founding of the village of Sob in the southern part of Njafaj suggest that the original migrant-settler established residence in unclaimed, empty forest or jungle, there are a few accounts that differ subtly by suggesting that the original migrant and village founder, before settling on a location in which to light his brush-clearing fire, first went to ask the permission of the *maad* at his court in Diakhao. Reliable estimates put the arrival of the first Gelwaar monarch in the Siin toward the end of the fourteenth century, while the oldest Serer villages, including Sob, date to two or three centuries earlier.[6] This suggests that, as myths of community origin evolve and change, one of the new elements being inserted into the story is the salience of a centralized state authority.

What difference does it make if one's historical memory emphasizes localist autonomy or long experience with a centralized state? It seems to make a great deal of difference in how one responds to the *contemporary* state. The data bear out the hypothesis that those who remember the Serer past with a greater emphasis on the centralized Gelwaar state are somewhat more likely to be supportive of the contemporary state and even show a greater willingness to make voluntary economic sacrifices for state authorities.[7] In contrast, a historical memory that highlights localist autonomy stands out in combination with factors like religious syncretism as a marker of those who are more unlikely to comply when the contemporary state asks for sacrifice (see the discussion below).

Before I discuss relationships between historical memories and political behavior, it is necessary to evaluate the sociology of variations in centrist versus localist historical memories by using a centrist historical memory index (0–100) as a dependent variable in multiple regression analyses.[8] Multiple regression analysis of this centrist historical memory index against a list of social-structural positioning variables (table 3) reveals that two typical indicators of domination are associated with having a historical memory that emphasizes central state authority. Age and gender (maleness) correlate positively with a historical memory of Serer political institutions that privileges the centralized Gelwaar state. This historical memory may positively orient older, male respondents to the centralized state of the postcolonial regime (see table 5). This is an entirely sensible and theoretically plausible finding, since elder men have had more to do with the state, know how it works and how to use it, and generally are more likely to benefit from it. This regression also confirms that some of the more disenfranchised—especially women and the young—may have a different historical memory, one that emphasizes localism and local autonomy and does not treat the state—any state—as an important part of traditional political culture. This data supports the general notion that it may be the young in the Siin who are the carriers, indeed the agents, of neotraditionalism, of revival of idealized memories of Serer institutions and culture. These groups thus stand out for their tendency to idealize a more autonomous Serer past.

Membership in the caste of Serer free farmers yields the numerically largest correlation coefficient and the greatest degree of confidence. Unlike members of the other three caste groups (castes associated with the Gelwaar household, customary Serer aristocrats, and members of low-caste groups), members of this free farmer majority seem much less likely to emphasize centrism in their historical memory.[9] Interestingly, this suggests that the greatest nostalgia for autonomous local control over land tenure and adjudicatory matters lies not among the descendants of aristocrats or the precariously positioned low castes but among this majority middle group.

Idealizing Historic Institutions of Authority: Serer, Colonial, Gelwaar, Muslim

This analysis considers how respondents ranked the most important and trustworthy institutions of authority in the Serer past.[10] I used their responses to construct a series of 0–100 indices for four types of historic authoritative institutions (Serer customary-historic authorities, the colonial state, the Gelwaar state, and Islamic leaders [marabouts]). Higher scores on these indices indicate a greater tendency to remember a given authority type as the historically most important and trustworthy institution for the well-being of the village in which the respondent lives. Table 6 summarizes findings from multiple regression analyses of idealization of each of the four types of historic authorities against the nine independent social-structural positioning variables.

With regard to idealization of the Serer customary authorities, the largest numerical correlation coefficient and the greatest degree of statistical confidence ($\beta = .113$, p-value $= .002$) is associated with the caste group of Serer customary aristocrats (*lamans, yal bakhs, saltigués*, and a few other specialists in matters of custom). Not surprisingly, those who belong

TABLE 5. Centrist Historical Memory by Social-Structural Position
(significance at 5% error level, N = 646)

Historical Memory	Structural-Positioning Variable	β Correlation Coefficient	P-Value (2-Tailed)
Centrist	Free farmer caste	-.194	.000
	Older	.121	.002
	Male	.106	.006

TABLE 6. Idealization of Historical Authorities by Social-Structural Position
(significance at 5% error level)

Historical Memory	Social-Structural Positioning Variable	β Correlation Coefficient	P-Value (2-Tailed)
Idealize Serer customary authorities (N = 727)	Serer aristocratic caste	.113	.002
	Older	.100	.009
	Animist	.081	.032
	Less educated	.072	.053
Idealize colonial state (N = 727)	More educated	.100	.007
	Not animist	.068	.066
Idealize Gelwaar state (N = 463)	Not Mouride	.167	.000
	Poorer	.142	.005
	Religiously syncretic	.136	.004
	Older	.116	.012
	High extralocal activity	.112	.030
	Male	.108	.051
Idealize marabouts (N = 593)	Muslim Mouride	.229	.000
	Younger	.175	.000
	Muslim non-Mouride	.174	.000
	Religiously orthodox	.115	.006
	Less educated	.092	.023

to Serer customary aristocratic caste groups are much more likely to idealize their predecessors and ancestors as the most important and trustworthy authoritative institutions in the past. While Gelwaar aristocrats have "moved on" into powerful and sometimes economically lucrative positions in the middle ranks of the political and bureaucratic machinery of postcolonial Senegal, the former *lamans, saltigués*, and other groups have, if anything, "moved down" into the stratum of the Serer free farmer caste. As expected, we find that the very small percentage of Serer respondents who openly identify themselves as animist are especially attached to customary institutions and practices.[11] In addition, age and lack of education also seem to figure in the image of the Serer customary idealist (although education lies just beyond our confidence interval, with a *p*-value of .053, correlation with a *lack* of education makes clear theoretical sense). The members of Serer society with the most positive historical memory of customary Serer authorities are thus older, probably less educated men and women who identify themselves as animist and, especially, who belong to the customary aristocratic castes.

When we turn from idealization of customary Serer aristocrats to the more socially unusual and controversial matter of idealizing the *colonial* administration, we find that only education and animism help explain this attitude. Although the data do not permit confidence, they do supply a statistically discernible hint that animists are less likely to wax nostalgic about the colonial state. This is expected, given the general attachment of this demographically small minority (5.8 percent) to institutions that seem authentically Serer and this group's general hostility to vectors of sociocultural change. Education, however, offers a much more reliable correlation: the higher the level of education, the more idealistic the image of the colonial state. This of course contrasts with the statistical nonsignificance of variables one might expect to be associated with a rosy memory of the colonial state, such as material wealth or membership in the Gelwaar caste (the best-positioned colonial collaborators in the Siin). Formal and informal in-depth interviews suggest that nostalgic memories of the colonial state are most salient as a contrasting foil to disappointment with and distrust of the postcolonial state. Thus the data in table 6 may suggest that the more educated, who are more familiar with the failings of the postcolonial state, are therefore more likely to turn to the colonial state as an idealized precursor to a discredited contemporary regime.

Idealizations of the Gelwaar state present a different and more complex situation. In some ways, those who idealize the Gelwaar state are reminiscent of those who idealize the Serer customary authorities. Older people, and possibly men as well (*p*-value for gender = .051), are more likely to idealize the Gelwaar state than are other groups: the young, who may have never lived under the Gelwaar regime, and women, whose contact with the Gelwaar state may have been more limited to simple predation. Moreover, Mourides are far less likely to have positive historical memories of the Gelwaar state.

At another level, idealization of the Gelwaar state underscores the degree to which cultural memory and social reality defy easy, Parsonian, tradition-modernity dichotomies. Romanticized notions of the old Gelwaar regime can be found among those who are poor, religiously syncretic (both stereotypical hallmarks of tradition), *and* who are also highly involved in extralocal social and economic relations (a hallmark of modernity). This makes sense given the tenuous position—in formal political and economic relations—of these individuals who have made a partial, but not especially remunerative, entry into commodified economic relations. They have rewritten the Serer past as statist, remembering fondly not the Weberian, legal-rational colonial state, as more educated monotheists do, but the Gelwaar regime, a state that seems traditional and authentic and, perhaps more significant, which serves as a critical counterpoint to a contemporary political-economic system that has failed to fulfill their aspirations or meet their needs. This salience of particular historical institutional legacies for particular social groups suggests the contingent mobilization of cultural symbols and historical memories as resources in contemporary relations and struggles.

The Gelwaar state provides the iconic idiom for an arbitrary, alien authoritative, predatory regime (invoked in the present day to disparage the Rural Council Law). Yet, as the data in table 6 suggest, some segments of Serer society do carry an idealized memory of that political system, indicating that invocations of the old Gelwaar regime are more complex than they might seem at first glance. These fond memories of the Gelwaar regime dovetail with the vilification of the postcolonial state, because the positive idealization of the Gelwaar regime sets up certain expectations regarding decentralization and federalism. It is possible to simultaneously vilify the current regime by derisively labeling it the *maad* and idealize the old regime of the actual *maad*, because the rap against the postcolonial state is that it is a new *maad* "that does not even know how to behave like a *maad*."[12] Once the contemporary state is understood as the new *maad*, there is an expectation that it will function like the old head of the old Gelwaar monarchy. Yet the postcolonial state categorically and emphatically rejects the federal division of authoritative responsibilities and consequent autonomy of the *lamans* and other customary Serer officials—a centerpiece of the Gelwaar system. Serer interpretations of what the new state *is* are rooted in complex, sometimes idealized memories of historical institutions, which, in the case of those noted in table 6, seem to set the contemporary state up for popular frustration, rejection, and vilification. The sociology of idealization for the Gelwaar state thus sets the stage for the sociology of rejection of the postcolonial state.

Finally, idealization of the Islamic Sufi marabouts is especially noteworthy because it is clear that, throughout the preindependence history of the Siin, marabouts played a minor role in social and political affairs. Marabouts did have a presence in the court of the *maad*, but even there they served only as scribes, who had little contact with Serer society outside court. There is little evidence of mass conversion of the free farmer or lower castes prior to the early to mid–twentieth century. Indeed, the defeat and dismemberment of Ma Ba Diakhou, an important jihad leader who wished to convert the entire Serer population by force, became a defining element in the cultural identity of the Serer of Siin as a non-Muslim people.

The maraboutic elite remains relatively peripheral today in this region, where mosques bring together small cells of highly motivated devotees, and where the vast majority of those who call themselves Mouride or Tijane cannot identify a marabout with whom they have had face-to-face contact or to whom they make regular cash or material payments. When pressed, most respondents state that they either make payment to the titular head of their brotherhood (the equivalent of a U.S. Catholic saying he or she pays a tithe to Pope John Paul II), or that they pay it "directly to the poor."[13]

For these reasons, those who rank the marabouts high when considering the most important and trustworthy officials in the Serer past exhibit a distinct form of "Islamic revisionism." In spite of the widely understood fact that marabouts have always played, and to this day continue to play, a rather marginal role in Serer social affairs, those who read them as a major actor in Serer history are engaged in an anachronistic projection of their present-day Islamic fervor onto the narrative of the Serer past. Consequently, we should expect this maraboutic idealism to be found largely among the most fervently Islamicized of the Serer of Siin.

As table 6 shows, respondents are much more likely to idealize the maraboutic role in the Serer past if they are Mouride, and a little less so if they are non-Mouride Muslims of another brotherhood (43.2 percent of all respondents call themselves Mouride, 13.8 percent Tijane, and 2.6 percent identify with other brotherhoods or refer to themselves as Muslim without a brotherhood). But religious affiliation alone is not the only factor: orthodoxy plays a significant role here as well. Syncretic Muslims are less likely to think that the marabouts have been major players in Serer history. This is a story told largely by the orthodox, who constitute a minority of the total Serer population (recall from table 3 that on the 0–100 orthodoxy scale, the mean is 41.6, the standard deviation 18.4).

Idealization of the historical maraboutic role is also a story that seems to appeal to the young and the less educated. These most devout Serer Muslims—individuals who are young, poorly educated, largely Mouride, more observant and strict, and much less likely to blend elements of *pangoolism* with their brand of Islam—stand out as a distinct category of outliers in this society. As will be shown, considerable overlap exists between "Islamic idealization" and a willingness to rupture established, seemingly traditional Serer relations and institutions.

Institutional Syncretism in Historical Memory

When Serer respondents discuss historically legitimate and trustworthy institutions of authority, they do more than simply idealize one kind of ruler. Sometimes a single respondent selects authorities from divergent, arguably contradictory, cultural frameworks for very high ranking in terms of most legitimate and trustworthy historic authorities. We can use the degree of cultural eclecticism or cultural consistency in ranking historic authorities to construct a "syncretic historical memory" index. For example, a respondent who ranks the Serer *saltigué*, or rain priest, number one, the chef de canton number two, and an Islamic marabout number three would generate a high score on this 0–100 index.

The index also captures responses suggesting that political institutions *should* be just as syncretic as they "always used to be." For example, a positive response to the following statement would yield a high score on this index: "If only the subprefect and the rural councilors came and worshiped the *pangool* of this village like the old Gelwaar *maad* used to, then the rains would surely still be abundant." This syncretic historical memory index gives us some sense of the degree to which institutional blending is already taking place as Serer respondents think about their political heritage. Syncretic historical memory is indicative of a syncretic worldview, which may help predict responses to contemporary political institutions and development planning.

As shown in table 7, only the degree of religious syncretism ($\beta = .305$, $p = .000$) and lack of education ($\beta = .095$, $p = .017$) account in a statistically reliable way for variation in syncretic historical memory. These findings may be more important for what they leave out. Syncretic historical memory cuts across socioeconomic, caste, religious, gender, and generational lines. Given the relatively high mean value of the 0–100 syncretic historical

TABLE 7. Syncretic Historical Memory by Social-Structural Position
(significance at 5% error level, N = 580)

Historical Memory	Social-Structural Positioning Variable	β Correlation Coefficient	P-Value (2-Tailed)
Syncretic historical memory			
	Religiously syncretic	.305	.000
	Less educated	.095	.017

memory index (63.7) and the relatively low standard deviation (only 14.4), we can say with some confidence that most Serer respondents tend to have a rather syncretic view of their political institutional heritage. As qualitative research leads us to expect, most Serer respondents exhibit a high degree of syncretism when it comes to religion, political culture, and historical memory, and this tendency cuts across socioeconomic stratifications.

This regression would seem to confirm the historical continuity of syncretism: those who believe in a past marked by a high degree of political syncretism also tend to be religiously syncretic. It is important to underscore that we should not expect syncretic historical memory and religiously syncretic contemporary behavior to have anything to do with each other. The finding that the religiously syncretic are considerably more likely to hold syncretic historical memories of political authorities underscores the not necessarily predictable point that syncretism in this society is not limited merely to the religious realm but also represents in itself an overall, probably consistent and holistic, worldview that transcends specific realms of action or attitude.

These findings also suggest that level of education may help explain a highly syncretic historical memory of political relations. The less educated one is, the more likely one holds syncretic beliefs about historic political relationships. It seems that higher levels of education weed out notions like "the *maad* always came and adored our *pangool*" or "the rains would be better if only the subprefect came and offered libations here."

It is worth noting that age is not one of the significant factors in this model. If we were witnessing, as the correlation with *lack* of education might suggest, a classical modernization process of "wiping out" superstition and traditional beliefs (components of syncretic historical memory), we should expect young people as a group to hold fewer syncretic historical memories of authority. The fact that age does not predict syncretic historical memory tends to give some credence to the supposition, based on nonquantitative observation, that neotraditionalism may actually be more widespread among Serer youth than among the generation who came of age in the decades just before and just after independence.

Patterns in Remembering Culture and Institutions

An analysis of these three general strands of historical memory reveals the outlines of possible relationships between sociomaterial factors and attitudes about tradition and culture. The results summarized in table 8 are diverse, suggesting not one or two clear-cut social cleavages in Serer society but a variety of conjunctural clusterings depending on the nature of the political attitude or historical memory in question.

While some of the data suggest stereotypical "traditionalism," as in the tendency for older, animist customary aristocrats with little education to idealize Serer customary tenure authorities (see table 8), no evidence exists for clear-cut matrices of "tradition" and "modernity" underlying political culture and historical memories. Rather, there is evidence for what might be called institutional lag effects, for the continued salience of particular elements of Serer political heritage meaningful for particular social groups in the present day.

One group does, however, stand out as a kind of outlier in Serer society. While conventional indicators of commodification or modernization explain relatively little of the variation in historical memories and political attitudes explored above, Islamic religious identification, especially highly orthodox adherence to Islam, which is quite rare in this society, does offer greater analytic leverage.[14] This is clearly so with regard to idealization of the marabouts as important historical actors, and clearer still in the analyses that follow.

Figure 3 demonstrates that this outlier effect of stark adherence to Islam extends to matters of direct economic significance, such as material wealth: Non-Mouride Muslims stand out as a distinctly well-off social category in the Njafaj region. Christians and animists occupy roughly the same stratum, and intriguingly, Mourides stand out as decidedly the poorest group. Membership in a non-Mouride brotherhood fits the argument developed above: the versions of non-Mouride Islam practiced in the Siin separate their adherents from the rest of Serer society, and interestingly, non-Mouride Muslims also stand out for being better off in material terms. If we find hints of a variable that denotes classical indicators of modernization, it is not education or extralocal involvement but affiliation with religious frameworks that, when adhered to in a strict orthodox manner, separates adherents from the rest of society. Like Weber's Protestant ethic, in this society such separation may be a precondition for capital accumulation.

TABLE 8. Summary of Historical Memories by
Social-Structural Position

Historical Memory	Social-Structural Positioning Variable	β Correlation Coefficient	P-Value (2-Tailed)
Centrist	Free farmer caste	−.194	.000
	Older	.121	.002
	Male	.106	.006
Idealize Serer customary authorities	Serer aristocratic caste	.113	.002
	Older	.100	.009
	Animist	.081	.032
	Less educated	.072	.053
Idealize colonial state	More educated	.100	.007
	Not animist	.068	.066
Idealize Gelwaar state	Not Mouride	.167	.000
	Poorer	.142	.005
	Religiously syncretic	.136	.004
	Older	.116	.012
	High extralocal activity	.112	.030
	Male	.108	.051
Idealize marabouts	Muslim Mouride	.229	.000
	Younger	.175	.000
	Muslim non-Mouride	.174	.000
	Religiously orthodox	.115	.006
	Less educated	.092	.023
Syncretic historical memory	Religiously syncretic	.305	.000
	Less educated	.095	.017

Mouridism, as noted above, seems to work in exactly the opposite way. It is important here to keep in mind that Mourides and non-Mouride Muslims differ most markedly in terms of religious orthodoxy. As figure 4 shows, the non-Mouride Muslims (like Christians) score noticeably higher than their Mouride counterparts on the orthodoxy scale presented above. Although it may seem odd at first, the most orthodox religious group are in fact animists. This makes sense when we recognize that the orthodoxy index measures internal consistency *within* the respondent's stated religious affiliation. So an animist who, for example, makes charitable payments directly to the poor would be observing the reciprocity-based

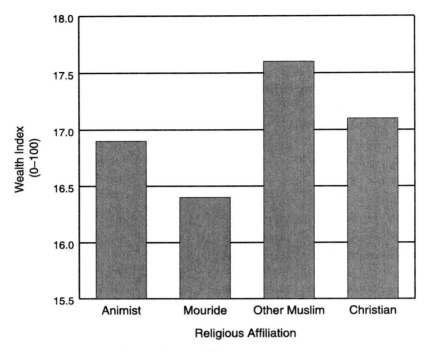

Figure 3. Mean wealth by religious affiliation ($N = 727$).

precepts of this religion and would score high on the orthodoxy scale, while an animist who makes a religious payment to a marabout or a Catholic priest would score very low on this scale. While most Serer who call themselves Muslim or Christian (the great majority, at 94.2 percent of the population) continue to worship the *pangool* and are therefore quite syncretic, those who identify themselves as animist (a small minority at 5.8 percent) are a much more religiously orthodox lot.

As the orthodoxy index suggests, Mouridism, the stated religion of 43.3 percent of respondents, is both a poor person's religion and a religion marked by much greater practical syncretism than other monotheistic religions practiced in the Siin. What makes non-Mouride Islam (and to a lesser extent, Christianity) an indicator of both distinctive historical memory and, as shown in figure 3, distinctive material accumulation is not the *choice* of religious affiliation or the *content* of religious dogma, but the degree of syncretism to which the religion is subjected. Monotheistic affiliation in this society by itself tells us very little. But monotheistic affiliation observed with relatively less syncretism is an important indicator of social distinctiveness.

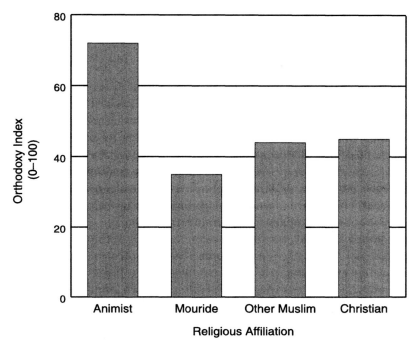

Figure 4. Orthodoxy by religious affiliation ($N = 727$).

Historical memory of political institutions and culture is neither constant nor unitary but varies according to key indictors of social structural positioning. Instead of a primordial Serer notion of tradition, we see clear evidence that some Serer informants disagree with others on what exactly tradition is and, by extension, why it is important. When institutions are adapted in terms of historical memory, such an adaptation conforms not to *the* unitary Serer notion of local culture but to a dominant one, leaving alternative, subaltern memories and potential adaptations as part of the rationalizations and complaints of those who are marginalized in the twin processes of institutional imposition and adaptation.

ENMESHING EFFECTS OF HOLISTIC WORLDVIEWS

There are clearly specific and contingent relationships between historical memories of political culture and social structural positioning, but historical memory and political culture cannot be reduced to epiphenomenal ideological "cover" for "real" material interests. Indeed, a close look at the data on a number of questions about contemporary political behavior shows that historical memory and cultural variables are sometimes more useful in explaining variation than are straightforward socioeconomic positioning and associated material interests.

Multiple regression analysis uncovers the degree to which concrete material and structural conditions (wealth, degree of extralocal engagement, education, caste, age, gender, and status as head of household) or more ideological-cultural variables, including historical memory, explain variations in political attitudes and behaviors. This analysis tests the relative significance of historical memory and cultural variables versus material and structural variables with regard to three questions of political behavior: willingness to turn land into a sellable commodity; support or opposition to the right to pawn land, an important agricultural practice in this region; and willingness to make voluntary economic sacrifices for the postcolonial state. As we shall see after exploring specific processes of institutional adaptation, these are crucial issues in the transformation of tenure, and by extension, of social relations in the Siin in the aftermath of commodification and state bureaucratic consolidation.

Selling Land When the Spirits Say Not To

The people of the Siin have been pressured to commodify social and economic relations since the early part of this century. As a result, the question of land sale has been a kind of elephant in the room for many decades. Should the Serer of Siin develop a market in land, given that many outsiders (from French colonial administrators in the 1920s to World Bank technical assistants in recent times) have suggested this would provide a solid basis for agricultural expansion? Or should they "preserve" what they perceive as traditional regimes of tenure based on inalienable custodianship on the part of lineage heads, rain priests, and in an indirect form, ancestral spirits themselves? Since land remains the major form of capital in this rural subsistence society, questions about the transformation of regimes of control and exchange of land remain salient and contentious. Norms of reciprocity, gift exchange, marriage, mutual attendance at family ceremonies (at which large quantities of capital may be informally transferred) are all tied up with the maintenance of socially acceptable systems of holding, managing, and transferring land.

The next chapter focuses on an innovative, institutionally syncretic response to this tension between commodification and "economic traditionalism." But for now, consider popular willingness to commodify land an important matter of contemporary political behavior and attitudes, variation in which is critical to understand. Respondents were asked whether they agree or disagree with the following statement: "If I were planning to sell a field, but the *saltigué* [rain priest] or the *pan* [shaman] told me that I should not sell it because the *pangool* [ancestral spirits] were opposed to the sale, then I should not sell the field." Those surveyed could respond in one of five ways: agree strongly, agree, don't know, disagree, or disagree strongly.

Reluctance to openly commodify land, especially when we invoked the ancestral spirits and mediators of their interests like the *saltigué* and the *pan,* remained quite high. Almost three-quarters of those surveyed (71.6 percent) agreed with the statement—that is, they would not violate the wishes of the *saltigué, pan,* and by extension, the *pangool* (see table 9). Yet 15.9 percent were willing to stick their necks out and declare their "independence from superstition," publicly announcing their willingness to turn their faces away from the past, toward a "bright" future of individual title, a free market in land, development, and progress.[15]

Taking responses to this question as a dependent variable, and indicators of social-structural positioning and historical memory as independent variables, multiple regression analysis reveals that indicators of material conditions and structural position fail to account for variation in willingness to commodify land and drop out of the equation (see table 10). Despite that fact the regression initially included social structural and material conditions variables like wealth, extralocal involvement, education, age, gender, household head status, and caste, none of these provided results that permit statistical confidence. Instead, the significant variables were all ideological and cultural. Those willing to defy custom and ignore the *saltigué* and the *pangool* in a land sale are likely to be religiously orthodox, are not likely to exhibit an institutionally syncretic historical memory, and are more likely to have a statist or centrist historical memory. These ideological factors prove the most compelling in explaining this important variance in response to the question of land sale.

These data corroborate earlier inferences about religious orthodoxy and syncretism. Those more strict in adhering to religious norms, and less willing to mix and match or blend religious traditions, are more likely to stand outside community norms and sell land in spite of custom, the wishes of the spirits, and the counsel of customary Serer authorities. This extends what we might infer from careful ethnographic and historical research: orthodoxy has the effect of extracting an individual from the network of social relations in which tenure matters are embedded. That web of relations is not animist as such (self-avowed animists constitute only 5.8 percent of the population, while self-reported Mourides constitute 43.3 percent), but it is decidedly syncretic.

TABLE 9. Opinion Regarding Ancestral Spirits and Field Sale
(in percentages, N = 724)

	Agree Strongly	Agree	Don't Know	Disagree	Disagree Strongly
I would not sell a field if the ancestral spirits opposed the sale	53.2	18.4	12.5	5.8	10.1

TABLE 10. Willingness to Commodify Land, by Social-Structural Position and Historical Memory-Culture Variables
(significance at 5% error level, N = 519)

	Ideological-Culture Variables	β	P-Value (2-Tailed)	Social-Structural Position Variables	β	P-Value (2-Tailed)
Would sell land against wishes of ancestral spirits	Religiously orthodox	.222	.000	none	—	—
	Syncretic historical memory	–.210	.000		—	—
	Centrist historical memory	.157	.000		—	—

As already noted, contemporary religious syncretism and a syncretic institutional memory are closely and positively related. Those who are willing to sell land against the wishes of the spirits tend not to think about the past in institutionally syncretic terms. This reinforces the comprehensive quality of orthodoxy discussed above. Orthodoxy is not simply a spiritual matter but is a generic issue of being closed to blending and hybridity. Those who lack a syncretic orientation seem to stand outside the community on important matters such as land commodification.

Finally, although it has a somewhat lower correlation coefficient (β = .157), a centrist or statist historical memory also stands out as a statistically robust indicator of willingness to commodify land. This also makes sense: it is the postcolonial state that, inadvertently, has emerged as the primary vector of commodification of land in this region (see chapter 5). Those with a statist historical memory seem to already accept the idea that the state can and should intervene in tenure relations, separating these matters from control by localist leaders like the *saltigué* or the *lamans*, removing them from concerns of ancestral spirits, and freeing land up for circulation as ordinary pieces of "property."

This regression, like the two that follow, indicate with some degree of certainty that ideology, culture, and historical memory matter—that they are not pure epiphenomena of material conditions and social structural conditions. If this were the case, if they were mere ideological window dressing, then those factors that undergird a variable like centrist historical memory (these include caste, age, and gender, as summarized in table 8) should become statistically discernible in the regression above. Caste, age, and gender drop out of this regression. This suggests that, although centrist historical memory varies in part according to whether one is of a certain caste, older, and male, centrist historical memory is not a pure function of these social structural factors. Rather, as is the case with any internally coherent and comprehensive worldview, centrist historical memory has an independent effect of its own on willingness to commodify land.

As we shall see in the two examples that follow, this is not to suggest that historical memory of culture is necessarily the *cause* of willingness to commodify land. There may be some kind of "interaction effect" between religious orthodoxy, centrist historical memory, and nonsyncretic institutional memory, on one hand, and willingness to commodify land, on the other. It is entirely conceivable that these ideological patterns are merely justifications or rationalizations for a willingness to sell land. That is, individuals who want to "modernize" their landholding, who want to be free to buy, sell, or do what they want with their fields without interference from old mystics and beings they cannot even see may *choose* to adopt a highly orthodox religion (such as a non-Mouride form of Islam). They may develop a historical memory in a centrist and nonsyncretic manner that justifies breaking the power of "traditional" syncretic relations and authorities.

While such an interaction effect is entirely plausible in theoretical terms, it does bring us back to two basic points that frame this discussion of the relationship between material and ideological factors. First, it does not undermine the fact that material conditions and social-structural positioning variables have dropped out of the equation, and that, for whatever reason, measurements of culture, ideology, and historical memory do a better job of making sense of variance in this key behavior.

Second, historical memories and associated cultural frameworks (like orthodox monotheistic religions) are entryways into much more comprehensive, systemic frameworks of meaning or worldviews. Once an individual, operating on the basis of purely instrumental calculation, "decides" that being an orthodox Tijane is the best way to get ahead and avoid interference in the process of capital accumulation, that individual may buy into not just one element of that worldview but the entire package. To turn to a somewhat trivial but graphic example, a new convert may like the idea of being able to say no to the *saltigué*, but upon adopting strict Tijanism, the convert also will be forced to give up drinking *sum-sum*, the wildly popular moonshine of the Siin, the drinking of which, most respondents agree, is a hallmark of Serer adulthood.

Now, the convert may choose to ignore that particular element of the coherent worldview that is Tijanism. Like most Serer, the new Tijane continue to get together with friends at a corner of the marketplace and idle away long hot afternoons over a few shot glasses of quasi turpentine *(sum-sum)*. In fact this is just what many Serer Muslims do. But once they do this, once they start mixing and matching practices, they are no longer adherents to an orthodox religion. Pulling themselves back into the fabric of Serer society, they fail to break away, and they lose the benefits of orthodoxy (separation) that may have attracted them in the first place. Failing to break away, they are more likely to be subject to the syncretic demands that emanate from within the syncretic institutional and comprehensive normative structure that is Serer society. While the alcohol prohibition is only a graphic example, it illustrates the dilemma, the ancillary, unexpected, independent predictive power of ideological and cultural systems. You buy into them because they offer raw material advantages. You may not get those advantages without convincingly adopting all or most of the coherent worldview, which may then force you to engage in actions that contradict your interests: giving up moonshine in order to say no to the spirits and sell your land. Once faced with this contradiction between the comprehensive demands of normatively contradictory holistic worldviews, most Serer have opted for the worldview that fulfills more of their holistic needs—the nonorthodox, Serer syncretic one. This, in turn, helps account for the limited social scope of both orthodoxy and accumulative economic behavior.

The Right to Pawn

Two other illustrations (attitudes about pawning land and willingness to make voluntary economic sacrifices or the state) complete my examination of the independent predictive power of ideological-cultural factors in contrast to material-structural variables. Both of these illustrations underscore the enmeshing effect of cultural values and historical memories that draw individuals into holistic, comprehensive worldviews.

The following example deals with the now common, but officially illegal, practice of pawning land. In the years between the world wars, a distinctive system of land exchange emerged known as *taile* pawning, which entails payment of a cash guarantee for indefinite usufruct rights in a field. Under this arrangement, the original field proprietor may regain pawned land simply by repaying the cash guarantee without interest at a reasonable point in time prior to a growing season. *Taile* pawning facilitated the partial commodification of tenure relations in the Siin by making land for cash exchanges commonplace. Increased flexibility of exchange facilitated the spread of peanut production by increasing the amount of acreage farmed in any given year. But at the same time, pawning "preserved" a Serer notion of control over land as inalienable custodianship on the part of lineage heads and their ancestral spirits. Pawned land was never really lost to the original controlling lineage. Even if land was pawned for generations and effectively transferred, no precedent for alienation was set: the fiction remained in place that original owners enjoyed the right to reclaim their fields whenever they chose.

Independent Senegal's 1964 land reform sought to restore what the Senghor regime saw as "traditional" African tenure egalitarianism by doing away with the tenure control of lineage elites, *lamans, saltigués,* and the *pangool* ancestral spirits they claimed to represent. In sweeping away "aristocratic accumulation," the state also swept away practices like pawning as vestiges of elite domination. Although many Serer initially welcomed this, discontent has spread with the reform, especially because of its effective ban on land pawning, an exchange mechanism central to the local tenure system.

To tap into contemporary attitudes on pawning, respondents were asked whether they agree or disagree with the following statement: "The proprietor of a field should have the right to pawn his land for an indeterminate period and reclaim it whenever he wishes." Table 11 indicates that responses again overwhelmingly favored the syncretic tenure option that slows the process of commodification. With regard to pawning, 19.5 percent *oppose* the syncretic route and, agreeing with the state, feel that field owners should *not* have the right to make these types of indeterminate loans. Table 12 helps us zero in on the sociology behind responses to this question.

TABLE 11. Opinion Regarding the Right to Pawn Land
(in percentages, N = 724)

	Agree Strongly	Agree	Don't Know	Disagree	Disagree Strongly
Field proprietors should have the right to pawn their land without a time limit	46.7	19.1	14.7	3.6	15.9

Here, a slew of variables survive the statistical significance test, but only two of them—age and education—clearly relate to material conditions, while the two caste categories represent social structural factors. The remaining seven variables in this regression model are ideological-cultural. The four most important variables all have to do with historical memory or religion, while education ranks next to last in predictive power.

These coefficients tell a story about who thinks what with regard to pawning, but the very rankings confirm the general findings of the previous analysis (table 10): again, nonmaterial, nonstructural factors seem to play major, independent roles in helping explain variation in an important matter of political behavior. Religious syncretism is the most important factor in predicting a respondent's position on pawning. The more religiously syncretic you are, the more likely you are to oppose pawning. Those who are animist, young, and Mouride, and who idealize customary Serer institutions of authority, also oppose the right to pawn. Conversely, being religiously orthodox, older, and more Muslim (but not Mouride) tends to suggest support for the pawning institution.

First and foremost, we should remember that we are exploring exactly who—in that 19.4 percent against the right to pawn—opposes a practice otherwise widely supported in Serer society (as chapters 4 and 5 make clear). There seem to be two groups here. The first group—the young and educated—state what the designers of the National Domain Law might expect: pawning is a practice of the past, and as tenure relations are "modernized" it will and should be swept away. Interestingly, this perspective should also find support among the wealthy and those who show willingness to accumulate land. But wealth offered no significant correlation, while the groups most willing to accumulate, identified in the previous analysis (table 10)—the religiously orthodox and the non-Mouride Muslims—actually support the pawning practice. Factors associated with modernization and commodification, then, do not provide a clear picture of who opposes pawning.

TABLE 12. Opposition to the Right to Pawn Land, by Social-Structural Position and Historical Memory–Culture Variables

(significance at 5% error level, N = 588)

	Ideological-Culture Variables	β	P-Value (2-Tailed)	Social-Structural Position Variables	β	P-Value (2-Tailed)
Oppose the right of a field proprietor to pawn land	Religiously syncretic	.284	.000	Younger	.177	.000
	Idealize Gelwaar state	.268	.000	Caste: Serer aristocratic	−.140	.000
	Animist	.199	.000	Caste: Gelwaar caste	−.091	.011
	Idealize Serer aristocracy	.180	.000	Education	.086	.016
	Muslim Mouride	.147	.000			
	Muslim non-Mouride	-.086	.019			

The second, more important group (if the beta-coefficients are any guide) is an intriguing subset of Serer society—syncretists and Mourides, many of whom are also animists who idealize the old institutions, especially the Gelwaar state. This combination, and the relatively small size of this group, may suggest that these respondents are of low caste, such as members of the former *ceddo* warrior caste. As noted above, caste underreporting is common, so we should not expect stigmatized castes to prove significant in regression models. But Mouridism has been a haven for people of low caste. *Ceddo* in particular, displaced by the collapse of the Gelwaar state, remain highly animist and syncretic in their practices but nominally affiliated to Mouridism. They and other low-caste individuals began making a living through farming only after independence (before this time, their attachment to the Gelwaar elite was their source of livelihood). They thus have limited access to land and are likely to receive only poor and small plots of land by means of a pawning regime. It would therefore make sense for them to oppose pawning and favor the state's land reform law.

Pawning is a Janus-faced institution, turned at once toward preservation of that which seems traditional and toward a future of commodified tenure relations. The data reflect this reality. But they also highlight the fact that the tenure regime is in fact bifurcated. The lower, less official, more popular tenure system is still undergoing gradual commodification, a process in which pawning is a vector of change that the most vulnerable groups tend to oppose. Some of these conclusions presage my discussion of the social significance of pawning as a syncretic tenure institution. For the time being, however, it is important to emphasize that, regarding the land exchanges mentioned above, we gain no analytic leverage on the complex patterns of support and opposition to pawning without the help of ideological and cultural variables that do not regress into insignificance when pitted against more concrete material and social structural factors.

Making Sacrifices for the State

Similar evidence of the salience of ideological and cultural variables arises during an exploration of the legitimacy of authoritative institutions. For the purposes of this study, I operationalize legitimacy as "willingness to make a voluntary economic sacrifice" when a particular authority asks for it. Respondents were asked to identify the authority for whom they would be most willing to pay taxes or make a donation. They ranked their top three choices from among six leaders: subprefect, president of the rural council, marabout, village chief, *laman*, and *mak a ndok* (eldest in a matrilineal extended family, and a vestigial historic authority figure).[16]

I present my complete analysis of the data gathered from this question (including the striking fact that 54.6 percent ranked the vestigial *mak a ndok* first) in chapter 6. For now, we will explore the sociology of respondents who included a state official—subprefect or rural council president—as one of their top three choices. Table 13 shows the percentage of respondents who ranked these two officials first, second, or third, and the percentage who never mentioned either of them. We can translate responses for these two officials into a single index, in which the highest score obtains when a respondent places the two state officials, in either order, first and second, and the lowest score is given when the respondent fails to mention either state officials. As the table suggests, a large fraction of those surveyed score very low on this "state legitimacy" scale. Indeed, the scale has a mean value of 24.5 and a standard deviation of 24.0, so two-thirds of all the responses rank below 50 on the scale.

TABLE 13. Percentage of Respondents Willing to Make a Voluntary Donation to State Officials
(N = 727)

	Ranked First	Ranked Second	Ranked Third	Not Mentioned
Subprefect	15.3	14.2	16.5	54.0
Rural council president	3.4	12.7	20.8	63.1

Multiple regression offers some sense of who finds the state legitimate, as summarized in table 14. These results further confirm the importance of historical memory and ideological factors. Two of the three significant regressors that meet the test are matters of historical memory. They rank first and third in terms of the absolute size of their correlation coefficients. The third regressor, education, is an extremely important social structural variable, so state legitimacy clearly is not simply a function of ideological factors. Historical memory of the colonial state apparently is twice as important as education in determining if one is willing to make a voluntary economic sacrifice for the contemporary state. This again confirms the statist historical memory thesis: despite the inherent contradiction between the colonial and postcolonial states (the latter supposedly having overthrown the former), for Serer respondents a positive orientation toward a state, any state—even the colonial state—correlates positively with finding the postcolonial state legitimate. Centralized states, in a way, are centralized states: how you feel about the one with which your people have had a long history is an important predictor of how you feel about the current set of arbitrary, alien imposed rules, practices, and leaders.

Interestingly, Islamic idealists—those who promote an anachronistic, reified notion of the importance of marabouts in Serer history—are noticeably less likely to make voluntary economic sacrifices for state officials. The regression on the legitimacy of the marabouts suggests, not surprisingly, that Islamic idealists are making their voluntary contributions not to the rural council president or the subprefect but straight to their marabouts. Regardless of who gets their money or their millet, the point is the same: with the exception of the very important education variable, other material and social structural factors drop out of this regression, leaving behind ideological-cultural variables that help reveal who finds the state legitimate enough to pay up, and who does not.

TABLE 14. Perception of State Legitimacy, by Social-Structural Position and Historical Memory–Culture Variables

(significance at 5% error level, N = 727)

	Ideological-Culture Variables	β	P-Value (2-Tailed)	Social-Structural Position Variables	β	P-Value (2-Tailed)
Perceive the state as legitimate	Idealize colonial state	.211	.000	Educated	.104	.004
	Idealize marabouts	–.066	.071			

CONCLUSION

Again, we should not interpret the data above to suggest that historical memories or other ideological factors cause anyone to pay taxes or the *addiya,* or that they lead individuals to ignore ancestral spirits and sell their land. The data presented in this chapter make three simple but compelling points. First, no unitary Serer historical memory of culture and informal institutions exists. Rather, memories, narratives, and idealizations vary according to caste, age, gender, education, wealth, stated religious affiliation, and degree of religious orthodoxy. Institutions and economic relations are subjected to questions of morality in the Siin as in Silicon Valley, but this does not mean that in either place we should expect to find unanimity on what is and should be considered moral about economic relations. Serer respondents seem to fashion divergent historical memories of the moral basis for political and economic relations in complex and probably pragmatic ways. These divergent memories suggest shifting, circumstantial underlying patterns of social cleavage.

Second, as we examine how Serer peasants have adapted a series of imposed state and market institutions so that they make sense in terms of historical memories of culture and institutions, we can proceed with some degree of confidence that the pertinent ideological-cultural factors are not simple epiphenomenal outgrowths of underlying material interests and circumstances. With regard to matters of land commodification, the right to pawn land, and the legitimacy of state authority, historical memory and other ideological-cultural variables seem to play an important role, indeed, a more important role than most material-structural factors in accounting for variance in key political behaviors. Historical memory does not entirely account for these behaviors, and the arrows of causality may point east, west, and elsewhere. But as we proceed to explore the intricacies of institutional syncretism, we have reason to suspect that something is going on here. Even though matters of historical memory and "institutional lag" do not tell the entire story, they probably represent significant pieces of the puzzle of how formal institutions change when they are imposed beyond their historical and sociocultural places of origin.

Finally, and perhaps most important, ideological-cultural factors, notions of tradition and historical memories may constrain everyday political and social behavior. Values and cultural attitudes that help constitute a holistic, comprehensive worldview can generate an enmeshing effect. Individuals may buy into a particular element of culture for instrumental reasons that reflect the interests and utility-maximizing behavior commensurate with their social structural position. But once individuals adopt such cultural attitudes, they may become unintentionally enmeshed in the holistic worldview that these values help constitute. Once so enmeshed, individuals may find that adherence to the systemic, comprehensive worldview demands ideologically consistent behavior that can cause direct violation of concrete material interests and utility maximization. The social outliers have attached themselves to more dogmatic moral frameworks (especially non-Mouride Islam) that demand separation from the matrix of Serer social relations, while most Serer have opted for the more pragmatic and eclectic syncretic moral framework that undergirds Serer culture and ongoing processes of institutional syncretism in the Njafaj region of Siin.

4 · Land Pawning as a Response to the Standardization of Tenure

A PAWN CONTRACT

In the last weeks of 1937, Birame Diouf and Waly Sene made an arrangement. In a few days, Diouf would have to pay almost two thousand CFA francs in head tax to the *jaraf* of Tukar, the village representative of the local king, himself a vassal of the French colonial state. If Birame Diouf refused, the king would send his *ceddo* warriors to Diouf's house, and they eventually would track him down and deliver him to the *commandant de cercle* at Fatick. Out in the eastern Saluum where they were building new roads, the corvée gangs could always use extra hands.

Rather than default on the tax, Diouf made a deal with his distant relative Waly Sene. Sene needed more land to farm. In the coming rainy season, Diouf would have three fallow fields. So Diouf offered a plot of about a hectare of land to Sene for his indefinite use, in exchange for a cash payment, a kind of guarantee, of twenty-five hundred CFA francs. In the local language, Diouf made a *taile* with Sene, a land pawn guaranteed by cash as collateral.[1] This particular *taile* contract would hold for over fifty years, until Diouf's great-grandson, Djignak Diouf, repaid the twenty-five-hundred-franc guarantee to Sene's descendant and, after some wrangling, regained his grandfather's plot.[2]

This chapter draws upon the experience of people like Birame Diouf and Waly Sene to explore how the Serer of Senegal's Siin region responded to and adapted models of individually held, alienable private property imposed in the early part of this century as the Siin was transformed into the heartland of Senegal's Peanut Basin. In the face of pressure to develop a market in land and to place ownership in the hands of individual farmers, the Serer produced an innovative system of exchange, the *taile* pawn, which accommodated the demands of a new economic order but did so in a way consistent with, indeed inspired by, a particular historical memory of culturally "authentic" patterns of ownership and exchange of land.

At one level, *taile* represents a syncretic adaptation of market relations in terms of informal rules, habits, and values that emphasize kinship relations and originality of settlement. At another level, *taile* exemplifies local dynamics of reconstruction of culture in response to colonialism. *Taile* relations are grounded on a reification of one among several possible notions of legitimate ownership and inheritance, crystallizing an understanding of "authentic" cultural practice that serves the interests of elder male lineage heads at the expense of other social groups.

This chapter explores the origins and significance of Serer land pawning in four steps. After briefly describing *taile* as a form of economic exchange, I draw upon the now hegemonic strand of local historical memory to reconstruct an image of precolonial Serer land tenure relations, placing local institutions of ownership and exchange in historical and cultural context. Next, I explore social and economic transformations associated with commodification and the simultaneous expansion of Sufi Islam in the 1920s and 1930s. I show how colonialism and Islamicization generated pressure for a standardization of new forms of property, new relations of ownership, and new types of exchange in the Siin. Against this background, I return to Birame Diouf, Waly Sene, and their arrangement, examining *taile* as a form of institutional syncretism that transformed imposed land tenure institutions by blending them with reformulated informal practices and values. Finally, I examine the legacy of this form of institutional syncretism, which sidetracked the establishment of freehold property relations in the Siin even as it facilitated the spread of the peanut economy, the crucial vector of capitalist transformation and colonial rule in the western Sahel. Through *taile*, Serer farmers built institutional arrangements for a *sustainable* process of local cash-crop commodification. In effect, this form of syncretism optimized specific local cultural and political goals, as well as the crucial economic goal of intensifying agricultural production *without* a wholesale, destabilizing transformation of the web of local social relations, patterns of authority, and systems of meaning.[3]

What Is Taile?

Taile has become a key term in the vocabulary of rural Senegal's informal economy. Even in the Siin, respondents use this Wolof term to refer to an exchange in which one party offers a valued item as collateral for a cash loan.[4] Although *taile* pawns have today evolved into exchanges of a wide variety of goods (jewelry, cloth, tools, animals, beds, and radios) for cash loans, in the 1920s, when these arrangements first became widespread, the chief valued commodity was land itself. In a superficial way, these *tailes* involving land resembled the kind of pawning prevalent at the margins of industrialized market economies: a valued item hocked as a guarantee against a cash loan.

Tailes differed from traditional market economy pawns in that they required no payment of interest and had no fixed term. Exchanges could even span several generations. Great-grandsons of the parties who negotiated the original *taile* terminated the contract simply by repaying the original loan amount in exchange for return of the pawned field.

The indefinite, multigenerational nature of the *taile* exchange was crucial. *Taile* allowed transfers of land for cash without affecting local notions of ownership because a *taile* transferred use rights to land without transferring title. Predominant local notions of ownership made a very clear distinction between use rights and title, and *taile* represented a syncretic adaptation that preserved this distinction even in the face of the increasing commodification of economic relations. Some new institutional economists have applied the term *redeemable sale* to such exchanges.[5] But this awkward appellation imposes more than it describes. *Redeemable sale* squeezes the square peg of an innovative, hybrid ontology of ownership and exchange into the round hole of dichotomous "traditional" and "modern" property regimes.

DOMINANT HISTORICAL MEMORY OF SERER-SIIN LAND TENURE INSTITUTIONS

As noted in chapter 2, the hegemonic version of "authentic" Serer-Siin tradition holds that precolonial land ownership and exchange were rooted in a sense of originality tied to episodes of migration to a new locale, settlement, and clearing of forestland by fire.[6] This emphasis on originality of settlement is not unique to the Siin or to the western Sahel. Rather, this type of originality is a structure of the *longue durée* of African history, a response to social tension that results in a pattern of cleavage, migration, and resettlement.[7]

The Laman–Yal Bakh *Contract*

Within the dominant narrative of Serer migration and village founding, the fire estate represented an archetypal model of property, and the *laman* and his lineage represented idealized "owners." This was especially true with regard to the complete meaning of ownership—creator, negative holder, holistic custodian. *Lamanic* "ownership" entailed the management of community goods in their material dimensions (rotation, fallow, tree access) and spiritual dimensions (relations with key *pangool* spirits that ensure soil fertility, good rains, abundant crops). Within this ontology of ownership, alienation or sale of land is problematic. But village founding myths include stories of the settlement of "second migrants," morality plays on how to incorporate the "stranger." These stories sketch idealized models of how to transfer land to newcomers from those who hold rightful title.

Although the first *laman* controlled a vast estate as a result of the bush-clearing fire, his lineage was too few in number to make productive use of all this land. He needed to attract settlers and incorporate them into the new community. As long as prospective settlers recognized the material and spiritual legitimacy of his claim (the primacy of the *laman's* control over land and the significance of the *pangool* of the *laman's* lineage), the *laman* granted them a portion of his fire estate. The newcomer received the right to cut or clear a certain parcel, known in Serer as a *bakh*. The holder of the right to clear such a space is thus the *yal bakh,* or "master of cutting."[8]

The crux of this relationship between *laman* and *yal bakh* was a recognition on the part of the latter that he held only *use rights* to the land, and that the *laman* retained ultimate "title" based on the originality of his settlement and the significance of his relatives, seen and unseen, for the well-being of the fire estate and the community. Once a *laman* made a grant of cutting rights, he could not summarily retake the fields as long as the *yal bakh* continued to use them. But if the *bakh* land fell into disuse and returned to the condition of *o kop ale* (wild, forestland, out of civilization), it would then revert to the *laman,* as holder of ultimate "title" in the form of holistic custodianship.[9]

Recognition of ultimate *lamanic* title entailed regular payments on the part of the *yal bakh.* Although details vary from village to village, in general the *bakh* holder had to provide a payment to the *laman,* often referred to as a *laax.* Such payments ranged from a largely ceremonial gift at the death of either party to the contract, to an annual deposit of a fraction of each harvest. Gifts usually consisted of some combination of agricultural products (millet, and since colonialism, peanuts) as well as alcohol.[10]

Although a *yal bakh* could not alienate his land, he was free to distribute it as he saw fit within his lineage. As generations passed and lineages expanded, the *bakh* holder's role took on increasing importance. After many generations of distributing fields within his own lineage, a *yal bakh* might even take over some of the material responsibilities of custodianship associated with the *laman,* such as management of the crop rotation and pasturing systems.[11]

Despite this increased autonomy, *bakh* holders continued to pay the ceremonial gift to the *laman*. The payment, however token and occasional, remained crucial because it reaffirmed the entire system of ownership and exchange. It reminded a young *yal bakh* that neither he nor his ancestors "created" the land. The payments underscored who was responsible for the fertility of the soil, the productivity of the land, and by extension, the well-being of the community. Perhaps most significantly, the payment underscored the gulf between fire master *(laman)* and cutting master at the level of *pangool*. While a master of cutting might eventually come to take on some of the material custodial responsibilities of a master of fire, his *pangool*, to the extent they were prominent at all, could not eclipse those of the pioneer-migrant who lit the first fire. Payment of the ceremonial gift to the *laman* announced the *bakh* holder's recognition that he would never hold "real" title to his land in the full, holistic custodianship sense.

Origin stories of the founding of the first fire estate and the first granting of a *bakh* to a newcomer are extremely important for contemporary land tenure relations because they establish, through larger-than-life metaphorical example, the parameters of moral, economic relations. Tales such as the one that follows, from the village of Tukar, teach basic principles: rightful ownership or control of property is a matter of original settlement and first use, and "original title" belongs not to an individual but to a lineage. These historical archetypes of ownership and exchange remain crucial in the present day because people came to understand new, commodified models of controlling and exchanging property within the cognitive frame of existing tenure arrangements, with their emphasis on originality of settlement, holistic custodianship, and lineage control.

Tales of Village Founding: The Example of Tukar

We can take as an illustrative example the story of Djigan Diouf and the founding of Tukar, a large and ancient community in the center of the thirty-village zone of my research.[12] Although several different versions of this story remain in circulation, most inhabitants of Tukar are familiar with a somewhat stylized, simplified account. This is probably because this generalized version of the narrative is sometimes taught to primary school students (in the U.S. equivalent of second and third grade) at the local state-run school, the École Kane Faye de Tukar.

This popular version opens with Djigan Diouf as the hero-migrant who journeyed out of the Wolof kingdoms to the north of the Siin during the reign of one of the first Gelwaar *maads* and set fire to the bush. He was followed shortly afterward by Fassamane Thiao, who is identified, even by his fiercely proud descendants, only as the *second* founder of Tukar. Fassamane asked Djigan for some land to farm, but he also went to see the *maad*, who authorized him to light a fire too. Even though Fassamane Thiao controlled his own fire estate, he offered a small amount of millet to Djigan out of respect for his status as the first founder.

After Fassamane, no other migrants lit bush-clearing fires. The popular version of the story highlights the arrival and settlement of Djemé Bahoum, a great hunter, as the third founder of Tukar. Bahoum offered to share some of his catch with Djigan, and eventually received his own *bakh* grant. His descendants continued to offer game as regular payment to Djigan's family. In similar fashion, ancestors of the Kamas, Fayes, Ndiayes, and other prominent families became Djigan's comrades and received substantial *bakhs*, around which the contemporary neighborhoods of Tukar are organized.

Not surprisingly, we find wide discrepancies between somewhat simplified, widely circulated village founding tales and more detailed, and perhaps more historically accurate, versions told by elders and key members of founding lineages. These simplified and probably less accurate stories are more significant to my study, to the extent that I explore not the effect of some primordial set of *actual* events on contemporary social relations but the way popular historical memory provides a larger-than-life model of how people ought to relate.

Comparison between expert and folk accounts nevertheless underscores key simplifications in the folk text. In the case of the village of Tukar, noteworthy distinctions exist between the generic account above and the much more detailed story told by a contemporary *lamanic* descendant of Djigan Diouf, Diaga Dibor Ndofene Diouf. As the *laman* Diouf recalls:

> All the fields that we farm came from the fields of Djigan Diouf. Anyone in the neighborhood who says otherwise, who says this or that thing had been started by his father—no. Everything was done by Djigan. It was he who came from Lambaye with his brother Ndik, and they created the village of Tukar.
>
> At first they settled a few hundred meters from here. Djigan had lit the fire that cleared all this territory, which extends all the way to the black lands, and he farmed all of that space. This all belonged to Njujuf,[13] and when the *maad* came, he said that Njujuf would never change, and would never move from here. Njujuf had its own special liberties. Among all the *maad a Sinig* who succeeded, no one tried to change Njujuf, no *maad* dared to try to seize our millet.[14] If they did, they would be cast off their throne. The *pangool* of Njujuf would attack them and cause them to lose their power. Our fields belong only to the inhabitants of Njujuf, and the *laman* is in charge of them.

In the days of Djigan, Fassar o Njafaj, an adventurer, came upon Djigan one day at the end of the harvest.[15] Djigan was going to have a very large harvest of millet. So Fassar said, "Ooh, you're going to have quite a bit of millet!" to which Djigan responded, "Tuuk!" [Shut up!]; and then he told Fassar to say "Kar-kar" [Just kidding]. It's from here that we get the name of the village, Tukar.[16]

So after that, Djigan took Fassar in and gave him someplace to sleep and shared meals with him. After a few weeks though, Fassar went to Diakhao.[17] I don't know what exactly he went to see the *maad* for and what they talked about, but Djigan just took care of the house in Fassar's absence. The *maad a Sinig* said to Fassar, "When you go back to Tukar, light a fire at Sagne Folo [in the northern part of Tukar], and there where the fire burns will become your new property." This is exactly what Fassar did when he got back.

Djigan stepped out of his house and saw this gigantic fire. He said to his brother Ndik, "That *paal* [blacksmith] who left all that baggage here has lit himself a fire!"[18] Djigan and his brother jumped on their horses and went to the edge of the fire, cutting down live trees to protect their *ndaak*.[19]

The next day the *paal* came back and said to Djigan, "The *maad a Sinig* greets you." He then recounted for Djigan his encounter with the *maad* and the division of the fields. So together they went to see the effect of the fire, and saw that it stretched behind Njujuf in the opposite direction, toward Xuuxnan [now in Ngangarlam]. All that space became the *ndaak* of Fassar o Njafaj.

Ironically, the popular account casts Djigan Diouf more clearly as the village founder, the primary figure responsible for lighting the bush-clearing fire. In that simplified version of the story, later migrants appear more deferential and subservient to Djigan. Moreover, unlike the folk version, the account by the *laman* Diaga Diouf suggests considerable tension between Djigan, the first founder, and Fassar (Fassamane from the popular version of the story). Fassar went behind Djigan's back to the *maad* and got secret permission to light his own fire. Djigan responded by calling Fassar's caste identity into doubt in an extremely serious manner—suggesting that he is in fact a blacksmith. Especially because of the fact that the *laman's* version implicates the Gelwaar monarch in this intravillage conflict, it seems to have a much wider narrative agenda than the folk version. The *laman's* account highlights in unmistakable terms the core antagonism between the Serer village founder on one side and the Gelwaar monarchs and their local allies on the other.

In light of the findings described in chapter 3, this is not surprising: the *laman* is part of the social group most likely to carry an antistatist historical memory. Our respondent, the *laman* Diouf, evidently has a complaint with the "second family" of Tukar, the descendants of Fassar o Njafaj (Fassamane Thiao). This is not surprising, given that in the present day the leader of the lineage of Fassar-Fassamane, became the first rural council president and Diaga Diouf was the last reigning *laman* in the area. Intriguingly, Diouf's rhetorical devices for discrediting the Thiao family include calling him a blacksmith and linking him to external conspiracy with the reviled Gelwaar *maad*.

The folk account glosses over this tension between two holders of fire rights in the same village. Fassar-Fassamane, even as a *laman* in his own right, pays his respects to Djigan as the original *laman*. More important, subsequent migrants establish contractual relations with and receive *bakh* grants from Djigan, not Fassar-Fassamane.

Expert accounts of village founding like that of the current *laman* of Tukar include considerable historical detail (especially for a tale preserved via oral history for some twenty-five generations) and clearly serve to advance particular political agendas in the present day. But such accounts, known to only a few initiates, are not meant to establish foundations for the *lamanic* lineage's claim to legitimacy and prominence. This task falls to vernacular accounts, which in the case cited above, actually do more to establish an order in which the descendants of the first *laman* figure prominently at the top of a social hierarchy.[20]

STANDARDIZING PROPERTY RELATIONS

To the architects of imperialism, commerce was a disembodied, almost Platonic force, one of the principal agents of natural social development. Incarnate in the real material interests of the likes of the Compagnie Française de l'Afrique de l'Ouest, the advancement of commerce stood out as one of the most central *missions civilisatrices* of French colonial policy. The advancement of commerce—whether that meant increasing imperial profits or turning "indolent savages" into commodity farmers—required colonial officials to introduce new socioeconomic and cultural infrastructure. Like today's processes of marketization in territories "reclaimed" from socialism, the initial imposition of commodity production for international markets in Senegal in the late 1800s depended on an extensive program of reformulating socioeconomic relations, political institutions, and supporting values and consciousness. New notions of work, property, and exchange were imposed. To support the new order, new legal and political institutions were created along with systems of enforcement, like corvée gangs and the infamous Code de l'Indigenat, which brought labor discipline to French possessions in Africa. When local values and social relations blocked marketization, these too had to be swept away. This was institutional imposition and modernizing transformation (see chapter 7).

At bottom, installing the infrastructure of the market was not just a matter of displacing antecedent forms of economic organization and unsupportive political and legal arrangements. It entailed a more profound "civilizing" process, one that imposed a new framework of values, habits, and informal rules, a new institutional infrastructure, and a new world-view supportive of a new socioeconomic order. This wider civilizing process provides the backdrop for the push toward freehold property relations in the Siin in the 1920s and 1930s.

Enforcing Commodification

The politics of collaboration in the Siin allowed the colonial state to placate commerce without making a tabula rasa of existing political structures.[21] By the time the French began to introduce large-scale production of peanuts for export in this region in the 1890s, the king of Siin (the *maad*) and the royal lineage as a whole (the Gelwaar) had long since settled into a cozy, lucrative collaboration with French administrators. Gelwaar monarchs lent their authority, somewhat limited legitimacy, and considerable coercive power to the colonial effort to convert the Serer into peanut farmers.[22]

Prior to World War I, the Serer were nevertheless slow to expand peanut production.[23] At first, most peasants were unwilling to include the new crop in their system of three-year rotation of *pod* (large millet), *maac* (small millet), and *tos* (fallow). The fallow year was crucial to the rotation cycle, providing both an opportunity for soil regeneration and a grazing space for cattle, whose manure ensured soil fertility.[24] Introducing peanuts threatened to alter this balance. Peasants would either have to reduce fallow areas (and, as a result, reduce the size of herds or send animals elsewhere during the growing season) or, less acceptably, reduce millet acreage.

Colonial administrators tried to apply the logic of the market and convince Serer producers that they could use cash earned from selling peanuts to fill the food gap that would result from reducing subsistence crop acreage. But, for producers whose system was well adapted to the vagaries of rainfall in the western Sahel, and who had little familiarity with avoiding starvation by using cash to buy food, this was a hard sell.[25]

Especially after World War I, the colonial administration turned to a more systematically enforced head tax to get the Serer to produce peanuts. Prior to the tax, commodification had spread rather slowly in the Siin. Peasants grew peanuts on marginal lands without significantly altering their three-year rotation system. While the Serer economy had long known manufactured commodities and money, socially significant transactions, such as payments of the bride price, had been only marginally converted to cash exchanges.[26] The only way the colonial state was going to force the Serer to grow large quantities of peanuts, it seemed, was to force them to *need* cash. The head tax fit the bill quite well. Those who could not or would not drum up the necessary cash to pay the head tax soon spent their days hauling sixty-foot palm tree trunks or hand paving the road from Mbour to Fatick.[27] The corvée gang provided Serer producers with extremely visible examples of the punishment awaiting those who tried to evade the tax.

In the early years, there were instances of organized resistance to the new head tax. In response to initial imposition of the tax in the village of Diohin in 1891, peasants staged a widespread but short-lived revolt against the local *saax-saax*, the tax collector for the *maad*. In Diohin and elsewhere, however, the combined coercive power of the *maad* and the colonial military easily overwhelmed spontaneous opposition to the head tax and eventually to peanut production itself.[28]

Implementation of the head tax was made possible in part by the collaboration of a significant minority of the Serer population, the *ceddo* warrior caste. Long habituated to living off the backs of the Serer peasant, the *ceddo* saw tax collection as an ideal basis for maintaining an economy of predation.[29] However, the handwriting was in fact already on the wall for this predatory caste. Their counterparts in conquered, dismembered Wolof kingdoms to the north had been turned into Muslim plantation hands in the aftermath of the colonial peace. The *ceddo* of Siin knew that they would lose the material basis for their caste distinctiveness once the colonial (or postcolonial, as it turned out) state chose to dispense with the Gelwaar regime of the Siin. Understandably wary of the shaky foundations of the local economy of predation, the *ceddo* of Siin took up this new raison d'être—tax collection—with special zeal.[30]

Because there was only one way for a Serer farmer to come up with the cash to pay the head tax, the delicately balanced rotation system was modified to make room for the peanut. In the years after World War I, the peanut became part of a new three-year rotation—millet (*pod* only), peanuts, and fallow.[31]

Standardization: The Colonial Regime

The politics of collaboration with the Gelwaar monarchy prevented colonial administrators from systematically imposing freehold property relations and thereby upending local tenure relations. Although such a policy would have greatly advanced the interests of commerce and "civilization," it also would have completely destabilized the system of village-level aristocratic control over land (the *laman–yal bakh* aristocracy), whose support had been vital to Gelwaar rule since the monarchy was established in the Siin in the fourteenth century. Maintenance of a legitimate local political elite who could ensure stability and quiescence on the cheap—the paramount concern of colonial policy after World War I—took precedence over more ideal plans to expand peanut production by making tenure more "secure."[32]

Colonial policy with regard to property relations, however, did not reflect a coherent, uniform respect for "customary rights." Despite reluctance to undermine collaborative political institutions, colonial administrators did seek to promote European norms of ownership and exchange when possible. To that end, decrees from 1906, 1932, and 1955 set out to "institute eminent rights in property, including registration and alienability of lands."[33] Moreover, in 1907 the Appeals Court for French West Africa drew on a "theory of succession of states" to argue that the colonial state, as the inheritor of the rights of the former Wolof kingdoms, could legally claim unused land in these territories because local kings had been "the absolute masters of people and goods, and by extension, sole proprietors of all lands without exception."[34] Although these interventions fell short of a complete reformulation of local land tenure institutions, they did serve to project European models of ownership and exchange into the rural sector for the first time.[35]

At a more subtle and significant level, administrators used a central mechanism of the civilizing process, the codification of customary law, to solidify the socioeconomic foundations for increased peanut production.[36] Colonial administrators sought to rationalize what they saw as the disorder and uncertainty resulting from overlapping local systems of property holding and inheritance. The process of codification of law helped idealize patrilineal holding patterns and marginalize and eventually eliminate competing models, especially matrilineality. The spread of Islam also served colonial interests, in that it provided moral and religious bases for patrilineal holding, adding further pressure to standardize land tenure toward a European freehold model.

Colonial legal codification simplified the complex bilineal systems of inheritance and control that had characterized the Siin before commodification. Control of the fire and cutting estates discussed above (the *laman–yal bakh* system) can be organized according to both patrilineal and matrilineal systems of inheritance, although matrilineal fire estates tended to be more ancient than their patrilineal counterparts.[37] While both matrilineages and patrilineages might control land, other goods were more clearly associated with one line or the other. Cattle holding as a form of savings, for example, was primarily a concern of the *tim*, or matrilineal family.[38] Moreover, a few specific classes of goods, such as jewelry and fabric, fell more strictly into a category of "women's goods," passed not matrilineally (brother to sister's son) but in a direct uterine line from mother to daughter. In a similar uterine pattern, some accumulation of cash even took place at the level of the *ngak*, or kitchen, an intrahousehold familial unit of consumption organized around a mother and her offspring.[39]

For our purposes, the most important pattern of ownership (outside the *laman–yal bakh* land tenure system) centered on "father's goods." Unlike cattle and land, certain goods, such as tools, guns, household furniture, carts, and a few other manufactured items, had long been considered the individual property of males, which they could pass directly to their sons.[40] Some analysts have suggested that, because these individualized patrilineal goods tended to include manufactured commodities like agricultural tools and weapons, it was only natural that, as the universe of manufactures expanded, such new items fell into the category of father's goods. However, given the heterogeneity of inheritance patterns and ownership arrangements, it seems more likely that new commodities (including cash earned from peanut production) were up for grabs in terms of patterns of ownership and inheritance. The fact that peanut cash and most new commodities became father's goods suggests not a kind of metaphysical correspondence between prior patrilineal goods and new commodities but a struggle in the aftermath of commodification, in which patrilineal modes emerged as the dominant system for controlling property.[41]

Patrilineal appropriation of new commodities and the proceeds of cash cropping contributed to the "standardization" of property, ownership, and exchange in the Siin. Men managed to take advantage of new forms of property, new relations of ownership, and new types of exchange by asserting that new goods were father's goods, and that the cash earned from growing peanuts should be "father's money," passed on directly to sons. This buttressing of male control of property moved Serer notions of ownership and control away from heterogeneous, overlapping systems (in which patrilineal and matrilineal inheritance existed side by side, and in which control at the level of the lineage, *ngak*, and individual was not unusual). In place of these systems, the Serer began to adopt a pattern of ownership that more closely conformed with the European standard of individual control, primogeniture, and alienability.

For French colonial officials, the most unproductive, backward form of property holding, the one least conducive to the grounding of "civilized" commerce, was matrilineality. In the process of codifying customary law and in selecting traditional leaders with whom to collaborate, Saint-Louis did its best to discourage matrilineal inheritance and to steer the Siin and other rural societies away from this "barbarism," toward forms of inheritance and property holding thought to constitute a better foundation for industriousness and commerce.[42]

For French colonial officials, matrilineality dispersed wealth into seemingly byzantine social networks in which title was uncertain and investments in soil fertility were unlikely to take place. In this sense, French colonial officials presaged what Thomas Bassett calls the "tenure evolution model," common in contemporary thinking at institutions like the World Bank, which holds that tenure systems necessarily progress toward more secure, more individual, and more alienable patterns of control.[43] Overlapping bilineal systems also complicated social control for French colonial officials. A 1939 report on Serer customary law describes how local producers took advantage of bilineal inheritance patterns to cheat French commercial houses out of repayments of debts. As they expanded peanut production, male heads of household accumulated considerable debts in seed and new tools. In good years, household heads repaid debts each year from their harvest proceeds. But in bad years (or simply when individuals chose to devote cash proceeds to marriage, baptisms, or other purposes) unpaid debts accumulated. Upon the death of a head of household, commercial houses and colonial officials expected an eldest son, as heir, to take over responsibility for his father's debts. Eldest sons quickly caught on to this surcharge on bereavement, and many of them fled to the household of their maternal uncles upon the death of their father. They claimed that under matrilineal custom they were in fact heirs to their *tokor*, or matrilineal uncles, not their fathers. Trading companies like Maurel et Prom and Buhan et Tessière found themselves saddled with massive numbers of defaulted loans and could find no heirs to take responsibility for them.[44] When control of land, cattle, peanut wealth, and other goods had been regrouped along patrilineal lines, the patterns of ownership and exchange of the Serer "made more sense" from the colonial point of view and lent themselves to much easier incorporation into the colonial legal framework and the underlying economic order. This was of course an act of James Scott's "authoritarian high modernist state simplification" par excellence.[45]

Standardization: The Importance of Islam

French colonial policy also took advantage of a crucial religious ally in the effort to standardize ownership and exchange in pagan enclaves like the

Siin. Since the days of Governor Faidherbe, colonial policy in Senegal had emphasized cooptation of Islamic Sufi leaders who were not openly hostile to the regime.[46] After the total defeat of the jihad movements of the 1880s, few rebellious religious leaders remained, and in the last decades of the nineteenth century and the early part of the twentieth century, the brotherhoods and the colonial regime settled into comfortable and mutually beneficial collaboration. As former warriors and displaced peasants of the defeated Wolof kingdoms joined the new brotherhoods, the marabouts provided a docile labor force to expand peanut production into so-called new lands of the Ferlo Desert and the eastern Saluum. Colonial officials posed no obstacle to the mass conversion, facilitating the process by which the brotherhoods replaced the old Wolof nobility as a new rural aristocracy.

This emergent version of Islam became an arena in which new cultural forms were constructed to suit the interests of those groups who could work their way to an advantageous position in the new order. Men seized upon Islam as a way to reorganize the distribution of wealth and control over resources in their favor. Even the highly syncretic brand of Sufi Islam preached by the Mourides allowed for no deviation on this score: patrilineal control of wealth and patrilineal inheritance became sacred tenets.

Although women were decidedly subordinated in the Siin prior to the arrival of Islam, they had enjoyed marginally greater social flexibility and influence before the advent of the Mouride, Tijane, and other Islamic brotherhoods. For example, control of cash in the *ngak* had enabled women to accumulate some resources outside the control of their husbands and brothers. Moreover, the ambiguities of inheritance and ownership in a bilineal system offered women occasional opportunities to control land and wealth. Bilineality can generate chronic conflict between uncles and fathers. A son may be able to play his father off his matrilineal uncle, and vice versa. When sons enjoy such opportunities, their chief ally, counselor, and coconspirator is often their mother. Likewise, situations in which lines of male control and power become unclear create openings for women themselves to play one off the other and assert their interests.

Islam served as the handmaiden of imperialism by helping to limit these types of opportunities built into heterogeneous property relations. Abelin sums up the usefulness of Islamic organizations to the colonial regime by noting, "The expansion of Islam in the territory of Senegambia promoted during this period numerous ideas which for many were not in contradiction with the logic and mode of thinking of Europeans. . . . Islam brought not just its religious ideas, but its *economisme* and its juridical body, all of which made it, ideally a 'temporal religion.' "[47]

Convinced of the notion that the preferred moral form of inheritance was from fathers to sons (with daughters receiving half the inheritance of sons under *shari'a* law), Islam as practiced by local marabouts encouraged the complete abandonment of matrilinealism, "a pagan, ungodly practice."[48] Gradual conversion to Islam, even in the recalcitrant Siin, contributed to a change in consciousness that greatly facilitated the process of standardizing norms of property and ownership along "normal" patrilineal lines.

In the Siin, Islam amounted to a vehicle for the accumulation of greater wealth and power on the part of one social group as societies reconstituted themselves in the aftermath of colonial domination. The move toward patrilinealization created a rather broad alliance of rural men, Islamic leaders, and colonial officials who, for rather different reasons, collaborated in a process of gradual standardization of property relations that promoted individualism and alienability.

TAILE AS AN ALTERNATIVE SYSTEM OF EXCHANGE

Birame Diouf and Waly Sene, with whom this discussion began, were familiar with the head tax, peanut expansion, and new commodities, as well as colonial and Islamic pressures for property standardization, patrilineality, and individual holding. Birame Diouf, for example, had converted to the Tijane brotherhood some years before he entered into a *taile* with Waly Sene.[49] In the years leading up to his *taile* contract, Diouf also faced exceptional demands, some of which would have occurred without the arrival of the peanut, others of which emanated from new economic relations. After one harvest, probably in 1936, in which Birame's yields were good, two of his sons took wives, at considerable expense to Birame. Some months later, during the rainy season of 1937, the only son of Birame's third wife fell ill with malaria. Birame took the boy to the local marabout, who, at the cost of a bull, promised to heal the child. The marabout spent almost two weeks preparing the necessary remedies, shortly after which the child died.

Then the rains of 1937 came. They began with force in June and continued into July. Birame Diouf's millet sprouted. The rains continued in an unprecedented torrent, inundating his young plants and effectively ruining the millet crop that year. The heavy rains created hardship for many farmers. Diouf, with all his recent losses, was ill prepared to face the crisis. By the time December came, he had no money to pay the head tax, and no cattle left to sell for cash. He discreetly sent word through relatives that he needed cash quickly and could offer a field in exchange.

Diouf would *taile* his field to Waly Sene before 1937 came to a close. Before turning to the contract itself, we should first consider a kind of "dual stratification," another by-product of commodification that bears on the origins of *taile* as an adaptation of new property relations in the Siin.

Dual Stratification

Once farmers like Birame Diouf had acquiesced to cash cropping, it became possible for merchants to extend markets for manufactured products into the countryside. The *escales*, villages designated as peanut collection and purchasing sites, became distribution nodes for an expanding range of manufactured items that worked their way into the ordinary life of the rural producer. Even more slowly, the Serer peasant started to use cash to gain access to new medicines, to travel outside the Siin, perhaps even to send a son to school.[50] As Birame Diouf found in 1937, in hard times the need for cash could be extreme.

However, acquisition of cash resources did not always follow lines of social stratification that existed in Serer society before commodification. While patterns of stratification were not clearly binary, many older, more aristocratic lineages that controlled fire estates and large *bakhs* felt less pressure to convert land to cash crop production, preferring instead to maintain precolonial land use arrangements. Aristocrats generally planted just enough land in peanuts to pay the head tax, continuing to keep significant acreage idle to maintain the integrity of the fallow system.

At the lower end of the precommodification status hierarchy, families of relatively more recent arrival in a village, and members of lower castes such as griots, artisans, and slaves, had less stake in the customary economic order and limited access to land.[51] For many of them, agriculture had never been a fully remunerative activity, and their holdings in livestock were generally quite marginal. When a new economic order emerged which permitted one to raise one's status simply by accumulating cash, these groups were among the first to seize new opportunities.

The caste system and artisanal work are especially significant in this regard. In the Siin, as in Serer and Wolof societies more generally, artisanal activity has been the object of considerable disdain on the part of the free farmer majority and the aristocrats. Handicraft workers of all kinds—blacksmiths, leather workers, potters, weavers, and woodworkers—were considered members of distinct and very clearly subordinate endogamous castes. Marriage between members of the free farmer or aristocratic groups and these castes remains the basis for de facto community exile even today.

The flood of imported manufactures both displaced a good deal of local handicraft production and commodified remaining and new artisanal work.

Blacksmiths, potters, and weavers—as well as masons and mechanics—
were paid with what one respondent evocatively called "silver objects for
living."[52] The commodification of artisanal work brought blacksmiths,
weavers, and griots into greater contact with new economic opportunities.
These groups, like the Wolof *ceddo* to the north, had little access to land,
and, since they needed to pay the head tax like everyone else, they were
eager to earn cash through novel means.

In addition, Islam provided new economic opportunities for members of
disdained castes. In the Siin, Islamic affiliation has generally been stronger
among griots and other low-caste groups than among free farmers and
aristocrats. The religion appears to offer a "universalistic out" for people
whose ascriptive characteristics trapped them into low social status.
Indeed, table 15 shows that even in the present day, we find that low-caste
groups are more well represented in the Islamic brotherhoods than others
members of Serer society.

It is especially striking that members of the low-caste group represent
the largest percentage of any caste in the most orthodox Muslim groups
(non-Mouride Muslims). As discussed in chapter 3, Mouridism itself, a
popular option in the present day for all castes, including the free farmer
majority, does not correlate very strongly with highly commodified economic relations, strong support for state intervention, and breaking with
Serer customary tenure and political institutions. But identification with
non-Mouride Islamic groups does in fact correlate with all these indicators
of cleavage from the wider Serer community.

An examination of the degree of religious orthodoxy exhibited by caste
group, regardless of exact religious affiliation, reveals that those of low
caste stand out as the most orthodox members of Serer society (see figure
5). While the Gelwaar and Serer aristocratic castes are also quite orthodox
in the present day, table 15 points out the degree to which this orthodoxy
is expressed within Christianity, rather than Islam or animism. Unlike
their free farmer neighbors, those of low caste tend to have much more
orthodox Islamic beliefs and practices, an observation that tends to confirm
the notion that egalitarian, universalistic Islam served as a social and economic "out" for the lowest members of Serer society.

To the extent that Islam also represented a vehicle for insertion into the
new economy, the tendency of lower status groups to more readily become
devout followers of Sufi marabouts put them at an even greater advantage
in the new economic order. In the Wolof regions to the north and east of
the Siin in the 1920s and 1930s, the Islamic brotherhoods emerged as dominant economic actors. Marabouts set up vast plantations worked by their *talibés* and used these estates to enrich themselves as a new agricultural elite.[53]

TABLE 15. Religious Affiliation by Caste Group

(in percentages, N = 707)

Caste Group[1]	Animist	Mouride	Other Muslim	Christian	Total	N
Gelwaar	2.97	35.64	18.32	43.07	100.00	202
Serer aristocratic	3.95	38.16	15.78	42.11	100.00	76
Free farmer	9.66	47.98	13.71	28.65	100.00	321
Low	0.93	45.36	23.15	30.56	100.00	108

1. For details on the categorization of castes into the four caste groupings, see chapter 3.

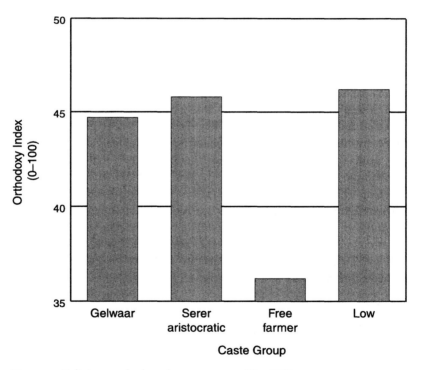

Figure 5. Religious orthodoxy by caste group (*N* = 727)

Although the brotherhoods did not emerge as a landowning elite in the Siin, they did represent magnets of economic opportunity for those who were willing to uproot themselves from Serer society, migrate into adjacent Wolof lands, convert to Islam, and become devout *talibés* (followers).[54]

Within the Siin, lower caste and marginal families were much more likely than free farmers or aristocrats to have a son, cousin, or brother who had converted to Islam. Conversion connected these emigrants to new sources of wealth outside the Siin, wealth that worked its way back to family members left behind in the pagan Siin.

Aristocrats and free farmers, partly due to their security of tenure, partly out of disdain for artisanal work and for Islam, were cut off from quick insertion in the new cash economy. As a result, a kind of double stratification emerged in the Siin. On the one hand, by the old measures of land, cattle, originality, and *pangool* affiliations, the old hierarchy was little altered. Yet, on the other hand, as lower caste groups and marginal families sought opportunities in the new cash economy or used their affiliation with Islamic institutions to gain access to cash resources, a parallel hierarchy based on cash emerged that amounted to, if not the diametrical inversion of the existing land-status hierarchy, then at least a significant rearrangement of key groups.

Birame Diouf, Waly Sene, and the Significance of Taile

Although accounts are somewhat sketchy, it would appear that there was an element of dual stratification at work in the 1937 *taile* between Birame Diouf and Waly Sene. Diouf's family claimed descent from the original *laman* of Tukar, Djigan Diouf, and lived, along with most others of the clan, in the neighborhood of Njujuf. Sene lived in the recently settled village of Ndokh, located at the outer reaches of the old Diouf fire estate, toward the frontier between Siin and the Wolof kingdom of Baol. Ndokh was established as a satellite village by migrants from the Njujuf neighborhood of Tukar. The inhabitants of the Ndokh "colony" saw themselves as dependent on the *laman* of Njujuf.[55] Sene, as a resident of Ndokh, was thus almost certainly a social subordinate to Birame Diouf, member of a powerful *lamanic* lineage.

Sene's descendants also note with considerable pride that Diogoye Sene, one of Waly's sons, was one of only two young men to serve in France during World War II. No conscripts were recruited from Ndokh itself, given its relative isolation, but Diogoye managed to work his way into military service because he had already migrated to Fatick, the regional administrative capital, where he was occasionally employed at the local commercial station of the Buhan et Tessière trading company.[56] The Senes lived in a satellite village of Tukar, yet they had made connections to the new economy at a rather early date.

As noted at the outset of this discussion, the combination of Waly Sene's accumulation of a sum of twenty-five hundred francs and Birame Diouf's urgent need for cash to pay the head tax in December of 1937 precipitated the *taile* of a plot of just under a hectare from Birame Diouf to Waly Sene. The exchange would remain in force until 1992, when Birame's grandson, Djignak Diouf, tried to repay the twenty-five-hundred-franc guarantee to Waly Sene's grandson, Niokhor Sene. That attempt to repay the *taile* pawn resulted in a series of harsh accusations, a near divorce, threats of supernatural retaliation, and appeals to the reviled legal machinery of the state.

Although the Diouf-Sene *taile* appears to have been based on dual stratification in which a land-rich aristocrat traded fields for cash from a subordinate with a toehold in the new economy, this was not a necessary ingredient of all *tailes*. Dual stratification only added to the already existing pressures for commodification of land that precipitated the *taile* innovation. The head tax and availability of new commodities created a need for cash. Given that, apart from cattle, the major form of wealth in the society was land, it naturally became increasingly important to find a way to translate land into cash and vice versa. As Abdoulaye Bara Diop points out, "Land pawns developed along with the need for money to address urgent necessities: ceremonial expenses, tax payments, fees."[57]

Taile is a form of exchange that worked within the exigencies of the new economy—especially the need to exchange wealth in fields for wealth in cash—but at the same time, it remobilized a *certain version* of traditional land tenure arrangements. By maintaining a clear ontological distinction between title and usufruct, and by transferring only usufruct and not title, pawns between ordinary producers like Birame Diouf and Waly Sene conformed to this local notion of legitimate property and moral exchange. Following the model of the holders of fire and cutting rights, it was not possible to accept what was implicit in the freehold model—fusion of usufruct and title that would permit transfer of the two together, that is, the sale of land.

LEGACIES OF *TAILE*

Commodity farming demanded a significant increase in acreage under production, which was greatly facilitated by *taile* pawning as a mechanism for moving land back and forth between lineages whose labor capacity and subsistence needs varied according to cycles of household expansion and contraction. By "preserving" a hegemonic version of traditional Serer ownership and exchange, land pawning successfully imbued new, partially commodified relations of exchange with authenticity and cultural legitimacy. By providing a locally acceptable mechanism for short-term, flexible exchange of land benefiting from what new institutional economists call "high self-enforcement" and "low transaction costs," pawning eased integration into cash-crop production and contributed to the spread of the peanut economy. Yet from the point of view of another classic developmental goal—the institutionalization of individualized freehold property—pawning was quite dysfunctional. It accommodated economic commodification in a way that preserved a local understanding of ownership as nonmarket, inalienable, lineage guardianship over the material and spiritual dimensions of land.

Taile shows us how institutional syncretism can advance cultural, political, and economic goals in creating sustainable processes of commodification and capitalist incorporation. Clearly, *taile* maintained authoritative resource management by masters of fire and *yal bakhs* while upholding the local ontology of property and exchange, as well as other social relations and cultural values supportive of the Serer land management complex. But this syncretic institution was also the most effective arrangement for the economic agenda of transforming the Serer into cash-croppers who could reliably pay their head tax and thereby help finance the burgeoning colonial presence in French West Africa. This was not, of course, an autochthonous Serer goal, but it was the crucial feature of the macroeconomic climate in which the Serer found themselves in the early decades of the twentieth century. Even though French colonial administrators envisioned and imposed their own trajectory of institutional change to maximize peanut production, these efforts at institutional imposition failed. Instead, Serer peasant farmers did the creative work of institutional reengineering, adapting their own culture and structures as well as the new model of freehold property and exchange. Syncretism in this case was important not just because it rendered formal institutions legitimate but also because it produced an institutional arrangement that incorporated the peanut into the existing land tenure and resource management system far better than any of the available institutional alternatives.

Then, as now, *taile* pawning suggested an important lesson for international and national-level planners and policymakers about deeply sustainable development. Land tenure and other economic interventions enjoy greater success when they are tailored to distinctive, heterogeneous patterns of local institutional syncretism. Syncretic institutions like *taile* can balance straightforward material goals of introducing new crops or techniques, increasing yield, or intensifying agriculture with the social-cultural importance of making use of, rather than demolishing, on-the-ground, culturally embedded structures of authority, exchange, and meaning. This simple lesson, unfortunately, eluded the designers of agricultural modernization schemes and land reform in postcolonial Senegal.

Transitions

The Siin Reordered

In the rainy season of 1974, the Ngahoye Pond was a sunbaked, cracked clay sink. Fifty years before, it's said, the place was very different. Most summers, Ngahoye used to flood well into surrounding millet fields. On hot August and September afternoons, the pond wore a teeming multicolored halo—half the perimeter crowded with women washing their indigo *pagnes* and *bazin boubous,* the other half barely accommodating the thirsty herds of one-hump cattle and interminable scruffy goats and sheep that had come from across the western Siin to drink. Further into the waters, in the hidden estuaries and narrow canals formed by a hundred half-sunk baobabs and tamarinds, children splashed and swam among the crocodiles. By all accounts the incarnation of ancestral spirits, Ngahoye crocodiles were benevolent and friendly, only very rarely taking a bite out of any of the youngsters.

But by 1974, things had changed at Ngahoye, indeed throughout the Siin as a whole. The difference was especially striking on a short stroll out of the *pind ke* (zone of human habitation) and into the *o kop ale* (wilderness).

The *o kop ale,* first of all, was a good deal farther away than it used to be. Back in the days of Birame Diouf and Waly Sene, it took only a few minutes of wandering beyond the last houses of Tukar or Ngan Fissel or most any other village to reach the pastures and forests of acacia, tamarinds, and baobabs, where children passed the night watching over their elders' herds.[1] By the summer of 1974, the young shepherds picked their way through peanut field after peanut field on their way out to the open land. When they arrived among a few sparse trees, the sad irony of the name they used for the place—"forest"—surely escaped those too young to recognize the consequences of a growing population's insatiable demand for fuelwood.

It wasn't just that drought and population growth were taking their toll on pond and forest. In the east toward Diakhao and the valley of the river Siin, something even more dramatic was happening. The Siin and its tributaries, which had once flowed with freshwater nearly all year round, were turning still, salty beyond use. Although freshwater still pooled in the river's floodplain after heavy rains, the Siin never really flowed anymore. Without the regular flushing of freshwater through the river mouth, the Atlantic worked its way up the valleys. Saltwater gradually crept into the vast aquifer under the Siin, contaminating a water table that had sustained communities in the Siin for almost a millennium. Every year a few more wells turned completely brackish, unsuitable even for washing animals, let alone drinking.

Despite severe strains on a delicate ecosystem, the immediate cause of death of the river Siin and its aquifer was not intense population pressure, agricultural expansion, and ecological change in the kingdom of Siin proper. Here the trees and pasture grasses that held moisture in the soil, although severely threatened as of 1974, were still saved from sudden and complete denuding by the mixed agropastoral system managed by customary aristocratic lineages. But in the headwaters of the Siin, in Baol to the north and the Ferlo Desert farther east, an entirely different mode of agricultural production had been put in place since the 1920s. Mouride plantation agriculture was intensive and expansive. The *talibés* who cleared the *daaras* had little concern for trees, and no time for goats. Pasture and forest only meant less land for peanuts, less yield for the marabout, less glory to God. As a result, the region of the headwaters of the Siin had long since been stripped bare for the peanut. The wasteland left behind, cleared of moisture-retaining trees and brush, could trap only a tiny fraction of the stingy Sahel rains, let alone feed the Siin River and aquifer.[2]

Plantation agriculture in the Mouride heartland vastly accelerated processes of environmental degradation that were playing themselves out more slowly in the Siin. The conservationist practices of the customary agropastoral system slowed, but did not contain, the environmental effects of a booming population cramped into a very limited geographical area. Thanks to vaccines against smallpox and tuberculosis, as well as marginal advances against waterborne diseases and improvements in nutrition, mortality rates had been falling fast since the 1950s. Population pressure resulted in some migration out of the Siin. Those blessed with education, connections, or luck tried their hands in Fatick, Kaolack, Dakar, and other towns. But many stayed behind to farm, resulting in a steady expansion in cultivated acreage. Moreover, the Serer of Siin continued to live up to their fabled "attachment to the soil," migrating in relatively small numbers to new agricultural lands in eastern Senegal. A large portion of the young men who did look for work in towns or in the new agricultural lands to the east tended to stay there for only a few years, often earning just enough cash to return to the Siin, marry, become established, and settle down to become elders.

As a result of increasing population pressure, the people of the Siin were forced to expand cultivated acreage in at least three ways. First, they moved into relatively more remote lands that had once been reserved for pasture. Second, fewer producers observed the three-year rotation of peanut-fallow-millet, dropping the fallow year entirely to either make more money (growing peanuts) or grow more food (millet) to feed expanding families. Finally, they turned to lands with extremely hard *jek* soil, once considered impossible to farm. Indeed, significant expansion into *jek* soil, made possible by the government-subsidized introduction of draft plows in the 1960s, bought the Siin a temporary reprise from demographic and environmental calamity, postponing the land scarcity crisis until the 1980s.

In the 1960s, the Serer took the gift of the plow eagerly and repaid the debt with reliable votes for Senegal's ruling Parti Socialiste and devotion to its head, Léopold Senghor, himself a "son of the Siin." The pond at Ngahoye may have dried up and their namesake river might be dead, but the Serer of Siin were now citizens of a free and independent nation. Apart from design changes in national identity cards and a two-color substitution in the national flag, independence from France meant less to most Serer than freedom from the *maad*. Since his ancestor signed the first treaty with the French in 1854, the king of the Siin, the *maad*, had collaborated closely with the colonial regime. In the 1800s, he was a stalwart French ally against Islamic resistance movements and even killed the most important jihad leader of the 1860s, Ma Ba Diakhou.[3] In this century, he collected the head tax, rounded up hands for corvée gangs, meted out punishments, and recruited young men to fight for (but not with) *fraternité, égalité,* and *liberté* in two European world wars. The *maad* and his associates did very well for themselves under French colonial rule. To this day, the Serer celebrate not so much independence from control by the *toubab* (white person) but from control by his henchman, the *maad*, to whom the Serer farmer was related, in an oft heard rendition, "the way the bottom of your shoe is related to your foot."[4]

But in fact, independence brought more to the ordinary Serer farmer than just the plow, a decade of gracious agricultural credits, and an end to the *maad's* hated regime. Senghor grounded his ambitions for independent

Senegal not just on a superficial Africanization of the official bureaucracy but also on a more profound transformation of political, economic, and social institutions to reflect what he saw as the principles and norms of African civilization. What *négritude* had done for the philosophy of literature, Senghor hoped to achieve at every level of society of an independent Senegal.

The crown jewel in Senghor's extension of *négritude* from comparative literature to comparative sociology was a land reform program promulgated by the 1964 National Domain Law. In the philosophical framework of *négritude*, rural Africa was the repository of a kind of spontaneous socialism, a communitarian ethic grounded in egalitarian land tenure relations. In this vision, contracts, elaborate mechanisms of exchange and lending, and certainly individual holding, were entirely unknown. To the extent that any such practices were present in rural Senegal circa independence, they were vestiges of "Roman law" left by French colonial rule. For Senghor, rural inequality in particular was a consequence of alien bourgeois tenure arrangements imposed and propped up by colonial legal and political systems. The National Domain Law set out to do away with these contaminants, restoring and modernizing communitarian African land tenure systems.

Senghor saw his literal revolution in land tenure relations as a first, catalytic step in a process of restructuring Senegalese society according to African socialist principles. Once land tenure relations were grounded on local norms, rural folk would naturally come to participate more fully and wholeheartedly in the political and economic life of the new country. In particular, their increased motivation, enhanced by government-subsidized inputs like draft plows, fertilizer, improved seeds, and so on, would result in considerable agricultural intensification and increases in peanut production. A growing rural sector would provide the economic base for the quantum leaps in industrialization, education, and social services that would bring Senghor's vision of African socialism to full fruition.

Bourgeois distortions in the rural sector were so extensive, however, that a time of transition would be required before the ordinary peasant became fully self-conscious of his new status in a new order institutionalized by legislation like the National Domain Law. Before the land reform was even put into effect in most parts of the country, Senghor undertook a process of "rural animation." For a few idealistic years, the Animation Rurale program sent young, educated cadres throughout the countryside to teach peasants about their new relationship to the state in the wake of independence, their new rights as citizens and how to act upon them, and their new role in a society guided by (their own) rural African principles and norms.[5]

A combination of fiscal crisis and imminent threat of animated peasants marching on parliament demanding increased producer prices killed Animation Rurale after just a few years. Nevertheless, the need to help peasants along in the transition to the new era of African socialism and the new National Domain Law's land tenure system remained. After the French withdrew price supports in 1968 and the bottom fell out of the peanut market, rural producers staged spontaneous, uncoordinated production strikes. Farmers in the central Peanut Basin, of which the Siin is the geographical and productive core, refused to plant peanuts (for which they were being paid, metaphorically, in kind), switching instead to their familiar pattern of autarkic self-sufficiency based on millet. By this time, it was becoming apparent that the transition to a new African socialist order—at least in the countryside—might require more time and persuasion than originally envisioned.

The 1964 law vaguely envisioned a new level of popularly elected local government, a system of rural councils that would play a central role in enforcing the new tenure regime. By the early 1970s, with an outburst of tenure litigation threatening to overwhelm existing courts of first instance, Senghor's government recognized the need to clarify and quickly put into place the new rural council system. Another mechanism to ease the transition back to African socialism (like Animation Rurale only minus the idealism), the new councils were grafted onto the administrative divisions of the country inherited from the colonial regime: *régions (cantons)* divided into *arrondissements (cercles)*, now further divided into *communautés rurales.*

Communautés rurales (rural communities) would be governed by a rural council, two-thirds of whose members would be elected every five years, with the other third chosen by the boards of the agricultural cooperatives operating in the *communauté rurale.* The rural councils would select among themselves a president to serve as the chair of the council and administrative head of the *communauté rurale.* The subprefect of each *arrondissement* (postcolonial nomenclature for *commandant de cercle,* but still a trained civil servant centrally appointed in Dakar) would serve as a "tutor" to the rural council, guiding it in the niceties of administering a budget, running a government, obeying the law, and so on. This proved a crucial design tension: were the rural councils elected representatives who might fulfill Serer cultural aspirations regarding land tenure, adjudication, and resource allocation (the state perhaps becoming a new master of fire)? Or were they administrative agents of a distant centralized state (a new version of the old *maad*)?

In 1974, the year Ngahoye Pond was but an eight-foot-wide mud puddle, the Siin (now twinned with another Serer kingdom to the east in the Siin-Saluum region) was preparing both for its first rural council elections and for the installation of the National Domain Law. Since that time, National Domain Law land tenure arrangements and the rural council as political and legal institutions have met with responses similar to the rope stall in the village marketplace or freehold property models. The Serer have drawn upon their own fluid, heterogeneous concepts of legitimate authority, rightful ownership, and justice to respond to these new institutional impositions. As we follow this response, we will see how various groups in Serer society are rereading both the National Domain Law and the rural councils in terms of competing frameworks of legitimate local culture. Multiple and sometimes incompatible processes of syncretism have been taking place over the last thirty years. Ironically, the exigencies of state building after colonialism pose new and more serious obstacles to making new, exogenously imposed institutions legitimate and meaningful through syncretic adaptation.

5 · Two Romanticizations

Tenure Confusion after the National Domain Law

> What's it about? The National Domain Law is about, very simply, a return from Roman law to Negro-African law, from the bourgeois conception of property to the socialist conception, which is also the traditional black African one. . . . It's about returning to Negro-African law and adapting it to the demands of our development.
>
> LÉOPOLD SENGHOR

> The National Domain Law is entirely negative—there is nothing good about it. Now, when someone loans a field, the other one can come along and "nationalize" it. This is not right—we have never heard of such a thing. Our ancestors had never heard of such a thing—it creates a great deal of hate between people. People have divorced their wives because of this.   HAMAD SARR

INTRODUCTION

The National Domain Law and Serer responses to it reveal overlapping and, in some ways, contradictory processes of romanticization and reconstruction of land tenure relations. On the one hand, Senghor's 1964 legislation was built on its own romantic notions about unproblematic egalitarian access to abundant commons land in a protosocialist rural Africa.[1] This vision of communitarian tenure relations was not entirely without basis in historical reality. Rather, the philosophy of *négritude* and African socialism read the history of land tenure relations in places like the Siin (ironically, Senghor's own homeland) rather selectively. Senghor's (and by extension, the state's) memory of *egalitarian* protosocialist African tenure practices ignored the decidedly authoritarian, hierarchical, patriarchal, local political institutions (the *laman–yal bakh* system discussed in chapter 4) that managed systems of *relatively* equitable access to land and other natural resources. Senghor's regime thus reified a version of "traditional" culture that revamped rural social relations along lines that both served the state's interest and advanced Senghor's larger project: grounding his Senegalese variant of African socialism in what were presented as real-world, historically authentic material relations of institutionalized equality.

Although equipped with resources for institutional and cultural construction that were far more rudimentary—hand tools to the state's bulldozers—peasants in places like the Siin have engaged in much the same process of reifying their own version of traditional land tenure systems in order to advance their own interests. As James Scott would be the first to remind us, Serer peasants are neither passive nor powerless in the face of this equipment.[2] The state may proclaim, promulgate, and inaugurate all it wants, but especially in Africa, states lack the coercive resources to promote their vision without some degree of voluntary cooperation from ordinary people like the Serer of the Siin region. Whereas the National Domain Law focuses on amorphous notions of communitarian control and egalitarian access, in the Siin local response to the National Domain Law idealizes specific customary institutions of authority (*lamans* and the *yal bakhs* in particular) as well as informal socioeconomic institutions like the *taile* pawn.[3] This chapter shows how institutional syncretism in the aftermath of the National Domain Law took the Serer beyond mechanistic "exit options" into more intentional and creative processes by which Serer farmers struggle to redefine, redirect, and reappropriate laws and institutions that flout local cultural frameworks and historical memories.[4]

In particular, the Senegalese state's *négritude*-inspired version of traditional land tenure relations has precipitated a defensive counterreification of what many see as their authentic land tenure practices and institutions, which they perceive as threatened with extinction in the face of "modernization" under the National Domain Law. A reform that had been intended to restore equal access to and efficient distribution of land under harmonious communitarian control has, by disregarding vestigial patterns of legitimate land tenure authority, yielded a distinctly bifurcated, Manichean, dual tenure system. In the upper or formal half of the dual tenure system, the National Domain Law reigns. Serer farmers treat this regime as fundamentally illegitimate and engage in unfettered opportunistic behavior in response to it. In the lower, unofficial half of the dual tenure system, a reified "law of *cosaan* (ancestral tradition)" governs imploded relations of trust within a collapsed community of close kin and allies.[5]

The legitimacy of the old *laman–yal bakh* system has been transferred to the smaller scale institution of the *yal mbind*, or household master. As the circle of trust collapses around the household unit, relations outside the household increasingly fall under the auspices of the National Domain Law, which facilitates a free-for-all of instrumental self-promotion. This schizophrenic system has resulted in an unintended increase in the insecurity of land tenure and disintegration of the Serer agropastoral system. Rotations are no longer enforced, fallow is a thing of the past, nitrogen-fixing trees are cut for fuelwood, and livestock, which must be led far outside the Siin to find pasture, take their restorative manure with them. The net result has been a rapid acceleration of ongoing processes of environmental degradation and soil depletion, with consequent declines in both subsistence and cash crop yields.

Demolition without Reconstruction

In a narrow sense, the National Domain Law was a success. In particular, the reform eliminated the semiofficial authority of old rural aristocrats like the *lamans* and *yal bakhs* of the Siin, as well as analogous officials in other regions. According to the logic of the land reform, local aristocrats of the Siin used their control of arcane local custom to accumulate resources in an unfair and unproductive manner. The reform was successful, then, to the extent that it broke the power of these "entrenched" rural aristocrats.

Yet in the Siin (as opposed to rural areas dominated by the Mouride or *daara* mode of production), this "success" entailed dismembering a relatively integrated and adapted system of control over land use, access, and exchange that enjoyed considerable social support and consent. After independence, but before the National Domain Law, *lamans*, and to an increasing degree *yal bakhs*, continued to perform duties associated with holistic custodianship (allocating land, coordinating field rotation, maintaining fallow and pasture, and limiting the cutting of trees for fuelwood, animal feed, and construction materials). In their capacity as relatives, community notables, elders, and most important, intermediaries with the spirit world, *lamans* and *yal bakhs* delivered substantive justice in conflicts over land allocation and use. Their proximity to litigants and the long-term nature of the relationships in question made it possible for them to intervene not just in the particulars of a given field conflict but also in the wider interpersonal, marital, familial, social, or supernatural contexts of a disagreement.

From the modernist point of view of the designers of the National Domain Law, integrated land management and substantive justice in the hands of rural aristocrats like the *lamans* and *yal bakhs* of the Siin meant arbitrariness, lack of accountability, and abuse of power.[6] These familiar indictments of "traditional" authority reinforced the central complaint of the modernist architects of the National Domain Law against rural aristocrats: they "owned" more land than they could possibly ever farm, let too much of it lie unused, and, in a newly independent, democratic-socialist society, could not be trusted to guarantee fair access to land for all those in the community who needed space to farm.

This broad generalization underscores the pitfalls of a unitary, *national* land reform policy like the National Domain Law. Whereas, in the Siin, customary aristocrats did not themselves cultivate acreage significantly greater than that of ordinary farmers, in the economically more important Senegal River valley, aristocrats were linked much more clearly to petty and not-so-petty accumulation.[7] Thus it makes more sense that the region was the target of an egalitarian African socialist land reform meant to break the back of customary lineage elites.[8]

With the indictments against traditional land tenure authorities clear, the solution was simple: an independent Senegal could not abide backward, unjust, arbitrary systems of tenure that relied on arcane and ascriptive claims to title and blocked fair access to land. The power of the customary aristocrats would therefore be broken through a simple transfer of control over land from the various customary rights-holders to the state, the agents of which would have the power to grant and withdraw land title and to resolve conflicts in the name of ensuring "maximum productive use."[9] "Maximum productive use" in practice became the "two-year usufruct" rule: anyone who farmed a field for two or more consecutive years gained legal claim to it.[10] The National Domain Law also banned land sales to prevent the emergence of a market in land, as well as effectively banning loans and pawns, considered instruments by which aristocrats ensured the subordination of commoners and those of low caste. The state itself would assume the role of land and resource manager: in the Siin, the state would become the new master of fire, although no one really knew how this might actually happen. The scheme made excellent sense on paper but overlooked one crucial element in practice: trust.

Energized by the simple, characteristically 1960s faith that the euphoria of independence could be channeled into political legitimacy and popular trust for formal state institutions, reform planners expected peasants like the Serer of Siin to naturally and quickly transfer their trust from *lamans* and *yal bakhs* to whomever happened to be charged with tailoring the National Domain Law to each region. When the state's representatives in the countryside (subprefects and prefects) tried to do this, it made the National Domain Law seem like another edict from on high. When the job was given to elected rural councils, peasants tried to syncretically adapt them but were thwarted by the state's unwillingness to pursue true democratic decentralization (see chapter 6).

TABLE 16. Authority Most Important
for Village Well-Being

Authority	Percent Who Ranked This Leader "Most Important" to Village Well-Being
Subprefect	36.2
Saltigué (rain priest)	17.3
Village chief	15.6
Marabout	12.5
Rural council president	10.2
Laman	8.2
Total	100.0
N	698

Upon initial implementation of the National Domain Law in the Siin, there was still some tension with the old customary authorities, but by the late 1980s overt resistance had been essentially eliminated. "The *lamans* and the *yal bakhs* exist no more," is how most Serer respondents approach the subject of customary tenure authorities today. Indeed, effectively displaced from tenure and land management responsibilities, the customary aristocrats seem politically marginal to most people in the Siin today. Table 16 shows that only 8.2 percent of 698 respondents considered the *laman* the most important authority for maintaining the well-being of their village in the present day.[11]

Outside the lands they administer for their own households and for a small number of close relatives and allies, *lamans* and *yal bakhs* no longer perform formal land management or adjudicatory functions. Quite significantly, however, they continue to perform their spiritual functions as the custodians of the shrines of ancestral spirits *(pangool)*, although such activities have been separated from the processes of material husbandry with which they had once been enmeshed.[12]

Land reform under the National Domain Law has precipitated at least three parallel processes of response. First, the law has been rejected and vilified as an alien, illegitimate imposition. Second, hand in hand and proportionate with rejection of the National Domain Law, we find a stark romanticization of the memory of displaced local institutions as more authentic, legitimate, and appropriate than their "modern" alternatives. Despite the formal reality of modernist demolition of customary Serer land tenure institutions, at an informal level the vestiges of idealized Serer land allocation patterns, exchange practices, and even a collapsed version of *laman–yal bakh* authority continue to organize agricultural relations within a collapsed circle of trust. Dual, overlaid, potentially discordant tenure systems now exist in the contemporary Siin. This institutional disorder has negative consequences in terms of security of tenure, agricultural productivity, environmental preservation, and the likelihood that farmers will make improvements to their land.

Vilification: The National Domain Law Has Destroyed Human Relations

The sweeping away of Serer land tenure institutions has precipitated simultaneous reification of remembered tradition and and vilification of the contemporary land tenure system associated with the National Domain Law. In response to the state's land reform, popular memories of the flexibility, proximity, efficiency, and fairness of "traditional" tenure institutions have grown increasingly idealized. At the same time, angry rejection of the National Domain Law has been most pronounced at points where the new regime, in its effort to restructure rural economic and social relations, most effectively demolishes the institutional and normative infrastructure of the old order.

The National Domain Law's approach to reformulation of rural society followed a medical pathology model characteristic of the heyday of modernization theory: once the state identified, isolated, and fixed the "subsystem" responsible for unequal access to land, it would be on the way to the "cure" for what it saw as stagnant agricultural practices, declining production levels, and stark urban-rural income inequality. As we have seen, the National Domain Law identified protobourgeois customary aristocrats as the obstacle to a "natural" state of productive, harmonious, egalitarian rural African socialism. The cure was simply to replace these authorities with more modern, state-formulated egalitarian institutions.

The modernist point of view failed to appreciate, in a classic Parsonian error, that land tenure authorities were not a single subsystem that could be isolated from the rest of the rural social order and reformed. Instead, *lamans*, *yal bakhs*, and the land tenure regime they managed were intimately intertwined with much wider networks of family relations, marriage, religion, labor pooling, and reciprocity. As a means of control over the most important form of agricultural capital and over the sacred foundation of local religious practice, land tenure in fact formed the social mesh that held together other networks and relationships. The rhetoric of rejection of the National Domain Law is vitriolic, and reification of remembered local alternatives quite pronounced, in part because the state's effort to eliminate rural aristocrats tore at the webbing of Serer social relations in general. This is why today in the Siin the mere mention of the words *national domain* is almost invariably followed by "has ruined relations between people."[13]

Detailing Rupture: Family, Marriage, and Reciprocity

Serer denunciations of the disruptive effect of the National Domain Law are rich and extensive, focusing to a great extent on how, in the words of the farmer Gorgui Faye, "This new law has completely ruined human relations because family is destroyed as a result of this 'National Domain.'"[14] Concretely, the National Domain Law is said to weaken bonds of family cohesion, ruin or block marriages, and interrupt circuits of reciprocity. A good deal of the rhetoric of hate between families inspired by the National Domain-Law focuses on marriage. In response to the seizure of fields under the reform's two-year usufruct rule (an act referred to locally as "nationalization"), antagonists have broken off marital engagements, banned visits between households, and sometimes divorced.[15] For example, Boucar Ngom insists that because Hamad Faye has seized a pawned field using the new law, he (Ngom) can no longer take a wife among Faye's relatives: "I was surprised when he took the field, because I had confidence in him, relations had been friendly between us. Then all of a sudden, brutally, he nationalized this field. I couldn't believe it. Relations are no good between us anymore. . . . I would not go over there and ask for a wife— that is no longer possible because I don't have any confidence there in him."[16] Ngom in fact goes beyond his own bad experience with Faye to condemn the entire National Domain Law for its disruptiveness: "The National Domain Law is entirely negative—there is nothing good about it. The Domain—all it has brought is bad. It's broken up relations between people. Women have been divorced over this."[17]

Faced with circumstances similar to those of Boucar Ngom, Latyr Farah Diouf explains the consequences of his opponent's invocation of the National Domain Law: "I would have preferred to have avoided the National Domain Law, because the administration is bad; it dirties the bonds of family between people. Once you do that [nationalize a field], people won't even marry between each other's families. Once there's been a problem of nationalization, it can last far into the future—for thirty years there can be no marriage between families, because someone went to the administration."[18]

Diame Sene v. Waly Koundoul Sene illustrates how rupture generated by the National Domain Law cuts off not just marital relations but also other circuits of social reciprocity—in this case mutual attendance at major family ceremonies like funerals. When Babacar Sene died, his brother Waly Koundoul Sene and his son Diame Sene both claimed they should inherit the fields of the deceased. Diame eventually invoked his right under the National Domain Law to the land he had helped his father farm, and thereby gained control of the fields. Bringing the land reform law into a conflict between nephew and uncle amounted to a very serious breach of family relations on Diame Sene's part, resulting in considerable lingering tension.

The full extent of the rupture became painfully clear when both families suffered tragic deaths within the following year. Diame Sene, reticent to get into any discussion of the dispute, nevertheless admitted with anguish that "when my son died, three years ago, Waly Koundoul Sene banned any of his family from attending the funeral." Given the fact they are such close relatives, this was a rather unexpected intervention on Waly Koundoul Sene's part. Almost a year later, the mother of Waly Koundoul Sene (grandmother of Diame Sene) died. She had lived for many years in Waly Koundoul Sene's compound. In the days after her death, Diame Sene made ready to go pay his respects at the initial, public funeral ceremony, but Waly Koundoul Sene sent word that Diame should "*defal ndank* [go slow, take it easy].[19] Don't come here. Something might happen to you here, and if it does, know that it will be your own fault for coming."[20] Diame Sene, in Waly Koundoul Sene's eyes, should live with the consequences of the rupture he committed by nationalizing the field: "Diame should know that he is the one who broke himself off from our family."[21]

Diame Sene admits that he was deeply hurt when Waly Koundoul Sene refused to let him pay respects to his own grandmother. He felt that "this was all because I won the field from him in the dispute, because I won it under the Domain Law."[22] The cutoff entailed material as well as emotional-spiritual consequences. By preventing Diame Sene from even attending his grandmother's funeral, Waly Koundoul Sene ensured that Diame Sene would not attend any of the informal gatherings held under the auspices of that ceremony at which inheritance arrangements are usually made.

Covering Rupture and "Shame of Accumulation"

Those who win land through the National Domain law exhibit a "shame of accumulation," a tendency to hide or make excuses for the fact they have violated egalitarian community norms for the sake of extraordinary individual or household material gain. This is entirely in keeping with the finding described in chapter 3 that those who are most likely to *openly* violate seemingly "traditional" community norms regarding property relations are those who already have "removed themselves" from the matrix of social and cultural relations, a removal most evident in the adherence of such individuals to nonsyncretic forms of Islam.

As anthropologists have understood at least since the days of George Foster, rural societies governed by extensive circuits of reciprocity and egalitarian distribution norms designed to promote food security tend to exhibit shame over accumulation.[23] This is even more pronounced in communities that rely on rain-fed agriculture for subsistence production and in which physical environmental conditions make famine a constant threat. Accumulation of land, food, supplies, and capital requires some *unwillingness* to share. Accumulation is difficult in a society organized around elaborate circuits of reciprocity and egalitarianism because the hardworking, successful, and lucky are always pressed to share in direct proportion to their good fortune. Communities in which nonsharing is normatively sanctioned and in which accumulation and stratification have taken place are probably less likely to survive famine, because too many of their population will be cut off from food supplies hoarded by nonsharers. Thus, we can surmise that, in settings close to the famine margin (especially societies that depend on rain-fed subsistence farming), there is a kind of social-evolutionary advantage to systems of reciprocity and to egalitarian norms that encourage both sharing and shame over accumulation. These are not backward vestiges of irrational tradition but rational, adaptive responses to specific socioenvironmental circumstances.

It is ironic, but telling, that shame of accumulation should inhibit popular acceptance of the National Domain Law. Despite its intention to return tenure relations to an egalitarian African socialist past, the system under the National Domain Law has instead made land more alienable and has precipitated the beginnings of petty accumulation. Tenure insecurity resulting from the collapse of their holistic land management system has effectively forced farmers in the Siin to use the new law to grab juridical title to as much land as possible, lest others with whom they had shared or made informal exchanges of land under the old system beat them to the punch.

Samba Faye v. Samba Yatt offers a good illustration of this shame of accumulation at work in the contemporary Siin. In 1971, Samba Faye received a field in *taile* pawn from his neighbor Samba Yatt. After a number of years in which Yatt, the original proprietor, asked Faye, the field taker, to accept repayment of the cash guarantee and return the field, Faye finally contacted a rural councilor and won a judgment in his favor granting him title to the plot. Faye insists that, since he took the field, "if we see each other, we greet each other. . . . Since we had the problem, at each ceremony of his, I go there, I attend and there is no problem between us."[24]

Faye is very careful to touch upon crucial external hallmarks of *masla*, or social harmony, between himself and his erstwhile rival, Yatt.[25] They do what is required of two neighbors who live in the same community and share bonds of reciprocity—greeting and mutual attendance at funerals, baptisms, marriages, and so on. Neither of them is an "outcast" or "zealot" who has renounced the "Serer way" of structuring relations between neighbors.

But that is the extent of their intercourse, because, as Faye puts it, "we do live in the same neighborhood, but Yatt is not my relative." This directly contradicts Yatt's version of their relationship. Reflecting on the decision to enter into the pawn arrangement in the first place, Yatt tells us, "Looking back on it now, I should have never taken the five thousand francs from Samba Faye, because he's a close relative."[26]

Something funny is going on here. The original field master and loser under the National Domain Law, Yatt, claims that the two men are "close relatives." The winner under the National Domain Law and original field taker, Faye, denies any lines of family relationship between the two men, and is thus able to insist that there has been no rupture. Both men are maneuvering for the best moral and social position around the shoals of social rupture and violation of community norms. Faye, the legal winner, is careful to both assert the minimum social *masla* and to establish that relations are good enough between them, because, after all, they are not relatives. Yatt, on the other hand, seeks to place the blame for a serious social violation squarely on his rival, Faye, by drawing Faye closer to him and claiming that he is not just kin but also a close relative. This of course strengthens Yatt's assertion that Faye, the winner, acquired his field in an illegitimate way simply because he used the land reform law to get it.

Faye is indeed a new accumulator, but an embarrassed one, not a proud one. His embarrassment and his desire to effectively deny his new social role are critical in understanding the failure of the state's land reform to fulfill one of its central goals, tenure security. The precise articulation that has emerged in the Siin between the National Domain Law and Serer notions of social reciprocity in tenure relations blocks the emergence of a class of proud accumulators. Those who win land under the law in fact hold that land *less securely* now because they feel compelled to justify—sometimes in elaborate ways—their control of land that they and others sense they should not rightfully possess, but that the state nevertheless sanctions and indeed encourages them to keep.

Defending and Using the National Domain: Overlapping Winners and Losers

In spite of the ubiquity of the rhetoric about ruining family relations, there are circumstances in which Serer farmers express support for the National Domain Law. In the midst of land conflicts, for example, we sometimes find stereotypical instrumental rhetoric: those who stand to lose under the new law denounce it as an abrogation of the moral basis of civilized society, while those who stand to benefit from application of the law occasionally praise it for advancing the rule of law and the clarity of procedure: "What is happening now is truly a lot better than the way things used to be. Some things are forbidden, and the law is there and it is enforced, and that is good. The *maad* now says the field is for you, and it's for you. We have a firm law, it's clear, and that's all there is to it."[27] This winner not only champions the generally reviled National Domain Law, he tellingly goes on to refute the notion that it has contributed to a loss of tradition: "The youth, they have a kind of knowledge that the elders lack, and the same is true the other way around. It's always been that way, and the National Domain has not changed anything. We don't have a problem of lack of respect for elders. . . . *Cosaan* is not forgotten."

Yet it is crucial to note that the respondent wants to have it both ways: he wants to hold the field he won under the National Domain Law and believe that "tradition" remains unaffected by his actions. This is consistent with the absence of clear-cut social groups that favor and oppose the reform. Most everyone denounces it, but will use it when it can be instrumentally useful for them. This may reflect the lack of stark land inequality in the Siin. The frequency distribution of number of fields controlled is rather narrow, with a mean of 2.5 fields and a standard deviation of 3.1. Even considering landholding patterns by caste group, we find little variation and no real evidence of stark distinctions between landlords and the landless, as figure 6 suggests.

The free farmer caste, the bulk of the population (about 45 percent), tend to engage in overlapping patterns of land exchange, of which pawning is the most important form. The majority of the population neither consistently pawns nor consistently takes fields in pawn. Among those households that offered land in pawn in the rainy season of 1993, 25 percent of these also received pawned land *in the same growing season*. If we

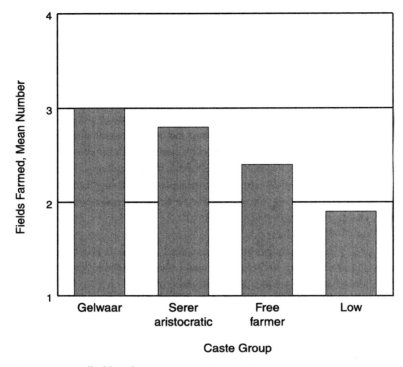

Figure 6. Landholding by caste group ($N = 727$).

were to explore this practice over more than one growing season, we would find a much higher rate of producers giving and taking land in pawn. Qualitative interviews suggest that the rate would be 75–80 percent over the course of ten years.

This flux stems in part from the fact that households usually shift from giving land to taking it in the course of the life cycle of a family. When children are young, provide insubstantial agricultural labor, require only limited amounts of food (which can be grown on a small amount of land) and demand cash outlays (such as school costs), families often pawn unneeded fields to earn cash. When families grow larger and children are old enough to be pulled out of school to work the fields, the demand for land increases and farmers "call back" their pawned land; they may seek to obtain additional plots as well (usually by offering cash to those who would like to pawn land). Thus farmers may sometimes stand to lose from the two-year usufruct rule of the National Domain Law, while at other times they may gain from it (by using the law to take control of pawned fields).[28]

Women Wanting Rupture: Gender and the National Domain

Looking within the household, particularly at gender relations, reveals somewhat different patterns with regard to family rupture and social harmony. Although women generally remain invisible to the National Domain Law itself, they naturally engage in their own struggles to maintain or gain control over the land they farm.[29] Despite the fact that these struggles often take the form of intrahousehold conflicts with men, the disputes analyzed for this study suggest that women often seek the intervention of extrahousehold authorities, from generic "elders" and village chiefs to rural council officials. These appeals to extrahousehold authority occur in spite of the fact that officials tend to ignore or marginalize women's claims to control their own fields. Evidence indicates that, when women go to the state, they are often quite willing to rupture familial relations. This contrasts markedly with most of the cases explored above, in which male litigants who benefit from the National Domain Law seek to conceal this fact or at least establish that such invocation of the state did not violate social *masla* and lead to rupture.

Siga Sarr v. Adama Diouf, for example, furnishes a typical illustration of the willingness of subordinate women to bring in the state and rupture familial relations. The female litigant, Siga Sarr, says, "I will go to the gendarmes if Adama Diouf doesn't give up the land. I don't care if he ends up in prison over it. In fact, I would bring that about if I could. I don't care if it ruins relations with the family either."[30]

Sarr is the second wife of the *yal mbind* (household master), Aliou Diouf, who has been away in Dakar for a few years. He left his brother, Adama Diouf, in charge of the household as the de facto *yal mbind.* Siga Sarr came into conflict with her brother-in-law Adama Diouf because he refused her labor, as well as that of her cowife Tening Faye, on the fields that all the members of the household used to farm collectively. Instead, Adama Diouf set aside a few fields and declared that these were for *his* family, and he did not want the help of his sisters-in-law in farming them, nor would he help them work their fields.

Sarr and her cowife, lacking other recourse or means to protest, accepted Adama Diouf's decision to end the collective labor arrangement.[31] But if Adama ends the long-standing shared farming scheme, Sarr insists that she and her cowife (who by now have pooled their labor) should farm the fields that belong to their husband—none of these should go to Adama Diouf. When, at the start of the rainy season, Sarr went out and planted peanuts in a prime field near the compound, Adama Diouf objected, insisting that the field was rightfully under his control as *yal mbind.*

Siga Sarr had no way to reach her husband in Dakar, with whom she communicated only when he chose to pay a visit to the village. In her words, "What else could I do? Adama wanted to take the field from me, so I had to go talk to the chief of the village."[32] Unfortunately for Siga Sarr, the village chief refused to hear her complaint, insisting that she should address it to her *yal mbind* and resolve it *within* the household. He told her that, as chief of the village, he had no power to intervene in "another man's affairs." Thus thwarted, Sarr turned to the state, asking a rural councilor to force Adama Diouf to let her farm the field near the household.

The state did not give Siga Sarr what she wanted. For that rainy season, Sarr lost the field, but Adama Diouf is supposed to compensate her for the peanut seed she planted. Sarr nevertheless intends to plant in the disputed plot again in coming years. And as she points out, she knows that taking Adama to the state authorities might have very serious consequences. He may end up in prison, and relations within the family may be ruined, outcomes to which Sarr's response remains clear: "I don't care."[33]

Siga Sarr v. Adama Diouf illustrates the circumstances under which rupture of familial relations is not just an acceptable but a desired outcome. It is important to set this dynamic in the wider context of a more general social unwillingness to invoke the National Domain Law for fear of rupture. Although we are dealing with questions of breaking familial relations in both cases, there is a clear analytic distinction between intra- and interhousehold relations, because they are embedded in very different dynamics of postcolonial social change.

Intrahousehold relations must be considered in the context of the homogenization of ownership and inheritance patterns over the past century, which has been moving toward standardized Euro-Islamic patrilineal norms. As noted in chapter 4, standardization and patrilinealization have drastically limited a once wide diversity of property and inheritance regimes. This has favored male elders and patrilineal control and tended to limit women's control over wealth. Moreover, in the aftermath of the passage of the National Domain Law, the authority of *lamans* and *yal bakhs* has collapsed onto the institution of the *yal mbind*, further concentrating economic and political power in the hands of male heads of households and limiting options available to women. Within the household, then, when women opt for rupture they engage in a form of resistance against a relatively new and especially gendered form of control that emerged as a result of colonial standardization and that has been aggravated by postcolonial land reform.

TABLE 17. Tenure Transformation Attitudes
by Gender
(in percentages, N = 727)

	Women	Men
Would sell land even if the *pangool* opposed	12.8	18.9
Oppose the right to pawn land	13.4	25.3

Interhousehold relations are embedded in slightly different processes of social change: the decline of community-based land management and adjudication systems, along with the weakening of pawning as an exchange mechanism. Women in fact seem more unwilling than men to rupture customary interhousehold tenure relations, as table 17 reveals. As we know, with the sudden imposition of the National Domain Law, the fabric of social relations *between* households has (apparently inadvertently) been undermined. Community relations at the interhousehold level have been sufficiently destabilized to provoke an anti-national-domain backlash, as people seek to understand why they can no longer trust their neighbors, invite their relatives to their funerals, or get back the fields they loaned.

Women are more sensitive to interhousehold rupture not because they have more at stake in the preservation of the *lamanic* land management system or *taile* pawning institutions per se—if anything, they have less at stake in the preservation of such institutions, given their marginality with regard to tenure control. Women are reticent to rupture tenure at the interhousehold level because of the fundamental *embeddedness* of tenure relations in the Siin: once the material webbing (land tenure relations) is ruptured, the tear cuts into layers of the social fabric (extended kin networks, marital arrangements, interhousehold domestic labor pooling, and festivals as mechanisms for communication, solidarity, and the redistribution of wealth) of more direct material salience to subordinated women in this society.

The fact that, by contrast, women seem willing to rupture intrahousehold relations speaks loudly to the profound transformation of the household itself since colonialism. Largely through standardization in the form of patrilinealization and family nuclearization, the household has itself been de-embedded. Matrilineal clans no longer accumulate capital in the form of cattle herds and therefore no longer provide women with some basis for material wealth and power independent of their husbands and fathers.

Matrilocality is a thing of the past—women now almost universally go to live with their husband or his family. Even a woman's extended patrilineal family is less able to intervene after marriage in the "internal affairs" of her husband's household. No wonder then that more than two-thirds of some one hundred women interviewed for this study would gladly see their nuclear family patriarch imprisoned by the state in a land dispute, yet ardently defend hallmarks of customary Serer tenure relations like *taile* pawning or supernatural prohibitions on land sale.

REIFICATION

> In the *laman*'s time, we never knew such scandal.
>
> Aissatou Sene, 1993

Reification in response to the National Domain Law focuses on elements of the Serer land tenure regime most at odds with the state's new "African socialist" values and objectives: the trust-based *jange o qol of* (take back your field) ethic that formed the basis for *taile* pawning, and the institution of the *laman*. By making two years of usufruct the de facto criterion for title, the National Domain Law effectively removed the keystone from preindependence tenure relations. It directly contradicted the Serer ontology of property, predicated on the *separation of* usufruct from title. This concept of property, linked to settlement patterns and lineage holistic custodianship, had long cemented the authority of *lamans* and *yal bakhs* as well as the *taile* pawning system of exchange. Promulgation of the new private-property-like notion of *fused* title and usufruct has generated nostalgia for all these institutions.

The Jange O Qol Of *Ethic*

Before the National Domain Law, those who received fields in pawn and other temporary usufruct transfer generally did not try to permanently seize these "borrowed" lands because of a widespread sense that, when confronted by an original proprietor who wanted to regain his land, one should not hesitate to utter the ritual phrase *jange o qol of* and then return the borrowed or pawned plot. Failure to do so resulted in violation of a widely understood *jange o qol of* ethic, leading to social sanctions (cutting off marriage alliances, familial visiting, and removal from reciprocity circuits, mutual aid, and labor pooling arrangements). Land tenure authorities *(lamans* and *yal bakhs)* blocked *jange o qol of* violators from access to land, forcing either compliance or migration out of the community.

Although historically it may or may not have stood as an icon of community harmony and interpersonal trust, now that it has been submerged into the *imaginaire* by the National Domain Law, the *jange o qol of* ethic has become an idealized touchstone for Serer community harmony and reciprocity. We find a typical indication of wistfulness for lost trust and the *jange o qol of* ethic in the remarks of the litigant Abdoulaye Dieng, who lost one of his best fields to Mahecor Cama. Cama had taken the field in *taile* pawn but eventually seized control of it under the National Domain Law. In response to this, Dieng complains, "If this had taken place in the past, there would have been no discussion. I'd have given back the money, and the other person would say, 'Jange o qol of.' That's all that would have to happen, no discussion, no fooling around, none of this business."[34]

But with this trust-based ethic trampled by the National Domain Law's "land for those who farm it" principle, it makes sense that *jange o qol of* has emerged as a kind of club that those who lose under the National Domain Law use to bash those who win. *Latyr Farah Diouf v. Hamad Ndong* offers a vivid picture of this kind of idealization used as an instrumental dispute tactic. In this conflict, Waly Fall had borrowed a field from its original owner, Latyr Farah Diouf. But Waly Fall pawned it (without Diouf's knowledge or consent) to a third party, whose heir, Hamad Ndong, seized it using the National Domain Law. The pattern of exchange in this case is not unusual, nor is the tendency of the loser to reify the amiability and communitarian qualities of a system under which he would have won. According to Waly Fall,

> If it had been up to me, well, we would have dealt with this under the "talking tree." That's where we used to meet together with the leaders of the village to talk about these problems. I would have stood up in the meeting, walked over to Hamad Ndong, and handed him the money in front of everybody. If he didn't take it, then I would have asked in a voice so that everyone could hear: "Hamad, why won't you take this money and give me the field back?"
>
> I would have proposed to Hamad that I give him some other little piece of land over there somewhere. It would have been much better to hear from him why he refused to give back the field. . . . If only the council of the elders had dealt with this problem, everything would have been fine by now.[35]

Whether the intervention of a council of elders in a "talking tree" meeting were in fact the instrumentalities of the *jange o qol of* ethic is neither clear nor particularly important. Councils of elders and "talking trees" have more to do with French colonial efforts to construct what they saw as "traditional" village gerontocracies than with the complexities of historical relations of power over land in the Siin. Most other portrayals of the *jange o qol of* ethic in practice depict a more low-key, private affair mediated by the language of *masla* (maintenance of social harmony, avoidance of ugly confrontation resulting from raw, naked disclosure of true feelings). Indeed, given the importance of *lamans* and *yal bakhs* as allocative authorities, most accounts suggest that a dispute of this kind would have traditionally been dealt with in a private meeting among Fall, Ndong, the original field proprietor, and the relevant *laman* or *yal bakh*. Community knowledge of the resulting problem (essential for the exertion of social pressure) would have stemmed not from a public meeting under a baobab tree but from gossip and rumor.

But accounts such as Fall's cannot be dismissed as the vindictive fantasy of those who suffer at the hands of the new order. His selection of nostalgic themes is not haphazard but reflects a response to features of the new land tenure system that most conflict with local historical memory regarding authority, property, and exchange.

For example, in principle the reform might be construed to empower younger people, whose access to land was formerly constrained by older customary officials. Waly Fall thus invokes a council of elders, as opposed to the *laman* or *yal bakh*, in his lament over lack of respect for the *jange o qol of* ethic. Elders represent an especially idealized institution of authority, on which nostalgia for a range of historic Serer institutions has collapsed. Fall increases the rhetorical impact of his remarks by incorporating this additional, gerontocratic strand of post–National Domain reification into his denunciation of lack of respect for *jange o qol of* norms.

Likewise, the National Domain Law introduces a new kind of public space—procedural, impersonal, and bureaucratic—for the adjudication of land problems. To the extent that this is a public space "contaminated" with alienness, we find a longing in remarks like Fall's for a more familiar, localist version of publicness. Even though *jange o qol of* interactions in fact tended to be discrete, one-on-one affairs, reification tends to agglomerate elements of "tradition." Fall thus evokes the sense that the National Domain Law has imposed an unfamiliar, threatening public space tainted with the alienness of the colonial and postcolonial states in place of an idealized, communitarian, familial "talking tree."[36]

In a discussion of the reification of tradition as an idealized contrast to the imposed National Domain law, Fall's imaginary public humiliation of his opponent in front of the council of elders under the "talking tree" carries significant symbolic weight. His assemblage of elements of lost "tradition" highlights the points of tension between the ethos and authority structures of the new order (procedural impersonalism, egalitarian resource access, and bureaucratic decision making) and those of an idealized past (trust, reciprocity, community harmony, and public decision making under the guidance of elders).

Lamans *and* Yal Bakhs

Where the new tenure system appears rigid and harshly impersonal in its proceduralism, *lamans* and *yal bakhs* are remembered as flexible and close to the relatives and neighbors whose land they managed. The National Domain Law and its enforcers seem like the local agents of a power "not from here" (a *commandement*), which either through ignorance or malice tramples community sensibilities and routines.[37] In contrast, rose-colored memories of the *lamans* and *yal bakhs* highlight their embeddedness in local culture, their altruistic concern for food security and community well-being, and their indispensability in managing unrealistically harmonious social relations in the preindependence Siin.

The key *lamanic* virtue, social proximity in a small-scale setting, facilitated minute season-by-season adjustments in land allocation at the level of the individual producer. Moussa Cama touches this chord of lament for the idyllic authority of the *laman* in discussing the conflict in which he is deeply embroiled *(Village of Ndokh v. Njujuf Quarter):* "When I think about problems like this, I think of the *lamans* that I know, and this is what they used to do: There'd be a couple, just two people, in a house, with small children, too small to really help in the fields, and too small to really add mouths around the bowl. The *laman* would take fields away from them, and give them to someone else who had needed more land to feed his family. That's what I knew the *lamans* to do."[38]

In Cama's case, the state has been unable to intervene in an extremely complicated land use conflict between his community, Njujuf, and the neighboring village of Ndokh. Their old *laman*-managed rotation system has collapsed, and both sides need land for subsistence farming and herding. Their collective acreage is the subject of complex struggles over patterns of pasture and cultivation, which state authorities consistently treat simply as a question of cutting out paths for livestock to get to water.

Set against this contemporary background, Cama's account of how a *laman* he knew would have dealt with a young family idealizes the old order in contrast to reviled features of the new system under the National Domain Law. For Cama, the *laman* was invested with enough authority (and wisdom, in this rosy remembrance) to adjust land allocation arrangements in a temporary, ad hoc fashion.

In a similar vein, Samba Marone, the chief of the village of Mboyen, reminisces over how his ancestor, a *yal bakh* and village chief, would have handled a land dispute in which Marone was embroiled. In this case, *Marone Men v. Guignane Cama*, a set of fields in Mboyen had been set aside for four young orphans to take control of when they grew old enough to farm. However, Guignane Cama, the widowed mother of these children, left the village of Mboyen because of conflict with her former in-laws, the Marone elite of the village. Guignane Cama took the children with her, and Samba Marone, the village chief, as well as a few of his relatives and their rural council allies, took the opportunity to gain control of the fields that had been set aside for the children.[39]

Marone expresses regret over what happened (he blames the rural council members for precipitating the land grab) and fondly remembers how his father would have dealt with the whole affair when he was responsible for field allocation: "My father, a *yal bakh*, he would have loaned the fields to relatives until someone in the village who lacked land needed them and asked for them. And if the orphans came back and needed them, then my father would have the opportunity and the power to take the fields back and give them to the boys."

This vision of the caring and modulated exercise of allocative authority contrasts sharply with Samba Marone's own use of the new land tenure system. True, he and his relatives did benefit from the departure of the widowed Guignane Cama because they took control of a number of fields set aside for her sons. They insist however that they will give these fields back to the orphans as soon as they are old enough to return and claim their father's land. The problem is that the National Domain Law has brought the rural council president and the rural councilor into this arrangement—both powerful men from outside the village. They have taken their cut, which was substantial: they got the two largest and most fertile fields of the lot.

Samba Marone admits, moreover, that if the rural council president and rural councilor refuse to give back their fields when the orphans return, he too might not give back the field he has taken. Under the National Domain Law, he technically has title to his field as long as the orphans do not return within two years, which they are unlikely to do given their young age. Marone recognizes the moral ambiguity of his position by waxing nostalgic for management of such a situation in the days of his father.

In addition to reification of the institutions of the *laman* and *yal bakh*, we find that idealized memories of *lamanic* concepts of ownership have become entangled with new principles of the National Domain tenure system. For example, Boucar Thioro Diouf, a member of a *ceddo* (pre-independence warrior caste) family, presents a fascinating synthesis of discourses of legality and originality of settlement: "The Serer [here Diouf uses *Serer* to refer to the free farmer caste] of today, you don't even dare to tell him, 'Get off my land': on the contrary, it's up to him to say it, because he is now the owner of the fields, *because it was his ancestors that deforested the land* in order to have fields to farm. Although my ancestors were there, living off his ancestors, now the Serer is more legal, that's the truth."[40]

In the old political economy of the preindependence monarchy (the Gelwaar regime), the *ceddo* warriors were a predator class who did not farm but lived off what they extracted from Serer free farmers. Independence put an end to the regime of the Gelwaar *maad*, shutting down the economy of predation and forcing the *ceddo* out of their position as enforcers and tax collectors and onto the land. Diouf sees the National Domain Law as creating a legal order that benefits free farmers at the expense of the old Gelwaar aristocratic elite (of which the *ceddo* were ancillary members). Thus, Serer free farmers have "become more legal."

Yet, in a syncretic discursive moment, for the former *ceddo* Diouf, originality and fire rights actually make Serer free farmers more "legal" in contemporary land tenure relations. Diouf ignores the "modern" and in fact legal basis to claim land (the two-year usufruct rule) and instead brings up the old question of *whose ancestors cleared the land* as the justification for contemporary tenure claims. His position points up how salient this reified local construction of ownership has become, even for someone whose social caste in fact stood to gain from the land reform, whose group really *was* made more "legal" by the reform.[41] For Diouf, *ceddo* displacement and social change are tied up in a bundle with independence, the end of the Gelwaar state, and land reform. It just so happens that Diouf throws into that bundle what appears to him a commonsensical way to think about ownership: the reified *lamanic* model based on lineage originality.

THE DUAL TENURE SYSTEM

Highly romanticized historical memories of the preform tenure regime present a systematic foil, a point-by-point alternative to the norms and institutions of the state's new tenure system. The result is not simply a rhetorical disjuncture between the de facto National Domain regime and the imagined, idealized alternative that many Serer wish was still in place. A comprehensive alternative set of institutions, practices, and norms persists in the highly localized, informal spaces out of reach of the National Domain system. The state's inability to fully institutionalize its new regime, combined with Serer localist reification of prereform land tenure institutions, has produced a bifurcated dual tenure system in the Siin.

In the dual tenure regime outlined below, incomplete or blocked processes of institutional syncretism have produced developmental dysfunctionality. The Serer have responded to postreform realities by maintaining two parallel tenure regimes, between which they maneuver as their interests require: a public sphere governed by the principles and institutions of the National Domain Law but completely lacking in popular legitimacy, and a radically contracted private sphere governed by the law of *cosaan* (ancestral tradition) but crippled as an effective resource management structure by its limited social scope.

Taile *and the Informal Tenure System*

Despite the installation of the National Domain Law, "the land for those who farm it" principle has not become a dominant or even widespread popular basis for thinking about land ownership in the Siin. Rather, beneath the formal reality of the new tenure system, *lamanic* tenure models remain extremely important to most Serer. This is especially evident when we consider *taile* pawning relations in the aftermath of the National Domain Law.

Tailes still take place with considerable frequency, outside the view of state officials. The state's egalitarian idealism aside, farmers in the Siin still need to make adjustments to acquire cash—for example, when children are young—and to expand their acreage when children grow old enough to farm. Subterranean, limited *taile* pawns continue to fulfill this need for flexibility in tenure relations. The *mētis* (practical) knowledge embedded in *tailes* retains its utility in spite of the state's inability to recognize, let alone make use of, such local practices.[42]

Subterranean *tailes* are central to a Serer sense of living under two systems of law, the National Domain Law and what an elected local official calls the "law of ancestral tradition." For many, like farmer Sombel Cama, the question of which law is more salient, more important in their lives, is really rather simple: "It [the National Domain Law] has become a law since the rural council started to push it, but we here, we don't really practice that law, because the person who gives you a field would not really refuse you any request."[43]

Field proprietors in Cama's community, Sob, remain tied to field takers in relations of reciprocity and mutual aid, a somewhat idealized framing given the fact that acts of nationalization (seizure of pawned plots under the authority of the National Domain Law) do occur. It is striking nevertheless that for Cama, the very persistence of a sense of reciprocity and mutual aid (however idealized) is enough to call into question the relevance of the National Domain Law.

Although comparative data for the period predating the National Domain Law are not available, of the 727 respondents surveyed in the rainy season of 1993, 30.1 percent reported that they either farmed land given to them in pawn or had fields out in pawn in that growing season. Among producers interviewed in the course of land litigation, 76.6 percent responded that they had been engaged in some form of land pawning in the previous five years. Many respondents, such as Gorgui Marone, testify openly to the fact, that, in full violation of the land reform law, they continue to practice *taile* pawning: "If I had the power, I would return to the old ways of the *lamans*. I still borrow fields in *taile* even today. I farm these fields for five years, maybe ten years, and then I give the field back to the original owner, like we always did."[44]

Survey data also suggest that the practice of giving and receiving pawned land is socially widespread. Interestingly, the use of multiple regression to explore who, in terms of socioeconomic and cultural indicators, takes pawned land, turns up very little in the way of results. That is, there are no significant variations with regard to age, wealth, education, extralocal involvement, caste, religion, or various forms of historical memory. The data suggest that being male or religiously orthodox indicates only a very slightly increased likelihood that one will take pawned land.[45]

Thus, those who take fields in pawn are equally likely to come from a variety of socioeconomic, religious, and ideological groupings from within Serer society. As table 18 suggests, much the same is true with regard to giving fields in pawn. Gender stands out as the most powerful predictor of involvement in pawning. Not surprisingly, the men who dominate tenure relations and control land are more likely to pawn land. There is also a slight tendency for those of the Gelwaar caste to pawn land, which offers some indication that they have translated their high preindependence political status into postindependence landholding. An equally weak correlation suggests that greater education leads to a decreased likelihood of pawning land. This is an interesting finding that might seem to confirm the notion that pawning is a "traditional" practice, one left behind by those who advance in the modern sector. If this were the case, however, we might

TABLE 18. Land Pawning, by Social-Structural Position and
Historical Memory–Culture Variables
(significance at 5% error level, N = 727)

	Variable	β *Correlation Coefficient*	P-*Value (2-Tailed)*
Give land in pawn	Male	.288	.000
	Less educated	.089	.013
	Gelwaar caste	.083	.020

also expect discernible positive correlations for variables like wealth, extralocality, or at least orthodoxy, and there are no such correlations. The low negative correlation with education may also say something about the nature of dodging survey questions: those who "know better" don't openly admit to engaging in borderline illegal economic relations.[46] Most important, these data confirm that *taile* pawning, although it began as a transfer rooted in dual stratification, has become an extremely widespread economic practice in the Siin.

This *taile* exchange system persists and appears widespread, but with two significant alterations. First, although respondents like Hamad Ndong claim to engage in multiyear *tailes,* these are rare and depend on a high degree of social proximity and mutual trust. To ensure that field takers will respect the *jange o qol of* ethic and resist the temptation to nationalize fields, unlimited-term *tailes* tend to take place only within a very contracted circle of trust. Second, outside that circle, most Serer farmers have turned to very short-term *tailes* to accommodate their need for flexible, personalistic mechanisms of exchange within the new realities of the National Domain Law's two-year usufruct rule.

The Collapsed Circle of Trust

Idealized vestiges of prereform *lamanic* tenure relations persist within a collapsed private realm, a circle of trustworthy relations that usually does not extend far beyond family members or close friends drawn from a common age-class or circumcision cohort. The National Domain Law is central to this collapse on a number of levels. First, by displacing the authoritative institutions of *laman* and *yal bakh,* it unraveled much of the webbing that formed the material basis for community-wide trust-based social relations. Functional social networks have gradually fallen from the level of the *lamanic* or *bakh* estate to the level of the household.

Second, the two-year usufruct law has effectively made long-term *tailes* illegal. The threat of nationalization leaves those who have fields to pawn extremely wary.[47] As Latyr Sene notes, "It's only by family connections or bonds of friendship that people loan fields now."[48]

Many land disputes in fact arise over failures to correctly perceive the boundaries of the newly shrunken circle of trust. Mamadou Dione, for example, pawned a field for twelve thousand CFA francs to a cousin he thought he could trust: "I could have given this field to any of my brothers. That's what I should have done. They would not have done this to me. Instead I gave the field to Malale Dione, whom I thought I could trust because he's a sort of cousin; his family are allies of my father's line."[49] With the encouragement and help of a mutual relative (who happened to be a former rural council president), Malale Dione seized the field under the National Domain Law. As a result, Mamadou Dione's circle of trust contracted even closer to the boundaries of his nuclear family.

The circle of trust is not shrinking with regard to land issues alone. Despite the multiplicity of causes and complexity of overlapping processes, most in the Siin feel that the land reform has precipitated a general sense of suspicion, increasing individualism, and disintegration of community integrity and solidarity. People in the Siin know that other forces are at work here—Western education, urbanization, new economic opportunities in a market based system, and what young people learn from U.S. television reruns. But these forces are abstract and distant. They see the breakdown within the real material relations of agricultural production that every farmer in the Siin knows to be fundamental to community wellbeing. Gorgui Faye chooses a decidedly Dostoyevskian image to convey the breakdown: "In the old days, when you went to ask a relative for something, he would give it to you without a problem. But in our times now—you see my shirt over there? I wouldn't even have the confidence to loan *that* to my own relative for more than two days, because he might try to keep it forever."[50]

After two days the relative would steal the shirt. After two years a person can nationalize a field. The language of distrust and social rupture has become the language of the National Domain Law, even down to its very structuring of time.

Short-Term Taile *Strategy*

To avoid the threat of field nationalization posed by the National Domain's two-year usufruct rule, short-term *tailes* of up to two years duration have become commonplace in relations in the lower, informal half of the dual

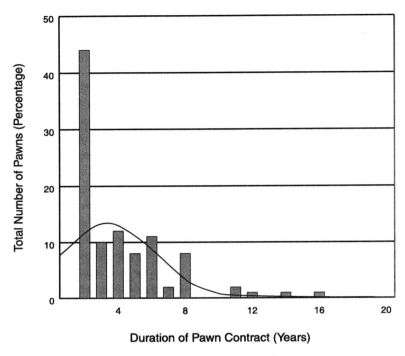

Figure 7. Frequency distribution of pawn contract duration ($N = 727$).

tenure system. Indeed, most *taile* pawns fall near or under the two-year de facto limit. Figure 7 shows the distribution of pawn duration (in years) reported by those who receive land through *taile* pawns. The mean duration is 3.7 years for a pawn, but the standard deviation is 5.6 years. As the graph makes clear, most pawn contracts now last for a period far shorter than the National Domain Law's cutoff for legal usufruct transfer.

Boucar Ngom v. Hamad Faye illustrates the widely accepted logic of the short-term *taile*. In about 1968, Ngom pawned a field to Faye. By 1990, Ngom's children had grown up, and they needed fields of their own. Ngom claims to have approached Faye over the course of several rainy seasons to try to get the field back, but each year just before the time of clearing the fields, Faye rebuffed him with a different excuse. Exasperated, Ngom thought he had found a way to get his field back and keep Faye happy at the same time: "I proposed this year to give back the seventy-five-hundred-franc guarantee that Faye had given me, and to get back the field, and then to give Faye another plot somewhere else. I suggested that after a few years I would give back the first field if he still wanted it."[51] Faye refused this request categorically, and eventually contacted friends in the rural council, with whose help and encouragement he seized the disputed field under the National Domain Law.

Ngom's request is striking for both the clarity and the apparent naïveté of his plan to switch his contract with Faye from a more customary long-term *taile* to a short-term arrangement. Perhaps Ngom was not too familiar with the dynamics of working around the National Domain Law, or perhaps he underestimated Faye's own experience with such maneuvers (a mistake that cost him the field). In either case Ngom lays bare the straightforward logic of the short-term *taile* loan: get Faye (the field taker) to give back the original pawned field, substitute an alternate field someplace else, and offer to give Faye the original field again in "a few years" (presumably, say, two).

Thanks to numerous experiences like Ngom's throughout the Siin, when field proprietors deal with prospective field takers outside the shrunken circle of trust, they are now unwilling to risk loaning their land for more than two years. When they do loan it, they make sure they have enough cash on hand every two years to repay the pawn and recover their land. If the field taker is then still interested in a *taile*, a new contract can be arranged for a different field. Field proprietors like Ngom thus can continue to engage in instrumentally useful, short-term *taile* loans without running the risk of "nationalization" associated with lending outside the circle of trust.

CONSEQUENCES OF THE DUAL TENURE SYSTEM

If security of tenure, improvements to soil, agricultural productivity, voluntary compliance with land management arrangements, and social peace constitute objective measurement criteria, then the dual tenure system emerging in response to the imposition of the National Domain Law is dysfunctional. By displacing an extant and locally legitimate land management and adjudicatory system, the National Domain Law has precipitated a not-so-syncretic response in the form of bifurcation. This has made tenure in land less secure and reduced the likelihood that producers will make long-term investments in their soil. The lack of coherent, community-wide land tenure institutions has meant a nearly complete collapse of the long-established rotation scheme, essentially bringing an end to fallow and pasturing. The dual tenure system's severe legitimacy imbalance has also made adjudication of disputes over land extremely problematic. Boundary disagreements, inheritance conflicts, and contested loans turn into chronic disputes that drain the resources of local officials and accentuate the insecurity of tenure (see chapter 6).

These institutional failures coincide with a long-term decline in agricultural productivity in the region. While environmental factors, fluctuations in international markets, and the state's withdrawal from
agricultural support programs of course have contributed to this decline,
the inefficiencies and contradictions inherent in the dual tenure system
have severely limited the ability of producers in the Siin to respond effectively to difficult exogenous circumstances.

Deterioration of Land Management Systems

Perhaps the most fundamental and unintended consequence of the dual
tenure system has been a rapid decline in fallowing. Even before the promulgation of the National Domain Law, Serer farmers were gradually
abandoning the fallow year in response to technological change, demographic expansion, and consequent land scarcity.[52] But the dual tenure
system triggered in response to the reform put much greater pressure on
fallow space for several reasons. First, the National Domain Law displaced
the political authorities responsible for fallow, crop rotation, and customary land management without installing equally effective "modern" alternatives. The reform seemed to accept the widespread misconception that
common-pool resource schemes are embedded in a harmonious and egalitarian moral economy. In fact, the common-pool land management system
of the Siin depended on the *authoritative* management of *lamans* and *yal
bakhs*, whose power and legitimacy were crucial to the maintenance of
practices like fallow (as well as crop rotation and animal pasturing,
although fallow is the key basis for all these practices).

Second, the National Domain Law's de facto ban on *taile* relations has
also inadvertently undermined the practice of fallow. The land reform had
done nothing to change the underlying social conditions that necessitate a
flexible form of short- to medium-term land transfer. But outside limited
circles of trust, producers in the Siin have turned to short-term *tailes*, of
one or two years' duration. Under such circumstances, it is inconceivable
for field takers to put pawned fields into fallow. In contrast, the long-term,
personalistic nature of prereform *taile* did in fact permit fallow, as one
respondent makes clear in typical terms:

> The National Domain Law does not please us the *baadolo* (peasant pro-
> ducer; free farmer caste) at all, because it has ruined many things here.
> In the past you could take a poor, worn-out field that had been loaned or
> pawned to you and put it into fallow for a couple of years, and then con-
> tinue to farm it afterward.[53] But now you would not want to even put it
> into fallow, because you know you have to leave it that way for at least

two years, maybe more in order to get any results. Nowadays, if somebody loans you a field, after two years they take it back because they
fear that if they let you farm it for three years, you'll try to seize it
under the Domain.[54]

The personalistic relationship between socially proximate and inter-
connected parties made it possible to fallow pawned land in the prereform tenure regime. A field taker might know, for example, that a field
proprietor had offered land in pawn while his children were young, and
that he would ask for his field back when they reached adolescence. For
the field taker, the time horizon of the contract was fairly clear, implying
relatively secure tenure for a decade, more or less. Given such long-term
usufruct transfer, it was in the interests of field takers to make an invest-
ment in soil fertility in the early years of the pawn arrangement.
Knowing they would farm a field for ten years, field takers habitually
left pawned fields in fallow and allowed livestock to pasture there for a
rainy season or two before starting to farm the plot intensively.
Contrary to the expectations of generations of technical assistants—
from French colonial administrators to World Bank agricultural
experts—a property regime grounded on the *inalienability* of land and
on lineage ownership, rather than individual ownership, actually provided greater incentives for soil improvement than more familiar models of freehold and commodified exchange.[55]

Furthermore, by tying control over land to demonstrated use, the
National Domain Law in effect encourages continuous planting. In the
context of the dual tenure system, it should come as no surprise that producers manipulate the ambiguities inherent between new tenure principles (two years of usufruct as the basis for title) in contrast to prereform
principles (usufruct transferable with consent of *laman, yal bakh,* or
sometimes *yal mbind*). A considerable number of the disputes analyzed
for this study essentially stem from efforts to take advantage of this gap
between de facto state law and the law of *cosaan* (ancestral "tradition").
Moments of inheritance, migration, or change in control of the household
are especially ripe for making such claims. As a result, for any given piece
of land we find multiple, competing claims to use-rights grounded in both
National Domain Law and local principles of access.[56]

Because the guiding principle of the National Domain Law is *mise en
valeur* (putting to use), a farmer who chooses to fallow a contested field
opens the door to rivals who can claim the field according to competing
tenure principles or simply by asserting that they will put it to immediate use. A number of rural council decisions even allude to this logic,

suggesting that a litigant lost a field because he "obviously controlled more than he could use" at a given time.[57] Thus, as early as the rainy season of 1993, only 8.4 percent of 711 respondents in twelve villages scattered around the western Siin practiced fallow. Among this small fraction of producers who continue to fallow, very few can let more than one field lie at a time. The mean number of fields that any given farmer had in fallow that year was 1.3, but the standard deviation was 0.5 fields. Put another way, of the forty-four farmers who practiced fallow that year, thirty-three of them fallowed one field or some fraction of a field. As these data confirm, the days when land custodians like *lamans* or *yal bakhs* orchestrated the setting aside of vast areas for pasture and refertilization are indeed over.

Most farmers continue to raise livestock but have been forced by the near elimination of fallow to send their animals to pasture outside the Siin, sometimes as far away as the Ferlo Desert or the eastern Saluum for a three-month rainy season.[58] The disappearance of fallow has predictably coincided with declines in soil fertility and in yields of both peanuts and millet. An agricultural system that for several centuries had sustained extremely high population densities and an intensive agropastoral system in marginal environmental conditions, shorn of its authoritative structures, is disintegrating.

De Facto into De Jure

The contemporary act of "nationalizing" fields under the National Domain Law amounts to stamping what had become de facto transfers of use rights and control with the official imprimatur of the state. The law pushes what had been understated, de facto long-term land transfers to become de jure, unequivocal declarations that land has changed hands. By effacing a subtle mechanism for long-term transfer and insisting on a greater degree of official explicitness in identifying "owners," the National Domain Law has replaced flexible allocation with a kind of rigid insecurity.

Previously, many long-term *tailes* amounted to tacitly acknowledged, de facto transfers of "title" (holistic custodianship responsibility). In such instances, field takers would tend to postpone requests from field proprietors for the return of a pawned field. After many years of farming a pawned field, field takers might hold off original owners by making excuses designed to delay recovery of the field until the following growing season: "Oh, I can't give it back this year, I've already seeded there." "Let me just farm here another year, because my brother is using my other fields, and except for this one, I have no other field for my millet."

In cases where original field proprietors accepted these excuses and delays went on for many years, they in effect chose not to fully exercise their right to regain their land. Although field proprietors might have accepted the de facto reality of the pawn-cum-transfer, it was common for them to continue to reassert their claim to de jure proprietorship by making at least a formal, almost ritual effort to repay the loan and regain the field at the start of each growing season.[59] Having accepted a de facto transfer, proprietors directed this gesture not at the particular field taker but at the wider community. By continuing to go through the motions of asking for the return of the field and accepting the fiction that the taker "only needs the field for one more year," field proprietors under the prereform system asserted to the community that one de facto transfer should not be taken as a wider precedent. The seemingly empty claim and farcical excuse reminded other potential field takers of the de jure reality of the proprietor's claim to holistic custodianship of his estate. In this way, the prereform exchange regime allowed some long-term *tailes* to become de facto transfers without undermining the basic logic of the *laman–yal bakh* model based on a clear-cut distinction between title and usufruct.

The abruptness of the National Domain Law lies in the fact that it swept away this rather delicate adjustment in the local tenure system. Overnight it turned what had been de facto arrangements carefully concealed by the try-to-reclaim-but-postpone charade into explicit de jure transfers. Field takers who were quietly gaining clear control over borrowed land were forced to step into the light of day and declare this intention publicly by making a direct claim before the rural council. Whereas the prereform system shielded field takers from *jange o qol of* sanctions, outright transfers under the National Domain Law not only violate that ethic but also invoke the authority of the state to achieve that end. Likewise, the old arrangement had enabled field proprietors to make "exceptions" to the ban on transfers of title, but did so in a way that did not establish precedents—that is, did not undermine their overall claims to control their *lamanic* or *bakh* estates in a holistic custodianship sense. By making partially ambiguous, de facto arrangements into clear-cut, de jure transfers of land, the National Domain Law undermined these claims to proprietorship and dissolved the material base of the political power of *lamans* and *yal bakhs*.

During the very years when Senghor's architects of African socialism were drawing up the land reform law, Serer farmers in the Siin were subtly adapting their own tenure arrangements with this reclaim-postpone mechanism. The architects in Dakar had no idea of this alternative project and inadvertently swept it away when they put their own idealistic reform in place.

CONCLUSION

Although the National Domain Law was crafted in the days of the seemingly unlimited legitimacy of the newly independent Senegalese state, its radical modernism and resultant bifurcated tenure system have squandered that legitimacy in the Siin. Given this backdrop, it is difficult to imagine voluntary Serer cooperation (not to speak of the danger of intentional sabotage) with state-sponsored interventions (be they in agriculture, adjudication, health care, education, taxation, local governance, democratization, or other realms) that require community contribution or participation. The simmering mood of defiance and passive resistance borne of such mistrust amounts to real danger in light of the fragile social basis for democracy in contemporary Senegal. Senegal's boldest effort to deepen democracy by expanding it to the *sujets* in the countryside—the Rural Council Law—met with a form of interpretive vilification born of mistrust sown in part by the National Domain Law.

Moreover, the reform represents a real missed opportunity on the part of the Senegalese state. The officials who designed and managed the National Domain Law failed to recognize the salience of prereform structures and values, and missed the chance to coopt these into new institutional arrangements. Such a process of cooptation could have helped circumvent the sense of loss that has led to nostalgia for, and eventually reification of, prereform institutions. Had the reform, for example, coopted the Serer innovation of *taile* pawning by making provision for a kind of trust- or oath-based mechanism of land exchange, it might have legitimated the entire reform effort and contributed to the process of developing agriculturally productive, syncretic institutions.

Despite the high romance built into President Senghor's vision of the National Domain Law, the result of such a process of incorporation of local values and locally legitimate patterns and institutions might have been a truly syncretic land tenure system. Such a system would have been rooted not in a single, static idealization of the rural African past but in a flexible incorporation of present-day popular memories of practices, rules, and values that seem "traditional" and are invested with authenticity and legitimacy.

Absent institutional syncretism, the National Domain Law met a fate quite common for policy and institutional initiatives in postcolonial societies. The realm of official state administrative hierarchies and formal rules (e.g., the National Domain Law) and the realm of local informal rules, habits and values (the vestiges of the *lamanic* tenure system) lost connection from one another. The state, as Goran Hyden has aptly put it, "floats above society." It is Peter Ekeh's two publics in the worst possible form: legitimation, trust, volunteerism, and indeed social capital formation remained linked to relations and practices of the informal, remembered, and idealized social and institutional relations. Naked self-interest—utility maximization unchecked by social or moral codes—governs the official realm. Vilification of the upper official institutional space feeds from and foments reification and idealization of the informal, unofficial realm.

This is the all-too-familiar, standard pattern of state-society relations in postcolonial Africa. But as the creation of *taile* pawning and the early effort to transform the rural councils suggest (see chapter 6), it did not have to be this way. Institutional bifurcation and a dysfunctional dual tenure system in response to the National Domain Law reflect the truncation and failure of syncretism. This is not the only form of local response to institutional imposition in Africa. The dynamics of syncretism suggest ways that cultural change and the local dynamics of legitimation can be harnessed for productive purposes to promote meaningful integration of state and society.

6 · "The King Has Come—
Now Everything Is Ruined"

*The Promise and Frustration
of Syncretic Rural Democracy*

On a cool evening in March 1992, the drums of the griots sent out an announcement: an old man, a revered old man, had just died. Next day, Djignak Diouf heard that it was old Matiasse Sene. Djignak Diouf harnessed up his horse, hooked the cart, and set off to pay his respects at the funeral. On the way he passed a field, the one that his grandfather, Birame Diouf, had given in pawn to Waly Sene, the father of Matiasse Sene. It was a good, rich field, and Djignak's family hadn't put a hoe in that soil for almost two generations.

This first phase of the funeral was an appropriately massive affair—Matiasse had many relatives and many connections. The imam from Bari, a Tijane marabout of some importance for the people of the Siin, had even been driven down in his blue Peugeot, now parked under a broad baobab. Out beyond that morsel of shade, a vast crowd sat on the hot sand just outside the courtyard. They sat there all afternoon, as the sun crossed the sky and the air shimmered with radiant heat. Off in the distance, women tended gigantic pots of cooking rice, stirring with spoons more like shovels. Children ran about gathering up fuelwood. It would be four in the afternoon before the crowd got their bowls of rice garnished with morsels of meat, the amount and quality of the cuts carefully apportioned according to the gender and status of those around the bowl. No matter. Matiasse had been a man of considerable stature. The more the crowd waited, the more they honored him on this the day after he had succumbed.

Djignak had to wait for the right moment to approach Niokhor, the eldest son of the deceased, about the field. It was a difficult decision for

Djignak. It wasn't such a great idea, such a tactful maneuver, to try to repay a fifty-year-old pawn right in the midst of the first funeral ceremony itself. On the other hand, there was something to be said for moving quickly. It was already March. In a few weeks Niokhor would clear the field and it would be impossible to try to get it back during that rainy season. Acting now meant acting decisively, before Niokhor settled into his new role as *yal mbind* and *yal qol*, master of the household and master of the fields. Before Niokhor redistributed plots among the family, there was a brief window of opportunity for Djignak to hand over the twenty-five hundred CFA francs and recover his grandfather's land.

These scenarios rattled about in Djignak's head as he waited in the hot sun for the rice. He glanced at his watch. Three in the afternoon. Somewhere on the other side of the crowd he heard the familiar jingle of the afternoon radio news broadcast from Dakar. He could make out the tune, but none of the headlines. Neither really changed all that much anyhow.

He waited. As the shadows started to lengthen and the sand beneath his rubber sandals radiated the last of its absorbed heat, the speeches began. The imam gave a long-winded benediction of sorts. The women had probably finished cooking but wouldn't dare bring the food during the speech making. The griots spoke for the family. They sang and told the stories of Matiasse. At last the women came with the bowls. They passed through the crowd, which ordered itself according to proximity to the deceased, proximity to the imam, age, sex, money, caste—some things that make you important anywhere, some just in this corner of Africa. Finally Niokhor said a very few words and everyone settled down with a "Bisimallahi" to their bowls.

This was the time. Djignak swallowed a few polite handfuls of warm rice, keeping an eye on Niokhor. The host predictably ate very little, rose and made the rounds of the bowls, greeting his guests. Djignak pulled away from his bowl, licked his hand clean, resisted the cries of "You haven't eaten!" and "You don't like it?" with a perfunctory "I'm full, thanks," and circled around the crowd to intercept Niokhor. They stepped discreetly away from the crowd, out of easy earshot.

"Njok."

"Nu yare jam."

"Jam somm a njeg u."

"Yaasam Roog a yirmin, Niokhor."

Greetings out of the way, Djignak proceeded to business: "Niokhor, I need to talk to you." Djignak pulled out the rolled-up bills and handed it to the bewildered Niokhor. As Niokhor unrolled it, confusion passed across his face at this inordinate funeral gift, some ten or twenty times a polite amount. Djignak clarified, "Here's the money you gave to my grandfather. I need the field on the road to Tukar."

Niokhor, stunned, didn't respond for a few moments. Then he called his brother over. He told him that Djignak had just insulted their late father. People nearby overheard, then began to murmur. Soon a wave of murmur passed across the crowd, then a wave of silence, followed by a curious turning of heads. They told Djignak he should leave. Some people thought that his close relatives ought to go too. Niokhor's brother told Djignak, "Don't stay, really. For your own sake, please don't stay now."

It took a few days for Niokhor to respond in a more precise manner. In the interim he had found himself with the twenty-five hundred francs in his pocket. He sent his uncle, a relative of one of Djignak's wives, with the cash and a message: "Niokhor says to tell you that he is nationalizing the field."

"He is nationalizing" it meant taking it under the authority of the state's local land tenure authorities, the rural councils. Niokhor and his father Matiasse before him had farmed the field on the road to Tukar all their lives. The rural councils enforced the National Domain Law, which said that anyone who farmed a field for two years or more owned it. For the new authorities, Niokhor's claim could not have been more secure.

Djignak Diouf asked "customary authorities"—the oldest descendant of the old master of fire of the region, notable elders of the community with various, unclear connections to the old *laman–yal bakh* land aristocracy—to step in and clear up the matter. They agreed that Niokhor Sene should conform to the old customs surrounding *taile* exchanges, and even though the original contract had been made decades before, Niokhor should relent, return the field to the Diouf family, and take back the original twenty-five-hundred-franc pawn amount.

At first Niokhor Sene brushed aside this advice and worked with the rural council, which ruled without much hesitation in his favor. Niokhor did not have to give back the field. But despite this judgment in his favor, in the end, he refused to win. He refused to keep the field under the state law. He tells us that his family, his mother especially, pressured him to give the field back to Djignak Diouf because, if he did not, it would cause irreparable rupture between the two families: ties of reciprocity and gift exchange would be broken immediately. Wives would be divorced and sent back to their parents. Relations between Dioufs and Senes would never be the same.[1]

So Niokhor Sene *voluntarily* renounced the rural council's decision in his favor and gave the field back to his neighbor Djignak Diouf. Sene heeded the warning of a local elder, who evoked a widely understood aphorism about state power and state adjudication: "Don't let the king [the state] come in, because once the king has come, everything is ruined . . . that closes the door between families forever."[2]

Niokhor Sene's refusal to win, his refusal to retain a field that he and his late father had farmed all their lives, gives us a sense of Serer responses to the elected local government system—the rural councils—established a few years after the National Domain Law. This chapter explores how the Serer response to these new rural councils (as well as associated technocratic resource management agencies) reveals the deep promise of democracy for syncretism, and the intense vilification and institutional dysfunction that results from breaking this promise.

Overview: Syncretism Foiled

Senegal's 1972 Rural Council Law established elected local councils throughout the countryside, largely to manage tenure relations under the partially implemented land reform.[3] State officials had come to realize that the National Domain Law had not captured the imagination and aspirations of rural Senegalese for a fairer, more productive rural order. For most Serer peasants, the National Domain Law was just another haughty promulgation from the *commandement* in Dakar, a bunch of grand speeches to politely applaud during political rallies and forget as soon as the subprefect's entourage of Land Rovers disappeared over the horizon. Moreover, the period of institutionalization of the reform actually coincided with *declines* in agricultural production (the period known as the *malaise paysan*),[4] along with marked increases in petty land litigation.

As the reform was gradually but incompletely implemented, it became unclear which rules applied, who was in charge, and what the tenure and land management regime really was. This undermined old systems of land allocation and dispute resolution like those managed by the *lamans* and *yal bakhs* of the Siin. Waiting for the new dispensation to "descend" from Dakar, some *lamans* themselves grew hesitant to assert their former authority, and more and more producers took their disputes to the new state courts.[5] In regions like the Siin, the National Domain Law was gradually and somewhat inadvertently sweeping away one of the more carefully constructed Rube Goldberg devices of colonialism—the quasi-federal reliance of the central administration on traditional local political elites to actually do the nitty-gritty work of governance with regard to tenure relations, pasturing, and natural resource management.

Enter the 1972 Rural Council Law: in a bold move underscoring the fact that Senegal was indeed once the vanguard of pluralist experimentation in

Africa, the state turned to rural democracy as a solution to the disorder induced by the land reform. The 1972 Rural Council Law took administration of land tenure out of the hands of the state's centrally appointed, uniformed civil servants (the prefects and subprefects) and gave it to new, democratically elected rural councils composed of and selected by ordinary peasants in small districts known as *communautés rurales* (rural communities).[6] It was thought that rural democracy would sweep into power respected community leaders who themselves embodied the values and cultural specificities of each microregion. These democratically elected officials would bring legitimacy to a tenure regime that so far had met with not just rejection but vilification as well.

In the early years, rural councilors read the National Domain Law in a way that generally upheld principles of the old master-of-fire tenure system, especially *taile* land pawning. Since they were democratically elected representatives, *this* seemed to be their job: make the basic principles of the law (equality and productivity) work in "Serer terms." This required rural councilors to be proximate, to know farmers, and to keep track of their various relationships and needs. The rural councilors, as members of the community, could do this. These were democratically elected masters of fire working in the form of a more or less legal-rational Weberian bureaucracy— a classic example of institutional syncretism in the making (the state might just be the master of fire).

But beginning in the late 1970s, the rural councils were instructed by their superiors in Dakar—prefects, subprefects, and extension agents— that they had erroneously interpreted the National Domain Law. Thinking and seeing "like a state," the subprefects, prefects, and other higher-ups wanted a simple, clear, easy-to-apply law.[7] "Two years of usufruct equals title" was the National Domain Law for the Dakar-appointed officials, and when their administrative subordinates (the rural councilors) did not seem to grasp this, they had to be tutored and overruled (the state, it turns out, is decidedly *not* the master of fire).

With the *lamanic* system marginalized and rural councilors vilified by farmers for their un-*lamanic* behavior, land and resource use became a utilitarian free-for-all. In this interest-maximizing nightmare, no one needed to sacrifice scarce farmland to make room for someone else's cattle. No one had to leave a field fallow and thereby give up the chance to make some cash growing peanuts. Nitrogen-fixing trees were cut down as a first come, first served resource. Within a few years, the intricate system of crop rotation in the Siin was collapsing. In the process, boundary disputes, inheritance claims, and petty land-related arguments formerly resolved by the *lamans* flooded the rural councils, who were rarely able to handle complex and important matters without the intervention of their administrative superiors, the prefects, subprefects, and extension agents. Rural democracy became illegitimate, irrelevant, the object of disdain and scorn because grassroots institutional syncretism had been explicitly and deliberately put to an end by representatives of centralized state authority.

The promise of democracy to advance institutional syncretism is itself the tragic element in the story. The Senegalese state, like most postcolonial regimes, has had considerable difficulty implementing genuine decentralization, let alone decentralization by means of handing over power to autonomous, democratically elected rural councils.[8] Now reined in, the rural councils, the lowest rung in the administrative hierarchy, show us the danger of playing fast and loose with democratic (and syncretic) representational hope. Despite progress in making the rural councils the new masters of fire, Serer peasants now understand the rural councils in a different historical light, as the latest manifestation of alien, arbitrary government, the reincarnation of the feared and reviled Gelwaar state that ruled the Siin from the fourteenth century until independence in 1960. In five centuries of dealing with this state and its king, or *maad*, Serer peasants developed sophisticated techniques of ignoring, circumventing, and sabotaging outside authority, techniques that have been redeployed in response to these new agents of the *maad*, the rural councils.

Serer peasants do not simply reject and vilify the rural councils, as they do the National Domain Law. They *interpretively vilify* the rural councils, reading them as the old monarchy and thereby expecting, as they expected from the old monarchy, quasi-federal respect for Serer institutional autonomy and a sense of responsibility to attend Serer ceremonies and "adore" Serer demigods (see chapter 2). They shun the rural councils not because they are an alien, arbitrary imposition and not simply because "they are the *maad*," but more precisely because they commit regular, oblivious offenses as they fail to even behave as a *maad* should.

Much as their grandparents blended freehold and *lamanic* holistic custodianship into *taile* land pawning, contemporary Serer peasants have attempted their own process of bricolage, trying to reassemble the legal-rational, democratically elected rural councils *and* their own systems of supernaturally sanctioned resource management into a new model of legitimate local authority. This took place against the backdrop of rapidly collapsing structures of local authority. For a time, it held out the promise that the ideological memory and institutional reality of the old *lamans* might be refashioned within the framework of elective local democracy. But the reality of sham decentralization made this impossible, leading to a process of interpretive vilification of the rural councils as alien, arbitrary, distant, and untrustworthy authorities.

Collapse and Transformation of Lamanic Authority

> My ancestor was a *laman*. His name was Demba Yandé, and he was *laman* over an area that included all of Puday and Tongoñ as well. [Respondent spontaneously reaches behind him for a log, which he plants in between us as we speak.] This is *laman*. The land belonged to my ancestor. The log is like a witness. You see, my ancestor burned the brush clear. He took a very large log as a "guarantee," proof that he was the master of all the space that he had burned. The *lamans* had all of that land, but now that the *lamans* are gone, the *communauté rurale* has taken everything over, taken over responsibility for the land.[9]

It's not at all clear what happened to the log that Hamad Sene's ancestor had saved as a marker of his *lamanic* office. Sene reaches for an ordinary log to give us a feel for what *lamanic* custodianship might have been about, but the actual relic itself is long gone. For people like Sene, the descendants of ancient *lamans*, all of that authority is in the past now. The government in Dakar would like peasants such as Sene to accept the rural council as the field and natural resource manager, and by extension, as the modernized version of Sene's own ancestor Demba Yandé, the new masters of fire. Yet, the local response to new state authoritative institutions is in fact far more complex.

Part of that complexity lies in the displacement of the old *lamans* and *yal bakhs* that had, up until the 1960s, maintained versions of land and resource management systems similar to the regime over which Demba Yandé presided.[10] The de jure replacement of customary authorities by the state's new rural council system has accelerated an ongoing process by which the territorial and demographic scale of *lamanic* authority had been gradually shrinking for some time. To make sense of adaptation of the new rural council system requires first stepping back and understanding three features of this accelerated transformation in Serer political and economic institutions.

First, the scale of *lamanic* authority, which had been slowly declining, collapsed rather suddenly in the wake of the Rural Council Law. Over many generations, the allocative resource management, fallow maintenance, and to some extent, adjudicatory functions of the *lamans* had slowly been transferred to *yal bakhs*, along the lines described in chapter

4. In older communities in the Siin, many *yal bakhs* had become functional equivalents of *lamans*.[11] Since the imposition of the rural council system, the *yal mbind*, usually the eldest male in a household, has taken on many of the land use, resource management, and even adjudicatory functions of the old *lamans* and *yal bakhs*. What had been ordinary heads of households have become scale models of the old *lamans* and *yal bakhs*, central figures in the allocation of fields and determination of cropping patterns for a single household. *Yal mbinds*, standing in for displaced *lamans*, are today presented as the semisacred repositories of legitimate Serer authority over land and local resources.[12]

The collapse of *lamanic* land tenure functions onto *yal mbinds* has put tremendous pressure on household heads to fulfill functions for which they are not especially well suited. Rotation and fallow schemes implemented at the household level, as opposed to the neighborhood or village scale, are relatively nonviable because it is very difficult for an ordinary-sized household to set aside, by itself, enough space to pasture even its own animals. The economies of scale achievable only through community land management are essential for viable pasturing in a physical and social environment like that of the Siin. Moreover, the collapse of *lamanic* functions and legitimacy onto *yal mbinds* accounts for a good deal of contemporary land litigation as disputants play one adjudicatory system off another.

Second, "elder" has emerged as the logical designation of high sociopolitical status as *lamans* and *yal bakhs* have transferred both political functions and popular legitimacy to *yal mbinds*. Among the very wide social category of *yal mbinds*, some are of aristocratic descent, but most are not. Yet all of them, by the very nature of the *yal mbind* office (senior male of a household), tend to fall into the amorphous designation of *o mag* (*les vieux*, "the elders").

As figure 8 suggests, elders (exemplified by the *mak a ndok*), unlike state officials, enjoy great popular legitimacy, ranking at the top of a list of six institutions for whom respondents would be most willing to make a voluntary economic contribution. The very low figure for *lamans* reflects their loss of de jure power but also underscores the transfer of legitimacy of historic customary authorities to generic elders.[13]

I deliberately included *mak a ndoks*, heads of matrilineal clans, as a "maximal test" for the legitimacy of elders because, had the term *elder* appeared on the survey, preliminary field tests suggest it would have received well over 95 percent of first-choice responses, and because *mak a ndoks* are relatively marginal authorities in the contemporary Siin. As a

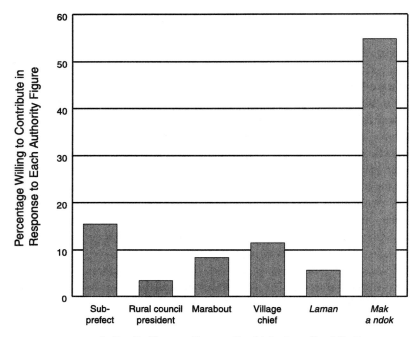

Authority Figures Requesting Voluntary Contributions

Figure 8. Percentage of first rankings among authorities for whom respondents were willing to make a voluntary contribution ($N = 704$). Serer respondents are familiar with the idea of leaders of all sorts asking for voluntary contributions of labor or material resources. Local historical memories are rich in the details, context, and meaning of colonial and postcolonial officials, Islamic and Catholic religious elites, the old Gelwar kings, local lineage-based authorities, and even extended kin all "requisitioning" the time, money, surpluses, and sometimes women and children of Serer families. Oral historical accounts typically include interpretive arguments about the relative merits or faults, morality or immorality, of such demands or requests. In this cultural-historical context, pretesting of this survey question suggested that respondents treated it as an assessment of the moral legitimacy of both the officeholder (the particular subprefect or marabout) and the office itself as institutional structure and historical claimant on personal resources.

result of the general move toward patrilinealism, very few *mak a ndoks* manage savings, cattle herds, or inheritance arrangements as they did two generations ago. Yet they enjoy far greater legitimacy than other authority figures because, for most Serer respondents, they are emblematic of a category of elders that function as repositories of the idealized legitimacy of the old *lamans*.

Finally, coincident with the collapse of *lamanic* legitimacy onto elders, a new social elite was rising—World War II veterans. For ordinary peasants, as for national political elites, the war constituted a transformative experience.[14] It brought the Siin into what was perhaps its first meaningful contact with the world outside the western Sahel.[15] The war experience forged a class of individuals who had acquired a new perspective on their own society as well as a new and unprecedented facility in working within the colonial state machinery. Veterans learned to speak French, albeit an unschooled, clumsy French. Nevertheless, this cohort, unlike their fathers, could converse in the language of the colonizer, and later, the language of the postcolonial state. Moreover, the Word War II generation learned to operate within the organizational structures and bureaucratic institutions of the colonial state. Unlike most other Serer, they were familiar with what are often referred to as "matters of *keit*," official business having to do with paperwork: filling out forms and responding to, working within, and when possible, manipulating a large bureaucratic organization.[16]

The World War II generation has in effect staged a quiet but extremely effective coup. They have managed to use their relatively superior knowledge of the French language as well as their relatively greater familiarity with the bureaucratic machinery of the state to elbow aside would-be contenders for rural councilor positions—especially the younger heads of *lamanic* and *yal bakh* lineages—and establish themselves as the local rural council elite. Of equal significance, they have assumed the legitimacy of the old *lamans* and *yal bakhs* by successfully presenting themselves as members of the new amorphous category of elders. Demographically, they are of course in the right slot. But they were also community heroes who had achieved something that very few before them had accomplished: they were taken by Europeans to a faraway land where they faced grave danger, *and they returned home.* We should not underestimate the degree to which this was an extraordinary accomplishment that set this generation apart as semimythical figures.

THE PROMISE: THE STATE MIGHT BE THE MASTER OF FIRE

Serer farmers have tried to transform the rural council system through dynamic institutional syncretism, even though the effort at syncretism has been systematically blocked and signs of syncretic outcomes are thus fragmentary. In the limited domains where rural councilors enjoy some autonomy, we still find evidence of this notion that "the state must be our master of fire."[17] We see this with regard to the practice of "suspending" disputed fields, the application of "environmental" logic to claims regarding trees, the incorporation of *cosaan,* oratorical proceduralism, and Serer notions of kin representation. Syncretism is always a two-way street, a reworking of both imposed institutional superstructure and local institutional infrastructure. Thus, Serer actors have also stripped down elements of Weberian bureaucracy (rights, equality *korom* [a Serer version of "quorum"], *keit,* and administrative hierarchy) and made them new features of Serer values, habits, and informal rules.

Field Suspension

Intended or not, the rural council practice of "suspending" the use of disputed fields before the rainy season blends legal principles of the National Domain Law with practices and expectations associated with the old masters of fire. If a land conflict remains unresolved by the time that clearing in preparation for the growing season usually gets under way (April to May in most locales), rural councils may suspend use of the contested fields, meaning that neither litigant will farm the disputed space that year. The field reverts to the national domain, and the rural council, as proprietor of that national domain, retains the power to temporarily grant the field to a third party to avoid wasting productive land.

In the years just prior to the Rural Council Law, the combination of population pressure, land scarcity, and a decline in the effective authority of *lamans* made the time before the rainy season a period of considerable potential conflict. As Hamad Faye, a staunch supporter of the National Domain Law (under which he successfully gained choice fields from a neighbor), puts it, "In the time of Kumba Ndofene Diouf [most celebrated of the last *maads*], people killed each other over these kinds of issues. Now people don't fight each other; people are not killed."[18]

Even a *laman,* whose interests generally are not served by the National Domain Law, confirms that considerable violence over fields accompanied the years after independence: "If it had not been for the National Domain Law, there would have been a lot of killing, because there are just too many people and not enough space for farming."[19]

However, field suspension was more than just another nice idea on paper, because it made sense in terms of a general Serer unwillingness to jeopardize subsistence crop production. In many of the land disputes examined in this study, uprooting or in any way threatening millet plants consistently meets with resistance bordering on moral revulsion. Hamad Faye captures the essence of this reticence to uproot the staple crop: "No peasant ever accepts someone who comes along and draws a boundary in your field taking away millet that you've already planted. Even if the elders had asked me to cede the land before the planting, it may have been possible, but when someone's already cultivated, you can't expect them to cede; . . . you would never give up even one single stalk of millet."[20]

Field suspension has become the expected norm when tensions extend into the spring land-clearing time. Ibou Sow, a Tukolor farmer in the largely Serer village of Ngarjam, accused both informal elders and rural council officials of discriminating against him as a Tukolor in his boundary conflict with Ndeba Sene, descendant of the local *yal bakh*. Sow is convinced he will not receive justice from the Serer authorities. But once the spring came, and the boundary remained where Sene would put it, Sow, like so many others in his position at this time of year, put the conflict aside for the growing season: "I do not agree with this result, but I will wait until next year. I must wait until after the harvest to bring it up again, . . . otherwise what will we eat?"[21]

Similar, although sporadic, illustrations of syncretism occur in the work of all of the authorities that constitute the rural council system. In an extremely heated conflict between two brothers in the village of Puday *(Aliou Faye v. Modou Faye)*, for example, the agent of the Water and Forests Service turned his usual role inside out.

Trees and "Environmental Logic"

Water and Forests Service agents are tree and pond specialists, agents of a classic Weberian, functionally specialized organization (as evident in the discussion of the *Puday Pond Conflict,* below). Nevertheless, in *Aliou Faye v. Modou Faye,* the local Water and Forests Service agent played the role of a *holistic* authority, intervening in a fashion reminiscent of a master of fire not just in the matter of a disputed palm tree but also in the deeper disintegration of the household itself.

In this dispute, two brothers who share the same father but different mothers came into conflict over trees, fields, and even the physical arrangement of the household in the years after their father became debilitated by a degenerative illness. As the father's authority as *yal mbind* (household master) declined, the two brothers vied for control. Their resource conflicts seemed to mask a deeper struggle over whose mother would inherit senior status once the father was gone. Their struggles burst out at every seam of potential conflict in the society, at what Lloyd Fallers would call the "trouble spots in the law."[22]

Among many other issues, the brothers Aliou and Modou Faye disputed the use of a palm tree situated just outside the compound. When their father was still well, he managed access to the palm leaves (used for making hut roofs, among other things), allowing each brother more or less equal use of the limited number of leaves. As the father became debilitated, the brothers fought over control of the field in which the tree was located. The rural council had stepped in a few years before, dividing the fields between the brothers in a manner that the elder brother, Modou, found unacceptable, but which did give Modou control of the field with the palm tree. He grumbles about this arrangement: "I was not in agreement with the division that the rural council did. Aliou is responsible for all of this, bringing in the rural council. I was obliged to accept what he did; there was nothing else I could do, but he [Aliou] insisted that he should still have access to the palm leaves."[23]

A few years later, Modou would not let Aliou cut leaves from the tree. He insisted that Aliou was not cutting these for his own use but intended to give the leaves to a relative of his mother's who did not live in their compound.[24] Aliou denied this accusation. They fought. Aliou claimed that Modou threatened to kill him.

Since they were at each others' throats over a tree (or at least the tree, the immediate catalyst for this demi-fratricidal outburst, appeared to the state authorities to be the nub of the conflict), the rural council president asked the local Water and Forests Service agent to deal with the matter. Given the nature of his dossier, he could have easily told Modou that he should let Aliou use the tree. He could have determined the truth of the accusation about giving the palm fronds to a maternal relative and issued a judgment on the acceptability of that practice. This would have been in keeping with the usual pattern of intervention in "tree matters."[25]

Unlike the representatives of the rural council, who simply told the men which fields they could farm, the Water and Forests Service agent set up a kind of provisional authority resembling that of a *yal mbind* when he declared that Modou, as the older brother, should serve as the *yal ndaxar*, or "master of the tree."[26] He should decide who would gain access to the tree and who would not. But he should behave the way a *yal mbind* ideally would behave—he should ensure unfettered access for all members of the household—especially his brother Aliou—who needed palm leaves.[27] In this sense the Water and Forests Service agent went well beyond his formal responsibilities as technocratic agent of the state. To truly deal with the tree issue, he effectively reconstructed a facsimile of *yal mbind* authority to create a viable tree-management regime within the household and prevent recurrence of conflict.

In the years after the Water and Forests Service agent's intervention in the palm leaf problem, Modou and Aliou fought over fields and over the positioning of a new granary around the household. Yet the tree problem did not resurface. By violating the very essence of his organization, functional specificity and procedural narrowing, by acting like a more *syncretic* authority, more in the vein of the old *laman*, the Water and Forests Service agent succeeded in patching together an arrangement that made conflict over the palm leaves less chronic.

In a sense, the Water and Forests Service agent took a more "ecological" approach to a resource management problem. Instead of just considering the palm tree, the availability of leaves, or the various uses to which they might be put, he looked at the wider context in which the tree was situated, the "ecology" or "environment" in the largest sense. The irony is that this kind of environmental approach, so celebrated in resource management circles, essentially promotes a retrogression in the typical Weberian understanding of the functioning of a modern bureaucracy: there is an element, not altogether explicit, of neotraditionalism in this ecological approach to resource management.[28] Narrow proceduralism must give way to a wider appreciation for the physical, social, and even cultural context, as well as to efforts to link natural resource interventions to resolution of deeper contextual problems. The double irony in this case is that the Water and Forests Service agent went beyond the palm leaves to rebuild the authority structure of the *yal mbind* without any self-consciousness about "ecological" approaches to resource management or neotraditionalism. Ironically, the Serer rural council president behaved like a classic Weberian bureaucrat. Yet the tree specialist, a Wolof from outside the Siin, behaved in a syncretic fashion, like a *laman*, in a spontaneous reaction to the circumstances with which he was confronted, a classic example of "*bricolage* from below."[29]

Incorporating Cosaan

In limited ways, rural council land management has been made to work with and support, rather than sidestep or demolish, Serer values, habits, and informal rules regarding adjudication and resource allocation. This incorporation of *cosaan* is evident in the reliance on elders, deference to customary legal principles, and a procedural emphasis on "witnessing."[30]

First, the rural councils have very clearly abandoned the notion that they are the court of first instance or the sole arbiters of land conflict. There are simply too many such conflicts. Rural councilors would be overwhelmed if they tried to deal with all of them. Instead, they rely regularly on elders and notables of the neighborhoods of the interested parties. As we have seen, "elder" is a euphemistic category that includes land tenure authorities that existed before the National Domain Law—*lamans* and *yal bakhs*. Rural councilors rely on these former officials because they tend to be a good deal more knowledgeable about historic field boundaries, the lines of conflict, and relationships of exchange between lineages. Moreover, rural councilors understand that litigants are far more likely to abide by decisions arrived at "among friends," within "the family," and especially, "with the help of the elder."

Second, as the rural councilor Cheikh Sene of the village of Ngangarlam points out, officials see their role as explicitly syncretic, because they must arrive at decisions that "balance two laws": "When we deal with a situation like this one *[Thimndane Gning v. Pierre Ngom]*, we need to try to take into account the law of the National Domain and the law of *cosaan*."[31] Sene and other rural councilors explain that if they try to simply apply the principles of the National Domain Law without balancing in the elements of the law of *cosaan*, the result would be violence and chronic disputes. By explicitly combining the legal principles they use to make their decisions, they seek to arrive at judgments that will not require calling in the gendarmerie. Given the extremely limited resources of the Senegalese state, let alone the paucity of crumbs that work their way down to the *communautés rurales*, the councilors really have no other choice but to undertake this kind of bricolage.[32]

This reliance on the law of *cosaan* even manifests itself in discussions about the training of rural councilors. Some rural council officials argue that their colleagues are untrained and unqualified to hold office not because they do not understand the National Domain Law but because they fail to uphold principles of the law of *cosaan:* "The problem is this: the rural councilors are chosen by election. There is no seminar to train them. . . . The main problem is their lack of training—for example, you have people seizing fields after they've taken the field in loan for two or three years. That is not normal."[33]

State law very clearly allows rural councils to seize fields that have been loaned for two years. But this *was* a serious violation of norms under the old law of *cosaan*. There may be a lack of training here, but if so, it is not a lack of training in the actual principles and procedures of the Rural Council–National Domain system. Rather it is lack of training in the syncretic principles and norms of what the rural council system could become, a system that Serer peasants have tried to refashion to conform to their own distinctly syncretic notions of what is "normal."

Finally, the centrality of personal witnesses in rural council procedure reflects a shift towards Serer *cosaan* norms. In popular Serer notions of fair adjudication, the presence or absence of witnesses is usually enough to establish the validity of a claim. We see this in *Sitor Cama v. Modou Sow*, a struggle by Cama to force Sow to keep his promise to return a field that Cama's grandfather had pawned to Sow's relative some two generations earlier. Sitor Cama insists there is really no ambiguity in the case at all: "I had witnesses there who saw and heard that Modou Sow said he would give me the field once Siou [a relative using the field 'temporarily'] moves away. The witnesses were there, and they will speak for me."[34]

Witnesses who will speak on one's behalf were also all that Pierre Ngom seemed to need to strengthen the credibility of his argument over field inheritance with his uncle Thimndane Gning: "If Thimndane Gning tries to touch those fields using the National Domain Law, well, there are many witnesses in the village who have heard the truth about this, and some of the witnesses are my relatives too."[35]

Pierre Ngom reveals the degree to which witnessing and testimony are linked to public oration in a community of people woven together by familial relations. A witness who is also a relative is *more useful* for Pierre Ngom than an "objective" external observer. An outside observer with greater objectivity is unreliable and has no basis for providing testimony. Individuals frequently express this preference for witnesses who are also relatives, for what would seem to be inherently biased sources from a Weberian legal-rational and impersonal point of view.

Rural councilors generally take into account this preference for personal oral testimony as the highest form of evidence. For example, when asked whether he felt that his intervention in *Thimndane Gning v. Pierre Ngom* would hold, the rural councilor Antoine Ndour replied by describing the most important parts of his adjudicatory intervention: "I do hope they will stick by the decision. I think they will. There were, you know, a lot of relatives present when we all talked together at the end. I made sure they all came. The relatives heard what was said, and they agreed with what I said. They witnessed the arrangement that we made."[36]

In his informal review of his procedures and operations in a specific case, this state official says nothing about the National Domain Law or rural council deliberations or the legal principles involved in inheritance and guardianship matters (issues at stake in *Thimndane Gning v. Pierre Ngom*). Rather, he focuses on what he considers crucial: family members were present, they consented, and they acted as witnesses.

Kin Representation and Moral Familism

Making rural councils syncretic has meant, in the eyes of most Serer people, making them function according to the personalistic norms and informal rules of the habitus associated with the old masters of fire. It is as if the Serer are struggling to reconcile tensions between what the literature has long construed as competing "role behaviors"—acting as kinsman versus acting as elected representative or other public official.[37]

For example, when Diame Sene got into an inheritance dispute, he did not file a formal complaint with the rural council as the law envisioned. He instead went to the home of a maternal uncle, Diogoye Faye, who himself happened to be a rural councilor, to get advice on how to deal with the matter. Diogoye Faye helped Diame win his claim not because this is how, while adhering to principles of bureaucratic impersonalism, Faye would treat anyone from the village who had land troubles. Faye intervened, of course, because Diame is his *ndokor*, his matrilineal nephew.[38]

When we dismiss Faye's behavior as nepotism, we implicitly expect that representative and bureaucratic structures like the rural councils would work "right" if only incumbents did not "contaminate" their duties as representatives and bureaucrats with their interests as kinfolk. But Serer farmers have been reinterpreting the office of rural councilor not so much as a position held by an official who acts according to the interests, norms, and procedures of the state but as a position for the representative-bureaucrat *as* kinsman, a relative who happens to have a place of power in the state apparatus, and who, although somewhat constrained by his presence in such an institution, can be expected to continue to behave as a relative. This is clear in the remarks of Gorgui Sene, a rural councilor in the Njafaj region, who is well aware of his status both as a representative-bureaucrat and a kinsman: "I am a rural councilor, but when there's a problem in the village, I prefer to deal with it as a traditional authority, not as a rural councilor. This is because people prefer that problems should be solved in a friendly way and that both sides should be satisfied."[39]

In spite of the fact Sene *is* the administrative authority, he sees no disjunction in playing the role of "elder" and prominent relative as he resolves a particular land dispute: "I asked everyone if they were happy with the arrangement and they all said yes. I did not make the division as a rural councilor, but as an elder of the family."[40] Serer litigants expect this role fusion. For example, in describing why the rural council president should step into his dispute, Cheikh Gakou does not refer to the objectivity, fairness, or democratic representativeness of the rural council president. Rather, he argues: "Yes, it is true that the rural council presidents have a role to play in problems like mine. Dokor [first name of the president] is in a good position to solve the problem, because of the lines of relatedness between himself and us—he is a relative, you know."[41]

It's really not clear on further inquiry *how* the rural council president, Dokor Ndour, is exactly related to Cheikh Gakou and Ndeba Gakou, the parties to the conflict.[42] Regardless of the *literal reality* of blood or marital relationship between the rural council president and Cheikh Gakou, Dokor Ndour is *perceived and categorized as a relative*, as someone who can be counted on to behave as befits a relative in a position of political authority. This nonspecific, possibly metaphorical relatedness is central to the success of the syncretic blending of elder-representative/bureaucrat that Serer farmers have tried to create.

Conversely, when a litigant feels no sense of kinship with an official like the rural council president, as is the case for Koly Diagne, one of the litigants in the Ndokh-Njujuf conflict, things change rather drastically: "I would not cede for the rural council president. . . . He doesn't live in the same house as me; *he may not even be a relative of mine.*"[43] If there's even some chance that the rural council president is not a relative, then it would be incomprehensible to cede when he asks. By implication, if he were *unequivocally not* a relative, the rural council president would have no legitimate claim whatsoever to ask farmers like Diagne to cede disputed land, to make a voluntary economic sacrifice.

In effect we see a system of "kin representation" in the making. Elected rural councilors do not serve a body of undifferentiated, equal-in-rights individual constituents. Rather, they function more like "corporatist delegates," the agents of the set of kin groups, lineages, and extended family networks who can credibly claim relatedness to them as elected representatives. At one level, of course, this seems strikingly unfair: those who have no relative in a rural council office are effectively shut out from democratic representation. In a society still stratified along endogamous caste lines, this may serve to disenfranchise entire categories of people who have no real relations of blood or marriage to political elites.

There are, however, very limited resources available to resocialize elected officials. In an ideal process of legal-rational, liberal state building, elected representatives would face sanctions for failing to represent all their individual, legally equal constituents. The infrastructural and normative transformations required to make those sanctions work in places like Senegal's Siin region have been discussed, promoted, financed, studied, and in their utter failure, lamented for as long as development has been on anyone's agenda. The fact is that the resources do not now exist (nor are they soon likely to be injected from the outside or accumulated from within by an altruistic developmental state or private entrepreneurial elite) to create a system of incentives for abandoning family, clan, regional, and ethno-linguistic loyalties in favor of proceduralism and impersonalism in representation and bureaucratic performance. Accepting that one lacks the means to promote such change via coercion, state building may be better served by making public-office holding and electoral representation work in accordance with the existing flow of political legitimacy in a society.

Kin representation is legitimate in the Siin. It is a local warp in the woof of the rural councils as syncretic structures. To make it more inclusive, to make it better approximate "universal" representation, one has to stay within the inner logic of this normative and institutional arrangement by making the boundaries of the concept of "kin" more fluid, by building on the usefulness of metaphorical, but perceived-meaningful, kinship relations.

Before I go on to briefly develop the idea of kin representation, it is important to point out that this disjunction between universalistic institutional ideals and particularistic practice is not unique to nepotistic bureaucrats in developing countries. Illustrations of this same disjunction exist in other parts of the world, where formal voting and representational, procedural, and civil rights are in practice inaccessible for certain categories of persons. Impersonalism and universalism are, for example, the very fabric of the U.S. constitutional order, yet we find particularism woven in from the very start in Article I's designation of African slaves as "three-fifths" of a person. Impersonalism and inherent rights are universal to all the people, as long as we agree on who "the people" are.

In much the same sense, the syncretic version of the rural councils I am describing here aspires to formal universalistic standards, but starts by proscribing the totalistic, ideal scope of the universal: one's nephew comes first. Once one has done everything possible for him, then one can try to apply the rules in a fair way to everyone else. This might seem to be an apologetic for discrimination and injustice: once all the claims of nephews have been addressed, there may not be much left for those who are not the nephew of somebody—no land left, or only the poorest plots with terrible soil or regular inundation.

Following the logic of syncretism, the most effective way to resolve this tension is *not* to "enforce the (liberal Western) rules," nor is it a wholesale transformation of values, habits, and informal rules. Rather, syncretism suggests that we seek a creative solution within the syncretic logic of local cultural-institutional change. A functional equivalent of impersonal, procedural fairness within the logic of a nonliberal cultural frame might be found by stretching the boundary and meaning of kinship itself.

In the liberal-individualistic sociocultural frame of the West, the challenge has been to truly universalize the concept of "the people," such that the propertyless, women, non-Europeans—once defined as children and incomplete or incompetent persons—can be recognized as juridically equal people. In a nonliberal context such as Serer society, the trick is not to reconceptualize everyone as homogenous individuals. Rather, the locally embedded solution may come within the idiom of familism and metaphorical relatedness by extrapolating the notion of kinship to the point that kin ties are so ubiquitous and interconnective that they establish universal or near universal inclusion.

We find that metaphors of kinship have been extended in Senegal to incorporate once heterogeneous ethnolinguistic and cultural groups. We see this in the popular-culture version of Cheikh Anta Diop's notions that Wolof, Serer, Tukolor, and other major Senegalese ethnic groups are in fact related as cousins, common descendants of the people (the rulers, to be precise) of Pharaonic Egypt.[44] The trickle-down influence of Diop's somewhat fanciful theories yields a sense of relatedness between ethnic groups that had once been in conflict (Wolof and Serer, for example). What the Serer call *ma sir,* "joking kinships," relations of ludic, perfunctory mutual insult that bind clans and ethnic groups as "joking cousins," seem to provide a cathartic mechanism for venting residual tension between rivals.[45] As a result, the northern part of Senegal, united by an intricate web of joking relations and pseudo-academic theories of common origin in a great civilization, exhibits low levels of interethnic conflict and a palpable sense of a relatively homogenous Senegalese national political community grounded in metaphorical kinship (we are all at least joking cousins, or we are all at least cousins descended from a common Egyptian civilization). In Senegal, the "scaling up" that sometimes accompanies ethnic reorganization has produced new imaginations of social relationships that posit new forms of relatedness among peoples who may not necessarily have anything to do with each other in terms of bloodlines or genealogical trees.[46]

We can treat the familist ethos of both the syncretic rural council and of extended metaphorical kinship not as a tribalist pathology but rather as a potentially useful (not to mention tangible and quite legitimate) social resource. The internal logic of this familism is not a logic of immorality, of personalistic greed and accumulation, of selling privileges of office to the highest bidder. Rather, it is a logic constrained by its own sense of appropriate behavior that places great emphasis on family, kinship, and the responsibilities of being a good son, daughter, or uncle. The wider the concept of relatedness stretches, the more closely the system achieves a goal of universalistic, reasonably fair access by drawing on cultural resources and notions of legitimacy that already operate within the society itself.

Familism is a potentially useful tool for building a socially embedded, nonliberal form of universalism. Unlike other social bases for exclusion (race in the United States comes to mind), kin relatedness can be conceived in metaphorical, negotiable, and malleable terms, as opposed to the quasi-genetic, ascriptive, unchangeable nature of many socially constructed notions of race. As long as the fluidity captured in *ma sir* relations and Diop's Egyptian stories establishes a meaningful new category of quasi kin, and as long as officeholders see it as their duty to "represent" all their kin and quasi kin, then familism can be a tool in the perfection of imperfect universalism. Ferreting the particularism (be it racial exclusion or nepotistic discrimination) out of universalistic institutions may indeed be a Sisyphean task. But the syncretic transformation of Serer rural councils underscores that widening the scope of inclusion and equal treatment will prove more successful if undertaken *from within* already existing and legitimate social and moral frameworks.

"Westernization" of Serer Culture and Practices

Syncretism entails transformation of *both* the newly imposed administrative hierarchies and formal rules of the rural councils, as well as the informal rules, habits, and values associated with Serer culture and customary law. Notions of rights and equality, as well as the bureaucratic procedures associated with *korom* and *keit*, reveal that institutional elements derived from the rural council structure have been incorporated into Serer culture by turning these elements into "naked objects," clusters of rules or relations shorn of their original sociocultural meaning and embeddedness.

Rights and Equality Made Serer.   Ideas about inherent rights have been pulled out of their Western-liberal social structural context and grafted into the matrix of social relations and values of the Siin. Serer youths, for example, proclaim a "right" to land or a "right" to feed their families. Many litigants invoke the discourse of rights to bolster their claims to space for subsistence farming. For example, the village chief of Ndokh posits a very common notion that the state and the law exist to protect a community's "right" to enough land for millet and cattle. He asserts, "We from Ndokh will do the absolute maximum possible to keep this space for our animals. We will go as far as we can, even all the way to Dakar, to assert our 'rights' to have a place to keep our beasts."[47] Neither the National Domain Law nor the Rural Council Law envisions any kind of right for a herder to have room to keep his beasts. Yet rights are so clearly the currency of relations with the colonial and postcolonial states that they have been transposed onto matters of the greatest social importance in Serer communities—subsistence farming and cattle.

The litigant Roger Sene fuses this sense of rights and tradition, indeed, rights to subsistence as an integral part of tradition, in rejecting the possibility that the state might ask him and his allies to give up their claim: "It is impossible that the state would ask us to cede—that cannot arrive, that cannot exist, because it is their duty to uphold our claim in this case, to uphold our rights when we demand that tradition be maintained in our access to pasture for our cattle."[48]

The idea of "rights" even finds its way into relations with the *pangool* (ancestral spirits) in a conflict between Dokor Diouf and his cousin Niokhor Dieng. As in most disputes, there are rumors that the litigants have sought the intervention of *pangool* spirits to ensure victory in the conflict or to harm their opponent. Diouf is a prominent figure of a spiritually powerful lineage in the community of the *laman*, and Dieng lives in a subordinate community. Diouf responds to the possibility that Dieng might have turned to the *pangool* for intercession: "Even if the *pangool* of Ndokh over there have some strength, Niokhor Dieng's request will not hold because he is not in the right. Because he never gave any money for the field, he should not get it back; he has no rights in this matter."[49]

Diouf could very easily assert that his requests to the *pangool* are much more likely to meet with favorable response than those of someone like Dieng for essentially ascriptive reasons (Diouf is a much closer "relative" of these *pangool* than Dieng). Yet he fuses the intervention of the *pangool* with the discourse of being " in the right" and "having rights," suggesting that the *pangool* base their intervention on some kind of determination of rights. Given that Diouf is already clearly the dominant player at the supernatural and status levels, this may be a way of coopting the only ground upon which Dieng might have a basis for his claim. Even so, it illustrates the tendency to integrate "Enlightenment rights" into basic elements of Serer cultural values.

We're not dealing with a "Serer liberalism" here, because the discourse of rights has been imported as a "naked" cultural-institutional object. The normative frameworks (or entailments) in which the rights discourse was embedded in Europe (social individuation and state-society relations as contracting among autonomous individuals) have been deliberately discarded to make possible the syncretic incorporation of "rights" in the normative-institutional framework of Serer society. While the sociological emphasis on the individual is completely lacking in this manifestation of rights in the Siin, we do find an incorporation of a "rights" discourse as a new warp in the woof of both subsistence claims and even relationships with ancestral spirits.

Ideals of "universal equality" are closely related to notions of inherent rights and follow this same pattern of syncretism via objectification. At one level, this new emphasis on universal equality dovetails with what Jean-Marc Gastellu refers to as the "traditional economic egalitarianism of the Serer."[50] As a vector for quasi-socialist, Enlightenment notions of equality, the National Domain Law emphasizes a static division of land in which every individual producer has, to the greatest degree possible, the same amount of land to farm as every other. In contrast, the *lamanic* Serer notion of economic egalitarianism was more closely rooted to a flexible allocation by lineage based on the changing needs of these corporate groups. In a demonstration of syncretism, both of these principles of equality now circulate. Cheikh Thiao exemplifies the familiar emphasis on actual needs when asked to respond to the redistributive goals of the National Domain Law: "You could say that it was intended to take away from some and give to others, . . . but my household isn't any better off than Malale Dione's in terms of land. We have pretty similar needs."[51] "Substantive equality based on need" is becoming a *perceived* principle of the rural council system, even though it was not designed to accommodate that idea of equality.

Notions of universal human equality have worked their way into the Siin from many directions (state-sponsored cultural transformation, formal education, French assimilation, liberation associated with the end of the Gelwaar kingdom of the *maad*). But Islamic religious universalism figures very prominently in the Serer appropriation via objectification of ideals of equality.[52]

Respondent Babacar Faye suggests the centrality of an Islamic cosmological narrative in the leveling of formerly inegalitarian caste and ethnic group relations: "It's true that things have changed, because now there are Fulanis who have become subprefects, there are blacksmiths who have become subprefects, and more even. But you know, in the colonial days, a good lineage really counted for something. There was one power, and there were the strong and the weak, even though we all do come from Adama and Awa [Adam and Eve]—Jola, Tukolor, Koroborop, Bambara, Toussaim, Serer, Toubab [Europeans], we are all descendants of Adama and Awa."[53]

On the one hand, this respondent insists that the old divisions based on caste and "good lineage" should still be important. On the other hand, he brings in the alternative leveling discourse of Islam, which suggests that caste, culture, lineage, and even race do not matter, since we are all members of the same universal human family.

Rereading Islamic religious universalism in a Serer way has depended on the successful incorporation of prominent icons of egalitarian universalism. For example, in a typical syncretic formulation, even the prophet Mohammed can be evoked to ensure good harvests in the Siin: "Now, we are in peace, and we thank God for all that he has done for us. Let God save us from evil, from the devil, and guide us toward the proper path. Let God continue to show us his mercy. Let the rainy season finish with good rains, as we all hope, and let God and Mohammed ensure our good harvests."[54] This benediction, which came spontaneously at the conclusion of an oral history interview, reflects a tendency of the Serer, along with many other peoples, Muslim and not, to draw new authority figures into local cosmology, a central concern of which is subsistence. In this fusion, the Prophet of God becomes another *pangool*, another spiritual force to which one can eclectically appeal to make sure the rains are good and the millet tall. We can say Mohammed has been "objectified" for syncretic purposes, because here he is invoked for localist objectives without concern or anxiety over restrictions on the use of his name or other religious institutional demands associated in less syncretic parts of the world with Islamic affiliation.[55]

Korom, Keit, and the *Voie Hierarchique.* Although training for rural councilors covers many other topics (procedures for voting, keeping records, rudimentary principles of the National Domain Law, special circumstances and methods for applying the law), very few of these elements of rural council training seem to be remembered, and none holds the position of prominence of the concept of *korom*.[56] When asked about the basic procedures to which rural councilors must adhere, rural councilor Doudou Ngued begins right away with *korom:* "For example, we know that we need to have a *korom*, that a majority of the members need to be present before we can begin to conduct any business, and that the majority makes decisions; and that goes in the *procés verbal* [official record of the judgment in French-style legal systems]. The subprefect and the rural council president must be present in order to have a *korom*."[57]

Likewise, rural councilor Antoine Ndour focuses on this same concept as the central element of rural council procedure: "In order for the rural council to discuss a matter that has to do with field disputes, we need to have a *korom* of the elected members."[58] *Korom* is a formalized element of "modern" institutional bureaucracy that dovetails extremely well with existing emphases in the Serer law of *cosaan* on publicness, oration, testimony, and witnessing in decision making. Something very much like *korom* has long been an element of what most Serer now remember as the "traditional" decision making mode—the council meeting in which the entire community gathers together under the supervision of elders. Such a meeting necessarily involves the entire community, all the parties concerned, everyone brought together. The notion that there is a modern institutional rule that in essence demands that meetings cannot be held unless everyone is present fits nicely with an underlying cultural emphasis on gathering the community together for the sake of orating, listening, and consensual decision making.

Korom illustrates how selected elements of rural council proceduralism are syncretically blended with Serer notions of *cosaan* and thereby become critical elements of the de facto, informal customs of officeholding. Similar dynamics occur with regard to written documents, which still carry a special type of mystique bordering on fear for many of those interviewed in this study.

Written documents, especially those associated with the state, can still evoke mistrust and anxiety. This was true even in the interviews I conducted: smooth and easy conversations often stiffened as soon as I took my pen and notebook "recording technology" out of my bag. The notebook, pencil, and pen themselves have long been the tools of census takers, military recruiters, and tax collectors. To the non- or semiliterate majority in these communities, these associations with outsiders engaged in processes of coercive extraction remain quite strong.

Broadening the historical lens somewhat, Islam, with its emphasis on the written word and the Arabic language as conveyors of divine blessing and insight, has long suggested in the Sahel a very different set of associations with the technology of literacy. Following this link, Arabic of course gives the Serer their term for paper and for the relations, practices, and concerns associated with paperwork and officialdom in general: *keit*. In the Siin, administration, extraction, regulation, provision of services, and surveying all fall into the broad ontological category of "matters of *keit*." Matters of *keit* thus usually invoke stereotypical patterns of fear and mistrust. For example, Pierre Ngom, embroiled in a land pawning dispute with some neighbors, indicates that he "takes the word of his neighbor and of the rural council president" as his promise that his field given in pawn will not be nationalized. He reports that "he has no written paper," because to have asked for one would have implied distrust on his part, would have indicated that either he himself, his neighbor, or the rural council president might have "been dealing unfairly" in the land problem.[59] As one rural councilor puts it, in clarifying his preference that disputes be resolved without the use of paper: "Because papers and documents and officials stamps, all those matters of *keit*—that is all the *maad* [precolonial, reviled king] being involved."[60]

As with *korom* and *keit*, Serer respondents have also seized the administrative *voie hierarchique* (administrative ladder or hierarchy) as a useful and culturally incorporable element of state machinery. Serer peasants generally understand that, if they are not satisfied with a rural council land decision, they can take the matter before the subprefect for review. Litigants know about this appeals structure, often referring to it as the *voie hierarchique*, the hierarchical path or administrative ladder, which peasants who are otherwise bureaucratically unschooled show great versatility in manipulating to their advantage. Says Bouré Fall, "In the past, you could end up with all sorts of corruption in a situation like this. Now, if you don't like what an official tells you, all you need to do is go above him, as I did. In the past, we had to live with what the canton chief decided, but now we can go above him, we can use the *voie hierarchique* to help us."[61] This respondent is a farmer with little literacy, fighting against the local schoolmaster, a man of considerable education and an administrative official. Yet Bouré Fall is not intimidated, because he has the *voie hierarchique* on his side, a tool he can use to promote his concrete interests.

These elements of legal rational bureaucratic practice and procedure—*korom, keit, voie hierarchique*—have been incorporated into, and thereby have transformed, Serer economic and political culture. To incorporate these new elements into Serer culture, they have been made into discrete objects, things that one can hold, observe, and categorize at a distance. One "has the *voie hierarchique*" on one's side. One must make a *korom*. Asking for a *keit* can be a rupture in relations; holding onto a *keit* can be a form of self-protection. Serer officials and litigants have found a way to strip down specific procedures and forms into discrete objects and tools that they can incorporate into their repertoire of modes of relating to power, coping with subordination, and every once in a while, resisting domination.

This objectification is clearly a central mechanism through which syncretism takes place. Hoping, as the early modernization theorists did, that newly imposed resource management and electoral institutions would "spread" their original organizational logic and normative framework throughout society is a pipe dream. Existing local cultural frameworks and institutional infrastructure will alter their ongoing logics of transformation to accommodate and adapt the vectors of modernity. New institutions

must be made to work within and not against this dynamic of local transformation. Syncretic incorporation via objectification may be part of the
solution, a mechanism by which functionally specific, seemingly traditional, but in fact hybrid institutions might emerge. This was happening,
in the early years, to the rural councils. We can still recognize marginal
vestiges of this process, in spite of the fact that the state took steps to prevent meaningful syncretic transformation of elected local government.

THE REALITY: THE STATE IS NOT THE MASTER OF FIRE

The democratic promise of the rural council system was, by design or not,
much more than elections and the legitimacy of mechanical representation. It held open the door for the takeover of low-level state offices by
ordinary Serer agriculturists who might carry into office their distinctive
worldview and transform the rural council system to make sense within
Serer historical memories and cultural expectations.

The Serer have tried to walk through that door. They have tried to
make the rural council system into neo-*lamans* and in fact have enjoyed
some success on the margins (evident in field suspension, environmental logic, *cosaan*-like procedures, kin representation, and the objectification of *korom*, *keit*, and the *voie hierarchique*). But then rural councilors
are tutored by the subprefects and prefects, reminded of their duty to
uphold the law, sternly rebuked as their judgments are revoked by their
administrative superiors, and warned that, as illiterate, untrained peasants, they should not deviate too far from a narrow interpretation of the
law and the functionally specific role they are to play in the overall
administrative framework.

Serer farmers know what is going on with the rural councils. They recognize the chain, they see when it is pulled from above, can feel when the
tenuous bonds of syncretism through which they have sought to transform the rural councils (and be *represented* by them) are sundered. In
those decisive moments, the rural councils lose their democratic credibility. They cease to represent and start to command. The idea that "the state
must be the master of fire" becomes a fantasy, masters of fire a revered
memory. Exposed, the rural councils become recognizable as agents of an
alien, conquering authority that does not know or care about Serer institutions, Serer beliefs, and Serer *cosaan*. Fourteenth-century conquest and
subjugation by a wandering Manding matrilineage (the Gelwaar), not to
mention the lessons Gelwaar kings, the *maads*, taught the Serer over six
centuries about the demands of centralized state building, remain a vivid

memory for the Serer. The rural councils have been recognized, reinterpreted and reworked within this trope. They are now the *maad baal,* the "dark king." And every Serer farmer knows, *o maad a gara—fop a yaqwa,* "the king has come—now everything is ruined."

Functional Specificity versus Syncretic Holism in the Rural Council System

The contrast between what the rural councils might have become— through syncretism—and their real position as agents in a functionally specific administrative hierarchy is especially clear when we compare rural council intervention in two particular land conflicts, *Village of Ndokh v. Njujuf Quarter* and the *Puday Pond Conflict.*

In *Ndokh v. Njujuf,* a case first described in chapter 5, state officials were faced with what they saw as an intractable (and stereotypical) conflict between herders and farmers competing to use the same space. The neighborhood of Njujuf (part of the ancient the village of Tukar) and the village of Ndokh (a recent colony set up by migrants from Njujuf) shared farming and pastureland under a land management scheme once directed by the *laman* of Njujuf. Before the 1972 Rural Council Law, the *laman* of Njujuf coordinated land use planning, assigning fields to individual farmers and setting aside pasture each year for common use. After the end of *lamanic* control, Ndokh and Njujuf *yal mbinds* met before the growing season to try to hammer out a *laman*-like arrangement for that year.[62]

But in 1990, a land conflict elsewhere in the territory of the former *laman* reduced Njujuf farmers' access to fertile farmland. The Njujuf farmers, who had access to pasture elsewhere, took their part of the well-fertilized Ndokh-Njujuf joint use area for millet planting and refused to set aside fields as common pasture.[63] The Ndokh farmers, who did not have the luxury of sending their cattle elsewhere for the rainy season, counted on the joint allocation of land with their relatives from Njujuf to pasture cattle. But by 1992, the Njujuf farmers had withdrawn so much land from joint use that the Ndokh cattle would suffer. The Ndokh faction complained to the Njujuf farmers that they should "respect the ways of our ancestors." The Njujuf farmers explained their loss of access to well-fertilized land elsewhere and their need for part of the Ndokh joint use area to grow enough millet to feed their families.

One day early in the planting period in 1992, a fight broke out between a farmer from Njujuf who had come to seed millet in a field where Ndokh herders were grazing their cattle. A crowd gathered and separated the combatants, who made violent threats and vows of revenge. Later that week, the state's agricultural resource management agent in the area, the CER chief, and several rural councilors used stakes to mark a network of paths cutting through the millet fields of Njujuf farmers, linking the tiny, scattered pasture spaces that belonged to the Ndokh herders so that their cattle could move freely between these micropasture plots and walk to nearby wells.[64] The arrangement was awkward, and no one was satisfied, but it held for that year.

The following year, 1993, the conflict became far more intense as the Njujuf farmers, responding to the fact of state intervention the previous year, refused to contribute any land to the joint pasture area. The CER chief made an even more haphazard staked-off path arrangement, which satisfied no one. Without the contribution of any Njujuf fields for pasture, there was simply not enough land to sustain the Ndokh livestock, regardless of the serpentine pathways laid out by the CER chief. After the CER official carefully cut the pathways a little wider, the farmers from Njujuf came out, took a look at their bisected fields, and tore out all the markers laid by the CER chief.

Four times that spring and early summer, the CER chief replanted the markers, and four times the farmers from Njujuf tore them out. The rains came, and the Njujuf farmers planted their millet across field and pathway. Accusations and threats flew back and forth between the two communities. Finally, the CER chief appeared again, a fifth time, to replace the boundary markers. This time he was accompanied by the rural council president, several rural councilors, and a force of some sixty gendarmes. They were expecting trouble, and it came in the form of a band of farmers from Njujuf armed with clubs, hoes, shovels, and a few axes. The outnumbered Ndokh contingent stood on their side of the joint land use area, rather less thoroughly armed. After the dust settled, the gendarmes had forcibly disarmed the Njujuf contingent, dragging five especially agitated individuals to the gendarmerie headquarters in Fatick, the regional capital, where they spent a few weeks in prison before being returned to Njujuf. When they got back, the growing season was well under way, and their comrades had capitulated in the struggle over the Ndokh joint use area—for that year.

Njujuf and Ndokh are intertwined by the physical geography of agricultural practice that grew out of a specific history of migration, territorial expansion, and collective land management. Although the state displaced the authority of the *lamans*, it did not create new institutions that could address the systemic problem here—that is, it did not balance the pasturing and agricultural needs of communities caught up in interlocking joint use systems. Instead, the state provides a series of functionally specific author-ities, each responsible for a different facet of land and resource manage-ment. The rural councils can grant clear title to individuals from Ndokh or Njujuf for land they have farmed (or set aside for fallow) for two years or more. The Water and Forests Service agent can tell them the best way to take care of and increase the number of *Acacia albidas* on those individu-ally held plots, and it might sometimes even be able to provide them with a few saplings. The CER chief, as demonstrated quite fully in the rainy sea-sons of 1992 and 1993, can thoroughly study the dynamics of pasture man-agement and develop the most rational routes linking fragmentary fallow microplots. But no one could tell the Ndokh faction what to do with their cattle if the Njujuf farmers insisted on using their fields for millet, and no one seemed to be able to tell the Njujuf group where they should plant their millet when they lost access to choice farmlands elsewhere.

State intervention in the *Ndokh v. Njujuf* conflict contrasts strikingly with adjudication of a similar land use conflict in the nearby village of Puday. Unlike *Ndokh v. Njujuf,* this conflict did not result in numerous visits by the CER chief, intimidation by the gendarmerie, or overnight stays in the prison in Fatick.

This case centers on the Ngahoye pond, just outside the village of Puday. In the dry season, Ngahoye is just a low-lying basin. In the rainy season, it becomes a full-fledged lake. In the course of almost a decade of poor rainfall, farmers with fields adjacent to Ngahoye gradually expanded their cultivated acreage into the pond itself. In 1993, rains were abundant. Ngahoye was full, brimming past the dry perimeter that had bounded it for many of the previous rainy seasons. But in June and July, before much rain had fallen and before it was apparent that the pond would fill, farm-ers around Ngahoye seeded millet well into the pond bed. As the pond filled, parts of their fields were inundated. By August, their rows of young millet extended right up to the water's edge. This physical arrange-ment left no access for livestock to reach the pond without trampling planted millet.

Many people in the village complained about the situation, mostly to the chief of the village, a man in his early sixties named Kory Gning. Gning asked farmers around the pond to cede the part of their fields clos-est to the water in order to create a ten-meter perimeter to give livestock access to the pond. This meant that the eight farmers who planted around the pond had to accept a considerable economic sacrifice that under normal circumstances would be unthinkable: give up land in which millet had already been planted.[65]

Gning met individually with the farmers and then held a community meeting, after which all eight farmers agreed to give up portions of their fields. Gning explains, "People had been coming to me pointing out that the pond was suffering. So I explained the problem to the farmers and everyone accepted what needed to be done. They all realize that they will lose a little bit, yes, but it's in the interests of everyone to expand the pond."[66]

Although this conflict had all the appearances of a classic farmer-herder dispute, and this was in fact how it appeared to the CER chief and the Water and Forests Service agent, farmers were not asked to give up millet for the sake of livestock. Rather, Gning argued that "we have to expand the pond because it belongs to our *pangool*." To most inhabitants of the village of Puday, the *pangool* of the founder's lineage and other ancestral spirits reside somewhere in among the trees at the center of the Ngahoye pond.

The village chief Gning suggested that the degradation of the pond, particularly expansion of adjacent fields, was having a negative effect on the *pangool* that lived there. The *pangool* were displeased with the condition of their pond, and this displeasure, according to Gning and others in the community, helped account for anemic rainfall for the better part of the last decade. Gning argued, "We [have] to expand the pond because it's always belonged to our *pangool*. This 'pushing' [expanding fields incrementally into the pond perimeter] has been a problem since the days of the colonials. But the *pangool*, you know, are for everyone. At the start of the rainy season, we make sacrifices there [in the Ngahoye pond] to ensure good rains. We also make sacrifices there if we're troubled by something. It's a very sacred place for us."[67]

Diaga Faye spoke for the eight farmers around the pond when he confirmed that the *pangool's* significance for the well-being of the community as a whole played an important part in his willingness to give up planted millet: "The pond has been there a very long time, since the days of our distant ancestors. When we came here, we found the pond here. We need to preserve it, we need to do this for the animals, yes, but also, maybe more importantly, for the *pangool*." Faye is particularly keen to point out that he did not give up the space because any adjudicatory or coercive authority asked him to do so. He yielded voluntarily because he saw a threat to a valued community resource: "It was not the presence of the president of the rural council or any authority that had anything to do with me giving up part of my field. It was instead that the people had seen and had judged that the rainy season's not working anymore, and therefore, we must maintain the pond. Maybe Roog will give us a chance to do this. I think it will help, and that Roog and the *pangool* will give us a good rainy season."[68]

A number of state officials had visited Puday in the course of this brewing conflict. They were ready to intercede, as they did in the Ndokh-Njujuf conflict, to carve out a space for cattle grazing and for access to the waters of the pond. But they were pleased to discover that the community had worked out its own arrangement without state intervention, without the use of coercive force. The contrast between the experience of the Puday community and the Ndokh-Njujuf conflict of the very same year was not lost on these officials. The CER chief himself brought up the two cases without solicitation, noting, "Puday is an example of how things should work. People recognized the limits, the borders of the pond. Everybody involved knew that they had overstepped the limits, and they arrived at an agreement without any trouble. Ndokh should have been like Puday."[69]

When asked to account for the difference between the conflict in Puday and the Ndokh-Njujuf conflict, which ended in violence and imprisonment, the CER chief argued, "In Puday, they gave up parts of their field because they all knew that they had encroached. They themselves showed us the boundaries of the fields; they were fully aware of where the boundary should have been. This problem in Puday, this was a problem that was handled in very good circumstances. It was quite different than Ndokh—there were not recalcitrants at Puday."[70]

Interestingly, however, neither the CER chief nor the Water and Forests Service agent was at all aware of the degree to which the Puday conflict had something to do with the community drawing on *pangool* symbolism to ask for voluntary economic sacrifices. Both of these officials had been assigned to the Siin for some time, yet their ignorance of this aspect of the Puday conflict was striking.[71] The CER chief, when asked about the importance of belief in *pangool* spirits in the resolution of the conflict, responded, "I had never heard of any *pangool* problem. In fact, I am not familiar with the term."[72]

Likewise, the Water and Forests Service agent saw this conflict neatly in terms of the functionally specific framework of his office: "I was called in because there was a problem of trees, and under the Forest Code this is the jurisdiction of the Water and Forests Service agent. The whole thing was essentially an environmental problem. There was even someone who had committed a felony for cutting a tree that he was not supposed to touch."[73] Yet when asked about the *pangool* dimension, he turned to another person present in the interview in search of clarification on what I was asking about. He then replied, "I was not aware of this side of it. This is the first time I've heard of it. I never even knew what a *pangool* was."[74]

State officials were completely unaware that in Puday a community leader had mobilized both parties to the conflict by invoking a holistic, locally meaningful explanation for why some should cede and others should gain, providing an acceptable, moral basis for making a voluntary economic sacrifice that the losers in the conflict apparently accepted. In the Ndokh-Njujuf conflict, no such reconstitution of a holistic land management framework ever emerged, and the conflict, not surprisingly, broke down into an intractable, ordinary calculation of raw instrumental material interests and an invocation of the coercive violence of the state.

Unaware of this contrast, state officials boiled the Ndokh-Njujuf and Puday conflicts down to issues of "character." This essentialist explanation, like all essentialist explanations, absolves people, especially political elites, of responsibility. If the Ndokh-Njujuf conflict had stemmed from some kind of innate characteristics of the "recalcitrants" who stirred up the conflict, then there really was nothing that the CER chief or the Water and Forests Service agent or the rural council could do to make things work out any differently. But the two conflicts in fact turned out very differently because of *a certain kind* of political intervention—the tapping of cultural memories of institutions for which a population is quite willing to make voluntary sacrifices. When political elites tap such a reservoir of legitimacy, the prospects for peaceful conflict resolution increase considerably.

As in the *Puday Pond Conflict*, institutions that can mobilize this legitimacy draw on institutional infrastructure—informal rules, habits, and norms (in the language of figure 1 in chapter 1)—to generate compliance with formal rules and the administrative structures that support them. Actors may choose to follow the rules and obey the institution in part because such cooperation is in their interest, but also because the holistic worldview to which they subscribe, manifested in values, habits, and informal rules, tells them it is moral to do so. Institutions that cannot draw support from infrastructure, as in the case of *Ndokh v. Njujuf*, depend either on the coercive power of administrative hierarchies or the utilitarian choice of actors to obey mere formal rules. The tragedy of the rural councils is that they were supposed to sink real roots in local institutional infrastructure, like Puday's village chief, Kory Gning. But instead, as in the Ndokh-Njujuf conflict case, they remain entirely formalist and superstructural, serving merely as title granters in a functionally specific bureaucracy.

The state was clearly wary of putting too much real adjudicatory, resource management, or revenue collection authority, in the hands of rural councils whose seats were filled by an electorate of mainly illiterate peasants choosing from a pool of candidates consisting of equally illiterate peasants. As a result, the 1972 law did not so much transform a system of rural administration established under colonialism as modify it slightly, leaving real local governmental power in the hands of the subprefect, an official appointed by bureaucrats in Dakar, removable only by bureaucrats in Dakar, and rather thoroughly insulated from the complaints or concerns of a local population. For a very brief time, the Rural Council Law spectacularly raised expectations that the institutional machinery of the state would be *given* to the Serer to freely rework in the image of their own historical memories and informal institutional legacies. The rural councils might let Serer peasants create neo-*lamans:* the state really would be the master of fire. Lack of real autonomy in land matters and incoherence of institutional design have rendered these supposedly responsive, proximate, substantively powerful authorities distant, alien, seemingly capricious, arbitrary, and lacking in real power with respect to their administrative superiors. *O maad a gara.* "The king has come."

INTERPRETIVE VILIFICATION: THE STATE IS THE DARK KING

This Is What We Call O Maad A Gara

> It is very dangerous for a *maad* to come here and try to deal with a problem. Because when the *maad* comes, he does whatever he wants, whatever pleases him. No one wants them, the *maads,* to come. Nobody wants to invite them into his home. We call this *o maad a gara* [the king has come]—it means that a line has been crossed, and things are no longer friendly at all. If someone calls someone else before the *maad,* that's it; it ruins everything.[75]

This sense of *o maad a gara* looms prominently in popular understanding of the rural councils in the contemporary Siin. The phrase has an axiomatic or iconographic quality: farmers understand that *o maad a gara* is a threshold in their relations. Once someone crosses the *o maad a gara* line, the breach is usually irreparable.

Consequently, we find a widespread tendency to avoid or limit blame for being the one to have committed the *o maad a gara* breach. For example, a witness to a land pawn between Latyr Farah Diouf and Hamad Ndong reveals the degree of sensitivity over "who went first":

> Latyr Farah Diouf went to see Dokor Ndour, the rural council president. Hamad Ndong thought that Latyr Farah went to see Dokor in order to make a complaint. But he didn't do that—he just went to get information.

But Hamad was angry, so he went to see Dokor himself, who then sent him to see the subprefect. It was the subprefect who stepped in at this point, and he gave the field to Hamad.[76]

At times, these machinations become almost comical, as litigants maneuver to demonstrate that their opponent set foot in the office of the rural council president first.[77]

The great irony in this squeamishness is that the officials of the rural council are not alien outsiders but are in fact members of the community. When asked, for example, if the term *maad* should apply simply to members of the territorial administration appointed in Dakar, most respondents agree with Ndeba Sene: "I mean the *maad*, the *buur* Siin, of course, and also the *jaraf* [village chief], the rural council president, the rural councilors."[78] When asked to clarify if this generalization would refer to a rural councilor who is also a relative of a litigant, Sene states, "Yes, even a rural councilor who is a relative is the *maad*."

In a variation on this theme of *o maad a gara* blame-shifting, Samba Faye, who won a field thanks to a rural council decision, finds himself in the unusual and enviable position of pointing out that it was his somewhat foolhardy opponent who first summoned the rural council. Faye does little to hide his delight at these circumstances—winning under state law without having to face the consequences of committing an act of *o maad a gara:* "Look, I didn't choose to go the rural council. I would have rather dealt with this problem by the intervention of the elders, *à l'amiable*, whatever. But I just got a summons. And, you know, the person who gets summoned doesn't have time to go around and call together the elders of the village. You just respond to the summons that was given to you."[79] Most winners under the rural council system don't have it as easy as Samba Faye. Instead it is not uncommon to find rural council winners like Cheikh Ndour, who tries to shift the blame for state intervention to impersonal social forces. Ndour argues that "it was the people of the neighborhood, not I, who called the rural council to arrange this problem."[80]

Others, like Latyr Farah Diouf, refuse to accept the "truth" that a relative or community member could have committed such a violation: "Maybe my cousin Hamad went to the authorities like that because he was encouraged by his uncle, Diomaye Sarr. Diomaye is a guy who has lived in Dakar a long time, and I think he's even part of the administration. Once Hamad had come under the influence of his uncle, well, maybe he was the one [Uncle Diomaye] who instigated this business with the *maad*."[81]

Respondents extend the *o maad a gara* logic to suggest that there would in fact be no reason to seek out the rural council system unless one were up to no good. We see this, for example, in the striking moral contrast between state and nonstate authority laid out by litigant Hamad Faye: "I've been through lots of problems, but I've never committed *tooñ* [blame, wrong, fault, error], so as to go to authorities.[82] I prefer that all I say be said with clarity and prudence, and that I avoid regretting what I say. God is master of all that is said and done, in any case."[83] Faye suggests here that being in the wrong, committing *tooñ*, is the reason that one goes to the authorities. The opposite of this degraded condition, a moral-religious virtue, is also rather revealing. Whereas going to the state is a matter of committing *tooñ*, what he prefers is a *God*-fearing clarity and honesty.

Orality and Being Heard

The rural councils are increasingly understood as being like the old *maad* in part because they so blatantly ignore, and at times explicitly violate, Serer norms with regard to adjudicatory procedure. One of the most important illustrations of this has to do with the state's obliviousness regarding "orality": speech making, discourse, being heard, and being listened to.

At one level, this desire to express oneself, to get to tell "one's own side of the story" in full, is characteristic of any subject people or anyone brought before a court, not just in rural Africa but in most societies.[84] The rural councils and related institutions thus seem arbitrary because they do not listen to people, do not provide the "proper" amount of time and space for litigants to say their piece. In this sense, Serer rejection is illustrative of the relationship between adjudicatory institutions and subordinate people in general.

But at another level, the Serer emphasis on orality and on being heard may reflect the discursive dynamics of a society grounded in oral tradition and relatively suspicious of writing technology. The technology of pen and paper, official written documents, even written religious texts, carry an element of alienness and menacing power for many Serer. In contrast, speech making, discursive mastery, storytelling, patience, listening until a speaker has said his *entire* piece (no matter how long-winded the speaker may be), are central to community relations and to the exercise of legitimate political authority in the Siin.[85]

Orality is of course a central component of the local understanding of respectful, procedurally correct adjudication. For example, Ibou Yatt, a litigant in *Ndokh v. Njujuf*, argues that "we must only have the opportunity to speak clearly before the rural council to get the problem solved in the right way."[86] Echoing this point, Hamad Faye, litigant in a different dispute, insists, "The officials should consult and ask the people involved.

They should gather information from them, and they should let everyone speak until they have said all that they want to say. Only then should they come in and divide things like this or that."[87] Presenting oneself through speech thus represents a central, perhaps the most important, mode of relating to power in Serer society. For example, in *Village of Sob v. Village of Diokul*, Ngor Mbede Dieng was on the losing side of a dispute between neighboring villages, adjudicated by the rural council president and the subprefect. Although Dieng disagrees with what the state officials decided in this case, he feels vindicated about his role in the struggle because, as he says, "we made our proposition to the authorities. If they had really understood our point of view, we would not have failed. Regardless of what they did, we discussed well in front of the rural council president. We saw the subprefect, we discussed with him as well for a long time. Why then was there failure? That is their problem, not ours—we showed our will."[88]

If speaking well, and thereby showing one's will, is the proper way for a respectable person to deal with an authority, then the converse is also true: being made to shut up is a significant form of disempowerment. A two-term rural council president, Mahecor Ndong, illustrated this point as he presided over a hearing in the land dispute *Amad Diatte v. Samba Faye*.[89] Once Faye had been declared the winner in this conflict, he proceeded to make a long speech in which he retold the entire narrative of the conflict, praised those who testified on his behalf, chastised his rival severely, and reiterated the rightfulness of his claim to the land in question. When a bystander asked Mahecor Ndong whether Diatte, the loser, would be allowed to respond, Ndong made clear the relationship between oration and power: "What, him? He has nothing to say. He is wrong; he should just sit there and accept. That's all he does. He does not speak."[90]

With unusual exceptions, litigants feel that the rural council system either tries to shut them up or does not listen to them very well or fully. This is a central reason why the rural council system fits the mold of an alien, arbitrary, oppressive authority. Ironically, proceduralism itself—not some self-conscious effort to rule arbitrarily—makes the state look like it is shutting people up and not listening well. At heart the rural councils are administrative courts established to apply a specific land tenure law, not the elected popular councils that would democratically incorporate into governance the values and vision of constituents. As such, the rural councils are not designed to intervene as a *holistic* authority. Rather, they are designed to narrow cases, zero in on precise claims, facts, and circumstances in a specific conflict, rather than explore the much wider relationships out of which conflicts emanate in a society undergoing rapid structural and cultural change.[91]

A holistic adjudicatory authority would have both the interest and the time to listen to long, flowery exhortations that may wander into family history, great deeds, or key events in relations between litigants. Adjudicatory authorities that narrow conflicts are procedurally bound to burn away all this extraneous chaff and, in doing so, are much more likely to cut litigants off, to force them to condense their testimonies and complaints into focused and succinct affidavit-like narratives, as opposed to oratorically impressive discourses.

For example, in the fraternal conflict *Aliou Faye v. Modou Faye*, the elder brother, Modou, sounds precisely this note of frustration over not being heard, not being allowed to speak: "When the rural council came, they didn't explain anything to me, they didn't ask me anything. The authorities came and did not let me have a chance to express myself at all. They just came with arrogance and divided everything up, and that was it."[92] After expressing his bitterness over what struck him as the arrogance of the state officials, Modou Faye paused for a moment and then expressed his thanks to me "for at least giving me the chance to talk about this. This is the first time anyone has asked me for my version of the story and given me the chance to tell what I think happened."

Bouré Fall feels much the same way about the state officials. In his case, *Latyr Diouf v. Bouré Fall*, a conflict over the placement of the boundary of a school's play yard that cut into Fall's millet field, the subprefect's procedure for resolving the conflict greatly irritated Fall: "The subprefect came down here and told me to replant the boundary markers that I had torn out [between Fall's field and the schoolyard]. He came and said it was not my turn to speak. Well, I took my turn anyway—I told him that I would be heard sooner or later."[93] The subprefect had denied Fall's right to speak, making him much less willing to voluntarily give up about ten square meters of a millet field for the expansion of the neighboring schoolyard.

This concern for being heard is by no means unique to the people of the Siin. But narrow adjudicatory proceduralism, which trampled the Serer emphasis on orality and on being heard, is precisely what we expect from a state administrative court, precisely what Serer farmers recognize as the behavior of an alien, external potentate of non-Serer origins, a kind of *maad*. For at least the old *maad* could, if positively disposed, hear you out. This Weberian procedural *maad* has no respect for orality.

A rechristening of the rural council as the *maad* is not all that is going on here. That rechristening has consequences because it establishes an expectation framework. *Maads* for centuries have at least kept their hands off *lamans* and tenure relations, showed respect for Serer *pangool* at key annual rituals, and, when they were willing to adjudicate, let individuals talk and looked at the whole picture. Serer vilification of the rural councils is *interpretive* because the rural councils' failure to meet the expectations created by the analogy of "rural council as *maad*" sets in motion a reading of the rural councils as a degenerate *maad* that fails to follow "normal" rules governing relations between Serer farmer and alien external authority.

Trope of the Maad: The State and the Rain Festival

The rural council system *becomes* the *maad* perhaps most vividly when these new state authorities are incorporated into planting-season rain festivals. These annual festivals vary from village to village across the Siin, but in general they consist of a few days of semisecret rites and public celebrations designed to ensure good rains and fertile crops. The festival of Raan in the village of Tukar offers a useful illustration of the contemporary state cast in the role of the *maad* during a community's most important ritual event.[94]

The Raan celebration occurs every year on the second Thursday after the appearance of the new moon in April. On the morning of Raan, the *laman* prepares a special offering of millet, sour milk, and sugar (a mixture called *foox*). Just after sunrise, he pays a solitary visit to the sacred pond that serves as the home of Luguuñ, the *pangool* that guided his ancestor, the founder of the village, on his migration from the north. The *laman* makes his offering to Luguuñ and spends the early morning in ritual prayer and meditation. He then begins a tour of the village, making ritual offerings of milk, millet, wine, and selected small animals at key shrines, trees, and sacred locations associated with particular *bakhs* and neighborhoods around the village. The *maad*, who in preindependence times came from his capital, Diakhao, for the Raan, attends some of these ceremonies but is careful to arrive after the *laman* and to avoid direct encounters with him.

Meanwhile, people begin to gather around the house of the *saltigué* (hereditary rain priest selected from the *laman's* lineage for oracular talent), who disguises himself with tree branches and leaves. He and his close associates have been drinking a powerful moonshine known as *sum-sum* throughout the morning. The *sum-sum* reportedly enhances the *saltigué's* vision of the future and of the supernatural realm. After sufficient preparation, the *saltigué* and his close companions emerge from his hut, mount their horses, and begin their own tour of some of the village's sacred locales. The *saltigué's* tour is timed to follow the *maad* but to eventually cross his path at a spot known as Nenem. Here, the *maad*, aware that the *saltigué* is coming, halts his entourage, waits until the *saltigué* passes before him, and then proceeds to his next destination.

The crowd that had gathered at the home of the *saltigué* has by this time begun a long, winding procession through the village, some on horseback, most on foot. Along the way, members of the crowd cut branches and leaves from the trees and adorn themselves in the manner of the *saltigué*. They also drape themselves with gris-gris (local amulets or charms), especially gris-gris designed to make the wearer impenetrable to knives. For the young men of the village, this is one of the high points of anticipation surrounding Raan. In the weeks prior to the celebration, young men regale visitors, outsiders, and the uninitiated (like myself) with promises "that you will see incredible things during Raan," and that "you will see people take out long, very sharp knives and try to stab themselves, but the knives will not penetrate their skin. The gris-gris are especially powerful on the day of Raan."[95]

Indeed, this group marching to the village center turns into a raucous crowd of shouting young men stabbing themselves (some, it seems, rather gently, others more forcefully) with all manner of rusty iron. Griots begin to arrive with their drums and fill the air with rhythms. Eventually, the celebrants reach a wide avenue that leads a few hundred meters to a kind of central open space or public square near the middle of the village. The crowd gathers at the southern end of this dusty avenue. The *maad* with his small entourage then arrives, also at the southern end.

This marks the beginning of the "running of the horses," a ritual that most contemporary respondents consider central to Raan. The horse riders from the crowd gather together and ride their horses at high speed to the northern end of the avenue, which abuts the central square. The *maad* follows alone on his horse, slowly. The griots sound out a beat reserved only for this day, this event. The Serer horse riders make a second dash, now southward, again followed slowly by the lone *maad*. They complete another round in this manner, going north and then south again. On the third run, the community riders and the *maad* rush northward together at high speed, followed by a group of griots, who walk slowly behind. Returning south for the third time, the *maad* again slowly follows the speeding Serer riders. Finally, everyone—*maad*, Serer riders, griots, and the crowd on foot—race north to the central square, where they take up their positions for the final act of the Raan.

The central open space is flanked on the east by the small Catholic church and on the west by warehouses built in colonial times to stock peanuts.[96] As the crowd moves into the square, the *maad* and his companions seat themselves along the western side, in front of the warehouse buildings. The village chief *(jaraf)* takes a position near the *maad*, on the same side. By this time, the *laman* and a small group of his lineage have arrived and seated themselves opposite the *maad*, along the eastern side of the square. The griots divide into two groups, one flanking the *maad* on the west, the other joining the *laman* on the east. The crowd, still stabbing and yelling away, gradually clears out in front of them.[97]

Once the space is cleared, the drumbeat accelerates. Members of the crowd break out in spontaneous bursts of dance in the middle of the square, racing almost as quickly back into the anonymity of the crowd. All around, young men whoop and holler and stab themselves with knives and machetes without penetrating their skin. At this point the *saltigué* and a few of his close associates arrive on horseback, from the south. The griots stop drumming. The *saltigué*, carrying a long spear, proceeds directly to the *laman*, dismounts, and waits for a moment. The griots of the *saltigué* begin a new drumbeat, fast and complex, peculiar to this part of the ritual. The *saltigué's* companions move about, shouting, swinging their machetes and clubs, working their way toward the center of the square. The *saltigué* himself then marches across to the west, faces the *maad*, and plants his spear perhaps two meters from the monarch. The *maad* does not move but responds matter-of-factly, saying, "Ndao, saltigué" (Bravo, *saltigué*). The *saltigué* storms back to the *laman's* side, waits a few moments, then rushes the *maad* again, somewhat menacingly, sometimes shouting taunts and insults. He repeats this process four times, each time rushing the *maad* and returning to the *laman,* each time accompanied by his griots and the increasingly feverish noise of his agitated companions. The *laman* remains seated and silent throughout. Once the *saltigué* has processed four times in this way, the *maad* and his entourage rise, mutter a few words of thanks or benediction, and then leave.

Respondents themselves are ambiguous about the exact meaning of menacing and taunting the *maad*, planting the spear before him, his slow march behind the racing horses, and the fact that he waits for the *saltigué* to pass when they meet during the village tour. Most focus on the fact that the *saltigué* is drunk at the time, that everyone is excited at Raan, that people say and do things during that event that they would never normally say or do.

Perhaps that is the point: people say and do things they never normally would. They normally would have never, for example, walked right up to the *maad* and planted a spear before him, taunted him, expected him to dutifully salute Serer horses and riders. That, in the era of the *maad's* domination prior to independence, would have resulted at least in a solid beating, possibly time spent shackled under the sweltering sun, or much worse. But at Raan, this is exactly what the *saltigué*, close relative and adjunct to the *laman*, is free to lead the community in doing. One of the many levels of meaning in this central community festival may be a replaying of the architecture of power in the Siin. The leader of the village-founding lineage commemorates his ancestors' migration and "creation" of the community, and then replays the various spiritual and political alliances that form the community. The external conqueror pays his respects too, but in a secondary, subordinate manner. Eventually both take up opposite positions at the central stage of the ritual drama. But the very presence of the external hegemon seems to be predicated on an opportunity to degrade him, to vent the community's anger at him, to let off steam for what the community suffered at his hand during the preceding year. Historically, the *maad* quietly acknowledged the spiritual leader of the community *(saltigué)*, accepted the berating, and quietly left—an unprecedented reversal of the usual relations of domination.

The Raan ritual is still practiced every year in the month of April in Tukar. Similar rituals take place in many other villages at more or less the same time. But the *maad* no longer attends these events, since the monarchy was disbanded upon independence. In the years since, representatives of the state sometimes have come to the Raan event. The subprefect attends as often as possible, usually every few years. From time to time the prefect of the *département* will even make an appearance. Since 1975, the rural council president has attended almost every year.

When any of these state officials show up for Tukar's Raan, they rarely make the rounds of the village's sacred shrines and trees in the morning. They attend the running of the horses and cheer but don't know how they might play a role. In the central square, they sit on the *west* side, in the position for the external conqueror, where the *maad* and his entourage used to sit. The *saltigué* and his group now rush up to the rural council president or subprefect four times, taunting and menacing them. A few state officials know to say, "Ndao, *saltigué*," but not many. When non-Serer authorities, like the subprefect or prefect, attend Raan, they usually have little idea what is being said to them, since so few of them speak Serer. By all accounts, it seems to them like a folkloric, colorful celebration, pagan incantations to try to control the coming rainy season, a moment for good community relations.

Yet the new *maad*, the new externally imposed hegemonic authority figure, has been incorporated into the community's most important festival in more or less the same role as the old *maad*. Rural council presidents and subprefects, for example, do not sit just anywhere in the central square. The dramatis personae of the Raan festival have really not changed, in spite of the fact that the Gelwaar regime has been dismantled. Only the actors who play the conqueror coming from the west have changed. The new players may not have quite mastered their lines or stage directions—sometimes they miss whole acts—but they are indeed there, in the show.

Not all Serer respondents read the symbolism of Raan and the presence of state officials in exactly this way. In fact, very few of them suggest that the rural council president or the subprefect is present so that the people of Tukar, represented by their *saltigué*, may belittle him as retribution for the arbitrariness, distance, neglect, or disruptiveness of the postcolonial state. But Serer respondents very clearly see a kind of consistency in the fact that subprefects and rural council presidents attend the Raan cere-mony and sit on the west side of the square. According to one *laman*, "The rural council president or the subprefect, they come here for our Raan out of respect for our *pangool* and for our *cosaan*. This is what the *maad* should do."[98] State officials should come because this is what the *maad* should do, and they, as the new *maad* should fulfill their responsibilities. Irregular and incomplete attendance only underscores the degree to which the new state authorities are not simply new faces in the role of the old *maad* but agents of a dysfunctional, degenerate *maad*. This is a *maad* that does not even bother to consistently or effectively respect local Serer cus-toms. Raan is indeed political theater, it's just that, unlike in Geertz's account of nineteenth-century Bali, this performance is a kind of farce, which, unbeknownst to many, reinforces the illegitimacy and alienness of vilified institutions of external domination.[99]

CONCLUSION

At the end of the day, the rural councils have largely failed to translate the promise of democratic legitimacy into popular acceptance of the National Domain Law or functional extension of the legal-rational bureaucratic authority of the state. If anything, the rural councils have, ironically, aggravated the alienness of the state. But the rural councils have provided the crucial foot in the door for the Serer, an opportunity to rework the lowest rungs of the state administrative-electoral machinery in terms that complement, rather than sidestep, Serer cultural expectations and histori-cal institutional legacies. They show us how institutional syncretism *might* have produced political legitimacy and developmental success; but tragically, the structural realities of the rural council system have short-circuited the process of institutional syncretism.

Both the potential success and the truncation are ironic and unintended consequences of the fact that the rural councils are socially proximate administrative agents chosen by popular election. They underscore the critical link between democratic institutional reform at the local level and syncretic cultural adaptation. Rural democracy naturally has made it possible for the Serer to redirect, reinterpret, and even adapt elected local government bodies. Democracy in effect promised the Serer the opportunity to *possess* local government in the fullest sense—first they staff it, then they rename it, and eventually they reappropriate it and direct it toward locally meaningful purposes in a locally meaningful style.

All this would amount to a disjunction between the goals of the state and the goals of local government bodies "captured" and syncretized by peasants embedded in local modes of production and economies of affection, if the rural councils really were elected *political* bodies that enjoyed some degree of local autonomy in establishing and executing policy.[100] If this were the case, local democracy would be the natural vehicle by which institutional syncretism would manifest its hybrid, locally legitimate, culturally meaningful rules and normative agenda. Central government might not understand and would probably not support such syncretic adaptation, but if the state could be convinced to sincerely decentralize and grant real local autonomy (not an unthinkable scenario in the era of structural adjustment), this type of syncretic takeover via local-level democratization would begin the process of drawing the state "down" toward society, yielding the beginnings of a developmentally viable state-society relationship in postcolonial societies.

Syncretism could resolve the governance conundrum of postcolonial societies.[101] Syncretism offers a viable means to transform alien, arbitrary, sometimes predatory postcolonial regimes (Young's Bula Matari) by reconfiguring them in terms of the deemed-historical values of local peoples and places.[102] Eschewing the *modernisant* displacement of traditional cultures and structures, syncretism recrafts and remobilizes tradition, harnesses local-scale legitimation and social capital for new purposes, and, in so doing, sets the stage for the normative consensus between state and society that undergirds effective regime building and sustainable governance.

Yet the tragedy of the rural council system lies in an all too common farce in local democratization schemes: these are not elected *political* bodies that enjoy real leeway in determining policy and making it work (an autonomy that would, above all, let the syncretic values and preferences of the electorate influence, shape, and define the local-level political space). Rather, they are *administrative agents* of the central government, under orders to implement key policies, like the National Domain, in accordance with the vision of the central state, as transmitted by tutelary prefects and subprefects. The rural councils are thus not really in a position to *adapt* the National Domain Law, to make sense of it for the constituents they supposedly represent, the Serer in the Siin, with their peculiar attachment to local peculiarities like *lamans* and *taile* pawning. Nowhere in Senegal are the rural councils in a position to tinker with the National Domain Law to make it make sense for any democratic constituency's local interests and peculiarities. They are dressed up as democratic representatives, but when faced with the real test of representation in rural Africa—the institutionalization of syncretic local values and practices—the rural councilors are told to stop being troublesome political representatives and shape up as administrative adjudicators and natural resource managers. They may want to uphold *taile* relations under the National Domain Law or incorporate *lamanic* notions of land custodianship, but when they seek to do so, rural councilors are reminded that their job is to *enforce the law*. And if they do not seem to "understand" the law, the subprefect and the prefect will be glad to educate them, and, when needed, overrule the adjudicatory decisions of "illiterate peasants." Syncretism holds the key to sustainable governance; truncated syncretism intensifies alienation and widens the chasm between society and postcolonial state.

Lacking the autonomy promised by representative democracy, the rural councils are vilified for *maad*-like alienness and arbitrariness. In the end, the democratic charade truncates the legitimacy-producing dynamic of syncretism. Just as *taile* was a productive, functional synthesis of freehold and *lamanic* holistic custodianship, the rural councils might have moved Serer society beyond the dead end of idealization of the largely defunct *lamans* and vilification of the postcolonial-state-cum-*maad*. The Rural Council Law had (and perhaps still has) the potential to generate a genuine, potentially dynamic blend of Weberian officeholder and supernaturally sanctioned lineage resource manager and judge. Instead, so far, we are left only with interpretive vilification. Cornered by the contradiction between the facade of democracy and the reality of administrative lackeyhood, the state, which *must be* the master of fire, is in the dispiriting end just another version of the *maad baal*, the "dark king."

7 · Culturally Sustainable Development

We have now followed three stories of local response to the imposition of formal state and market institutions in the Siin region of west-central Senegal. This matter of local responses to colonialism, Westernization, commodification, capitalist incorporation, development, and charitable (and not-so-charitable) aid constitutes a rich and underspecified realm of research. We know intuitively that peasants, the young, women, urban migrants, refugees, the landless—name your preferred category from among subordinate populations—simply do not accept the systems of production and domination I have placed under the rough heading "institutional imposition" without some effort to protect their own interests. A variety of literatures have sprung up around both the amorphous analytic sense that they do respond somehow and the oft-unstated normative preference for the idea that such response actually matters.[1]

In my exploration of Serer adaptation of three imposed institutions (freehold property relations, the 1964 land reform, and the 1972 democratic local government reform), I have tried to be much more specific about one kind of response, one process of dealing with institutional imposition. I have argued that if we care about what happens to imposed formal structures, if we want to understand why they "work" (or don't) in the Siin, the western Sahel, sub-Saharan Africa, and most rural parts of the formerly colonial world in general, then we had better not ignore the salience of local history, local culture, and institutional vestiges in popular responses to modernization, forced and voluntary.

This "preimposition" social detritus matters for at least two reasons. First, even if local institutions and culture exist only as historical memories, those memories can define—indeed provide vivid, quasi-mythic icons for—moral social, economic, and political interactions. This is important because the new institutions of resource-poor postcolonial states live or die according to the degree to which they garner popular consent and voluntary compliance. Along these same lines, historical memories of preimposition institutions and culture matter because they provide a rubric for the popular adaptation of newly imposed "modern" structures. I have argued that we need to understand the nature of this localist adaptation because it has the potential to greatly increase voluntary compliance with new formal structures or, conversely, sap promising new formal institutions of their last drop of popular legitimacy.

We have seen illustrations of both extremes, illustrations that suggest the circumstances under which localist adaptation sometimes yields syncretic blends, sometimes Manichean polarization pitting reified tradition against vilified modernity. Chapter 4 offers a clear illustration of syncretic blending. Between the world wars, the French colonial regime tried to standardize property relations in the Siin along freehold lines, hoping to eventually turn the "best peasants" in the Peanut Basin into a reliable African yeoman class. This plan bore unexpected fruit because the Serer neither commodified landholding nor developed a market in land. Instead they produced a new, syncretic exchange mechanism, the *taile* pawn. This type of land pawning made possible land-for-cash exchanges (a "modernization" of Serer economic relations) *and* buttressed the land tenure authority of masters of fire (a reinforcement of "traditional" economic relations).

Taile land pawning was dysfunctional for some developmental objectives, functional for others. Short-term, revocable land pawns only reinforced the idea that "real" ownership meant holistic custodianship in the hands of the leader of the master of fire's lineage. Clearly, the "Serer into yeomans" cause took a few steps backward. At the same time, the syncretic *taile* pawning institution was entirely functional for the expansion of peanut production, because it provided a socially acceptable mechanism for flexible, short-term exchange of land. This made it much easier to increase acreage under cultivation at a time when farmers were struggling to maintain millet production and satisfy their need to "grow cash" in the form of peanuts.[2]

In spite of this partial functionality, the independent state of Senegal had a very different historical memory of "authentic" African land tenure systems than did the Serer of Siin. The simple egalitarianism of Senghor's African socialist National Domain Law probably made sense for areas where something like bourgeois accumulation threatened to produce real landlessness.[3] But in the rural sector (where most of the national domain is located anyway), it amounted to a one-size-fits-all solution that not only disregarded diverse local notions of "traditional" African land tenure but also trampled the syncretic and useful institutional compromises (e.g., *taile*) that peasants like the Serer of Siin had developed over several decades of responding to commodification and institutional imposition.

Thus, the 1964 land reform, in spite of its restorative rhetoric and its pedigree (child of the once highly legitimate independence regime), was itself another institutional imposition. It began the process of driving legitimate informal institutions underground, cutting off the possibility for syncretic adaptation of the state's new norms of ownership and exchange. The resulting gap between a state-sanctioned official realm and the highly legitimate informal realm has aggravated a classic "two publics" split.[4] Only the increasingly romanticized informal realm enjoys legitimacy, popular consent, and a sense of sociocultural appropriateness. Formal, official institutions are vilified as not just the antithesis but also the antagonists of the romanticized traditional. They have come to stand only for lack of local consultation and lack of respect for local institutions and norms.

The state hoped that the democratically elected rural councils would alleviate this legitimacy gap. But in perhaps our most intriguing illustration of institutional adaptation, the plan backfired. Local democracy seemed to promise local staffing and local autonomy, which might have been vectors for institutional syncretism whereby elected Serer rural councilors would draw upon Serer values and institutional legacies in the performance of their duties. It seemed at first that the state might indeed be the new master of fire. But this interpretive syncretism turned to interpretive vilification. Rural councilors have not been permitted to govern "in a Serer way," as their electoral constituents want, but have been reminded to "uphold the law" and "follow correct procedure" because they are really just agents of the central administration. Serer farmers have seen this kind of centralized, arbitrary, extractive authority before, and they simply call it like they see it. The rural councils are hardly the new masters of fire: they are just the *maad baal*, the "dark king," all over again, the precolonial monarch of the Siin.

This particular rereading in terms of local culture and historical memory has specific entailments that only deepen the state's troubles. The metaphor "state as *maad*" aggravates popular rejection because the new state does not play by the old rules of the game, does not respect the limitations that had restrained the feared precolonial *maads*. That old system was at least based on a federal compromise in which a dominant king and court did freely steal from, prey upon, and sometimes arbitrarily punish the Serer peasantry, but left intact Serer religious and land tenure institutions. At least the old *maad* showed up for rain festivals, adored the ancestral spirits, and left land tenure matters to Serer customary aristocrats. The new state does none of this, doesn't even know how to behave like a *maad*, and consequently, is not to be trusted.

It is important to underscore that African government and market institutions have long been considered dysfunctional because they do not work according to rules laid out in Dakar or Harare or Paris. Yet this project argues that there is a pattern, a logic, and a process to that dysfunctionality. Across a wide variety of heterogeneous cultural zones (of which the Siin is just one illustration), the formal institutions of would-be centralized states have been and are being reworked into something else. That something else usually is informed by dominant (and sometimes subordinate) historical memories of precolonial institutional infrastructure and culture. The precise articulation between the remembered and the imposed is a vital factor in sorting out where and why disintegrating institutions left behind by decomposing African states collapse in some places and function in others.

The purpose of this book, then, is to highlight the ways that distinct, idiosyncratic local histories and cultures, and the sometimes tattered institutions that embody them, matter. This matrix of cultural memory and institutional vestiges matters in the specific stories of the spread of commodified economic relations in the Peanut Basin and the attempt to consolidate the local-level authority of a legal-rational centralized state after independence. These accounts reframe our conceptualization of institutions, formal and informal, offer a typology of articulations between imposed and local institutions (of which syncretism is a part), and suggest the outlines of a culturally sustainable form of development.

FORMAL AND INFORMAL INSTITUTIONS IN FLUX

> Formal rules, even in the most developed economy, make up a small part of the sum of constraints that shape choices; a moment's reflection should suggest to us the pervasiveness of informal constraints. . . . Persisting informal constraints produce outcomes that have important implications for the way economies change.
>
> Douglass C. North, Institutions, Institutional
> Change, and Economic Performance

This case study of Serer institutional syncretism shows that we cannot begin to tackle problems of institutional performance in developing countries as long as we ignore or oversimplify not only the role of informal institutions but also the complex processes of historical change and social contestation that envelop institutions and culture at the community level in developing societies. As Douglass North suggests, even economics, a discipline that at best *tolerates* messy questions of subjectivity, values, and worldview by conjuring up a few residual variables, increasingly recognizes the salience of the informal institutional realm.

In this latest spin of the social science rediscovery wheel—the slapping-of-the-forehead, "of course!" realization that institutions *do* in fact matter—we find a steady analytic drift toward the informal realm. Just as political scientists rediscovered the state, then democracy, in turn civil society, and at last political culture, the institutionalist revival follows a similar path.[5] The now not-so-new institutionalism of North, Elinor Ostrom, and others has paved the way for analysts like Robert Bates to argue for a return to the behavioral and normative underpinnings of choice, preference, and institution formation.[6] Economics itself is finally recognizing, with the rise of behavioral economics, the embeddedness of utility in culturally framed constructions of that which is useful.[7]

In this turn to the cultural and the informal, it seems that informal institutions already have everything that markets, legal systems, and elected local government are supposed to develop. They enjoy high levels of self-enforcement: people willingly follow informal rule systems without being forced to comply. Serer peasants regularly choose not to win, and give back fields that official law would grant them. Informal institutions enjoy low transaction costs: parties deal with one another willingly and easily, pawning land, exchanging gifts, and helping out with harvests, without the need for specialized intermediaries or costly watchdogs to make sure that people follow the rules. They command popular legitimacy and inspire willingness to engage in voluntary economic sacrifice. Although government officials, journalists, and development planners constantly bemoan such "profligate waste" and "the excesses of festivities," no one has to direct families to spend well beyond their means for the lavish public feasts that accompany baptisms, marriages, funerals, circumcisions, and other major life events and that redistribute wealth to extended kin, neighbors, and total strangers within well-established informal institutional networks.[8]

Yet the informal realm, what I refer to as the infrastructure of institutions, becomes something of an explanatory morass to the extent that analysts are unwilling to get into its messy hows and whys. In most cases, the informal realm is simply posited, like an axiom in Cartesian geometry, as a more "traditional" alternative, which, because it is somehow closer to ordinary, nonelite actors, *must* reflect their interests and values better than more distant, formal rules and hierarchies. Without probing into whether, why, and under what circumstances it might be true, it is easy to simplistically and unproblematically invoke an informal institutional/"traditional" culture matrix as a widely understood icon for the kind of idealized sociocultural "fit" that seems to elude formal state and market regimes.[9] If official markets, bureaucracies, courts, and so on could somehow attach themselves to or tap this reservoir, if they could somehow graft enough of the informal institutional realm onto themselves, they might seem more legitimate and culturally acceptable, improving the performance of formal institutions and advancing the cause of development.[10]

In the preceding chapters, I have drawn uneasy inspiration from this growing emphasis on informal, culturally rooted institutions as repositories of low transaction costs, smooth information flows, and high self-enforcement. As my portrayal of institutional disjuncture in response to the National Domain Law and interpretive vilification of the rural council system suggests, considerable practical legitimacy is to be found in the informal infrastructure of institutions. Clearly, the rural councils have been more successful when they worked with the informal rules, habits, and values associated with the old *lamanic* order (witness the contrast between resolution of the *Puday Pond Conflict* and *Ndokh v. Njujuf* described in the previous chapter).

But we cannot simply treat institutional infrastructure and cultural legitimacy as taken-for-granted, static sociohistorical givens. Instead, I argue that our task is much more difficult and in fact requires a further intellectual division of labor. This book shows that if we are to understand both the inherent legitimacy potential of institutional infrastructure and culture, and, perhaps more important, their effect on the performance of institutional superstructure, then we must consider more carefully the entire web of historical transformations and social contestation that envelops all elements of institutions, their upper, formal aspects as well as their lower, informal or cultural ones.

To that end, those who focus keenly on organizations and formal rules as such need to incorporate, rather than fear or dismiss, the basic relativist/constructivist insight of late-twentieth-century, nonpositivistic social science. Both culture in general and the informal institutional infrastructure that manifests cultural values can never be reduced to unitary historical or social absolutes, because they are in a condition of what we might think of as quantum flux across two dimensions. That is, they are in flux across time because true definitions of that which is historically authentic and culturally legitimate for a particular community or people varies as years pass: it is more a matter of dominant historical memories than of static tradition. That which constitutes traditional Serer religion, culture, and legitimate land tenure relations, as the preceding chapters have shown, can and does shift over time as memories of authentic culture and local history are rewritten, sometimes subtly, sometimes crudely, to include new elements and exclude or neglect other elements. Any serious effort to invoke the power and salience of culture and institutional infrastructure will be reduced to romantic, increasingly meaningless ruminations about peasant or traditionalist ideal-typical Others if we do not continuously reground our analysis in this ongoing reworking of that which successfully seizes the semantic high ground of the "traditional."

Informal institutions and local culture are also in flux across social cleavages (across "space," to round out the physics imagery). If changing historical memories constantly reshape the content and nature of institutional infrastructure and culture, then we must ask ourselves: Are these historical memories uniform across classes, genders, religious groups, and social factions? If not, when we find a dominant definition of authentic tradition, whose historical memory is this—which group or groups rewrote history and established "tradition" in a manner most favorable to themselves? Without a sensitivity for ongoing processes of social contestation, without a recognition of the reign of hegemonic definitions of culture and the gurgling forth of would-be counterhegemonic alternatives, attempts to invoke the mobilizational potential of institutional infrastructure and culture will eventually end up in a familiar cul-de-sac of empirically disengaged abstractions about the premodern, the nonurban, the "wrong" side of a slew of Parsonian pattern variables or their more contemporary stalking horses.

Sensitivity to relativistic flux across two dimensions—the degree to which notions of authentic culture and institutional infrastructure change over time and vary according to social group—is not simply a matter of intellectual purity that should interest ethnographers or historians who want to tell the most accurate story about cultural change in the face of modernization and development. This book has shown that the process of rewriting culture over time and through social contestation has a direct effect on (a) the relationship between "quaint" institutional infrastructure and "serious" formal rules and administrative hierarchies of state and market structures, and by extension, (b) the performance of these "harder" and more weighty institutions of adjudication, representation, production, property holding, and exchange.

In the preceding chapters, I have tried to go beyond a simple and mechanical concern for *grafting* locally legitimate informal infrastructure onto alien formal superstructure and thereby, through some unspecified alchemy, making the formal institutions "work better." The idea of tapping the informal institutional reservoir of legitimacy misses the fact that formal, modern institutions do not exist in a vacuum from processes of spontaneous popular adaptation. Markets, courts, elected local councils, and other formal institutions, once imposed—and especially once they are abandoned through underfinancing or state retrenchment—become *raw materials* in the local process of rebuilding institutions in response to structural change.

From a developmental point of view, what matters is the *kind* of articulation between formal rules and administrative hierarchies and the informal rules, habits, and cultural values that emerges out of processes of institutional imposition and local adaptation. This book suggests the rough outlines of a spectrum of such forms of articulation.

SYNCRETISM WITHIN A TYPOLOGY OF INSTITUTIONAL ARTICULATIONS

Newly imposed, modern institutions are most likely to "tap a reservoir" of informal legitimacy in the aftermath of a process of genuine institutional syncretism. Institutional syncretism is a process of refashioning all levels of institutional structure (administrative hierarchies, formal rules, informal rules, habits, and values) by drawing on elements from both newly imposed institutional structures and remembered "traditional" institutional arrangements. Syncretism is a process of creative bricolage, whereby the elements that make up new and old institutions become raw materials in the fabrication of a new, blended, innovative institutional arrangement at all levels of an institutional structure. Genuine syncretism anchors one end of a spectrum or typology of articulations of institutions in the aftermath of imposition, as shown on the lower left in figure 9. This schematic builds on the conceptual sketch of institutional structures presented in chapter 1. In graphical terms, the schematic representation of syncretism in the lower left of figure 9 expresses the creative recombination of institutional elements with distinctive crosshatching at every level of an institutional structure.

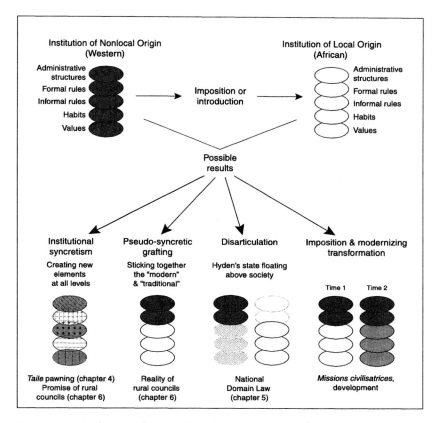

Figure 9. Articulations of institutions after imposition and syncretic response.

For example, *taile* land pawning emerged as the result of institutional syncretism combining a European model of freehold private property and the Serer notion of lamanic holistic custodianship (see chapter 4). *Taile* is governed by the *lamans* but generates a form of exchange that state officials can recognize and support. It posits an entirely new formal rule: a cash-for-land swap is acceptable. It roots this rule in a new interpretation of an old informal *lamanic* principle: use rights transfers (of the kind *lamans* and *yal bakhs* had made for centuries) are normatively sanctioned for everyone and can be made, ad hoc, by any two individuals. It creates a new informal rule as well: the revocation of the pawn contract, an act that preserves *lamanic* ideas of nontransferability of holistic custodianship at the same time it offers a functional equivalent for marketlike rapid movement of land.

Finally, at the level of habits and values (the cultural infrastructure of institutions), *taile* makes compromises with materialistic accumulation and individualism without requiring the wholesale reformulation of culture and the social order along Western liberal lines. To be sure, *taile* lets the Serer behave in a more accumulative fashion and permits a greater degree of emphasis on individual utility calculation in the allocation of land. But it does this in a context in which core values—collectivism, animism, and holistic custodianship-affirming community celebrations (like the Raan festival in Tukar)—remain central. This is the developmental power of institutional syncretism: it permits cultural change and adaptation, and it can provide a basis for a new institutional order more functional in a capitalist economy or a legal-rational state. But it offers a way to achieve these accommodations without a Parsonian syndrome of wholesale, unilinear transformation of all dimensions of culture and society.

Genuine institutional syncretism offers the mechanism for "modernization" (understood as the promotion of the institutions needed to function under capitalism and legal-rationalism) *while maintaining* meaningful connections to legitimacy, community, and stability-promoting values, habits, informal rules, formal rules, and administrative structures. This is the recipe for a sustainable modernity. It rescues culture and "traditional" institutions—to which nonelites continue to feel great loyalty—from the trash heap of backwardness and shame over a lack of "civilization." Deemed-traditional culture, channeling meaning and legitimacy, can, through institutional syncretism, render state, market, and modernity itself sensible, moral, and worthy of participatory sacrifice.

The recombination of new and old institutional structures does not always produce this kind of fluid, coherent recombination of institutional elements at all levels. In postcolonial settings, it is far more common for syncretism to consist of the mere "sticking together" of institutional superstructure (administrative structures and formal rules) derived from the modern West and institutional infrastructure (informal rules, habits, and values) derived from someone's idealization of a "traditional" non-Western social order. As depicted in figure 9, there is recombination in this pseudo-syncretic grafting, but there is little or no transformation of the contents of institutional elements. In graphical terms, figure 9 expresses this by showing local institutional infrastructure (light shading) stuck underneath non-local ("modern") institutional superstructure (darker shading).

Senghor's African socialist original vision of the National Domain Law, discussed in chapter 5, followed this model: he grafted the formal rules and administrative structure of a socialist legal rational regime to *his* notion of traditional Serer informal rules of communal landholding, habits of mutual aid, and values of collectivism. Pseudo-syncretic grafting is the spirit behind authoritarian justifications for single-party regimes. Especially in Africa, but also in Indonesia and other parts of Asia, single-party government has been represented as an adaptation of Western liberal democracy (superstructure) that incorporates non-Western cultural emphases on consensus decision making and community integrity (infrastructure).[11] The nature of this grafting makes it possible to idealize both the "preserved local culture" and the imported modern structures: neither of them is subject to transformation or creative adaptation. By keeping democratic formalities and traditions of unity and consensus hermetically sealed from each other and from deliberation, contestation, and transformation, pseudo-syncretic grafting provides a useful tool for claiming cultural authenticity without permitting the social and political process that actually can generate legitimacy (that is, genuine institutional syncretism).

This has been the fate of Senegal's rural councils. At first, Serer farmers and officeholders subjected them to genuine syncretism, with some degree of success (see chapter 6). However, when the state forced the rural councils to behave as administrative agents, it truncated the process of syncretism and forced a graft. The rural councils would remain part of the legal-rational administrative hierarchy of the Weberian modern state, and they would interpret the land reform as a set of literal, formal, codified rules as written in Dakar and applied uniformly throughout Senegal. Yet, the state essentially *declared* that the rural councils express and embody the values, habits, and informal rules of local Serer culture, just as Mobutu, Suharto, or Museveni in Uganda have declared that single-party rule expressed African or Indonesian values. The facade of syncretism is there, but the political and social process whereby syncretism actually combines imposed and local elements (administration, formal rules, informal rules, habits, and values) to make them legitimate, useful, and innovative is too destabilizing for a state unwilling to really decentralize local government and far too threatening for dictators unwilling to consider real pluralism.

Grafting of the kind manifested in the rural council and National Domain Laws has the potential to degenerate into a form of institutional disarticulation in which imposed, modern institutions exist solely as administrative hierarchies and formal rules but never sink roots in or develop their own corresponding and supportive informal rules, habits, and values. Thus the faded lower circles on the left side of the disarticulation schematic in figure 9. Conversely, local, traditional institutions lose their administrative structures (e.g., they abolished the *lamans* for the sake of socialist development), while their formal rules lose official status (e.g., *taile* essentially was banned). Thus the faded upper circles on the right side of the disarticulation schematic in figure 9. The local, the from-here, the deemed-traditional then exists only at the level of informal rules, habits, and values. Once local institutions become disarticulated from any superstructural elements, it becomes easy to idealize their infrastructural remnants of the traditional order. Given that new "modern" institutions fail to establish coordination with local informal rules, habits, and values, it becomes easy to vilify the superstructural elements of the new "modern" order. We in effect begin to *see* Hyden's state "floating above society" in irrelevance.[12] We understand the debilitating bifurcation in Ekeh's "two publics" in perhaps more precise terms.[13]

This is more than just a simple, reflexive traditionalist backlash, because it entails a specific and important trajectory of institutional and cultural transformation. Memories of alternative local structures and values may harden into a retrospective link to a past golden age, offering the hope of a utopian alternative to an unwanted or unpalatable present. Once dominant historical memory is filtered through this particular lens, it sets the stage for rejection, avoidance, circumvention, and sabotage of imposed modern institutions, pushing a society down the path of institutional collapse and economic stagnation.

Thus, formal institutional development failure is not simply a matter of state weakness or a lack of implementation resources. It is also not a matter of some kind of politically mobilized ideological opposition to regime goals, or a class-based conflict over state development policies. These more familiar explanations of development failure take us only so far in understanding the inability of even a stable, relatively consolidated African state (like Senegal) to impose its law and its model for agrarian reform on a politically quiet region relatively close to the capital and major transportation and communications infrastructure.

The backlash against the land reform, described in chapter 5, made largely displaced local institutions and normative frameworks into a highly romanticized antithesis to an equally reviled official state land tenure system. The contrast is Manichean in its melodramatic moralizations, and developmentally disruptive in its preservation of two overlapping and completely contradictory tenure regimes. The election of new local government bodies, described in chapter 6, was supposed to help address this split. Serer constituents at first thought they were voting into office new masters of fire, Serer peasants who would use genuine syncretism to make the state operate "in a Serer way." But when it became fully apparent that rural councilors were not their elected representatives but administrative agents of the state, Serer voters came to recognize, reject, and ultimately shun and disparage the rural councilors as contemporary manifestations of the "dark king," the hated preindependence ruler of the Siin. Naming and understanding the state in this way set the stage for interpretively vilifying it, because the postcolonial state could not even live up to what Serer farmers had been able to expect from the preindependence monarch (respect for local religion and custom; hands-off local land-tenure authorities).

This typology of institutional-cultural articulations implicitly includes one more category as a kind of zero-point antipode to institutional syncretism. Imposition and modernizing transformation has always been the implicit logic behind civilizing missions, religious evangelism, developmentalism, and modernization schemes of the Marxian and liberal variety. Some would say it is the logic behind the global promotion of free market capitalism and democratization in the current era. It in fact *recognizes* the articulation between formal organizations and culture, between institutional superstructure and infrastructure at the heart of this analysis. In the logic of a civilizing mission, administrative structures and formal rules are imposed or adopted as part of the project of desirable and intentional social change. Following a kind of Parsonian, systems theory approach, the presence of these administrative structures and formal rules—the implantation of elections, free markets, private property regimes, the church, environmentalist nongovernmental organizations, and so on—will *of necessity transform* underlying informal rules, habits, and values to correspond to and support new, modern institutional superstructure. Thus in the schematic of imposition and modernizing transformation in figure 9, we see the lower infrastructural elements of institutions starting out light in color (local) but over time becoming darker (more "modern") as a result of mere contact with more modern institutional superstructure (darker upper circles).

The truth is that if this were possible, analytically we should treat it as the most direct way to deal with the imposition or introduction of new institutions in culturally distinct settings, to get past the problems of interpretive vilification and localist idealization that have mired progressive developmental reforms like the National Domain Law and the rural council system. If one indeed could wholly replace distinctive forms of local culture and institutional infrastructure with informal rules, habits, and values that supported egalitarian land reform, democracy, free market capitalism, environmentalism, and so on, imposition and modernizing transformation would work. In truth, this has only really worked in societies where the carriers of premodern culture and institutional infrastructure have been wiped out through genocide or massive demographic exclusion (as in the United States, Argentina, Australia, and perhaps Johannesburg and Pretoria from about 1948 to 1985). Astonishingly, this approach to institutional change has been fully rehabilitated by the post–September 11, 2001 projects of "robust" democracy promotion and nation building, especially in Afghanistan and, more ambitiously, in Iraq.

Setting aside genocidal displacement and apartheid, there are two serious obstacles to imposition and modernizing transformation. Genuine transformation of culture and institutional infrastructure to support new superstructure requires extraordinarily expensive mechanisms of reeducation and resocialization to construct a hegemonic culture wholly alien to subordinates. In some ways, this was what the French colonial project of assimilation did in the urban coastal enclaves of Senegal (the Four Communes). It is worth noting that this worked reasonably well when carried out slowly over almost two centuries in a very limited geographic-demographic space. Efforts to extend it to the interior of Senegal collapsed in the face of the monumental costs of wholesale social engineering. In the post-9/11 world, it remains to be seen whether the new imperial power, the United States, is willing to shoulder the sacrifices, pay the bills, and muster the collective concentration and commitment of will to eradicate premodern institutional infrastructure and build a new sociocultural order in the newly "liberated" nations.

Imposition and modernizing transformation may also strike some as unethical for their effect of radical cultural homogenization. They effectively consign to the dustbin of history a universe of distinct local values, habits, and informal rules, each of which developed slowly to help a great variety of peoples solve the economic, ecological, and social problems of a thousand distinct contexts.[14] To the extent that this means the eradication of, say, female genital mutilation in the name of the universalization of bodily integrity as a human right, few may lament the loss of diversity. To the extent that this means the end of animist religion, extended family networks of solidarity and support, barn-raising-style labor-pooling arrangements, folkloric rituals marking the passage of life, and the integration of people with each other and their environments, some may see a cost in the sense that Karl Polanyi did when he considered the cultural demolition needed to build capitalism in the West.[15] This normative concern may mean nostalgia for the extinction of *National Geographic* magazine and the celebration of cultural exotica it helped invent. By contrast, it may have to do with cultural integrity as a kind of inherent social or human right. Or it may mean concern for the demise of the human stock of cultural and ideational diversity, a stock that may hold functionally useful norms or bits of wisdom that are of use to an alienated, materialist, homogenized liberal world. Cultural homogenization may wipe out the normative and ideational equivalents of Taxol, a potential cancer cure waiting to be found in the genetic diversity of the rain forest. By this logic, we preserve diversity for the sake of our own instrumental, as yet undefined, gain.

SYNCRETISM, NATIONAL DEVELOPMENT, AND SENGHOR

Institutional syncretism should seem somewhat familiar from a Senegalese point of view. This is because, at one level, it is closely related to programs of hybridization (then known more straightforwardly as Africanization) promoted most clearly by the likes of Léopold Senghor, and, in a different way, Julius Nyerere on the other side of the continent.

The comparison with Senghor is especially a propos given the subject matter of the last two chapters—the process by which Senghor's "own people" (at least for symbolic purposes) have rejected and to a certain extent reworked the very institutions the president-poet himself envisioned as the vehicles that would blend the best of European "modernity" and African "traditional" culture. The broad outlines of Senghor's model were essentially sound, with the exception of one key element. How is it possible to imbue national-level modern Weberian institutions (like the National Domain Law or the rural council system of elected local government) with the legitimacy of local, time-tested, cherished informal rules, practices, and values when those informal structures of legitimation vary widely from subnational community to subnational community? Even more problematic, how can such a process of hybridization be not merely envisioned but also engineered, from above?

Senghor's *négritude*–African socialist vision, perhaps most concretely realized in the form of the National Domain Law itself, amounted to his own, seemingly personal, idealization of traditional African culture and institutions. Senghor's syncretic institutional vision presupposed a *national* cultural base of subjectively meaningful, highly legitimate institutional infrastructure. These were never very precisely defined when it came to matters having to do with land tenure and local governance. The African side of the African socialist version of institutional syncretism seemed to have had something to do with egalitarianism in land access, nonhierarchical decision making, and harmonious community resource management.

If the last few chapters have demonstrated anything at all, it is that this decidedly nonhierarchical, utopian idealization of the rural African past, especially with regard to matters of land tenure, could not have been more disconnected from the reality of historical memory in the Siin. In this corner of Senegal, historical memory of traditional, legitimate rules, values, and practices focuses not an harmony or equality but on *authority*. While it may not be true elsewhere (and this is fundamentally the point), in this particular region we find a tremendous nostalgia for historic institutions that could manage resources, guard trees, set aside fallow and pasture space, direct crop rotation, and generally act authoritatively to manage resources and adjudicate in a society that was decidedly not egalitarian and harmonious but laced with multiple, overlapping patterns of domination and inequality.

The Senghorian vision for institutional syncretism of course missed the 180-degree dichotomy between its version of idealized authorities and tenure relations and the vision cherished by many Serer in the Siin.[16] But this particular error is not nearly as important as the supplanting of numerous, heterogeneous local institutional nostalgias like that of the people of the Siin by one grand national narrative of nostalgia. As was so often the case with his reflections on the negotiation between African and European culture, Senghor fundamentally had it right. But his was the right solution for a time that has not yet come and may not come for generations. The "scaling up" of nostalgia behind the Senghorian, statist version of institutional syncretism ultimately points in the right direction. But it points only in the vaguest possible way toward a universally welcome destination so far down the road that it is almost invisible, so remote that there is no obvious path to begin to follow.

Like his very philosophy of *négritude*, Senghor had the right kind of solution for the kind of person that he was: one man uniquely situated so far out in the vanguard of cultural hybridization that he has left his people, his entire country, many decades behind. *Négritude,* for example, was the moral-philosophical solution for a highly educated, culturally assimilated African who needed to find a way to square the circle of his embrace of Western education and material culture with Western racism and his rediscovery and revalorization of his origins and heritage.[17] It made a good deal of sense to Aimé Césaire and to Franz Fanon and, in a way, even to Ralph Ellison. It remained completely indecipherable and meaningless to Hamad Sarr and Sombel Cama and Mahecor Ndong and thousands of Senghor's rural compatriots who have not yet begun to think about making the kind of journey of personal, psychological, and cultural transformation that their onetime president traversed long ago.

Likewise, the nationally centered institutional syncretism of the National Domain Law, the *négritude* of land reform, is the same kind of developmental solution for a society that has not yet made the long, difficult, probably tragic journey down the road to distillation of its many distinct historical memories and institutional legacies into one homogenized cultural narrative. Both with regard to the National Domain Law and to *négritude*, Senghor will surely be recognized one day as a tremendous visionary. The kind of institutional syncretism he sought to impart (some Serer peasants would say impose) could one day make sense in a Senegal in which the scaling up and unification of historical memories has in fact taken place. But until that time comes, the national arena, despite its appeal to ardent modernists as the seemingly most efficient tool of integration and economic progress, is not where meaningful institutional syncretism will take place. Institutional syncretism, as the designers of Rural Council Law understood but could not implement, requires a radical and sincere democratic decentralization as the price for rendering a modern state and market culturally legitimate.

CULTURALLY SUSTAINABLE DEVELOPMENT

At its empirical heart, institutional syncretism is almost by definition an issue of micropolitics. It takes place within communities bounded by relative commonality in terms of hegemonic historical memories of culture and institutions. An emphasis on popular adaptation of culture and institutions thus requires a close understanding of the specific history and ethnography of a tremendous number and variety of distinct locales. This is especially true in sub-Saharan Africa, where colonial and postcolonial processes of state consolidation and nation building have not corresponded to socially and historically meaningful boundaries but have instead left as their legacy societies extremely fragmented in terms of historical memory of culture and institutional heritage.

The ethnic, cultural, and linguistic heterogeneity of African societies underscores one of the more difficult, but vital, lessons of this book: we may understand institutional syncretism in one very small area well enough to begin to think about alternative development prescriptions and policies, but how do we generalize from there? This project illustrates institutional syncretism among one subset (out of seven) of one ethnocultural block (out of eleven) in Senegal. *Lamanic* heritage, holistic custodianship, and *taile* pawning per se will not explain responses to the National Domain Law or the rural council system among the Jola in the

Casamance region of southern Senegal, nor among the Tukolor of the Senegal River valley, nor even among the Serer of neighboring Saluum. We must sooner or later face the messy, challenging reality that the social, historical, and cultural heterogeneity of even some of the most integrated African nation-states condemns macroscopic, national-level development initiatives grounded on one-size-fits-all institutional imposition to failure. Serious sustainable development will be grounded on careful regional tailoring to address the peculiarities of adaptation driven by regional differences in historical memory and institutional legacy.

Regardless of the microspecificity of the case examined here, this book suggests a general pattern of institutional-cultural transformation that can contribute markedly to developmental sustainability. The lesson of institutional syncretism is that the adjective *culturally* belongs in front of that elusive grail "sustainable development." A development that is sustainable must, in addition to meeting a host of other requirements, also be *culturally* sustainable. It must enjoy enough popular legitimacy to garner consent and voluntary economic sacrifice, or in another lexicon, to keep self-enforcement high, transaction costs low, and information flows unobstructed.

The experience of the Serer of Siin argues forcefully for institutional syncretism as a reliable path to culturally sustainable development. Development schemes and state institutional interventions that ignore, bypass, or seek to eliminate institutional vestiges and historical memories of local culture cut off the possibility of producing syncretic blends and thereby reduce the likelihood that development will be met with voluntary sacrifice and willingness to participate. Formal institutional initiatives that work with, coopt, or transform themselves by incorporating local institutional heritage upheld in dominant historical memories as authentic and legitimate stand a better chance of rallying a population toward formal developmental goals.

The kind of cultural sustainability discussed in this project greatly complicates the business of development, especially at the national level, because it demands intensive study of local peculiarities of institutional legacy, history, and culture. To really work, it requires a multiplication of effort in which land reforms, health care provision, legal interventions, democratic local government, and even, one might argue, educational curricula are closely tailored at a rather small-scale community level.

In the aftermath of structural adjustment, the collapse of state socialism after 1989, and the dismantling of statist regimes throughout Africa in the last decade and a half, this localist reformulation has already been taking place in a somewhat ad hoc fashion. Centralized state regimes simply do not play a major role in directing local development or launching expensive new initiatives. Deregulation, privatization of parastatal marketing boards, and wholesale dismantling of extension, credit, and technical services that could not be privatized have amounted to a rather rapid state withdrawal from the rural sector in societies like Senegal since the late 1980s.[18]

With the semiconscious dismantling of the once omnipresent African state, rural communities have been left to fend for themselves. In part, this autarkic turn of events has allowed substate actors—from regional governments to single villages—to negotiate their own projects and funding from the international donor community, especially the nongovernmental organizations. The Ministries of Agriculture, Development, Interior, and Planning have effectively devolved a good deal of sovereignty onto localities. Although this has been done in a nonsystematic manner (localities cobbling together whatever initiatives they can in order to fill a vacuum created by state withdrawal), it has in effect made a subnational political unit (a village or cluster of villages, a *région*, or sometimes an ethnolinguistic community) a much more salient player in the development process.[19] This devolution and decentralization opens the door to tailoring development initiatives to make use of the results of syncretic processes in order to produce true culturally sustainable development.

The sustainability of marketization, state-building, good governance, and the promotion of democracy—all manner of institutional transfers and impositions in the name of "development"—depends on tapping local circuits of cultural legitimation and voluntary compliance. Institutional syncretism uses local acts of creative adaptation to craft new strands of legitimation binding the institutional vectors of developmental modernity to history, culture, place, and meaning. As we have seen, syncretism thus holds the key to rendering modernity and development comprehensible, morally sensible, and worthy of sacrifice—and, thereby, sustainable.

CONCLUSION

Especially as states withdraw or are forced to dismantle themselves, local institutions, and the historical memories and culture in which they are embedded, become increasingly important in finding local solutions to the institutional challenges of modern economic and political relations: finding ways to market cash crops, obtain inputs, secure credit, exchange land and labor, apply justice, govern democratically, and so on.

This brings us back to an underlying, simple lesson at the heart of this project. Histories and cultures matter, and they complicate theorizing, generalizing, and planning. They matter because they determine the flow of consent and legitimacy without which institutions must rely on cumbersome coercive mechanisms of enforcement. They animate and help explain "local responses," help us understand popular avoidance, circumvention, and sabotage of even the most well-intentioned and benevolent development interventions. They complicate simply because there are so many of them, because taking seriously the mobilizational potential of historical memory, local culture, and institutional infrastructure means recognizing their diversity and their sui generis qualities.

These numerous and disparate notions of "our people's past" and "our heritage" amount to a kind of antimodernist revenge in a world increasingly directed by powerful institutions that work best when they homogenize and standardize human difference. Indeed, the machinery of market capitalism, centralized state authority, and one-size-fits-all democratic pluralism are increasingly blocked not by some systemic counterideology à la the old Soviet ideal but by the innumerable and disparate bits of detritus of history and culture left behind by the hundreds of thousands of peoples who were never asked if they wanted to be a part of some shining new "universal," never asked if they thought they might have something distinctive of their own to contribute to the crushing, monolithic economic and political norms of an emergent "global civilization."

Like errant birds sucked into the jet engines of modernity, these local histories and culture clog the machinery of progress, increasing transaction costs and creating irregular pockets of nonconformity in the otherwise seamless global topography of rational, modern market and state institutions. There is no simple solution here; no single retrofit will work because of the great heterogeneity of the detritus to which so many cling. Yet whether the engineers of the national political-economy and global development open their eyes and take advantage of it or not, real efforts are under way on the ground, in the villages and neighborhoods, to retrofit the sometimes merciless, unstoppable rotors of the engines of modernity. The machinery is being refashioned by a hundred thousand humble amateurs, *bricoleurs* who find a hundred thousand innovative ways for at least a few of the sparrows or hawks, or whatever nests in the local trees, to pass through the spinning blades.

Notes

1. "BUYING ROPE IS A YOUNG MAN'S JOB"

1. The Serer of Siin are one among seven distinct ethnolinguistic groups that together form the ethnic umbrella category "Serer." For the sake of simplicity and conformity with local self-identification, I use the term *Serer* to denote the Serer subgroup of the Siin region, also known in ethnographically precise terms as the Sinig, Siin-Siin, or Serer-Siin. For more complete reflections on the distinctions among Serer subgroups and the choice of ethnographic labels in this work, see chapter 2.

2. Throughout this book, I set the terms *tradition* and *modernity*, when unqualified, in quotation marks to call attention to, critique, and ultimately supplant this taken-for-granted but empirically false dichotomy and the discursive framework it helps constitute. This is a book about the agency of a poor peasant people in the world's most marginalized region who creatively adapt and reinvent their culture and historic lifeways (their "tradition") as well as the formal organizations and rules that are supposed to make them more developed, more productive, and freer ("modernity"). They reject, reshape, and reinvent both that which is frozen in the primordial past under the misnomer "tradition" and that which is reified as the pathway to an idealized, unattainable future under the heading "modernity." This book, like the people whose struggles it recounts, seeks to destabilize and move beyond the safe, easy, but illusory tradition-modernity trope. We are forced, then, as we write and think about these terms, to remember they are part of a deeply embedded and deeply erroneous way of looking at history and notions of change. Working within the constraints of the written word and the limitations of today's conceptual frameworks, I do my best to avoid these terms. But when forced to employ them, like James Ferguson in his discussion of the discourse surrounding "development," I place *tradition* and *modernity* in quotation marks as if to protect my arguments, findings, and ability to make sense from the semantic and conceptual radioactivity of these words. See Ferguson, *The Anti-politics Machine*.

3. On prebendal elites, see Joseph, "Class, State, and Prebendal Politics," pp. 21–38; Sklar, "The Nature of Class Domination in Africa," pp. 531–52. On agricultural policies, see Bates, *Markets and States in Tropical Africa.* On modernization schemes, see World Bank, *Accelerated Development in Sub-Saharan Africa.* On bloated states, see Young, *The African Colonial State in Comparative Perspective.*

4. Callaghy, "The State and the Development of Capitalism in Africa." For similar expressions of deepening, seemingly intractable crisis, see also Chabal, "Introduction"; and Van de Walle, *African Economics and the Politics of Permanent Crisis.*

5. Chabal, "The Quest for Good Government and Development in Africa," pp. 447–62; Keeton, "Mbeki to Promote African Recovery Plan at G8 Summit."

6. To borrow from the evocative work of Bayart, *The State in Africa.*

7. Ekeh, "Colonialism and the Two Publics in Africa," pp. 91–112.

8. Putnam, *Bowling Alone,* pp. 22–28.

9. Young, *The African Colonial State in Comparative Perspective,* pp. 1–12.

10. Putnam, *Bowling Alone,* pp. 22–28.

11. Hyden, *No Shortcuts to Progress.*

12. Diamond, *Developing Democracy;* Chazan, "Between Liberalism and Statism."

13. Sklar, "Democracy in Africa," pp. 11–24.

14. Mbembe, "Provisional Notes on the Postcolony," pp. 3–37; Bayart, *The State in Africa.*

15. Parsons, *The Structure of Social Action.* For a succinct and cutting review of the durability and revival of these tropes of teleological change, see Alexander, "Modern, Anti, Post, and Neo."

16. Especially in the last years of modernization theory, a wealth of studies considered the subtlety of the nonlinear relationship between "traditional" societies and processes of "modernizing" change. By the 1970s, the wholesale dismissal of much of modernization theory led to the unfortunate neglect of much of this valuable work on the comparative study of social change. Riggs, *Administration in Developing Societies;* Bendix, "Tradition and Modernity Reconsidered," pp. 292–346; Whitaker, "A Dysrhythmic Process of Political Change," pp. 190–217; Rudolph and Rudolph, *The Modernity of Tradition;* Price, *Society and Bureaucracy in Contemporary Ghana.*

17. Almond and Verba, *The Civic Culture,* p. 3.

18. See especially ibid., pp. 3–32.

19. Lucian W. Pye, introduction to *Political Culture and Political Development,* ed. Lucian W. Pye and Sidney Verba (Princeton: Princeton University Press, 1965), p. 4.

20. Pye, "Political Culture," p. 218. Although he acknowledges its roots in national character, Pye calls political culture "more explicitly political and hence more restrictive than such concepts as public opinion or national character" (p. 219). See also Pye, introduction, p. 8.

21. Lakoff, *Women, Fire, and Dangerous Things.*

22. Deutsch, *Nationalism and Social Communication.*

23. See Almond and Verba, *The Civic Culture,* pp. 12–32; Pye, introduction, pp. 17, 23; Verba, "Conclusion," pp. 529–42; Pye, "Political Culture," pp. 221–24.

24. One of the flaws in conceptualizations of political culture that rely heavily on Talcott Parsons is the notion of orientation. Rosenbaum argues that Almond and Verba's approach to orientation offers "so unbounded a definition that an investigator would have to spend an interminable amount of time compiling an elephantine list of orientations to be sure nothing politically relevant escaped notice" (Rosenbaum, *Political Culture,* p. 5, as cited in Patrick, "Political Culture," p. 274). Carole Pateman, Brian Barry, Richard Fagen, Robert Tucker, and others critique Almond and Verba for a static concept that ignores the possibility that "a 'democratic' political culture—such as the 'civic culture'—is the *effect* of 'democratic' institutions." Barry, *Sociologists, Economists, and Democracy,* p. 51; Pateman, "Political Culture, Political Structure, and Political Change," p. 292.

25. Putnam, "Institutional Performance and Political Culture."

26. The central text of the return to the state literature is Evans, Skocpol, and Reuschemeyer, *Bringing the State Back In.* With regard to the early stirrings of a normative shift toward analysis of democracy in southern Europe and Latin America, see especially O'Donnell, Schmitter, and Whitehead, *Transitions from Authoritarian Rule.* For a more complete exploration of the democratization framework, see Diamond, *Developing Democracy;* Migdal, "Studying the Politics of Development and Change"; Schmitter, "Idealism, Regime Change, and Regional Cooperation."

27. Keane, *Democracy and Civil Society;* Bratton, "Beyond the State"; Chazan, "Planning Democracy in Africa"; Chazan, "Africa's Democratic Challenge," pp. 279–307.

28. For the paradigmatic overuse of this primordialist, Manichaean distinction between civic and ethnic, see Kaplan, *Balkan Ghosts.* For a critical dismantling of this trope of oversimplification, see Lemarchand, "Genocide in Comparative Perspective."

29. Compare, for example, Putnam's definition of "civic community" and Almond and Verba's 1963 construction of the civic culture concept. Putnam et al., *Making Democracy Work,* p. 6.

30. Ibid., pp. 121–62.

31. Borrowing of course from Banfield, *The Moral Basis of a Backward Society.* Although the term was certainly not developed with sub-Saharan Africa in mind, it does "travel" reasonably well to other settings in which kinship networks seem, at first, to undermine modernization and the effectiveness of Weberian legal-rational institutions.

32. Putnam, *Bowling Alone,* pp. 22–28.

33. In a sense this is exactly what is happening in sub-Saharan Africa in the aftermath of the cold war. The throwing up of hands is most starkly visible in the extreme cases where—in the neoliberal civic culture lens—un-civic

underlying cultures have bubbled to the surface and actually washed away not just democracy, bureaucracy, and free markets but also the state itself (Somalia, Liberia, Sierra Leone, and the former Zaire). Even in less cataclysmic cases, frustration with lack of electoral rotation and with mismanagement and corruption have diverted resources away from an entire region increasingly characterized as a tribalist basket case.

34. Arrow, *Selected Papers of Kenneth J. Arrow*, pp. 45–80; Olson, *The Logic of Collective Action*.

35. North, *Structure and Change in Economic History*, pp. 59–68, 201–10; Bates et al., *Analytic Narratives*, pp. 231–38; Ostrom, *Governing the Commons*, pp. 1–102.

36. North, *Structure and Change in Economic History*, pp. 208–9; Bates, "Contra Contractarianism," p. 399. On behavioral economics, see the work of Matthew Rabin.

37. Sikkink, *Ideas and Institutions*.

38. Hall, "Policy Paradigms, Social Learning, and the State," pp. 275–96.

39. March and Olsen, *Rediscovering Institutions*, pp. 143–72.

40. This echoes the long-established sociological distinction between role structures (organizations) and rule structures (formal rules), both of which can be considered components of an institutional arrangement.

41. Hart, *The Concept of Law*. For an excellent review of the foundational work on the formal and informal aspects of institutions, see also Brinks, "Informal Institutions and the Rule of Law."

42. Bourdieu puts it more precisely when he refers to the habitus as "a system of lasting, transposable dispositions which, integrating past experiences, functions at every moment as a *matrix of perceptions, appreciations and actions*, and makes possible the achievement of infinitely diversified tasks, thanks to analogical transfers of schemes permitting the solution of similarly shaped problems." Bourdieu, *Outline of a Theory of Practice*, pp. 80–81 (emphasis in original).

43. Institutional organizations do not simply rely on correspondence or shared logic with one set of informal rules, habits, and values or with one institutional practice, but in fact draw on many kinds of informal rules, habits, and values to support their operation. Likewise, institutional practices correspond to, or share logic with, more than one administrative structure or one single set of formal rules.

44. Scott, *Seeing Like a State*, pp. 11–52.

45. See the discussion of "imposing and modernizing transformation" in chapter 7, as well as figure 9, for a more complete look at this widespread process of externally induced change.

46. Badie and Birnbaum, *The Sociology of the State*. See also Evans, "Government Action, Social Capital, and Development," pp. 1119–32; Evans, *Embedded Autonomy*.

47. Eckstein, *Division and Cohesion in Democracy*. Nor should it be limited, from a policy point of view, to the search for synergistic relations between

unchanging state bureaucracies and historically static, local cultural and social traditions. See Evans, "Government Action, Social Capital, and Development."

48. Giddens, *Central Problems in Social Theory*, p. 5.

49. See North, *Structure and Change in Economic History*.

50. Bourdieu, *Outline of a Theory of Practice*, pp. 80–81 (emphasis in original).

51. Ibid., p. 80, emphasis in the original. Bourdieu also offers this nugget about how the habitus provides a shared framework of meaning, a common code: "If witticisms surprise their author no less than their audience, and impress as much by their retrospective necessity as by their novelty, the reason is that the *trouvaille* [effort (at being witty)] appears as the simple unearthing, at once accidental and irresistible, of a buried possibility. It is because subjects do not, strictly speaking, know what they are doing that what they do has more meaning than they know *[sic]*" (p. 79).

52. Ibid., p. 82.

53. Ibid., p. 72. Once initiation is complete, readers can proceed to the "dialectics of the internalization of externality and the externalization of internality."

54. On "development discourse," see Escobar, *Encountering Development;* Ferguson, *The Anti-politics Machine*.

55. Scott, *Seeing Like a State*, pp. 11–52.

56. Achille Mbembe would echo Foucault in pointing out that the state imposition (the work of Mbembe's *commandement*) structures the way ordinary people conceive of the exercise of power in general. Mbembe, like Bayart, thus draws attention to how the metaphors and images of state corruption—"a goat eats where it's tethered"—have infiltrated everyday human interaction. See Mbembe, *On the Postcolony*.

57. Young, *The African Colonial State in Comparative Perspective*, pp. 1–12. In Kikongo, this means the "crusher of rocks," Young's appellation, borrowed from the colonial-era mercenary Henry Stanley, for the outsized, hypertrophic, enormously transformative colonial (and postcolonial) states.

58. Watts, "Capitalisms, Crises, and Cultures I."

59. Ibid., p. 15.

60. Ibid., pp. 11, 13, 18.

61. Watts, "Capitalisms, Crises, and Cultures I," p. 6; Watts, "The Shock of Modernity."

62. Watts, "Capitalisms, Crises, and Cultures I," pp. 11–19.

63. Stewart and Shaw, *Syncretism/Anti-Syncretism*, pp. i, 1–3. My project evokes the language of syncretism in this latter sense. Debate with proponents of the former sense, while of some concern to specialists in religious anthropology, seems to divert us into the sterile analytic dead-end debate between primordialism (religion is an extant body of unalterable knowledge and rules of divine origin, making syncretic blending a heretical dilution) and constructivism (religion is spiritual in function but at heart socially constructed and therefore subject to syncretic blending as a natural part of processes of change).

64. Bassett, "Introduction," p. 4.

65. Alvarez, Dagnino, and Escobar, eds., *Cultures of Politics/Politics of Cultures.*

66. See Laitin, *Hegemony and Culture,* pp. 76–96.

67. For example, Robert Price's study of the role behavior of Ghanaian bureaucrats shows how officeholders fail to reconcile the formal and organizational demands of Weberian legal-rational bureaucracy with the informal obligations and value structure of a "moral familist" ethic, informal rules, and habits. See Price, *Society and Bureaucracy in Contemporary Ghana;* Bendix, "Tradition and Modernity Reconsidered"; Whitaker, "A Dysrhythmic Process of Political Change."

68. Lévi-Strauss, *The Savage Mind,* pp. 16–36.

69. Riggs, *Administration in Developing Countries.*

70. Rudolph and Rudolph, *The Modernity of Tradition.*

71. Herskovits, *Continuity and Change in African Cultures;* Carter, *National Unity and Regionalism in Eight African States.*

2. THE SERER OF SIIN

1. See Aujas, "Les Sérères du Sénégal," pp. 293–333; Dupire, "Chasse rituelle, divination et réconduction de l'ordre socio-politique chez les Serer du Sine," pp. 5–32; Guigou, "Les changements du système familial et matrimonial"; Lericollais, *Sob;* Pelissier, *Les paysans du Sénégal;* Becker, *Les Serer Ndut;* Klein, *Islam and Imperialism in Senegal;* Mbodj, "Un exemple de l'économie coloniale"; Gastellu, *L'égalitarianisme économique des Serer du Sénégal;* Delpech, "Dynamismes sociaux et conflits d'autorité dans une communauté rurale serer du bassin arachidier Sénégalais."

2. Laitin, *Hegemony and Culture,* p. x.

3. See Crowder, *Senegal.*

4. See Vaillant, "The Problem of Culture in French West Africa." See also Crowder, *Senegal,* pp. 51–57; Hymans, *Léopold Sédar Senghor,* pp. 23–142.

5. Vaillant, "The Problem of Culture in French West Africa," pp. 3, 10; Crowder, *Senegal,* pp. 51–55.

6. This realization took the form of Senghor's "active assimilation" theory, a core element of his philosophy of *négritude,* which suggested that, as Africans adopt universal norms and institutions of French civilization, they should transform them in accordance with the particular genius of their own culture and heritage. See Senghor, *Liberté I,* pp. 39–69, 87–97; Crowder, *Senegal,* p. 126.

7. On the gradual integration of Senegalese peasantries into imperial commodity production, see Pelissier, *Les paysans du Sénégal,* especially pp. 224–44; Lericollais, *Sob,* for an excellent exploration of the impact of commodification in the Serer-Siin; and Moitt, "Peanut Production, Market Integration, and Peasant Strategies in Kajoor and Bawol before World War II."

8. As suggested by Cruise O'Brien and echoed by Villalón, this is truest with regard to the Baye Fall subsect of the Mourides, rather than the Mouride

movement as a whole. Cruise O'Brien, *The Mourides of Senegal;* Villalón, *Islamic Society and State Power in Senegal.*

9. For a thorough and definitive dismantling of the problematic discourse surrounding this term, see Love, "Talking about 'Tribe.' "

10. Klein, *Islam and Imperialism in Senegal,* p. 5; Dupire et al., "Résidence, tenure foncière, alliance dans une société bilinèaire," pp. 417–52; Gravrand, "Les Sereres," pp. 78–84; Colonel du Genie Pinet-Laprade, "Notice sur les Serers par le Colonel du Genie Pinet-Laprade, Commandant Superieur de Gorée," 1864, Archives Nationales du Sénégal, 1G33, pp. 1–5.

11. Dulphy, "Coutume des Sérères de la Petite Côte," pp. 237–321.

12. Pinet-Laprade, "Notice sur les Serers par le Colonel du Genie Pinet-Laprade," pp. 3–10.

13. U.S. Geological Survey, "Historical Rainfall: Senegal-Gambia," 1995, available on-line at http://edcsnw3.cr.usgs.gov/senegal/gifs/snglrain.gif, 16 April 2002; United Nations Food and Agriculture Program, "Preliminary Assessment of 2001 Cereal Production in Africa," FAO Rome, December 2001, available on-line at http://www.fao.org/giews/english/esahel/saho16e/saho16e.htm, April 16, 2002; Pelissier, *Les paysans du Sénégal,* pp. 3–10.

14. In a much quoted formulation, Paul Pelissier notes, "In contrast to the area occupied by Wolof farmers, usually devoid of trees, the Serer country appears as a sort of park, with carefully selected and well-placed trees throughout." For Pelissier's complete and still authoritative description of the physical, agricultural, and socioeconomic characteristics of the "parc Serer," see *Les paysans du Sénégal,* pp. 260–74.

15. Klein, *Islam and Imperialism in Senegal,* pp. 5–11; Reverdy, *Une société rurale au Sénégal,* pp. 7–9; Boulègue, *Le Grand Jolof, XIIIe–XVIe siècle,* pp. 18–21.

16. Klein, *Islam and Imperialism in Senegal,* pp. 6–8.

17. Ibid., pp. 8–11; Pelissier, *Les paysans du Sénégal,* pp. 206–9; Gastellu, *L'égalitarianisme économique des Serer du Sénégal,* pp. 32–36.

18. Dupire, "Classes et échelons d'âge dans une société dysharmonique," pp. 5–42; Becker, *Les Serer Ndut.*

19. Pelissier, *Les paysans du Sénégal,* pp. 230–42; Pinet-Laprade, "Notice sur les Serers par le Colonel du Genie Pinet-Laprade," pp. 10–17.

20. These include light-skinned, slightly demonic djinns; clever forest-dwelling dwarf wrestlers; and nocturnal, tree-dwelling monkeylike creatures that kidnap lone travelers. In addition, there is widespread belief that apparently ordinary human beings might be cannibalistic, supernatural creatures known as *naqs,* roughly translated as "witches" or "vampires" or perhaps more precisely as "soul eaters." For more detail on Serer religious beliefs and practices, see Becker, *Traditions villageois du Siin;* Becker, *Les Serer Ndut;* Dupire, "Chasse rituelle, divination et réconduction de l'ordre socio-politique chez les Serer du Sine"; and for a somewhat less scholarly but still informative treatment, Gravrand, *Civilisation Serer: Cosaan;* and Gravrand, *Civilisation Serer: Pangool.*

21. Dupire et al., "Résidence, tenure foncière, alliance dans une société bilinèaire," pp. 417–52; Gastellu, *L'égalitarianisme économique des Serer du Sénégal,* pp. 177–85; Guigou, "Les changements du système familial et matrimonial," pp. 46–48.

22. Diop, "Le tenure foncière en milieu rural Wolof," pp. 48–52; Lericollais, *Sob,* pp. 32–33, 45–46; Pelissier, *Les paysans du Sénégal,* pp. 196–203.

23. Pelissier, *Les paysans du Sénégal,* pp. 184–90.

24. Becker, *Traditions villageois du Siin;* Lericollais, *Sob,* pp. 16–19, 48–51; Pinet-Laprade, "Notice sur les Serers par le Colonel du Genie Pinet-Laprade," pp. 1–11.

25. André Lericollais and Charles Becker, personal communication, July 1993. This frontier had once been a no-man's-land, largely uninhabited because of frequent cattle and slave raids across the border. Consolidation of French colonial rule put an end to this chronic low-grade warfare and made it possible to establish settlements in what was otherwise desirable open land near the border. See in particular the exploration in chapter 6 of land conflicts involving the village of Ndokh.

26. Klein, *Islam and Imperialism in Senegal,* pp. 181–84.

27. Becker, Diouf, and Mbodj, "L'evolution demographique regionale du Sénégal et du Bassin Arachidier (Sine-Saloum) au vingtième siècle."

28. ORSTOM has, in recent years, been renamed the Institut de Recherche pour le Développement but is still widely known in the Siin by its former, and less politically correct, acronym. In the spirit of respecting local naming conventions, I use the old acronym.

29. This unique source details age, gender, marital and family status, education, migration, and dry-season labor activity for the entire zone population of thirty-five thousand. Thanks to the assistance of Charles Becker, an ORSTOM researcher who has published extensively on the Serer and rural Senegal, and to the generosity of Dr. François Simondon, then director of the Njafaj research project, I was given access to the demographic data set for the entire zone population.

30. For a complete overview of this research project, see ORSTOM, *Projet Niakhar.* Note also that *Serer* and more precise terms such as *Serer-Siin* and *Serer-Saluum* refer both to the ethnic groups and to the languages they speak.

31. As suggested by many of the contributors to the comprehensive methodological volume edited by H. Russel Bernard, *Handbook of Methods in Cultural Anthropology.*

32. For a general discussion of the concepts of "defining initial exemplar" and the "prototype effect," see Lakoff, *Women, Fire, and Dangerous Things,* especially the discussion of Eleanor Rosch's work, on pp. 40–54.

33. Pelissier, the authoritative chronicler of Senegalese rural communities, summed up the long colonial fascination with the Serer when he dubbed them "le type même de paysannerie egalitaire et 'anarchique.' " *Les paysans du Sénégal,* p. 198.

34. Suret-Canale, *French Colonialism in Tropical Africa.*

35. Barry, *Le royaume du Waalo;* Crowder, *Senegal.*

36. L. Geismar, as cited in Guigou, "Les changements du système familial et matrimonial," p. 27.

37. For the definitive overview of the rise of the Mouride brotherhood and their agricultural economic base, see Cruise O'Brien, *The Mourides of Senegal.* For an authoritative primer on *daaras* and Mouride agricultural colonies, see Villalón, *Islamic Society and State Power in Senegal,* pp. 118–19.

38. Klein, *Islam and Imperialism in Senegal,* pp. 63–149.

39. Ibid., pp. 193–218.

40. These types of latent, partially stated assumptions about the general social, institutional, cultural, and political characteristics of African peasantries occur in a variety of literatures and approaches. For an exemplary dismantling of this discursive frame, see Timothy Mitchell's analysis of Richard Critchfield's *Shahhat, an Egyptian* (Mitchell, "The Invention and Reinvention of the Egyptian Peasant," pp. 129–46).

41. Oral histories recorded for this study that are especially rich in data on village founding include Diaga Dibor Ndofene Diouf, oral history interview, 14 October 1993; Aissatou Sarr, oral history interview, 21 September 1993; Ndiogoye Thiao, oral history interview, 12 August 1993; Babacar Faye, oral history interview, 30 September 1993; Siga Marone, oral history interview, 2 October 1993; Diaraf Dibor Sarr, oral history interview, 20 September 1993; Ngor Wagane Ndour, oral history interview, 29 September 1993; Dione Falilou Diouf, oral history interview, 2 October 1993. Note that, throughout this volume, in order to protect the anonymity of respondents, I have changed the names of Serer individuals interviewed in dispute interviews and oral history interviews.

These accounts generally correspond with Becker's collection of village founding stories from the western Siin. Becker, *Traditions villageois du Siin;* on Serer origins in the Fuuta, see also Delafosse, *Haut-Sénégal-Niger;* Geismar, *Recueil des coutumes civiles de races du Sénégal;* Joire, "Decouvertes archeologiques dans la region de Rao, pp. 249–333.

42. See Barry, *La Sénégambie du XVe au XIXe siècle;* Boutillier and Caussé, *La demographie du Fouta-Toro.*

43. For this reason, Pelissier refers to the Serer, somewhat romantically, as the "people of the double refusal." They both refused to accept conversion to Islam and, in their migration, refused to adopt the language and culture of the people they encountered, the Wolof. *Les paysans du Sénégal,* pp. 192, 198; regarding the Serer migration out of the Fuuta, see also Dupire et al., "Résidence, tenure foncière, alliance dans une société bilinèaire," pp. 444; Lericollais, *Sob,* p. 16; Hesseling, *Histoire politique du Sénégal,* p. 49.

44. For a particularly thorough review of this literature, see Guigou, "Les changements du système familial et matrimonial," p. 39.

45. Pelissier, *Les paysans du Sénégal,* pp. 180–203; Diop, "Le tenure foncière en milieu rural Wolof," pp. 48–52.

46. In some cases, the founder asked "permission" to occupy the space from the precolonial king of Siin, known in Serer as the *maad*. This was often true even in villages that predate the fourteenth-century conquest of the Serer by the lineage of the *maad*, the Gelwaar, discussed below. In villages founded after the arrival of the *maad*, some founding tales entirely omit the presence or relevance of the *maad*. Both these types of anachronisms may reflect selective readings of the past designed to privilege or deny the relevance of centralized state authority, a subject to which we will return in chapter 3.

47. Arendt, *The Origins of Totalitarianism*, pp. 156–89.

48. Evidence exists for both matrilineal and patrilineal inheritance of the office. Dupire and colleagues offer a fascinating, although somewhat inconclusive, analysis of possible relationships between the two patterns of descent and the historical origins of various waves of migrants to the Siin. Ancient patrilineal fire estates in the northwest of the Siin suggest linkages to Tukolor or Halpulaar patrilineality in the Fuuta. Matrilineal inheritance of the fire estate outside the kingdoms of Siin and Saluum suggests pre-Gelwaar land tenure patterns, even though informants in the Siin themselves argue for a linkage between Gelwaar matrilineality and the matrilineality of Serer fire estates. See "Résidence, tenure foncière, alliance dans une société bilinèaire," pp. 418, 445.

49. Given that most Serer informants use the term *laman*, I use this designation to refer to the master of the fire estate. Nevertheless, terms like *yal naay* or *yal ndaak* may better represent land tenure institutions of the Siin for two reasons. First, *yal naay* and *yal ndaak* follow the general Serer-Siin syntactical construction for the "owner" or "custodian" of an object (e.g., *yal mbind* = "master of the compound," or household master). Second, *laman*, used to designate a similar Wolof institution, either is a term applied to the Serer through colonial codification of custom, or it raises the insoluble chicken-and-egg dilemma: did Serer migrants name an institution that they taught to the Wolof during their migration from the Fuuta, or did they borrow this land tenure structure from the Wolof? On *laman* as used by the Wolof, see Diop, "Le tenure foncière en milieu rural Wolof," p. 49.

50. Pelissier, *Les paysans du Sénégal*, p. 189; Lericollais, *Sob*, pp. 22, 29; Diop, "Le tenure foncière en milieu rural Wolof," p. 48.

51. Lericollais in particular highlights the importance of the *sas* in the agricultural system of the Serer. He cites the well-known proverb "five *sas* fill a granary of millet" to underscore the degree of environmental adaptation behind Serer agricultural practice. Lericollais sees this sophistication of land management and soil conservation as a distinctly Serer form of local knowledge, arguing that densities of *sas* planting are much higher in villages of more ancient Serer settlement. He notes rates of 15 *sas* per hectare in areas of ancient Serer habitation, but only 3.5 such trees per hectare in Tukolor communities in and near the Siin. Although written in the late 1960s, when faith in emerging Green Revolution technology minimized attention to local, "traditional" forms of knowledge, his study nevertheless makes a clear link

between successful farming systems and the culturally embedded, ecologically adaptive practices of a peasant society. *Sob,* pp. 29, 26, 45.

52. Ngor Mbede Dieng, dispute interview, 26 October 1993.

53. For a discussion of the role of *pangool* in Serer belief systems in general, see Dupire, "Chasse rituelle, divination et réconduction de l'ordre sociopolitique chez les Serer du Sine," pp. 5–32. On the spiritual aspects of the office of *laman,* see Diop, "Le tenure foncière en milieu rural Wolof," pp. 48–49; Abelin, "Domaine national et développement au Sénégal," p. 517; Dupire et al., "Résidence, tenure foncière, alliance dans une société bilinèaire," p. 440.

54. Collation of the many versions of the list of Gelwaar kings of Siin yields the number of generations born since the arrival of the first Gelwaar rulers. Using a standard of thirty years per generation places the arrival of the first Gelwaar ruler, Maisa Waly Dione, on the coast of the Siin around 1385.

55. De Kersaint-Gilly, "Les Geulowars," pp. 99–101; Sarr, "Histoire du Sine-Saloum," pp. 225–81; Diop, "L'impact de la civilisation Manding au Sénégal," pp. 689–707.

56. Sarr, "Histoire du Sine-Saloum," pp. 225–30.

57. Noirot, "Notice sur le Sine-Saloum, Pays de Sine," pp. 167–68.

58. Diop, "L'impact de la civilisation Manding au Sénégal," pp. 692–95.

59. Doudou Yatt, elite interview, 29 October 1993; Sarr, "Histoire du Sine-Saloum," pp. 225–81.

60. Diop, "L'impact de la civilisation Manding au Sénégal," pp. 695–705; de Kersaint-Gilly, "Les Geulowars," pp. 99–101; Klein, *Islam and Imperialism in Senegal,* pp. 11–17.

61. Even in the early centuries of the Gelwaar regime, the Siin was not an isolated rural enclave but was situated very near important trans-Saharan trading routes, highways along which caravans carried gold, slaves, ivory, and forest products northward in exchange for salt, iron tools, weapons, and other items heading south. The westward push of the Mali empire (of which the Gelwaar expansion may have been an episode) may have been directed at finding new sources of ocean salt to make up for lost salt mines in the desert of present-day Mali and Mauritania. Although the precolonial economic history of Siin and Saluum salt production remains to be written, there is evidence that the salty marshes along these two estuaries were commercially exploited as part of the forest-Sahel-Sahara long-distance trade networks as early as the twelfth century. See Diop, "L'impact de la civilisation Manding au Sénégal," pp. 690–92; Klein, *Islam and Imperialism in Senegal,* pp. 1–32.

62. Klein, *Islam and Imperialism in Senegal,* pp. 18–20.

63. For further elaboration on the origin of castes in West Africa, see Tamari, "The Development of Caste Systems in West Africa," pp. 221–50; Tamari, "Les castes au Soudan occidental"; Frank, "Caste versus Craft," pp. 169–88; Richter, "Further Considerations of Caste in West Africa," pp. 37–54.

64. Klein, *Islam and Imperialism in Senegal,* pp. 13–17; Sarr, "Histoire du Sine-Saloum," pp. 247–51.

65. Doudou Yatt, elite interview, 29 October 1993.

66. Here we have an illustration of Philip Curtin's argument regarding the night-and-day difference between New World chattel slavery and slavery on the African continent: in the administration of a very young, very old, or otherwise enfeebled *maad*, a powerful *grand farba*, himself technically a slave, might effectively run the kingdom. See Curtin, *Economic Change in Precolonial Africa*.

67. Klein, *Islam and Imperialism in Senegal*, pp. 13–14; Sarr, "Histoire du Sine-Saloum," pp. 249–50.

68. Latyr Sene, oral history interview, 30 September 1993.

69. Poggi, *The Development of the Modern State*.

70. In the marvelously adaptive retrospective logic of the *pangool* system, if the estates have splintered or the lineage has died out, this is clearly evidence of the decline of the relationship with the benevolent and supporting *pangool*.

71. As is the case across much of sub-Saharan Africa, accusations of being a "witch" or "vampire" increase in times of social dislocation, economic crisis, or political uncertainty. For an authoritative social history of this phenomenon, see White, *Speaking with Vampires*.

72. Diaraf Dibor Sarr, oral history interview, 20 September 1993.

73. Indeed, every *laman* and *saltigué* I interviewed for this study insisted that it was his ancestor and his ancestor alone with whom the *maad* had consulted before the Gelwaar victory over Ma Ba Diakhou (discussed in more detail below).

74. Similar processes of diverting the lost material struggle into the supernatural realm are evident in the Muskogee Redstick movement in the southeastern United States at the time of Indian removal, in Native American Ghost Dance movements on the Great Plains in the late nineteenth century, and in the mythico-histories of Hutu refugees in Tanzania after the 1972 genocide in Burundi, to name a few examples. Martin, *Sacred Revolt;* Mooney, *Ghost Dance Religion and the Sioux Outbreak of 1890;* Liisa Malkki, *Purity and Exile.*

75. This Portuguese deformation of the term *buur* Siin, "king of the Siin" in the Wolof language, appeared as a place-name on fifteenth- and sixteenth-century European maps. Given that, in the Siin and in Saluum, the monarch was referred to by the title *maad*, this may reflect the possibility that the Portuguese used Wolof translators or came to know the Serer kingdoms through Wolof-speaking intermediaries.

76. This same "anterior communities" thesis helps explain the creative response of Ngoni peoples in southern Africa to the pressures of Boer colonization, and of peoples of the forested interior of the southeastern United States to federal westward expansion. Ngoni peoples located *behind* front lines of European expansion were neither decimated like the Khoikhoi of the Cape, nor drained by constant skirmishes, as were the Xhosa along the Fish River frontier. Indeed, groups such as the Mthethwa and the Zulu were able to develop the *impi* age-regiment (a military unit organized around a generation cohort of young men who had shared rites of initiation), instigating the *mfecane* (time of troubles) process of rapid state consolidation and expansion.

Similarly, the Spanish colonial presence in Florida, the French expansion up the Mississippi, and the westward push of the United States inland from the Piedmont wiped out a large number of indigenous groups. Yet peoples located farther inland, like the Muskogee of central Alabama, had more time to reorganize their society to take advantage of the new trade in furs and other commodities and to elaborate new cultural structures that reintegrated scattered populations and provided a basis for resistance to European expansion. Martin, *Sacred Revolt;* Peires, "Paradigm Deleted," pp. 295–313.

77. See for example Pasquier, "En marge de la guerre de succession"; and Law, *From Slave Trade to "Legitimate" Commerce.*

78. In the late 1700s and early 1800s, Islamic revival movements had already emerged as powerful means to unify and mobilize communities to respond to the challenges posed by an emerging capitalist Europe. Revitalized Islam fueled the state-building efforts of Muhammad 'Ali of Egypt in the early nineteenth century, and even earlier, in the late 1700s, solidified the regime of Usman dan Fodio among the Hausa-Fulani of what would become northern Nigeria. See Lapidus, *A History of Islamic Societies;* Hiskett, *The Sword of Truth;* Rivlin, *The Agricultural Policy of Muhammad 'Ali in Egypt.*

79. Old states and communities were consolidated into vast new empires; some—like the Fuuta Tooro–based regime of El Hajj Umar Tall of the 1870s, or its successor, the last major jihad state, Samory Touré's regime—spanned areas as vast as the great medieval trading empires of Ghana, Mali, and Songhai. See Batran, "The Nineteenth-Century Islamic Revolutions in West Africa," 6:537–54.

80. Faidherbe's generation served in Algeria when colonial policy sought to undermine the power of Islamic leaders considered a threat to the colonial regime. This proved to be an utter failure, rallying the Algerian population around *shari'a* law and Islam, and raising the imams and the ulema almost to martyr status. Officials like Faidherbe took a basic lesson from 1840s Algeria and turned it into policy in 1860s Senegal: rather than fight the popularity and legitimacy of Islamic institutions, try to coopt them. Klein, *Islam and Imperialism in Senegal,* pp. 40–42.

81. For a glimpse into these early anthropological notions of cultural evolution, see Lewis Henry Morgan's savagery-barbarism-civilization schema, cited in de Maille, "Introduction to the Bison Book Edition," p. xviii. For an alarming and influential contemporary echo of this teleology, see Kaplan, "The Coming Anarchy."

82. See the fairly explicit discussion of this strategy in Pinet-Laprade, "Notice sur les Serers par le Colonel du Genie Pinet-Laprade," pp. 12–24, as well as in Klein, *Islam and Imperialism in Senegal.*

83. See Klein, *Islam and Imperialism in Senegal,* pp. 63–93.

84. Chief among the allies was Lat Dior, *damel* of the Wolof state of Kajor, who, having resisted Islam most of his life, recognized the power of Ma Ba Diakhou's movement, submitted to the razor, and threw his lot in with the marabout just after the conquest of Saluum. Lat Dior eventually confronted

the advancing French empire head on and was defeated, but he is lionized in contemporary Senegal as a heroic military and political figure who struggled to maintain African independence.

85. These included skirmishes over the size of European outposts on the coast of the Siin, conflicts over payment of commercial levies to the royal court for the right to trade in the kingdom, and squabbles over "arbitrary justice" against European commercial agents and others who held European citizenship rights. Pinet-Laprade, "Notice sur les Serers par le Colonel du Genie Pinet-Laprade," pp. 22–34; Noirot, "Notice sur le Sine-Saloum, pays de Sine," pp. 167–68.

86. Babacar Faye, oral history interview, 30 September 1993; Sarr, "Histoire du Sine-Saloum," pp. 260–62; Klein, *Islam and Imperialism in Senegal,* pp. 90–93.

87. Sarr, "Histoire du Sine-Saloum," pp. 225–81.

88. Diaga Dibor Ndofene Diouf, oral history interview, 7 March 1993; Babacar Faye, oral history interview, 30 September 1993; Daly Ndeye Faye, oral history interview, 14 June 1993; Sombel Cama, oral history interview, 17 September 1993; Latyr Sene, oral history interview, 30 September 1993.

89. Klein, *Islam and Imperialism in Senegal,* pp. 114–29.

90. Pinet-Laprade, "Notice sur les Serers par le Colonel du Genie Pinet-Laprade," pp. 28–34.

91. Even before the establishment of the first formal educational institution—the École des Otages—tutors regularly visited the court at Diakhao to teach young Gelwaar princes to read, write, and behave like "civilized" nobles. Although these educational efforts in situ generally failed (indeed, this period witnessed the rise to power of several *maads* who stood for the very antithesis of the ideals of French educational training: self-confident nonliteracy, brawling, uncontrolled appetites for drink, food, and women), this intervention did eventually result in the incorporation of a scribe literate in French as a permanent member of the *maad's* court. These scribes replaced the *petits-marabouts* that had provided literacy services (in Arabic) to the Gelwaar court for centuries. Scribes, selected with the guidance of the colonial administration, were recruited not just for their knowledge of France, Rousseau, or the intricacies of the *passé simple* but also for their usefulness as spies at the Gelwaar court.

92. Today the founder of the Mouride brotherhood is the most prominent anticolonial national hero, patron saint, and embodiment of Senegalese national cultural identity. Reproductions of the only known photograph of Bamba are everywhere—from ministerial offices in Dakar to small-town barber shops. Ironically, the portrait has a decidedly ghostlike air, in which all but the marabout's face is hidden behind a loose fitting, flowing white garment that reaches down to and obscures his feet, reinforcing the popular sentiment that the founder of Mouridism was so holy, so supernaturally endowed with *baraka,* so otherworldly in his vision and saintliness, that he had no need for his feet to come in contact with the ground. See also Cruise O'Brien, *The Mourides of*

Senegal. To varying degrees, the other major brotherhoods (the Tijanniya, Qadiriyya, and Layennes) followed versions of this Mouride model as well.

93. While the Baye Fall were never the numerical majority of Mourides, they were the backbone of the movement as a force for social reconstitution in the aftermath of colonial conquest and for the transformation of the Mourides into peanut producers. Today the Baye Fall are a small subgroup whose doctrines render them heretical to some Mourides. Yet they remain a kind of idealized, extreme version of Mouridism, helping to establish some of the core values of the movement through a kind of caricature.

94. Pelissier, *Les paysans du Sénégal,* pp. 307–9.

95. Ibid., pp. 309–11.

96. Of the remaining 17 percent, 34.5 percent self-identify as Catholic or Protestant and 5.8 percent as animist.

97. The second largest brotherhood in Senegal, the Tijanniya or Tijanes, also developed a presence in the Siin by similar means. The Niassenes, an offshoot of the Tijanniya, are often thought of as a Serer brotherhood because they are based in the city of Kaolack, in the former kingdom of Saluum. In Njafaj, the site of this study, 43.3 percent of respondents identify as Mouride, 13.8 percent as Tijane, and 2.6 percent as Khadir or Baye Fall Mouride.

98. These include Koranic verses written in Arabic on scraps of paper used as key elements in the amulets made for sale, as well as the use of Arabic terminology, blessings, and prayers intertwined with *pangool*-oriented animistic healing and intercessionary rites.

99. *Surga,* a Wolof term for "follower, underling, or worker," has taken on a slightly different meaning among the Serer of Siin, where it is used to describe a seasonal migrant agricultural laborer. It is thus analogous to the more widely circulated *navetane.* David, *Les navetanes.*

100. In Kaolack and Fatick, Serer migrants from rural regions like Njafaj encountered Serer-speaking peoples who had lived in these towns for some time. Both Kaolack and Fatick are sometimes referred to as Serer cities because they are located in the heart of the former Serer kingdom of Siin (Fatick) and Saluum (Kaolack). Both are administrative centers that grew up around colonial outposts located near enough to the former Gelwaar capitals to oversee affairs in the kingdoms. Both communities seem to have been founded around or near existing Serer villages. They are now ethnically quite mixed and include very large percentages of Wolof, Tukolor, and Halpulaar populations, along with many Serer inhabitants whose experience is naturally more urban than that of Serer in rural regions like Njafaj.

101. The French phrase means "the very model of the African peasant" and is quoted from Pelissier, *Les paysans du Sénégal,* p. 198.

3. "TRADITION" IN THE SIIN

1. I thank Charles Becker, François Simondon, and Ernest Faye of ORSTOM for making this collaboration possible.

2. I am especially indebted to the team of surveyors who implemented the questionnaire with perseverance and skill: Ousmane Faye, Moussa Sarr, Abdou Diouf, and their indispensable leader, Saliou Diouf. All the surveyors live in the Njafaj region, speak fluent Serer-Siin (as well as fluent Wolof and French), and are trusted by respondents. They conducted weekly visits to each household in their sector, posing a regular set of questions about health, nutrition, and sanitation. My survey was separated into discrete sections (socioeconomic background, tenure practices, rankings of authoritative institutions on a number of criteria, and agree-disagree statements regarding historical memory of culture and legitimacy of authority) that the surveyor could, when necessary, pose separately during repeated visits.

3. I randomly selected twelve from among the thirty villages in the zone of study. Within these villages, I randomly selected a fraction of the households. I divided household members into six categories: (1) male head of household, (2) female head of household (if there was no male head) or eldest female, (3) other senior males (over age 45), (4) other senior females (over age 45), (5) junior males (age 20–45), and (6) junior females (age 20–45). Within each category in which there was more than one possible respondent, respondents were chosen randomly. This intrahousehold stratification was necessary for two reasons. First, it was important to include the eldest male and female respondents for a supplemental series of questions directed primarily at household heads. Second, given that this project centers on historical memories of tradition, purely random, unstratified sampling would have provided a distorted picture because it would have failed to take into account the dynamics of cultural leadership and deference in these communities. The young still very much tend to defer to some elder, any elder, when discussing their opinions about "tradition." Group interviews in particular taught me that the narratives of elders set the boundaries within which the young might improvise to establish their own narratives, or out of which they might wish to escape to establish their own counterversion of "tradition." A purely random sample would have been somewhat less useful in trying to capture this dynamic. As I stratified it, the sample captures the opinions and behaviors of the young but is slightly skewed toward elders in order to address my theoretical concern for the dynamics of intergenerational deference and leadership in the elaboration of *both* dominant and dissenting historical memories of culture and "tradition."

4. The high nonresponse rate for this question, 17.3 percent, is noteworthy. The question was posed just after the most difficult period of the agricultural cycle, late summer and early fall, the end of the "time of suffering," when subsistence producers who depend on their anticipated new harvest and have little extralocal economic resources are probably undernourished and may be one environmental or agricultural calamity away from famine. Asking about food stocks is an understandably delicate matter, especially at this time of year, and shame over lack of means may have led many who would have responded negatively to this question to simply refuse to answer.

5. Amad Dieng, oral history interview, 28 August 1993.

6. Becker, *Traditions villageois du Siin.*

7. The inverse relationship, a statist historical memory caused by contemporary idealization of the postcolonial state, is not borne out by the analysis, as indicated in the discussion below.

8. This 0–100 scale recodes responses from several questions such that a respondent with the strongest possible emphasis on a centralized state would receive a score of 100. The scale is built from responses to four questions: (1) Who was the most important authority in this community prior to the arrival of Europeans here? (Rank the top three from among six choices: canton chief, *maad, saltigué, laman,* marabout, and village chief.) (2) What do you think of this statement (agree strongly, agree, don't know, disagree, or disagree strongly): "In the period before the Europeans came here, if you did not agree with the amount or locations of fields that the *laman* gave you to farm, you should and could go consult the *maad* in Diakhao to address this problem"? (3) What do you think of this statement (agree strongly, agree, don't know, disagree, or disagree strongly): "The *maad* had nothing to do with the *pangool* [ancestral spirits] of this village"? (4) What do you think of this statement (agree strongly, agree, don't know, disagree, or disagree strongly): "In the period before the arrival of the founder of this village, all the land around here belonged to the *maad* in Diakhao"?

9. This is borne out both by a separate analysis of variance between centrist historical memory, and caste group in general, and by multiple regression of each caste category against centrist historical memory. In the regression, the other three cast categories fail to yield statistically significant results, although the regression coefficients and their signs are consistent with theoretical expectations and qualitative findings. (Gelwaar caste: $\beta = .047$, $p = .405$; stigmatized castes: $\beta = .021$, $p = .676$; Serer aristocratic caste: $\beta = -.112$, $p = .613$.)

10. Respondents ranked the top three from among (1) canton chief, a local representative of the colonial administration, (2) Gelwaar *maad*, (3) *saltigué*, or rain priest, (4) *laman*, (5) marabout, and (6) village chief. For each type of authority (colonial state, Gelwaar state, customary Serer, or Islamic), we can draw on the 1 through 4 rankings to construct a scale of idealization for that authority type. For example, higher rankings for *both* choices in the customary Serer category *(laman, saltigué)* result in a higher score on the 0–100 index variable that rates degree of idealization of Serer customary authorities.

11. This is not to suggest that animism alone predicts attachment to "tradition," and that Islam or Christianity by themselves indicate some lack of attachment to "tradition." The very low level of animist self-reporting masks the degree to which very large numbers of those who report that they are Muslim or Christian offer libations to ancestral spirits, follow highly syncretic versions of the monotheistic religions, and exhibit strong attachment to other nonreligious elements of what they consider to be "traditional" Serer culture.

12. Quote by Babacar Faye, oral history interview, 30 September 1993.

13. As table 3 reveals, even Mourides and non-Mouride Muslims most commonly make their religious payments (either *asaka* or *addiya*) "directly to

the poor." This is a very common form of religious tithing in the Siin, and most respondents, whether Muslim, Christian, or animist, consider it entirely acceptable to pay what they call a religious tithe *not* to a religious official in the organization to which they (perhaps nominally) belong but directly to the poor with whom they have contact. This most commonly refers to individual acts of ad hoc charity directed toward distant kinfolk and neighbors in need. It often follows historic lines of caste subordination and dependence: for example, griots formerly in the service of particular free farmer families can call upon, and often receive charitable support from, their former patrons in the caste hierarchy.

14. As discussed in chapter 1, my use of terms like *orthodoxy* and *syncretism* does not indicate a normative ranking of religious (or other) practice by degree of conformity to a predetermined notion of pure or ideal behavior, belief, ritual, or custom (*orthodoxy* as a normatively preferred standard, *syncretism* as an impure deviation from standard). With regard to institutions, the thrust of this book is quite the opposite: to underscore the ubiquitous, quotidian nature of the effort at syncretism, and the utility of coherent and successful syncretic institutional outcomes. With regard to the discussion of religion here, orthodoxy and syncretism simply anchor opposite ends of a continuum defined by the degree to which respondents creatively blend (or do not blend) values, norms, rituals, and practices derived from more than one religious or cosmological framework. For more on this and other ways of treating syncretism and orthodoxy, see Stewart and Shaw, *Syncretism/Anti-Syncretism*.

15. The quote marks enclosing "independence from superstition" and "bright" are intentional and important. Tenure modernization schemes of this kind have failed to deliver the development and progress they initially promised.

16. *Mak a ndok* was included in part simply to gauge the legitimacy of customary authority figures. However, respondents were extremely likely to rank first a customary authority, especially if that authority were a plausible kinsman. With this in mind, I chose *mak a ndok* from among a number of other possible customary authorities because the "office" of eldest member of the matrilineal family is vestigial in the Siin today: matrilineal family networks have largely collapsed. When they exist, they tend to operate at small-scale, intrahousehold levels. For example, one of the primary historic functions of the *mak a ndok* and matrilineal clan was the accumulation and maintenance of cattle herds. Processes of colonial codification of law, commodification, and Islamification have transferred wealth, like cattle, that was once in the hands of the *mak a ndok* into systems of patrilineal ownership and inheritance (see chapter 4). Thus, when respondents were asked whether they keep a percentage of their cattle with their matrilineal uncles, 97.6 percent responded that they have *no cattle whatsoever* in the control of their matrilineal clan. Matrilineal property holding is largely dead, and the *mak a ndok* no longer functions as a community or even familial authority. Yet, as

a striking illustration of the lack of legitimacy of most state and formal authorities, 54.6 percent of respondents ranked an authority figure that has lost much of its institutional power, the *mak a ndok,* as the leader to whom they would be most willing to make a voluntary contribution.

4. LAND PAWNING AS A RESPONSE TO THE STANDARDIZATION OF TENURE

Earlier versions of this chapter appeared as "Institutional Syncretism and the Articulation of Modes of Production in Rural Senegalese Land Tenure Relations," *African Rural and Urban Studies* 4, no. 2–3 (1997): 59–98, published by Michigan State University Press, and as "The Market Meets Sacred Fire: Land Pawning as Institutional Syncretism in Inter-War Senegal," *African Economic History* 25 (1997): 9–41. Reproduced with kind permission from both of these publications.

1. The word *taile* is pronounced TIE-lay.

2. This account of the *taile* pawn between Birame Diouf and Waly Sene, to which I will return later in this chapter, is based on a series of interviews with descendants of the two parties and with adjudicatory officials in the land dispute that broke out when the Dioufs reclaimed the field from the Senes in 1992. Djignak Diouf, dispute interview, 11 July 1993; Niokhor Sene, dispute interview, 15 September 1993; Tening Faye, dispute interview, 3 October 1993; Mahecor Ndong, elite interview, 26 July 1993.

3. For a similar case of cash-crop intensification making use of and reworking, rather than clearing away, local, embedded institutions and culturally defined social objectives, see Netting, Stone, and Stone, "Kofyar Cash-Cropping," pp. 299–19. For a similar example of reconciling cultural embeddedness with exigencies of early capitalist transformation in western European industrialization, see Schuster, "Workers and Community," pp. 777–97.

4. As discussed in chapter 2, this use of an apparently Wolof term in Serer is the subject of etymological and ethnographic uncertainty. The Serer migration through the Wolof heartland has left the patterns of cultural influence between these two groups somewhat obscure. Diop and Abelin argue that the Wolof adopted key land tenure institutions such as the *laman* from the Serer. Shared terminology between these two groups may also stem from colonial selection: administrators' first contact with local land tenure systems took place in Wolof communities. When they "discovered" analogous institutions among other ethnic groups like the Serer, they may have applied already familiar Wolof terms to describe Serer institutions. This line of argument suggests the transformative power of colonial codification of culture: most contemporary Serer treat Wolof terms like *taile* and *laman* as perfectly natural, historically rooted Serer concepts, elemental to the *cosaan* (original "tradition") of the Siin. Diop, "La tenure foncière en milieu rural Wolof," p. 48; Abelin, "Domaine national et développement au Sénégal," p. 516.

5. See for example Ensminger, "Changing Property Rights," p. 8.

6. Notions of originality and village founding tales discussed here emerge primarily from the now-hegemonic narrative of Serer history and tradition. Traces of rival versions of "real" Serer tradition regarding ownership and exchange do persist. For the sake of brevity, I have excluded from this chapter a complete exploration of these rival versions, which fall into three categories:

1. More heterogeneous patterns of village settlement, which deemphasize the significance of a solitary village founder. Especially common among women, these versions may represent the vestiges of historic conflict with the *laman-bakh* aristocracy (discussed below).

2. Reinterpretations of precolonial Serer society from the point of view of Enlightenment concepts of rights and citizenship. These versions are especially common among young men who have grown up since independence.

3. Omission of the role played by the *maad* in establishing claims to land. This is a highly significant omission that suggests a conscious assertion of the autonomy of Serer land tenure claims with respect to state authority in general, and it may represent a reaction against independent Senegal's restructuring of land tenure relations through the 1964 National Domain Law. In this version of Serer tradition, hostility to the National Domain Law has been translated into an erasure of the role of any state—postcolonial or Gelwaar—in establishing authentic local land tenure relations.

7. In light of Braudel's structures of the *longue durée*, in much of sub-Saharan Africa, cleavage, migration, and resettlement in response to social tension have come to represent an archetype, an established pattern that structures, indeed limits, responses to social tension. See Braudel, "Histoire et sciences sociales," pp. 725–53; Bayart, *The State in Africa*, pp. 30–36.

8. Even today, this practice of clearing dead, unwanted brush constitutes a definitive signal of claim to usufruct. A master of cutting is one who has been "officially" sanctioned to perform this annual rite of clearing on a given set of fields and is, therefore, a holder of usufruct rights. On grants of land from *laman* to *yal bakh*, see Diop, "La tenure foncière en milieu rural Wolof," p. 49; Lericollais, *Sob*, pp. 19–20, 48; Abelin, "Domaine national et développement au Sénégal," p. 516.

9. Diop, "La tenure foncière en milieu rural Wolof," p. 49.

10. Dupire et al., "Résidence, tenure foncière, alliance dans une société bilinèaire," pp. 438, 440; Diop, "La tenure foncière en milieu rural Wolof," p. 49; Abelin, "Domaine national et développement au Sénégal," pp. 517–18.

11. In the last years of the colonial era, lines of authority between *lamans* and *yal bakhs* were becoming increasingly unclear. Many large fire estates had

long since been fragmented into *bakhs*, resulting in gradual devolution of *lamanic* authority. Moreover, with the coming of independence, the imminent collapse of the Gelwaar state destabilized other institutions of "traditional" authority, like that of the *lamans*. Abelin goes farther in this vein, calling the devolution of *lamanic* powers to *yal bakhs* a consequence of increasing individualism. See "Domaine national et développement au Sénégal," p. 521.

12. For complete reproductions of village founding myths in the northwestern Siin, see Becker, *Traditions villageois du Siin.* My account of the founding of Tukar draws primarily on interviews with Kumba Ndofene Thiao and Diogoye Diouf, as well as the schoolmaster Etienne Diop regarding versions of the tale recounted in the École Kane Faye de Tukar, the local primary school. Kumba Ndofene Thiao, interview, 3 July 1993; Diogoye Diouf, interview, 6 March 1993; Etienne Diop, interview, 19 April 1993.

13. Name of the original neighborhood of Tukar, founded by Djigan Diouf and current home of his descendants.

14. *Maad a Sinig*, or "King of the Sinig people," is the full title in Serer-Siin for the *maad* who rules the people of the Siin, sometimes referred to as the "Sinig."

15. Fassar o Njafaj is the person referred to in the folk account as Fassamane Thiao.

16. Djigan was alarmed that Fassar would announce, for anyone to hear (including the pernicious spirits that might bring plague or locusts), that Djigan was about to enjoy a bountiful harvest. In Serer and Wolof custom, one avoids drawing attention to success or good fortune for fear that evil spirits will take note, become jealous, and intervene. Especially in Wolof communities, for example, at the sight of a newborn baby, one responds by saying, "Oh, what an ugly baby you have." This is understood to mean that one is complimenting the baby, but that evil spirits will not catch the reversal of meaning and will overlook the child. Should one slip and offer a compliment or comment on how much millet someone is about to harvest, one should add quickly, *Kar-kar*, to ward off the attention of evil spirits, who presumably perked up their ears at the noisy compliment.

17. Diakhao is the capital of the kingdom of Siin, where the *maad* lived and held court. Given the age of the village of Tukar, Diaga Diouf's version of the tale both establishes the original claim to title on the part of his lineage and accommodates migrants who came centuries later, in the era of the *maad*, for whom Fassar would seem to be a stand in.

18. Diaga Dibor Ndofene Diouf, in a variation not found in any other versions of this story, refers to Fassar o Njafaj as a blacksmith, the lowest caste above slave.

19. They cut green, young trees to prevent the fire from burning into their *ndaak* (their "little piece," that is, their fire estate).

20. This distinction is quite suggestive with regard to the problem of "goose chase" ur-texts like *Conversations with Ogotemmeli*, by the anthropologist Marcel Griaule. Follow-up field evaluations of Griaule's seminal

research on Dogon cosmology have failed to uncover traces of the extremely complex creation myths and cosmologies elaborated in Griaule's interviews with a Dogon elder named Ogotemmeli in the 1930s and 1940s. The lack of correspondence may lie in a distinction between "folk" and "expert" knowledge: Ogotemmeli may have recounted an extremely elaborate version of Dogon mythology known only to a small number of initiates. At the vernacular, or folk, level, the "egg of creation," the "seven vibrations," or the dog star Sirius carry virtually none of the rich symbolic content found in expert accounts. To the extent that Griaule and subsequent students of African cosmology have used *Conversations with Ogotemmeli* as an "ur-text," inattention to folk-expert distinctions severely limit its usefulness as a basis for making sense of African religion and philosophy at a general level. See Van Beek, "Dogon Restudied"; and Griaule and Dieterlen, "The Dogon," pp. 83–94.

21. This preservation of rural African institutions contrasts markedly with land tenure policies in postcolonial Senegal, which, within a few years of independence, instituted a National Domain Law, which "fait table rase des droits traditionnels." Abelin, "Domaine national et développement au Sénégal," p. 525. See further discussion in chapter 5.

22. Klein, *Islam and Imperialism in Senegal,* pp. 114–25; Dione Falilou Diouf, oral history interview, 2 October 1993; Gorgui Marone, oral history interview, 22 October 1993; Selbé Sarr, oral history interview, 1 October 1993.

23. Lericollais points out that the peanut was produced "mostly as a condiment in the local economy" in the early part of the twentieth century. *Sob,* p. 78.

24. Pasturing livestock on the fallow fields enriches the soil with fresh manure. But at the beginning of the rainy season, when little vegetation remains for grazing, animals must be penned to keep them trampling or devouring the staple crop. The integration of livestock into the system makes possible much more intensive farming but requires authoritative coordination and management. See Lericollais, *Sob,* pp. 22–24; Pelissier, *Les paysans du Sénégal,* pp. 189, 224; Diop, "La tenure foncière en milieu rural Wolof," p. 48; Dupire et al., "Résidence, tenure foncière, alliance dans une société bilinèaire," p. 441.

25. Indeed, given price fluctuations and the fact that poor rains reduce yields of cash as well as subsistence crops, this remains a hard sell today. And given that population expansion and environmental degradation have only narrowed the already thin margin between subsistence and famine, it should come as no surprise, as James Scott has pointed out, that food security values remain quite powerful in today's decidedly more commoditized Siin *(Weapons of the Weak).*

26. For a thorough discussion of the place of the Siin in trans-Saharan and other precolonial trading systems, including evidence suggesting that the Siin actually exported cotton cloth, see Guigou, "Les changements du système familial et matrimonial," p. 45.

27. Sombel Cama, oral history interview, 27 September 1993; Dione Falilou Diouf, oral history interview, 2 October 1993.

28. Correspondence, Administrator of Sine-Saloum to Director of Political Affairs, 24 June 1892 and 25 May 1892, Archives Nationales du Sénégal, unclassified documents.

29. Dione Falilou Diouf, oral history interview, 2 October 1993; Babacar Faye, oral history interview, 30 September 1993.

30. As Cruise O'Brien describes in detail, colonial conquest of the Wolof kingdoms of Kajor, Jolof, and Baol precipitated dramatic social upheaval, in which the social function of the *ceddo* warrior caste disappeared virtually over night. See *The Mourides of Senegal.*

31. The other variety of millet, *maac,* gradually faded from Serer diets. The precommodification rotation system included both *pod* and *maac* varieties of millet as a hedge against drought and famine. The two varieties sprout and mature at different phases of the rainy season—one early, the other late. Should the rains prove poor in the first weeks of the rainy season but pick up by the end, the first variety *(pod)* will fail, but the second *(maac)* will not, ensuring a minimal subsistence yield. Strictly from a subsistence point of view (that is, putting aside the purchasing power generated by the peanut), the displacement of *maac* by the peanut pushed the Serer producer closer to the famine threshold. See Lericollais, *Sob,* pp. 28, 43, 79, 87, 89.

This new three-year rotation would last until the 1960s, when a rapid demographic expansion put tremendous pressure on fallow land. By the mid-1980s, the practice of fallow had all but disappeared, and the *pod*-peanut-fallow rotation had almost completely collapsed, seriously undermining the agropastoral system that for generations had maintained soil fertility in conditions of intensive farming and poor rainfall. Lericollais, *Sob,* pp. 79, 102; Abelin, "Domaine national et développement au Sénégal," p. 502.

32. Abelin, citing Étienne Leroy, notes the degree to which colonial officials, beginning with Faidherbe, sought to "protect" customary law and land rights. He refers to a 1904 decree that declared valid "the rights upon which the natives' collective property are based in cases where native chiefs hold such rights as representatives of the collectivity." "Domaine national et développement au Sénégal," pp. 513–14.

33. Diop, "La tenure foncière en milieu rural Wolof," p. 51.

34. Abelin, "Domaine national et développement au Sénégal," p. 514. The appeals court ruling represents a remarkably fanciful—and useful—projection of Sun-King-style absolutism onto the decidedly less centralized, more federal and pluralist political structures of the Wolof kingdoms.

35. Jean Chabas argues that, even when ostensibly engaged in preservation of customary law, administrators sought to project "standard" European principles so as to advance commercial interests: "The colonial legislator limits himself to declaring that he recognizes and respects indigenous rights, all the while searching to establish outside of those rights a new regime which conforms to his interest in giving the French and *assimilés* who trade with native Africans security comparable to what they would enjoy if they made similar

contracts in France." Cited in Abelin, "Domaine national et développement au Sénégal," pp. 514–15.

36. Arguing for lack of intervention in local structures of authority, Lericollais unintentionally captures the essence of codification as a form of transformation when he notes, "We must emphasize that the French administration never directly intervened in the tenure problems of the Siin: until the present day, they limited their regulation to matters of customary legislation, to which the great majority of peasants remain attached" (*Sob*, p. 22). This very business of tinkering with customary legislation had direct and profound implications for land tenure institutions and practices.

37. Dupire et al., "Résidence, tenure foncière, alliance dans une société bilinèaire," pp. 418–22; Ngor Wagane Ndour, oral history interview, 29 September 1993; Xemess Diouf, oral history interview, 28 September 1993; Diaraf Dibor Sarr, oral history interview, 20 September 1993.

38. The submatrilineage, or *ndok*, organized at the level of the kitchens within households, had been the primary locus of saving and cattle holding. Lericollais, *Sob*, pp. 37, 60, 65, 96; Guigou, "Les changements du système familial et matrimonial," p. 9; Dupire et al., "Résidence, tenure foncière, alliance dans une société bilinèaire," p. 437; Diaraf Dibor Sarr, oral history interview, 20 September 1993; Ngor Wagane Ndour, oral history interview, 29 September 1993.

39. In polygynous households (the norm among the Serer), an entire compound, or *mbind*, is organized around a male family head, but the *mbind* is in turn divided into various *ngaks*, each centered on a single cowife and her children. Dupire et al., "Résidence, tenure foncière, alliance dans une société bilinèaire," pp. 437–42.

40. In his 1864 description of the Serer, Pinet-Laprade, especially keen to find any trace of "civilization," highlights this pattern of patrilineal inheritance and specifies a few father's goods of the era. "Notice sur les Serers," pp. 18–20.

41. For analogous processes, see Colson, "Possible Repercussions of the Right to Make Wills upon the Plateau Tonga of Northern Rhodesia"; Mann and Roberts, introduction.

42. Dulphy, "Coutume Sérères de la Petite-Côte," p. 217; "Agents indigènes traduits en justice: Observations sur les états de jugements," Rapport sur la fonctionnement de la justice indigène, August 1923, Archives Nationales du Sénégal, Séries 6M/316.

43. See Thomas J. Bassett, introduction to *Land in African Agrarian Systems*, ed. Thomas J. Bassett and Donald E. Crummey (Madison: University of Wisconsin Press, 1993), pp. 4–5.

44. Dulphy, "Coutume Sérères de la Petite-Côte," pp. 297–98. Dulphy, the administrateur-adjoint des colonies who prepared the report, does not tell us if the agents of Maurel and Prom knew enough about bilineal systems to search for the matrilineal nephew of the deceased debtor. Presumably if they had, matrilineal nephews would have soon begun claiming that they followed patrilineal customs and inherited from their fathers, not their maternal uncles.

45. Scott, *Seeing Like a State,* pp. 32–38.

46. During his junior military service in Algeria, prior to his assignment as governor of Senegal, Faidherbe had come to appreciate the danger of attempting to undermine and eradicate locally legitimate Sufi notables. See Klein, *Islam and Imperialism in Senegal,* pp. 79–82, 221.

47. Abelin, "Domaine national et développement au Sénégal," pp. 514, 515.

48. Serigne Ibra Faye, elite interview, 23 October 1993.

49. Djignak Diouf, dispute interview, 11 July 1993.

50. For a thorough analysis of new cash needs that developed as commodification spread in the Siin during the interwar years, see Lericollais, *Sob,* pp. 95–96.

51. Griots, artisans, and other casted groups relied for their subsistence production on small plots of land loaned to them by their patron lineages. These fields were generally poor, and plots shifted from year to year. As the *ceddo* warrior caste gradually lost their former function in the economy of predation, they fell into relatively landless status, like other low-caste groups. See Lericollais, *Sob,* p. 45.

52. Ndiogoye Thiao, oral history interview, 12 August 1993.

53. See Cruise O'Brien, *The Mourides of Senegal;* Behrman, *Muslim Brotherhoods and Politics in Senegal.*

54. With its high population density and intensive, delicately balanced agropastoral system (which had successfully incorporated the peanut and earned the veneration of French colonial officials as the model peasant agriculture system in Senegal), the Siin was effectively off limits to the maraboutic *daara* mode of agrarian expansion. See Geismar, *Recueil des coutumes civiles de races du Sénégal,* p. 23; Pelissier, *Les paysans du Sénégal,* pp. 189, 198, 203, 224.

55. Gorgui Marone, oral history interview, 22 October 1993; Matiasse Gakou, dispute interview, 6 July 1993.

56. Niokhor Sene, dispute interview, 15 September 1993; Tening Faye, dispute interview, 3 October 1993.

57. Diop, "La tenure foncière en milieu rural Wolof," p. 51.

TRANSITIONS: THE SIIN REORDERED

1. Birame Diouf and Waly Sene were parties to a 1930s land exchange (*taile* pawn) described in detail in chapter 4.

2. By the 1970s, this area itself had been left behind by the marabouts. Decades of overproduction of peanuts had robbed the soil of nutrients. Sufi plantation owners had since moved east into "virgin" territory, including government-protected forests like Khelcom. In 1991, Mouride leaders issued an *ndigel,* or religious edict, calling for followers to help clear this designated wilderness zone. They came by the thousands, including a large number of employees of the government's Water and Forests Service (Service des Eaux et Forêts). For a very thorough exposé of the Khelcom affair, see Coulibaly, "Khelkom," p. 5.

3. An accomplishment for which the governor of Senegal sent his "deepest appreciation and congratulations," along with forty-three Arabian horses, two hundred muskets, and some miscellaneous perfume and jewelry.

4. Sombel Cama, oral history interview, 27 September 1993.

5. Markovitz, *Leopold Sedar Senghor and the Politics of Negritude.*

5. TWO ROMANTICIZATIONS

Epigraphs: Léopold Sédar Senghor, président de la République du Sénégal, radio address, 1 May 1964, as cited in Abelin, "Domaine national et développement au Sénégal," p. 508; Hamad Sarr, dispute interview, 26 August 1993.

1. For a discussion of President Senghor's vision of an egalitarian tenure reform that would restore an African socialist notion of communal tenure, see Debène, "Regards sur le droit foncier Sénégalais," pp. 79–83.

2. Scott's classic *Weapons of the Weak: Everyday Forms of Peasant Resistance* virtually set the intellectual agenda for a generation of scholarship on unconventional forms of response and resistance on the part of subordinate rural populations confronting capitalist incorporation and the consolidation of the legal-rational authority of the state.

3. *Taile* pawning is itself an adaptive local response to commodification informed by memories of precolonial tenure institutions (see chapter 4).

4. Quote from Hirschman, *Exit, Voice, and Loyalty.*

5. *Cosaan*, a crucial term in the cultural vocabulary of the Siin, refers to ancestral tradition, a corpus of inherited values, social norms, and informal rules perceived to be deeply rooted in the history of the region and constitutive of the Serer-Siin as a culturally distinct people.

6. I draw on Fredric Jameson and James Scott in thinking of modernism as an unproblematic faith in the ability of systematic, planned, centrally designed, and centrally organized actions to transform systems of production, governance, domination, inquiry, and meaning-allocation so that they will yield socially beneficial effects. See Jameson, *The Ideologies of Theory*, pp. 178–208, 195, as cited in Appiah, *In My Father's House*; Scott, *Seeing Like a State.*

7. LeRoy, "L'émergence d'un droit foncier locale au Sénégal," pp. 109–40.

8. The National Domain Law makes even more sense given the relative developmental importance of the Senegal River valley in contrast to the Siin. In the Senegal River valley, abundant water for year-round irrigated farms has led the state and the international development community to attempt large-scale production of sugar, cotton, and even wheat. The contemporary macroeconomic marginality of the Siin, in contrast to the centrality of the Senegal River valley, helps explain the implementation of a one-size-fits-all land reform so strikingly out of sync with tenure realities in one region, yet plausibly tailored to address problems of access and inequality in another.

9. From its inception in 1964, the National Domain Law envisioned the establishment of a new layer of democratically elected rural councils to govern new territorial administrative units known as *communautés rurales* (rural communities). The rural councils were to implement the state's control over the national domain and to serve as courts of first and last instance in land conflicts. The state was very slow to set up the new rural council system, so that, in practice, control over the national domain fell at first to existing agents of the centrally appointed territorial administration, that is, the governors, prefects, and subprefects who presided over *régions, départements*, and *arrondissements*, respectively. The legislation actually establishing the rural council system was not enacted until 1972; and in the Siin, three more years would pass before the first rural council was established. See Debène, "Regards sur le droit foncier Sénégalais," pp. 84–88; Caverivière, "Incertitudes et devenir du droit foncier Sénégalais," pp. 95–115.

10. The 1964 law itself established a principle of maximum *mise en valeur* (putting to use) of the "national domain." Article 2 of the law grants the state control of all rural lands for the sake of maximizing its productive use: "The state controls the lands of the National Domain in order to assure their use and rational exploitation." Article 15 moves toward the two-year usufruct rule by establishing that the state has the power to seize *(désaffecter)* land "as a result of insufficient exploitation, if the interested party ceases to personally exploit the land, or for reasons of general interest." As local representatives of state authority applied these very broad principles of tenure control, working definitions were established for "insufficient exploitation" of land. In the Siin region and throughout most of rural Senegal, farming during at least two consecutive rainy seasons became the official definition of "sufficient exploitation." Gouvernement du Sénégal. "Loi no. 64–46 du 17 juin 1964 rélative au domain national." For further background on the National Domain Law, see Diop, "La tenure foncière en milieu rural Wolof," p. 48; Abelin, "Domaine national et développement au Sénégal," p. 516; Niang, "Réflexions sur la réforme foncière Sénégalaise de 1964," pp. 219–27.

11. See chapter 3 for a complete description of the survey from which these data are derived, as well as an overview of its findings.

12. This may help explain why survey respondents considered the *saltigué*, or traditional "rain priest," the second most important authority for village well-being, after the subprefect, a state-appointed local government official. *Saltigués* once worked closely with *lamans* and were generally a prominent member of a *laman's* lineage. Their duties tended to focus on the supernatural side of land and natural resource management, whereas the duties of *lamans* tended to fuse material and spiritual matters. As the entire *lamanic* resource management system has been stripped of its material power, but retains its dimension of spiritual custodianship, it makes sense that *saltigués*, more so than *lamans*, still seem important for community well-being.

13. Koly Diagne, dispute interview, 16 September 1993.

14. Gorgui Faye, oral history interview, 19 July 1993.

15. Building on the name of the land reform, the Loi sur la Domain Nationale, Serer peasants have perceptively seized upon the words *domain* and *nationale* as the key, active ingredients of the new tenure system and turned them into verbs in Serer-Siin. Thus, they use phrases like "Oxe domain-a o qol es" (He domained my field), or more commonly and simply "Oxe nationalizé o qol es." Indeed, the term *to nationalize* has taken on the generic meaning of "seizing without moral right or authority." Strikingly, a rural councilor explained this concept to me by trying to make it apply to what he saw (quite insightfully) as a material possession about which I probably felt as Serer producers feel about their fields: "For example, if we talk about you loaning your car to somebody: if you loaned it to me for two or three years, and then you needed it back, and you asked me for it back, and I told you, No, I'm not giving it back because I've nationalized it, well, that's not honest, that's not logical." (Abdou Dione, elite interview, 19 October 1993.) The National Domain Law has not only ruptured social relations but has also in some ways transformed the very discourse of social rupture.

16. Boucar Ngom, dispute interview, 19 October 1993.

17. Ibid.

18. Latyr Farah Diouf, dispute interview, 3 June 1993.

19. Waly Koundoul Sene sent the message in Wolof, not Serer. In the Siin, Wolof is widely spoken among those whose economic and social relations link them to other parts of Senegal. Moreover, some phrases, like *defal ndank*, have acquired an idiomatic quality even among those who are not fluent Wolof speakers.

20. Ibid.

21. Waly Koundoul Sene, dispute interview, 19 October 1993.

22. Ibid.

23. See Foster, "Peasant Society and the Image of Limited Good."

24. Samba Faye, dispute interview, 16 September 1993.

25. *Masla*, as used by the Serer of Siin, refers to a strong emphasis in interpersonal relations on maintaining social harmony and avoiding ugly confrontations that result from raw, naked disclosure of true feelings. It is a crucial norm in Serer, as well as in many other preindustrial societies, in which the individual is subordinated to the social group.

26. Samba Yatt, dispute interview, 26 August 1993.

27. Calling the contemporary state the *maad* (the Serer term for the preindependence monarch of the Siin) is not just an elision of nomenclature but also a more systemic incorporation of new law and authorities into an established framework of popular historical memory regarding extravillage state authority. Hamad Faye, dispute interview, 16 October 1993.

28. For more detail on the duality of pawning patterns, see tables 17 and 18.

29. It is rather rare for women to formally make use of the National Domain Law to gain control of fields from their husbands or other men. Rural councils do tend to favor male control of fields. If, in a case of tenure ambiguity, the rural council can find a male head of household to serve as *yal qol* (field

master), he will become the officially designated titleholder of the fields used by everyone in the household, including women. Women tend to deal with the National Domain Law primarily in cases where they live in households without men and thus serve as their own *yal qol* (although such a title is rarely used with reference to a woman).

30. Siga Sarr, dispute interview, 25 August 1993.

31. *Siga Sarr v. Adama Diouf* also provides a clear illustration of the inner workings of polygynous households from the point of view of subordinated women. The solidarity of cowives like Siga Sarr and Tening Faye can belie the widespread notion, especially among progressives in the West, that polygyny constitutes an invariable mechanism for gender domination, a reliable tool for female disempowerment. In a context of overarching patriarchy and considerable gender inequality in control over rural capital, polygyny may actually increase the economic power of subordinated women by setting up natural alliances between cowives who are better able to *collectively* resist their husbands and other patriarchs than they might be in the isolation of monogamy. This is not to suggest that polygyny offers similar possibilities for empowerment in the political economy of urban, commodified settings.

32. Siga Sarr, dispute interview, 25 August 1993.

33. Ibid.

34. Abdoulaye Dieng, dispute interview, 19 October 1993.

35. Waly Fall, dispute interview, 3 June 1993.

36. It is as if Fall had been visited by, or was channeling, Amitai Etzioni. See Etzioni, *The Spirit of Community*.

37. For complete discussion of the *commandement* concept, see Mbembe, "Provisional Notes on the Postcolony," pp. 3–37; Mbembe, *On the Postcolony*.

38. Moussa Kama, dispute interview, 7 July 1993.

39. Samba Marone, dispute interview, 29 August 1993.

40. Boucar Thioro Diouf, oral history interview, 18 October 1993, emphasis added.

41. The *ceddo* were not tied to the old *lamanic* aristocracy but, as direct dependents of the *maad*, did not control much land of their own—they lived off predation instead. With the land reform, they stood to gain access to land and convert themselves into farmers. Although they were (and remain) quite unhappy about their change of vocation, as the *ceddo* became sedentarized they stood to gain from a two-year usufruct rule without which they would remain dependent on customary Serer land tenure authorities—*lamans* and *yal bakhs*—for access to land.

42. This disjuncture of vision, of course, illustrates very clearly James Scott's contrast between the organizational logic and epistemological constraints of the simplifying state and local actors armed with *mētis* knowledge.

43. Sombel Cama, oral history interview, 27 September 1993.

44. Gorgui Marone, oral history interview, 22 October 1993.

45. Gender and degree of religious orthodoxy stand out (β = .203 and .053, respectively), and both of them make theoretical sense. Men, who are more

likely than women to be publicly involved in the management of tenure relations, naturally appear more likely to take pawned land, as the positive correlation coefficient suggests.

46. This supposition is somewhat borne out by the fact that the educated
are somewhat more likely ($\beta = .086$, $p = .016$) to favor the right to pawn (see
table 12 in chapter 3). They would like to be able to pawn land, because it is
especially useful for people who have some degree of social mobility (and are
therefore likely to be away from their fields often), but are sufficiently clear
on the rules of the nature of the National Domain Law not to admit engaging
in this illegal activity.

47. It is very important to note that "those who have fields to pawn" includes
not only aristocrats but also the vast middle stratum of Serer society, who operate both as field proprietors and field takers, depending on circumstances.

48. Latyr Sene, oral history interview, 30 September 1993.

49. Mamadou Dione, dispute interview, 23 October 1993.

50. Gorgui Faye, oral history interview, 19 July 1993.

51. Boucar Ngom, dispute interview, 19 October 1993.

52. For a complete discussion of environmental and agricultural transformations prior to and during the era of the National Domain Law, see
"Transitions" (the section between chapters 4 and 5 in this volume).

53. This reference to a multiyear fallowing period may reflect the fact that
long-pawned fields were overfarmed, lacked soil nutrients, and therefore
required longer fallow times.

54. Gana Kama, oral history interview, 15 June 1993.

55. For a comprehensive review of the "tenure evolution" paradigm com-
mon to colonial administrators and postcolonial development experts, see
Bassett, "The Land Question and Agricultural Transformation in Sub-Saharan
Africa," pp. 3–31.

56. A point made with great insight and depth by Sara Berry. See *No
Condition Is Permanent*.

57. Latyr Farah Diouf, dispute interview, 3 June 1993.

58. Accompanied by a group of young men who had made many of these
seasonal transhumant journeys in their youth, the geographer André
Lericollais has produced a fascinating documentary that recreates one such
migration out of the Siin into the Ferlo Desert to the north.

59. For example, Samba Yatt, in his conflict over a field he had pawned to
Samba Faye, claims to have tried to get back his land for seventeen consecutive
rainy seasons. Although he never turned to community or state authorities to
force Faye to return the field, he nevertheless reminded Samba Faye, year in and
year out, that he (Yatt) retained a claim to the land and protested Diouf's use of it.

6. "THE KING HAS COME—NOW EVERYTHING IS RUINED"

1. This account of the outbreak and resolution of the 1992 land conflict
between Djignak Diouf and Niokhor Sene completes the presentation of the

first phase of this pawning relationship introduced at the beginning of chapter 4. This account draws on interviews with the litigants Djignak Diouf and Niokhor Sene and a number of their relatives and officials involved in the adjudication of the dispute. I have synthesized several accounts of the death of Matiasse Sene, his funeral, and Djignak Diouf's unexpected repayment of the pawn guarantee. This narrative thus represents a consensus version of a story about which individual respondents sometimes contradicted one another. Djignak Diouf, dispute interview, 11 July 1993; Niokhor Sene, dispute interview, 15 September 1993; Tening Faye, dispute interview, 3 October 1993; Mahecor Ndong, elite interview, 3 June 1993.

2. Antoine Ndour, elite interview, village of Bari, 19 October 1993. Interestingly, Antoine Ndour, the elder who echoed this widely understood formulation of state poisoning, is himself also an official of the very rural council he vilifies. Ndour is an elected rural councilor for the village of Bari.

3. The official title of the law is "Loi no. 72–25 du 19 avril 1972 relative aux communautés rurales." *Journal Officiel de la République du Sénégal*, no. 4224 (13 May 1972). The law established both the rural communities and their governing bodies (rural councils) and is widely known simply as the "Rural Council Law" or "rural council reform."

4. Gellar, Charlick, and Jones, *Animation Rurale and Rural Development*.

5. These *tribunaux départementaux* served as courts of first instance for the approximately 150,000 people of each *département*, an administrative unit below *région*, the largest territorial administrative national unit. Ba, "Les centres d'expansion rurale du Sénégal entre la dynamique paysanne et les structures d'état," pp. 621–31; Niang, "Le reforme de l'administration territoriale et locale au Sénégal," pp. 103–9.

6. The rural councils were in fact only partially democratically elected. Two-thirds of their members were selected in community balloting every five years, and the remaining seats were set aside for direct appointment by state designated agricultural cooperatives operating in the *communauté rurale* (rural community). Rural council elections took place every five years. Once a council was chosen, it selected from among its members a president.

7. In this case, seeing "like a state" refers to the authoritarian, high-modernist, *simplifying* vision James Scott explores in *Seeing Like a State*.

8. Vengroff and Johnston, *Decentralization and the Implementation of Rural Development in Senegal*.

9. Hamad Sene, dispute interview, 28 August 1993.

10. For a more detailed description of the workings of the *lamanic* land and resource system, see chapter 4.

11. Diop, "Le tenure foncière en milieu rural Wolof," pp. 48–52.

12. Western imaginings of rural African patriarchy aside, in the Siin the extraordinary primacy of the *yal mbind* is a relatively recent phenomenon. Until a few decades ago, *yal mbinds* did not exert such complete control over land allocation, crop rotation, resource management, or dispute resolution (see below).

13. It is striking that Serer respondents continue to find Islamic marabouts relatively illegitimate. Marabouts do regularly request voluntary economic sacrifice in the form of payments (some in the Siin pay an annual *asaka* [Wolof rendering of *zakat,* a formal Islamic tithe]). Marabouts often put out calls (known as *ndigel* in Wolof, or religious edicts) for their followers to clear the marabout's fields, harvest his millet, or shell his peanuts. Yet in keeping with the anti-Muslim tendencies of the Siin, these *ndigel* still fall on deaf ears.

14. The world wars constituted a formative experience for the generation of political elites that would lead colonies in Africa and Asia to independence after 1945. Time spent overseas, and educational contact with young elites from other colonies and with progressives and socialists from the metropole, helped shape leaders of the independence movements across the colonial world. The Léopold Senghors, Ho Chi Minhs, and Julius Nyereres of the colonies circulated in Paris and London in the midst of the struggle against fascism and the elaboration of both liberal democratic ideology undergirding the Atlantic Charter and the UN Universal Declaration of Human Rights and the socialist critique of fascism and imperialism. By their own accounts, their struggles back home reflected the mood of liberation in Europe. Morgenthau, *Political Parties in French-Speaking West Africa,* pp. 109–16.

15. Although Senegalese combatants were probably more numerous in World War I than World War II, their social impact as veterans in the Siin was less pronounced for at least two reasons. Anecdotal evidence suggests that the Siin sent fewer combatants to the first world war than the second. Moreover, the timing of independence was such that the World War II generation (not that of World War I) was in its social-status prime and thereby well positioned to take advantage of the new political and economic opportunities afforded by the new postcolonial regime.

16. *Keit* is the Serer-Siin (and Wolof) adaptation of the Arabic term *keitun,* meaning "paper." The term is used to refer literally to pieces of paper but also, as in "matters of *keit,*" connotes paperwork, bureaucracy, and officialdom in general. See the discussion under *"Korom, Keit,* and the *Voie Hierarchique"* later in this chapter.

17. Xemess Diouf, oral history interview, 28 September 1990.

18. Hamad Faye, dispute interview, 16 October 1993.

19. Diaga Dibor Ndofene Diouf, oral history interview, 14 October 1993.

20. Hamad Faye, dispute interview, 16 October 1993. Many respondents offer similar formulations, such as Mbaye Ndao, a litigant in Puday: "I was always against what was done. . . . Perhaps if it had been done before the seeding time, it would have been different, I might have been able to accept, . . . but [not] with the millet already planted." Ndao and Diouf exemplify comments also made by Moussa Cama, Kory Gning, and Diaga Faye.

21. Ibou Sow, dispute interview, 18 October 1993.

22. Fallers, *Law without Precedent.*

23. Modou Faye, dispute interview, 25 July 1993.

24. Given that questions of the disposition of the two mothers in the emerging new order constitute the apparent center of the problem, it should come as no surprise that Modou exploded at the notion (or invented the story, depending on whom you believe) that Abdou was using the tree for the benefit of one of his maternal relatives. Aliou Faye, dispute interview, 25 July 1993; Modou Faye, dispute interview, 25 July 1993.

25. The same Water and Forests Service agent intervened in the case of *Cheikh Gakou v. Ndeba Gakou,* a very similar conflict over the office of *yal mbind,* this time between the younger brother and the eldest son of the deceased head of household. In this case, the Water and Forests Service agent chose not to establish a new regime for access to the valuable resource of tree branches and leaves, nor did he get anywhere near the disintegration of the authority of the *yal mbind,* which was at the heart of the conflict. Rather, he behaved as a functionally specific state technician concerned with tree management. For example, at one point, Ndeba Gakou accused Cheikh Gakou of gratuitously cutting branches from the tree that he had no intention of using. The Water and Forests agent looked at the situation and saw that the tree was intact, that it had not really been cut. According to Cheikh Gakou, "he tore up" the paper summoning Cheikh Gakou to an ad hoc hearing in front of the tree to assess the damage and "told us to stop bickering and left." Cheikh Gakou, dispute interview, 19 October 1993; Ndeba Gakou, dispute interview, 25 August 1993.

26. Dokor Ndour, dispute interview, 6 July 1993.

27. Aliou Faye, dispute interview, 25 July 1993; Modou Faye, dispute interview, 25 July 1993.

28. On the environmental approach in resource management circles, see Berkes, Folke, and Colding, *Linking Social and Ecological Systems;* Costanza and Wainger, *Ecological Economics;* Röling et al., *Facilitating Sustainable Agriculture.*

29. See the discussion of syncretism from below and from above in Stewart and Shaw, *Syncretism/Anti-Syncretism,* pp. i, 1–3.

30. As noted in chapter 5, the term *cosaan* (ancestral tradition) is used in a similar fashion in other Serer languages, as well as in Wolof. While we know, and this study reinforces the fact, that *cosaan* changes and is subject to social contestation and construction, various actors at times find it in their interests to present *cosaan* as if it were unchanging, primordial, and embedded in static historical memory and culture. In contemporary Serer society, *cosaan* is often evoked to convey a sense of historical continuity, a connection to the specific way of life and worldview of Serer localities, as well as to establish a contrast with values, habits, and institutions of non-Serer origin that may be portrayed as inimical or threatening to local lifeways.

31. Cheikh Sene, elite interview, 27 July 1993.

32. This certainly reflects the sense of a number of rural councilors in the Siin. Antoine Ndour, dispute interview, 19 October 1993; Amaissa Diouf, elite interview, 27 August 1993; Cheikh Sene, elite interview, 27 July 1993.

33. Amaissa Diouf, elite interview, 27 August 1993.

34. Sitor Cama, dispute interview, 28 July 1993.

35. Pierre Ngom, dispute interview, 15 September 1993.

36. Antoine Ndour, elite interview, 19 October 1993.

37. For perhaps the most thorough analysis of the problematic of competing role behaviors and its impact on state-building and modernity in Africa, see Price, *Society and Bureaucracy in Contemporary Ghana*.

38. *Diame Sene v. Waly Koundoul Sene* is one among several conflicts that reveal how rural councilors integrate their work as elected state officials and their role as relatives and neighbors.

39. Gorgui Sene, elite interview, 17 June 1993.

40. Ibid.

41. Cheikh Gakou, dispute interview, 19 October 1993.

42. The most tangible link seems to be the fact that some distant nephews of Dokor's recently accompanied a young man from Dokor's village, who happens to have the name Ndour (as common as Jones is in London), to take a young bride from the household of Cheikh Gakou.

43. Koly Diagne, dispute interview, 16 September 1993.

44. Informants for this study, for example, readily identify Serer burial mounds (made by laying the roof of the deceased's hut over the burial plot, then covering this roof with two to three meters of dirt, resulting in a small hillock) as "Serer pyramids." When pressed on this nomenclature, informants indicate that this is "proof that we came from Egypt . . . like Cheikh Anta said." Gorgui Faye, oral history interview, 19 July 1993. On Diop's theories, see Diop, *L'Afrique noire precoloniale*.

45. These "joking kinships" are not limited to the Serer of Siin and their neighbors but are widely found across the Sahel (known, for example, as *basse teray* among the Songhai, *sinankowa* among the Bambara of Mali) and indeed in many parts of the precapitalist developing world. Their role in patterns of interethnic cooperation and nation building in Senegal represents an intriguing area for further research. For the most authoritative work on Senegalese joking kinships, see Ndiaye, "Correspondances ethno-patronymiques et parenté plaisantante," pp. 97–128. For background on joking kinship in general, see Radcliffe-Brown, "On Joking Relationships," pp. 195–210; Griaule, "L'alliance cathartique," pp. 242–58; Douglas, "Social Control of Cognition," pp. 361–76; Stevens, "Bachama Joking Categories," pp. 47–71; Freedman, "Joking, Affinity, and the Exchange of Ritual Services among the Kiga of Northern Rwanda," pp. 154–65; Kennedy, "Bonds of Laughter among the Tarahumara Indians."

46. Nagel and Snipp, "Ethnic Reorganization," pp. 202–35.

47. Matiasse Gakou, dispute interview, 6 July 1993.

48. Roger Sene, dispute interview, 6 July 1993.

49. Dokor Diouf, dispute interview, 28 August 1993.

50. Although he conducted research outside the Siin, in Serer communities located in the midst of the neighboring Wolof kingdom of Baol, Gastellu's

findings closely match the dominant version of cultural memory presented here, in which the preindependence *lamanic* order used holistic custodianship and redistribution of lands to maintain relatively equal access to land and other resources. Gastellu, *L'égalitarianisme économique des Serer du Sénégal.*

51. Cheikh Thiao, dispute interview, 25 August 1993.

52. The end of the regime of the *maad* as the end of slavery figures quite prominently in Serer conceptualizations of human equality. As Matiasse Sene notes, "In 1960, the Serer man became free, slaves became maternal relatives with whom you shared the same household. There was no more 'Aaah, this family there was my slave.' We are all equal now." Diokel Ndiaye, oral history interview, 29 September 1993.

53. Babacar Faye, oral history interview, 30 September 1993.

54. Gorgui Marone, oral history interview, 22 October 1993.

55. To be sure, the Serer are not unique in this regard. Catholicism's incorporation of Norse, Celtic, and Teutonic Gods into the panoply of saints is just one among many similar illustrations of the blending of imported monotheistic religious symbols and rules with the material concerns and motifs of local society and cosmology.

56. I use a transliteration of the term *quorum* as it has been incorporated into Serer structures of pronunciation *(KOR-om)* and grammar (*o korom ke* for "the quorum"), rather than the "correct" spelling of the original term in French (and English), to highlight the degree to which this term has been adapted to fit into not only Serer language but also Serer notions of the proper procedures that accompany decision making and adjudication.

57. Doudou Ngued, elite interview, 3 March 1993.

58. Antoine Ndour, elite interview, 19 October 1993.

59. Pierre Ngom, dispute interview, 15 September 1993.

60. Modou Tine, elite interview, 4 August 1993.

61. Bouré Fall, dispute interview, 26 August 1993.

62. Diaga Dibor Ndofene Diouf, elite interview, 7 March 1993; Matiasse Gakou, dispute interview, 6 July 1993.

63. Fields in the Ndokh-Njujuf joint use area were well fertilized because the three-year rotation, which included a year of fallow pasture, ensured a reliable input of cattle manure and mitigated the problem of soil depletion. These fields were thus prime space for growing the most important crop, millet. Moreover, as descendants of the *laman*, the Njujuf faction had access to far more land than the Ndokh faction. Thus, the Njujuf group could pasture their livestock on less desirable, less well fertilized fields elsewhere.

64. The CER chief, or *chef de CER* as he is locally known, is the state administrative agent in charge of a local Centre d'Expansion Rurale (CER). These centers were designed to bring together a variety of support services for agriculture (introducing new seeds and tools, credit, marketing, and access to fertilizer, saplings, and other inputs). CER chiefs also provide technical services and advice in matters relating to land use and resource management (except in the case of water and forest resources—the Water and Forests Service, or

Service des Eaux et Forêts, has its network of local extension agents for these matters). Their notorious underfunding, much aggravated since structural adjustment, has left them mostly unable to directly influence matters of agrarian change or sustainable resource management in Senegal.

65. Given the economic and nutritional realities of living largely on rain-fed agriculture in such a harsh climate, this prohibition on touching planted millet makes sense as part of a set of food-security values. Social relations, tenure patterns, and notions of moral and legitimate conflict themselves have naturally been structured by long experience with the concrete reality that, in this ecosystem, and given locally available technology, social conflict that reduces community millet production can lead to famine. Moussa Fall, dispute interview, 7 July 1993; Hamad Faye, dispute interview, 16 October 1993; Mbaye Cama, dispute interview, 25 July 1993; Diaga Faye, dispute interview, 25 July 1993.

66. Kory Gning, dispute interview, 21 August 1993.

67. Ibid.

68. Diaga Faye, dispute interview, 25 July 1993. In the religious cosmology of the Serer-Siin, Roog is the supreme, unitary, distant, creator God.

69. Abdou Touré Diop, elite interview, 23 August 1993.

70. Modou Diara Sagne, elite interview, 23 August 1993.

71. The failure of state officials to tap this reservoir, to grasp the cultural significance of the *Puday Pond Conflict* in contrast to *Ndokh v. Njujuf* is a curious by-product of the Senegalese state's otherwise laudable effort to mitigate ethnoregional political mobilization and promote interethnic familiarity, understanding, and harmony. With some exceptions, officials of the state's territorial administration (prefects and subprefects) and extension agents (CER employees, Water and Forests agents, dispensary nurses of the public health network, and teachers) are deliberately *not* assigned to their ethnic home regions throughout most of their careers. This has produced the desired result of using the relations between local level state representatives and ordinary citizens to promote a national cultural identity in addition to historic ethnoregional identities. But it can exacerbate the cultural alienness of the state. The policy, based on a simple "not-where-your-people-are" rule, does not include systematic ethnographic training or deliberate promotion of cross-cultural understanding, which might better position state officials to recognize elements of local institutions and culture that might be harnessed to advance state policy. This of course assumes that state officials *aware* of useful local traditional practices and values would be *willing* to see them as resources of potential benefit to the state, as worthy of what amounts to official recognition. The unfortunate and critical truth is that most state officials remain sufficiently high modernist to consider quasi-traditional authorities and local institutions and values as a priori obstacles to the development policy of a modern, legal-rational, democratic-socialist state. This a priori assumption, far more than *lack* of mutual understanding or information, accounts for not just the alienness of state officials but also the failure of state rural development policy in general. On high modernism, see Scott, *Seeing Like a State*, pp. 11–52.

72. Abdou Touré Diop, interview, 23 August 1993.

73. Modou Diara Sagne, interview, 23 August 1993.

74. Ibid.

75. Ndeba Sene, dispute interview, 18 October 1993.

76. Wagane Diouf, dispute interview, 3 June 1993.

77. For example, a litigant in a bitter inheritance dispute insists, "I only went to Dokor [the rural council president] because Pierre did first. I saw Pierre over there talking to Dokor once, and I felt that I had to do the same thing." Thimndane Gning, dispute interview, 27 July 1993.

78. Ndeba Sene, dispute interview, 18 October 1993. *Buur* is the Wolof equivalent for *maad*. The two are used in similar, but not identical, ways in the Siin. Historically, both refer to the old "king of the Siin." But in contemporary usage, *buur* tends to be used to refer to the administration in general, to the government or the state in Dakar in an abstract sense. *Maad,* on the other hand, evokes in a more specific way the style of rulership and institutionalized behavior of the old preindependence kingdom. So the use of *maad* tends to be associated with a proximate authority that engages in direct and tangible acts of arbitrary extraction of resources such as land, livestock, and labor. The idea that the rural councils are the *buur* is simply a statement of empirical fact. The idea that the rural councils are the *maad* is a more precise form of interpretive vilification.

79. Samba Faye, dispute interview, 16 October 1993.

80. Cheikh Ndour, dispute interview, 18 September 1993.

81. Latyr Farah Diouf, dispute interview, 3 June 1993. Thimndane Gning reveals very much the same kind of suspicions about his nephew Pierre Ngom, with whom he is locked in a conflict over field inheritance. Gning, unwilling to directly question the morality of a nephew who has sought out the help of rural council officials, suspects that one of these officials, Antoine Ndour, must have been influenced by someone else: "I think that there were some people around Antoine Ndour who were telling him to make some kinds of arguments that he should get the field and he should go to the state to do it." Thimndane Gning, dispute interview, 27 July 1993.

82. In Serer-Siin, the Wolof term *tooñ* can convey both wrongdoing committed on the part of the speaker and wrongs committed against the speaker. In conventional Wolof usage, *tooñ* generally carries the latter meaning.

83. Hamad Faye, dispute interview, 16 October 1993.

84. Clifford, *The Predicament of Culture.*

85. Indeed, in many of my more formal interviews (such as oral history interviews), respondents wove elegant oratorical formulations into their responses, typically in the opening and closing of the session or at the introduction of key topics about which they were especially knowledgeable. Such rhetorical flourishes generally met with praise and commentary from the attendees at the interview session, who were quick to note, rank, and compare an individual respondent's status in the community as a person "who knows how to talk" or who "has words."

86. Ibou Yatt, dispute interview, 7 July 1993.

87. Hamad Faye, dispute interview, 16 October 1993.

88. Ngor Mbede Dieng, dispute interview, 26 October 1993.

89. However, he was, at this time, simply an ordinary rural councilor, and the meeting was officially being run by Mahecor Ndong's handpicked successor and subordinate. The actual president was present and opened the meeting, but, as in many other such sessions, once things got under way, Mahecor Ndong took over as the real presiding force.

90. Mahecor Ndong, elite interview, 26 July 1993. Ironically, Mahecor Ndong himself has sometimes been treated in the same way. By 1990, opposition to Ndong's considerable influence on the rural council had expanded and become well organized. The subprefect eventually became aware of his role as a rural councilor of extraordinary influence in the community, and when the rural council dealt with matters that touched on Ndong's own personal landholdings or those of his allies, the subprefect stepped in to temper his influence. The mode of such disempowerment is striking, as an observer of rural council proceedings in the dispute *Saliou Ndiaye v. Yiigu Faye* notes: "During the rural council meeting that made the decision, Mahecor Ndong was not allowed to speak on the subject. It was the subprefect that made him keep silent." Wagane Diouf, dispute interview, 3 June 1993.

91. For further exploration of this contrast between procedural narrowing and substantive holism in African postcolonial and colonial legal orders, see Mann and Roberts, introduction; Chanock, *Law, Custom, and Social Order;* Falk Moore, *Social Facts and Fabrications.*

92. Modou Faye, dispute interview, 25 July 1993.

93. Bouré Fall, dispute interview, 26 August 1993.

94. This account of Tukar's Raan celebration is based on my own participant observation of the 1993 event, on numerous informal discussions with participants about the nature of this and other Raan festivals, and on interviews with the *laman, saltigué,* village chief, rural council president, and subprefect. Diaga Dibor Ndofene Diouf, oral history interview, 14 October 1993; Mbassa Faye, elite interview, 7 March 1993; Diaraf Seck Tine, elite interview, 20 September 1993; Dokor Ndour, elite interview, 4 March 1993; Hamad El Walid Diop, elite interview, 27 October 1993.

95. Daouda Tine, interview, 21 July 1993; Gorgui Gning, interview, 11 August 1993.

96. It is indeed ironic, or perhaps it is by design, that the central ritual event of Tukar's Serer animist tradition takes place in a space now bordered by structures that represent principal vectors of sociocultural transformation in the Siin. Only the mosque is missing from this space, perhaps a testament to the degree to which Islam remains a far less invasive alien presence.

97. Although most informants offer no interpretation for the standard positioning of the parties, others argue that it reflects the fact that, when the Gelwaar first arrived in the Siin, they came from the coast, to the west of Tukar. This corresponds to the Serer historical experience of the Gelwaar

conquest (they first settled on the coast and then moved up the valley to the Siin River) but does not incorporate anthropological and historical scholarship indicating that the Gelwaar had migrated from Gabou, a province of the old Mali empire to the east.

98. Diaga Dibor Ndofene Diouf, oral history interview, 14 October 1993.

99. See Geertz, *Negara*.

100. Here, I extend and tinker with Goran Hyden's vision of an uncaptured peasantry in *No Shortcuts to Progress*.

101. In Hyden's work, *governance* refers to the successful management of a regime structure, whereas *regime* extends beyond the mundane formal rules, constitutions, and administrative structures of the state to include the forms of legitimation and the normative frameworks through which state and society collaboratively set the moral terms for effective leadership, responsibility, accountability, consent, and dissent. See Hyden, "Governance and the Study of Politics," pp. 1–26.

102. Young, *The African Colonial State in Comparative Perspective*.

7. CULTURALLY SUSTAINABLE DEVELOPMENT

1. See for example Scott, *Weapons of the Weak;* Berry, *No Condition Is Permanent;* Chase, ed., *The Spaces of Neoliberalism;* Carney, ed., *Sustainable Rural Livelihoods*.

2. The phrase is from Dione Falilou Diouf, oral history interview, 2 October 1993.

3. Especially in the 1950s, severe inequalities in urban and semiurban access to both agricultural and residential land had emerged as a serious social problem, which the 1964 National Domain Law did address rather directly. For a more complete discussion of this issue in the broad historical context of land tenure relations in Senegal, see Moleur, "Genèse de la loi relative au domaine nationale," pp. 11–55.

4. Ekeh, "Colonialism and the Two Publics in Africa," pp. 91–112.

5. Regarding the rediscovery of the state, see Evans, Skocpol, and Reuschemeyer, *Bringing the State Back In*. With regard to the early stirrings of a normative shift toward analysis of democracy on southern Europe and Latin America, see especially O'Donnell, Schmitter, Whitehead, *Transitions from Authoritarian Rule*. On the rediscovery of institutions, see North, *Structure and Change in Economic History*. On the political culture revival, a representative key text is Putnam, *Making Democracy Work*.

6. Bates et al., *Analytic Narratives*, pp. 23–63.

7. On behavioral economics, see the work of Richard Thaler, Matthew Rabin, and others, including Jolls, Sunstein, and Thaler, "A Behavioral Approach to Law and Economics," pp. 1471–50; and O'Donoghue and Rabin, "The Economics of Immediate Gratification," pp. 233–50.

8. See "Gaspillages Ceremonielles," *Le Temoin* (Dakar, Senegal), (May 1995), for a typical journalistic lament.

9. See for example Ensminger, "The Political Economy of Religion," pp. 745–54.

10. For an illustration of this type of proposition, see Ensminger, "Changing Property Rights."

11. Mobutu's use of "Zairianization" and Suharto's use of *pancasila*—both pseudo-syncretic ideologies used to justify single-party authoritarianism as reflective of local cultural tradition—illustrate perfectly the close affinity between grafting and central-state and elite projects of regime justification. This contrasts markedly with the inherently decentralizing tendency of genuine syncretism. See Callaghy, *The State-Society Struggle;* Emmerson, *Indonesia's Elite.*

12. Hyden, *No Shortcuts to Progress.*

13. Ekeh, "Colonialism and the Two Publics in Africa."

14. This homogenization is the implicit central theme of the critique of globalization as acquiescence to the promulgation of U.S. culture and lifestyle in the process of global market integration. See for example Tomlinson, *Globalization and Culture..*

15. Polanyi, *The Great Transformation,* pp. 77–85.

16. As noted in chapter 3, the Serer version does not consist of a unitary vision but of multiple visions of authentic and legitimate historic institutions. All these idealizations nevertheless share this basic concern for authority, for reliable, trustworthy leadership that provides renewed certainty and predictability in a resource-management and exchange environment that has grown increasingly chaotic.

17. For an excellent and succinct summary of Senghor's intellectual biography, see Vaillant, "The Problem of Culture in French West Africa."

18. Olukoshi, Olaniyan, and Aribisala, *Structural Adjustment in West Africa;* Fall, "Labor under Structural Adjustment Program in Senegal."

19. In the Njafaj region of Siin, for example, a community self-help organization founded on the initiative of local farmers, the Associations des Paysans de Tukar, received little help, let alone notice, from any level of the Senegalese government when it worked with a Dakar-based nonprofit development organization, Environnement et Développement du Tiers Monde, to plan an irrigated farming project. Nor was the official state development bureaucracy a player as this isolated, community self-help organization negotiated with a U.S. nonprofit, Lutheran World Relief, for a thirty-thousand-dollar grant to begin the irrigated gardening project. Initiatives such as this are not unique to the Siin, nor are they new. But their multiplication underscores the increasing marginalization of formal state institutions in the dynamics of development at the grassroots. See Krishna, Uphoff, and Esman, eds., *Reasons for Hope.*

Glossary

Note on orthography: In general I have tried to avoid French transliterations of Serer, Wolof, and other local terms and place-names, giving preference instead to the orthographic conventions most common in contemporary literacy training in Serer and Wolof. However, given the complexities of linguistic and cultural blending in Senegal (names and transliterations imposed, borrowed, and syncretically reworked form Arabic, French and many local languages), this is not always easy or practical. Thus, following Leonardo Villalón's approach in his study of a nearby Serer urban center *(Islamic Society and State Power in Senegal* [New York: Cambridge University Press, 1995]), I have not applied a single orthographic correctness across the board, favoring clarity and familiarity at the expense of strict linguistic consistency. Thus, I use French transliterations when they are already widely recognized *(Mouride,* for example) and when more linguistically accurate renderings might prove unfamiliar *(Murid).*

Similarly, I have used French transliterations of a few place-names and all personal names. Given their inherent subjectiveness (this is what people call themselves), it makes sense to follow patterns of most common usage when it comes to people's names. Since birth certificates, identity cards, and other official state documents generally play a crucial role in structuring how people conceive of their own names, French orthographic conventions *(Diouf* as opposed to *Juuf, Thiao* as opposed to *Caw)* continue to determine the spellings of names except among a very small minority who, conscious of this influence, have chosen to adopt a local as opposed to the French spelling (for example, a Faye who has changed her name to Faay). Finally, a similar principle applies to the name of the people at the heart of this study: while French has offered many renderings of their name *(Sérèr, Séreer,* and *Sérere),* and strict local orthographic convention produces *Seereer,* it appears here as *Serer* to balance ease of recognition and local-language accuracy.

arrondissement   (French) Territorial administrative division in Senegal. *Arrondissements* are composed of *communautés rurales* and combine to form *départements*.

asaka   (Serer-Siin, Wolof, from Arabic) Wolof and Serer-Siin rendering of Arabic *zakat*, "Islamic tithe." Many Muslims in rural Siin pay what they refer to as *asaka* to a Sufi marabout, often in the form of a fraction of their millet or peanut harvest, although the *asaka* is sometimes paid in cash. Some Serer-Siin Muslims make occasional payments, referred to as *addiya*, to Sufi leaders.

baadolo   (Serer-Siin and Wolof) Ordinary rural producer and noncasted member of the majority free farmer group. Widely used in Serer-Siin, the term is roughly equivalent to *peasant* but is without strong social-theoretical or teleological connotations. It is sometimes used pejoratively to mean "country bumpkin," and is sometimes normatively inverted to mean "simple, decent farming folk." The Serer-Siin term *quokh-quokh* is also used as a synonym. Alternate spelling: *badolo*.

bakh   (Serer-Siin) Cut area; land area or estate managed by a "master of cutting," a *yal bakh*.

Baol   Precolonial Wolof kingdom located on the northern frontier of the Serer kingdom of Siin.

Baye Fall   (Wolof) A Mouride subsect founded by Cheikh Ibrahima Fall in the late 1800s. This group incorporated Wolof *ceddo* into Mouridism through emphasis on labor as an expression of religious devotion.

buur   (Wolof) Wolof term meaning "king," used interchangeably in the Siin with *maad*, title of the monarch of the Siin, chosen from the Gelwaar matrilineage.

ceddo   (Serer-Siin and Wolof) Low status, endogamous warrior caste in Siin, Saluum, and most Wolof states.

CER chief   (French) Technical assistance agents assigned to an *arrondissement* by the Service des Centres d'Expansion Rurale, an agricultural assistance agency of the government of Senegal. Each *arrondissement*-level Centre d'Expansion Rurale is staffed by an agent (known to most in the Siin as the *chef de CER*) who provides advice on land use, crop varieties, irrigation, pasture, inputs, marketing, and other matters related to increasing agricultural productivity.

chef de canton (French) Colonial official, equivalent in territorial administration to a contemporary prefect of a *département*.

commandant de cercle (French) Colonial official, equivalent in contemporary territorial administration to a subprefect of an *arrondissement*.

communauté rurale Smallest territorial administrative division in Senegal, made up of twenty to forty villages. These divisions were established in a 1972 reform to decentralize administration and establish a local-level venue for adjudicating land disputes arising under the National Domain Law.

département (French) Territorial administrative division in Senegal composed of *arrondissements*. *Départements* combine to form *régions*.

farba (Serer-Siin, Wolof) In Siin and some Wolof states, an agent of the king, often responsible for resource extraction and labor recruitment.

fire estate Space cleared by the historic fire set by a village founder upon arrival in a new territory. In ensuing generations, the fire estate was managed by the eldest male in the lineage of the village founder, who holds an office referred to as *laman, yal naay,* or *yal ndaak.* Ancestral spirits *(pangool)* associated with the founding lineage are thought to inhabit the fire estate and ensure the fertility of its soil.

Fuuta Tooro Precolonial kingdom located in the Senegal River valley, whose inhabitants were largely from Tukolor and Halpulaar ethnic communities.

Gelwaar (Serer-Siin) A Manding matrilineal clan that migrated to the Siin and Saluum River areas in the late fourteenth century and established centralized states incorporating the local Serer population into a federal system.

grand farba	(Serer-Siin and French) Official in the Gelwaar kingdom of Siin, leader of the *ceddo* warriors, and head of the military.
grand jaraf	(Serer-Siin and French) Official in the Gelwaar kingdom of Siin, representative of the Serer free farmer caste, and head of the royal council.
griot	(French, Serer-Siin: *gewell*) Member of an endogamous, low-status occupational caste whose functions include ceremonial drumming, poetry, praise singing, the dissemination of information, and the maintenance and recounting of community oral history.
gris-gris	(French, Serer-Siin: *teex*) Amulets or charms worn for supernatural protection or to ensure good fortune or success. These objects are made with bark, herbs, animal products, and other ingredients of spiritual significance. Since the spread of Islam, gris-gris often include verses of the Koran that have been written in Arabic on slips of paper and sewn into the amulet.
Halpulaar	Second largest ethnic group (17 percent) in Senegal. This ethnolinguistic group is widely dispersed throughout the Sahel and, consequently, is known by a number of different names, including Peul, Peulh, Fula, Fulbé, Fulfulde, and Fulani. The common language of these peoples is Pulaar. Some Halpulaar pastoral practices and elements of language overlap with those of the Serer, suggesting a shared history, possibly in the Senegal River valley. The Tukolor ethnic group (see below), also Pulaar speaking, is often included in the Halpulaar category.
imam	(Arabic) Islamic religious official. In Siin and other parts of rural Senegal, the title *imam* suggests a clerical official who presides over services at a mosque, in contrast to a marabout, whose spiritual and material responsibilities may be wider ranging.
jange o qol of	(Serer-Siin) Literally, "take back your field," a phrase used to denote the termination of a *taile* pawning contract. The person who paid a cash guarantee for use of a field is expected to graciously restore the field to its lineage proprietor when the latter repays the cash

	guarantee. The person returning the field uses this phrase to signal respect for customary notions of the inalienability of land.
jaraf	(Serer-Siin, Wolof) In Siin and some Wolof states, a village-level representative of the king; now a common term for village chief. Alternate spelling: Diaraf.
Jola	Fifth largest ethnic group (4 percent) in Senegal; concentrated in the southern Casamance region. Jola and Serer ethnic groups consider each other related, at least as *ma sir,* or "joking cousins." Alternate spelling: Diola.
Jolof	Precolonial Wolof kingdom located to the north of Siin, regional hegemon in the area north of Gambia River, including in its sphere of influence the Serer kingdoms of Siin and Saluum in the fifteenth and sixteenth centuries. Alternate spellings: Diolof, Djolof.
Kajor	Precolonial Wolof kingdom located to the north of Siin. Alternate spellings: Kajoor, Kayor, Kayoor, Cayor, Cajor.
laman	(Serer-Siin and Wolof) Title of inherited customary office of land custodian, responsible for land allocation, management of crop rotation and fallow, and land conflict adjudication. The term is widely used in Siin and some Wolof areas to denote the "master of fire," the eldest in a lineage whose ancestor first used a brushfire to clear land for farming and habitation.
lamanic	Of or having to do with the office of the *laman* or with the system of tenure relations, resource management, and adjudication maintained by the *laman.*
maad	(Serer-Siin) Title of the king of Siin, chosen from among the Gelwaar matrilineal clan. The office of the *maad* was discontinued upon Senegal's independence in 1960, and it was partially restored in ceremonial form in 1990.
maad a Sinig	(Serer-Siin) Full title of the Gelwaar king of Siin (see *maad*).
mak a ndok	(Serer-Siin) Eldest of a matrilineal clan, formerly responsible for management of matrilineally inherited goods, such as cattle.

marabout	(Arabic, Wolof, Serer-Siin) Islamic Sufi religious leader, in Senegal, associated with an Islamic brotherhood, or *tariqa,* such as the Mourides or Tijanes. Marabouts are understood to be endowed with extraordinary *baraka,* or divine grace, which puts them in a special position to intercede on behalf of their followers in spiritual matters. The term is sometimes translated as "living saint."
ma sir	(Serer-Siin) Joking kinship or joking cousins, relations between ethnic groups or lineages within ethnic groups characterized by rituals of humorous mutual insulting, possibly a mechanism for nonviolent expression of intergroup tension.
mbind	(Serer-Siin) Compound or household, usually made up of more than one *ngak,* or cooking unit. *Mbind* also can connote "inhabited space" or "community space," in contrast to *o kop ale,* which suggests uninhabited land or "wilderness."
Mouride	(Wolof, Serer-Siin) Second largest and politically most significant Sufi Islamic brotherhood in Senegal, founded by Cheikh Amadou Bamba in the 1880s, in part through incorporation of the Wolof *ceddo* warrior caste into a new syncretic form of Sufism. By the mid–twentieth century, Mouride leaders controlled a considerable portion of peanut production in Senegal, and they remain powerful agents for political mobilization.
National Domain Law	1964 legislation establishing a land reform program intended to "restore" African socialist egalitarian landholding patterns. The program works largely through the principle of "land for those who farm it," in which two years of usufruct translates into de facto title.
naq	(Serer-Siin) Soul eater, a person with unique supernatural abilities who is compelled to "consume" the souls of others in order to stay alive. *Naqs,* sometimes translated as "witches" or "vampires," are not readily discernible from ordinary people.
ndigel	(Wolof) Religious edict issued by a Sufi marabout. *Ndigels* in Senegal cover a wide

variety of matters over which marabouts would like to mobilize their *talibés,* or followers. *Ndigels* are most commonly issued to encourage followers to pray, fast, provide collective labor on the leader's plantation, or until recently, go to the polls to support ruling party candidates.

o maad a gara (Serer-Siin) Literally, "the king has come." This widely used phrase is meant to convey the illegitimate and arbitrary intervention of an outside authority, and it usually implies social rupture.

pan (Serer-Siin) Traditional healer or shaman who provides both medicinal and supernatural services. In the Siin and other parts of Senegal, such an individual may also be called a marabout, although more orthodox Muslims take umbrage at such usage of the Sufi title.

pangool (Serer-Siin) In the animist religion of the Serer of Siin, ancestral and allied spiritual beings associated with a lineage. *Pangool* intervene directly in human affairs, sometimes as benevolent guardians and guides, sometimes as malevolent tormentors. Maintenance of positive relations with the *pangool* is thus a major concern of spiritual life.

pangoolism, pangoolisme (English, French, Serer-Siin) Term sometimes used to refer to the animist religion of the Siin, central to which are the *pangool* ancestral and allied spiritual beings.

Peanut Basin Zone of concentrated cultivation of peanuts for export in west-central Senegal. The Peanut Basin includes, in the north and east, the Mouride shifting agricultural production and, in the south, the Serer intensive agropastoral system.

prefect Official appointed by Senegalese government to manage affairs in a *département,* a territorial administrative unit.

Pulaar Language spoken by Halpulaar and Tukolor ethnic groups. The language bears some relationship to the Serer-Siin language, which may suggest common historical origins in the Senegal River valley area.

Raan	(Serer-Siin) Annual rain and fertility festival in the Serer-Siin village of Tukar. Among other elements, the festival includes reversal of political roles and metaphorical taunting of representatives of the centralized state.
région	(French) Territorial administrative division in Senegal. *Régions* are the largest subnational territorial units and are composed of *départements*.
rural council	Elected council governing a *communauté rurale* (rural community).
saax-saax	(Serer-Siin) Village representative and tax collector for the *maad,* king of the Siin.
saltigué	(Serer-Siin) Rain priest and spiritual guide in the lineage of the *laman;* an inherited office. The *saltigué* is responsible for some fertility rites and relations with ancestral spirits.
Saluum	Precolonial Serer kingdom located along the estuary of the Saluum River to the southeast of the Siin, established by the Gelwaar matrilineage. Unlike the Siin, the Saluum was conquered by an Islamic jihad leader in 1862. Alternate spelling: Saloum.
Serer	Third largest ethnic group in Senegal (15 percent). This ethnic umbrella term encompasses at least seven culturally distinct subgroups, the largest and arguably "most typical" of which are the Serer-Siin.
Serer-Siin	One of seven major subgroups of the ethnic umbrella category "Serer." The group is characterized by an intensive agropastoral production system, high degree of animist-inspired religious syncretism, and legacy of both local customary and centralized state political institutions.
Siin	Serer kingdom located along the estuary of the Siin River, today the south-central portion of the Peanut Basin. This kingdom was established in the late fourteenth century when a Mandé matrilineal group, the Gelwaar, migrated to the area and incorporated Serer inhabitants into a centralized, but federal, state. Alternate spelling: Sine.

Sine-Saloum	Territorial administrative unit of the colonial regime, roughly combining the area of the Serer kingdoms of Siin and Saluum. Inherited by the postcolonial state upon independence, it was split into two new administrative *régions* (Fatick and Kaolack) in 1984.
Sinig	The ethnolinguistic subgroup of the Serer who live in the Siin region; also known as Siin-Siin or Serer-Siin.
Sossé	Manding ethnic group believed to have inhabited the Siin-Saluum estuary region prior to the arrival of the Serer. Alternate spelling: Socé.
subprefect	Official appointed by Senegalese government to manage affairs in an *arrondissement*, a territorial administrative unit.
taile	(Serer-Siin, Wolof) A pawn of a valued object for a cash payment. In the Siin region, the term denotes a common form of exchange of land, in which a cash payment or guarantee is made in return for use rights to a field. The original field proprietor may reclaim land by repaying the original pawn sum, without interest, at any time. Pawns permit partial commodification of land without undermining the notion of ownership as holistic custodianship on the part of a *lamanic* lineage and ancestral spirits.
talibé	(from Arabic: *talibun;* literally, student) In Senegal, the followers of an Islamic Sufi marabout.
Tijane	(Wolof from Arabic) Largest Islamic Sufi brotherhood in Senegal, derived from the wider North and West African Tijanniya movement. Senegalese Tijanes adhere to a distinctive version of Sufism that is somewhat less syncretic than that of the Mouride brotherhood in terms of practice and doctrine. Alternate spelling: Tidiane.
Tukolor	Fourth largest ethnic group (7 percent) in Senegal. This group is thought to share common origins with the Serer in the Senegal River valley. They are related to the Halpulaar, with whom they share a common language (Pulaar). Alternate spelling: Toucouleur.

Walo	Precolonial Wolof kingdom located north of the Siin, around the mouth of the Senegal River. Alternate spellings: Waalo, Oualo.
Water and Forests agent	(French) Technical assistance agent assigned to an *arrondissement* by the Water and Forests Service *(Service des Eaux et Forêts)*, a natural resource management agency of the government of Senegal.
Wolof	Largest ethnic group (43 percent) in Senegal. Their language and, to a lesser extent, culture have become nearly universal in Senegal, especially in urban settings.
yal bakh	(Serer-Siin) Literally, "master of cutting." The *yal bakh* is the eldest in a lineage that has been granted usufruct rights to a set of fields by a *laman*.
yal mbind	(Serer-Siin) Literally, "master of the compound," or "household master"; usually the eldest male in household. As the offices of customary land-tenure elites *(lamans, yal bakhs)* have been destabilized, many of their land management and adjudicatory responsibilities have collapsed onto *yal mbinds*.
yal naay, yal o naay	(Serer-Siin) Literally "master of fire," referring to the inherited customary office of a land custodian responsible for land allocation, management of crop rotation and fallowing, and land conflict adjudication. The term refers back to a village founder who, upon migrating to a new territory, first used brushfire to clear a vast territory for farming and human habitation. This term is synonymous with *laman*, although the latter, more Wolof term, is more widely understood throughout Senegal.
yal ndaak, yal ndaak le	(Serer-Siin) Literally, "master of a little piece," an alternative title referring to the land custodian responsible for land and resource management in the space cleared by a village founder's historic brushfire. See also *laman* and *yal naay*.
yal qol	(Serer-Siin) Field proprietor or custodian; literally, "field master." The term conveys temporary use patterns rather than title or ownership.
zakat	(Arabic) Islamic tithe, widely referred to as *asaka* in rural Siin (see entry above).

Bibliography

INTERVIEWS

The persons listed below were interviewed in the context of disputes over land, in their capacity as state or customary officials, or in formal recordings of oral histories. This list does not include a large number of more informal interviews conducted both individually and in groups. Note that on this list, as well as in the citations in the text, names have been changed to protect the anonymity of informants.

Cama, Gana, oral history interview, village of Gajak, 15 June 1993.
Cama, Mbaye, farmer, dispute interview, village of Puday, 25 July 1993.
Cama, Moussa, farmer, dispute interview, village of Tukar, 7 July 1993.
Cama, Sitor, farmer, dispute interview, village of Tukar, 28 July 1993.
Cama, Sombel, farmer, oral history interview, village of Sob, 27 September 1993.
Diafatte, Gorgui, farmer, dispute interview, village of Dam, 14 August 1993.
Diagne, Koly, farmer, dispute interview, village of Tukar, 16 September 1993.
Diagne, Maimona, dispute interview, village of Lem, 29 August 1993.
Diatte, Amad, farmer, dispute interview, village of Ngonin, 11 August 1993.
Dieng, Abdoulaye, farmer, dispute interview, village of Pultok-Diohin, 19 October 1993.
Dieng, Amad, oral history interview, village of Puday, 28 August 1993.
Dieng, Ngor Mbede, farmer, dispute interview, village of Diokul, 26 October 1993.
Dieng, Niokhor, farmer, dispute interview, village of Tukar, 14 August 1993.
Dione, Abdou, rural councilor, elite interview, village of Lem, 19 October 1993.
Dione, Bocar, farmer, interview, village of Tukar, 21 June 1993.
Dione, Maisa Waly, farmer, interview, village of Tukar, 5 March 1993.
Dione, Maisa Waly, farmer, interview, village of Tukar, 9 May 1993.
Dione, Malale, dispute interview, village of Bari, 27 August 1993.

Dione, Mamadou, farmer, dispute interview, village of Bari, 23 October 1993.

Diop, Abdou Touré, CER chief, elite interview, village of Ngayokhem, 23 August 1993.

Diop, Amad, farmer, dispute interview, village of Mbinondar, 5 June 1993.

Diop, Bouré, farmer, dispute interview, village of Ngayokhem, 26 August 1993.

Diop, Etienne, schoolmaster, École Kane Faye de Tukar, interview, village of Tukar, 19 April 1993.

Diop, Hamad El Walid, subprefect, *arrondissement* of Tattaguine, elite interview, village of Ngayokhem, 27 October 1993.

Diouf, Adama, farmer, dispute interview, village of Gajak, 25 August 1993.

Diouf, Amaissa, rural councilor, elite interview, Njafaj region, 27 August 1993.

Diouf, Boucar Thioro, farmer, oral history interview, village of Ngan Fissel, 18 October 1993.

Diouf, Diaga Dibor Ndofene, *laman,* oral history interview, village of Tukar, 7 March 1993.

Diouf, Diaga Dibor Ndofene, *laman,* oral history interview, village of Tukar, 14 October 1993.

Diouf, Diogoye, farmer, interview, village of Tukar, 11 April 1993.

Diouf, Diogoye, farmer, interview, village of Tukar, 6 March 1993.

Diouf, Dione Falilou, village chief, oral history interview, region of Njafaj, 2 October 1993.

Diouf, Djibril, farmer, dispute interview, village of Tukar, 22 July 1993.

Diouf, Djignak, farmer, dispute interview, village of Tukar, 11 July 1993.

Diouf, Dokor, farmer, dispute interview, village of Tukar, 28 August 1993.

Diouf, Latyr, farmer, dispute interview, village of Ngayokhem, 26 August 1993.

Diouf, Latyr Farah, farmer, dispute interview, village of Mbinondar, 3 June 1993.

Diouf, Wagane, farmer, dispute interview, village of Mbinondar, 3 June 1993.

Diouf, Xemess, farmer, oral history interview, village of Sob, 28 September 1993.

Fall, Bouré, farmer, dispute interview, village of Ngayokhem, 26 August 1993.

Fall, Moussa, farmer, dispute interview, village of Tukar, 7 July 1993.

Fall, Ndongo, farmer, dispute interview, village of Lem, 29 August 1993.

Fall, Waly, farmer, dispute interview, village of Mbinondar, 3 June 1993.

Faye, Aliou, dispute interview, village of Puday, 25 July 1993.

Faye, Assane, farmer, dispute interview, village of Pultok-Diohin, 16 June 1993.

Faye, Babacar, farmer, oral history interview, village of Ngan Fissel, 30 September 1993.

Faye, Daly Ndeye, farmer, oral history interview, village of Ngonin, 14 June 1993.

Faye, Diaga, farmer, dispute interview, village of Puday, 25 July 1993.

Faye, Doudou, farmer, dispute interview, village of Mem, 5 June 1993.

Faye, Gorgui, farmer, oral history interview, village of Tukar, 19 July 1993.

Faye, Hamad, farmer, dispute interview, village of Logdir, 16 October 1993.

Faye, Jacques, farmer, dispute interview, village of Diohin, 6 October 1993.

Faye, Malick, farmer, dispute interview, village of Sob, 5 June 1993.

Faye, Mamadou, farmer, dispute interview, village of Tukar, 23 August 1993.

Faye, Mbassa, *saltigué*, elite interview, village of Tukar, 7 March 1993.

Faye, Modou, farmer, dispute interview, village of Puday, 25 July 1993.

Faye, Moussa, dispute interview, village of Ngonin, 21 July 1993.

Faye, Samba, farmer, dispute interview, village of Diohin, 16 September 1993.

Faye, Samba, farmer, dispute interview, village of Pultok-Diohin, 16 October 1993.

Faye, Serigne Ibra, marabout, elite interview, village of Ngayokhem, 23 October 1993.

Faye, Simone, farmer, dispute interview, village of Ndokh, 6 July 1993.

Faye, Tening, dispute interview, village of Ndokh, 3 October 1993.

Gakou, Cheikh, farmer, dispute interview, village of Ngonin, 19 October 1993.

Gakou, Matiasse, village chief, dispute interview, village of Ndokh, 6 July 1993.

Gakou, Ndeba, farmer, dispute interview, village of Ngonin, 25 August 1993.

Gning, Baba, farmer, oral history interview, village of Sob, 20 July 1993.

Gning, Gorgui, farmer, interview, village of Tukar, 11 August 1993.

Gning, Kory, village chief, dispute interview, village of Puday, 21 August 1993.

Gning, Thimndane, farmer, dispute interview, village of Ngangarlam, 27 July 1993.

Kane, Niokhor, farmer, dispute interview, village of Lem, 18 October 1993.

Marone, Gorgui, farmer, oral history interview, village of Gajak, 22 October 1993.

Marone, Samba, farmer, dispute interview, village of Mboyen, 29 August 1993.

Marone, Siga, farmer, oral history interview, village of Sob, 2 October 1993.

Mbacké, Aliou El Hadj, marabout, elite interview, Darou Mousty, 26 April 1993.

Ndiaye, Diokel, farmer, oral history interview, village of Sob, 29 September 1993.

Ndong, Mahecor, rural councilor, elite interview, village of Tukar, 3 June 1993.

Ndong, Mahecor, rural councilor, elite interview, Njafaj region, 26 July 1993.

Ndour, Antoine, rural councilor, elite interview, Njafaj region, 19 October 1993.

Ndour, Antoine, rural councilor, elite interview, village of Bari, 19 October 1993.

Ndour, Cheikh, farmer, dispute interview, village of Tukar, 18 September 1993.

Ndour, Dokor, rural council president, elite interview, Njafaj region, 4 March 1993.

Ndour, Dokor, rural council president, dispute interview, village of Tukar, 6 July 1993.

Ndour, Mamadou, farmer, dispute interview, village of Bari, 6 May 1993.

Ndour, Ndoukou, farmer, oral history interview, village of Gajak, 23 October 1993.

Ndour, Ngor Wagane, village chief, oral history interview, Njafaj region, 29 September 1993.

Ndour, Pierre, farmer, dispute interview, village of Ngangarlam, 15 September 1993.

Ngom, Amakoudou, farmer, dispute interview, village of Godel, 4 September 1993.

Ngom, Babacar, farmer, oral history interview, village of Godel, 3 September 1993.

Ngom, Boucar, farmer, dispute interview, village of Pultok-Diohin, 19 October 1993.

Ngom, Bouré, farmer, dispute interview, village of Logdir, 19 October 1993.

Ngom, Pierre, farmer, dispute interview, village of Ngangarlam, 15 September 1993.

Ngued, Doudou, rural councilor, elite interview, village of Tukar, 3 March 1993.

Ngued, Mahecor, rural councilor, elite interview, village of Tukar, 6 March 1993.

Sagne, Modou Diara, Water and Forests Service agent, elite interview, village of Ngayokhem, 23 August 1993.

Sarr, Aissatou, farmer, oral history interview, village of Puday, 21 September 1993.

Sarr, Cheikh, farmer, dispute interview, village of Bari, 25 August 1993.

Sarr, Cheikh, farmer, dispute interview, village of Ngonin, 19 October 1993.

Sarr, Diaraf Dibor, village chief, oral history interview, village of Tukar, 20 September 1993.

Sarr, Diomaye, farmer, dispute interview, village of Mem, 16 September 1993.

Sarr, Gor, farmer, dispute interview, village of Mem, 6 July 1993.

Sarr, Hamad, farmer, dispute interview, village of Tukar, 26 August 1993.

Sarr, Selbé, farmer, oral history interview, village of Sob, 1 October 1993.

Sarr, Siga, farmer, dispute interview, village of Gajak, 25 August 1993.

Sene, Cheikh, rural councilor, elite interview, Njafaj region, 27 July 1993.

Sene, Diame, farmer, dispute interview, village of Tukar, 28 August 1993.

Sene, Gorgui, rural councilor, elite interview, Njafaj region, 17 June 1993.

Sene, Hamad, dispute interview, village of Puday, 28 August 1993.

Sene, Latyr, farmer, oral history interview, village of Sob, 30 September 1993.

Sene, Ndeba, farmer, dispute interview, village of Logdir, 18 October 1993.

Sene, Niokhor, dispute interview, village of Ndokh, 15 September 1993.

Sene, Roger, farmer, dispute interview, village of Ndokh, 6 July 1993.

Sene, Waly Koundoul, farmer, dispute interview, village of Ngonin, 19 October 1993.

Sow, Ibou, farmer, dispute interview, village of Logdir, 18 October 1993.

Thiam, Mamadou, rural councilor, elite interview, Njafaj region, 23 October 1993.

Thiao, Cheikh, farmer, dispute interview, village of Bari, 25 August 1993.

Thiao, Kumba Ndofene, farmer and ally of former rural council president, interview, Dakar, 3 July 1993.

Thiao, Mbissime, farmer, dispute interview, village of Tukar, 22 July 1993.

Thiao, Ndiogoye, farmer, oral history interview, village of Puday, 12 August 1993.

Tine, Daouda, landless farmer, interview, village of Tukar, 21 July 1993.

Tine, Diaraf Seck, village chief, elite interview, Njafaj region, 20 September 1993.

Tine, Modou, rural councilor, elite interview, Njafaj region, 4 August 1993.

Tine, Niokhor, farmer, dispute interview, village of Gajak, 25 August 1993.

Yatt, Doudou, nephew of current *linguere,* elite interview, Dakar-Usine, 29 October 1993.

Yatt, Ibou, farmer, dispute interview, village of Tukar, 7 July 1993.

Yatt, Samba, farmer, dispute interview, village of Mem, 26 August 1993.

ARCHIVAL SOURCES

The following archives were consulted in the course of this project.

Archives du Tribunal Départemental de Fatick, Fatick, Senegal (various unclassified court records).

Archives du Tribunal Départemental de Kaolack, Kaolack, Senegal (various unclassified court records).

Archives du Tribunal Régional de Kaolack, Kaolack, Senegal (various unclassified court records).

Archives Nationales du Sénégal, Dakar, Senegal, in particular:

Séries 6M: Justice Indigène.

Séries B and G: correspondence and treaties.

BOOKS AND ARTICLES

Abelin, Phillipe. "Domaine national et développement au Sénégal." *Bulletin de l'Institut Fondamental d'Afrique Noire* 41, no. 3 (1979).

Abitbol, Michel, and Naomi Chazan, eds. *The Early State in African Perspective.* Leiden, Netherlands: E. J. Brill, 1988.

Alexander, Jeffrey. "Modern, Anti, Post, and Neo." *New Left Review* 210 (March–April 1995).

Almond, Gabriel A. "Comparative Political Systems." *Journal of Politics* 18 (1956).

Almond, Gabriel A., and Sidney Verba. *The Civic Culture*. Princeton: Princeton University Press, 1963.

_____, eds. *The Civic Culture Revisited*. Boston: Little, Brown, 1980.

Alvarez, Sonia E., Evelina Dagnino, and Arturo Escobar, eds. *Cultures of Politics/Politics of Cultures: Revisioning Latin American Social Movements*. Boulder, Colo.: Westview Press, 1998.

Anderson, Benedict. *Imagined Communities: Reflections on the Origin and Spread of Nationalism*. London: Verso, 1983.

Anderson, J. N. D. *Islamic Law in Africa*. London: Frank Cass, 1970.

Anderson, Perry. *Passages from Antiquity to Feudalism*. London: Verso, 1974.

Appiah, Kwame Anthony. *In My Father's House: Africa in the Philosophy of Culture*. Oxford: Oxford University Press, 1992.

Arendt, Hannah. *The Origins of Totalitarianism*. 1948. Reprint, New York: Harcourt, Brace, Jovanovich, 1979.

Arrow, Kenneth. *Selected Papers of Kenneth J. Arrow: Social Choice and Justice*. Cambridge: Harvard University Press, Belknap Press, 1983.

Aujas, L. "Les Sérères du Sénégal (Moeurs et coutumes de droit privé)." *Bulletin du Comité d'études Historiques et Scientifiques de l'Afrique Occidentale Française* 14 (1931): 293–333.

Azarya, V., and Naomi Chazan. "Disengagement from the State in Africa: Reflections on the Experience of Ghana and Guinea." *Comparative Studies in Society and History* 29, no. 1 (1987): 106–31.

Ba, Abdou Bouri. "Essai sur l'histoire du Saloum et du Rip." *Bulletin de l'Institut Fondamental d'Afrique Noire*, ser. B, 38, no. 4 (1976).

Ba, Thierno Aliou. "Les centres d'expansion rurale du Sénégal entre la dynamique paysanne et les structures d'état. Médiation ou frein pour un développement autogestionnaire?" *Mondes et Développement* 13, no. 52 (1985): 621–31.

Badie, Bertrand, and Pierre Birnbaum. *The Sociology of the State*. Trans. from the French by Arthur Goldhammer. Chicago: University of Chicago Press, 1983.

Banfield, Edward. *The Moral Basis of a Backward Society*. Chicago: Free Press, 1958.

Barker, Jonathan. "Political Space and the Quality of Participation in Rural Africa: A Case from Senegal." *Canadian Journal of African Studies* 21, no. 1 (1987): 1–16.

Barry, Boubacar. *Le royaume du Waalo: Le Sénégal avant la conquête*. Paris: Editions Karthala, 1985.

_____. *La Sénégambie du XVe au XIXe siècle: Traite négrière, Islam, conquête coloniale*. Paris: Editions l'Harmattan, 1988.

Barry, Brian. *Sociologists, Economists, and Democracy*. Chicago: University of Chicago Press, 1978.

Bassett, Thomas J. "The Land Question and Agricultural Transformation in Sub-Saharan Africa." In *Land in African Agrarian Systems*, ed. Thomas J.

Bassett and Donald E. Crummey. Madison: University of Wisconsin Press, 1993.

Bassett, Thomas J., and Donald E. Crummey, eds. *Land in African Agrarian Systems*. Madison: Wisconsin, 1993.

Bates, Robert. "Contra Contractarianism: Some Reflections on the New Institutionalism." *Politics and Society* 16 (1988): 399.

_____. *Markets and States in Tropical Africa*. Berkeley: University of California Press, 1981.

Bates, Robert, Avner Grief, Margaret Levi, Jean-Laurent Rosenthal, and Barry Weingart. *Analytic Narratives*. Princeton: Princeton University Press, 1998.

Bates, Robert, Valentin Mudimbe, and Jean O'Barr, eds. *Africa and the Disciplines*. Chicago: University of Chicago Press, 1993.

Batran, Aziz A. "The Nineteenth-Century Islamic Revolutions in West Africa." In *General History of Africa*, ed. Committee for the Drafting of a General History of Africa, 6:537–54. Berkeley: University of California Press, 1989.

Bayart, Jean-François. *The State in Africa: Politics of the Belly*. New York: Longman, 1993.

Becker, Charles. "La Sénégambie a l'époque de la traite des esclaves." *Revue Française d'Histoire d'Outre-Mer* 64, no. 235 (1975): 203–24.

_____. *Les Serer Ndut: Études sur les mutations sociales religieuses*. Paris: Université de Paris, Paris-Sorbonne E.P.H.E., 1970.

_____. *Traditions villageois du Siin*. Dakar: CNRS-LA, 1984.

Becker, Charles, Mamadou Diouf, and Mohamed Mbodj. "L'evolution demographique regionale du Sénégal et du Bassin Arachidier (Sine-Saloum) au vingtième siècle, 1904–1976." In *African Population and Capitalism: Historical Perspectives*, ed. Dennis D. Cordell and Joel W. Gregory. Boulder, Colo.: Westview Press, 1987.

Becker, Charles, and V. Martin. "Essai sur l'histoire du Saalum." *Revue Sénégalaise d'Histoire* 2, no. 1 (1981): 3–24.

Behrman, Lucy. *Muslim Brotherhoods and Politics in Senegal*. Cambridge: Harvard University Press, 1970.

Bell, Daniel. *The Coming of Post-Industrial Society*. New York: Basic Books, 1973.

Bendix, Reinhard. *Kings or People: Power and the Mandate to Rule*. Berkeley: University of California Press, 1978.

_____. "Tradition and Modernity Reconsidered." *Comparative Studies in Society and History* 9 (April 1967): 292–346.

Berkes, Fikret, Carl Folke, and Johan Colding. *Linking Social and Ecological Systems: Management Practices and Social Mechanisms*. New York: Cambridge University Press, 1997.

Bernard, H. Russel, ed. *Handbook of Methods in Cultural Anthropology*. Walnut Creek, Calif.: Alta Mira Press, 1998.

Berry, Sara. *No Condition Is Permanent: The Social Dynamics of Agrarian Change in Sub-Saharan Africa.* Madison: University of Wisconsin Press, 1993.

Bohannan, Paul, and Philip Curtin. *Africa and Africans.* Prospect Heights, Ill.: Waveland Press, 1995.

Bouat, Marie-Claire, and Jean-Louis Fouillard. *Les Finances publiques des communes et des communautés rurales au Sénégal.* Dakar: Editions Clairafrique, 1983.

Boulègue, Jean. *Le Grand Jolof, XIIIe–XVIe siècle.* Paris: Editions Karthala, 1987.

Bourdieu, Pierre. *Outline of a Theory of Practice.* Geneva: Editions Droz, 1972. Reprint, Cambridge: Cambridge University Press, 1977.

Boutillier, Jean-Louis, and Jean Caussé. *La demographie du Fouta-Toro (Toucouleurs et Peulhs).* Dakar: Mission Socio-économique de la Vallée du Fleuve Sénégal, 1959.

Bratton, Michael. "Beyond the State: Civil Society and Associational Life in Africa." *World Politics* 31, no. 3 (April 1989).

Braudel, Fernand. "Histoire et sciences sociales: La longue durée." *Annales* 13 (1958): 725–53.

Brinks, Daniel M. "Informal Institutions and the Rule of Law: The Judicial Response to State Killings in Buenos Aires and São Paulo in the 1990s." Paper presented at the Conference on Informal Institutions and Politics in the Developing World, Weatherhead Center for International Affairs, Harvard University, 5–6 April 2002.

Bryant, Christopher G. A., and David Jary. *Giddens' Theory of Structuration: A Critical Appreciation.* London: Routledge, 1991.

Burton, Virginia Lee. *Mike Mulligan and His Steam Shovel.* Boston: Houghton Mifflin, 1939.

Callaghy, Thomas M. "The State and the Development of Capitalism in Africa: Theoretical, Historical, and Comparative Reflections." In *The Precarious Balance: State and Society in Africa,* ed. Donald Rothchild and Naomi Chazan. Boulder, Colo.: Westview, 1987.

_____. *The State-Society Struggle: Zaire in Comparative Perspective.* New York: Columbia University Press, 1984.

Carney, Dana, ed. *Sustainable Rural Livelihoods: What Contribution Can We Make?* London: Department for International Development, 1998.

Carter, Gwendolyn. *National Unity and Regionalism in Eight African States.* Ithaca: Cornell University Press, 1966.

Caverivière, Monique. "Incertitudes et devenir du droit foncier Sénégalais." *Revue Internationale de Droit Comparé* 38, no. 1 (January–March 1986): 95–115.

Chabal, Patrick. "Introduction: Thinking about Politics in Africa." In *Political Domination in Africa,* ed. Patrick Chabal. Cambridge: Cambridge University Press, 1986.

_____. "The Quest for Good Government and Development in Africa: Is NEPAD the Answer?" *International Affairs* 78, no. 3 (July 2002): 447–62.

Chanock, Martin. *Law, Custom, and Social Order*. London: Cambridge University Press, 1985.

Chase, Jacqueline, ed. *The Spaces of Neoliberalism: Land, Place, and Family in Latin America*. Bloomfield, Conn.: Kumarian Press, 2002.

Chazan, Naomi. "Africa's Democratic Challenge." *World Policy Journal* 9, no. 2 (spring 1992): 279–307.

_____. "Between Liberalism and Statism: African Political Cultures and Democracy." In *Political Culture and Democracy in Developing Countries*, ed. Larry Diamond. Boulder: Lynne Rienner, 1994.

_____. "Planning Democracy in Africa: A Comparative Perspective on Nigeria and Ghana." *Policy Sciences* 22 (1989).

Clifford, James. *The Predicament of Culture: Twentieth-Century Ethnography, Literature, and Art*. Cambridge: Harvard University Press, 1988.

Clozel, F.-J. *Les coutumes indigènes de la Côte d'Ivoire*. Paris: Librairie Maritime et Coloniale, 1902.

Colson, Elizabeth. "The Impact of the Colonial Period on the Definition of Land Rights." In *Colonialism in Africa, 1870–1960*, ed. V. Turner. Vol. 3: *Profiles of Change: African Society and Colonial Rule*. Cambridge: Cambridge University Press, 1971.

_____. "Possible Repercussions of the Right to Make Wills upon the Plateau Tonga of Northern Rhodesia." *Journal of African Administration* 2 (1950).

Comaroff, Jean. *Body of Power, Spirit of Resistance: The Culture and History of a South African People*. Chicago: University of Chicago Press, 1985.

Coquery-Vidrovitch, Catherine. "Towards an African Mode of Production." In *Perspectives on the African Past*, ed. Martin Klein and G. W. Johnson. Boston: Little, Brown, 1972.

Coquery-Vidrovitch, Catherine, and Henri Moniot. *L'Afrique noire de 1800 à nos jours*. Paris: Presses Universitaires de France, 1992.

Costanza, Robert, and Lisa Wainger. *Ecological Economics: The Science and Management of Sustainability*. New York: Columbia University Press, 1991.

Coulibaly, Abdou Latif. "Khelkom: La mort programmée d'une forêt." *Sud Hebdo* 155, no. 1 (2 May 1991): 5.

Critchfield, Richard. *Shahhat, an Egyptian*. Syracuse: Syracuse University Press, 1978.

Crowder, Michael. *Senegal: A Study of French Assimilation Policy*. London: Methuen and Company, 1967.

Cruise O'Brien, Donal. *The Mourides of Senegal*. Oxford: Clarendon Press, 1971.

_____. *Saints and Politicians: Essays in the Organization of a Senegalese Peasant Society*. London: Cambridge University Press, 1975.

Curtin, Philip D. *Economic Change in Precolonial Africa: Senegambia in the Era of the Slave Trade*. Madison: University of Wisconsin Press, 1975.

David, Philip. *Les navetanes: Histoire des migrants saisonneirs de l'arachide en Senegambie des origines à nos jours.* Dakar: Les Nouvelles Editions Africaines, 1980.

Davidson, Basil. *The Black Man's Burden: Africa and the Curse of the Nation-State.* New York: Times Books, 1992.

de Kersaint-Gilly, F. "Les Geulowars: Leur origine d'aprés une légende trés en faveur dans le Saloum oriental." *Bulletin du Comité des Études Historiques et Scientifiques de l'Afrique Occidentale Française* 3, no. 1 (1920).

de Maille, Raymond J. "Introduction to the Bison Book Edition." In *The Ghost Dance Religion and the Sioux Outbreak of 1890,* by James Mooney. Lincoln: University of Nebraska Press, 1991.

Debène, Marc. "Regards sur le droit foncier Sénégalais: Un seul droit pour deux rêves." *Revue Internationale de Droit Comparé* 38, no. 1 (January–March 1986): 77–94.

Delafosse, Maurice. *Haut-Sénégal-Niger.* 1912. Reprint, Paris: G.-P. Maisonneuve et Larose, 1972.

Delpech, Bernard. "Dynamismes sociaux et conflits d'autorité dans une communauté rurale serer du bassin arachidier Sénégalais." Paper presented at Deuxième Colloque Africain de Psychiatrie, Dakar, 5–9 March 1968.

Deutsch, Karl. *Nationalism and Social Communication.* Cambridge: Technology Press of the Massachusetts Institute of Technology, 1953.

———. "Social Mobilization and Political Development." *American Political Science Review* 55 (September 1961): 493–514.

Diamond, Larry. "Class Formation in the Swollen African State." *Journal of Modern African Studies* 26, no. 4 (1987).

———. *Developing Democracy: Toward Consolidation.* Baltimore: Johns Hopkins University Press, 1999.

Diamond, Larry, Juan J. Linz, and Seymour Martin Lipset, eds. *Politics in Developing Countries: Comparing Experiences with Democracy.* 2d ed. Boulder, Colo.: Lynne Rienner, 1995.

Diop, Abdoulaye Bara. "Le tenure foncière en milieu rural Wolof (Sénégal): Histoire et actualité." *Notes Africaines* 118 (1968): 48–52.

Diop, Abdoulaye Sokhna. "L'impact de la civilisation Manding au Sénégal: La genése de la royauté Gelwar au Siin et au Saalum." *Bulletin de l'Institut Fondamental d'Afrique Noire,* ser. B, 40, no. 4 (1978): 689–705.

Diop, Cheikh Anta. *L'Afrique noire precoloniale.* Paris: Editions Karthala, 1960.

Douglas, Mary. "Social Control of Cognition: Some Factors in Joke Perception." *Man* 3, no. 3 (September 1968): 361–76.

Dulphy, M. "Coutume des Sérères de la Petite Côte (Cercle de Thiés)." In *Coutumiers Juridiques de l'Afrique Occidentale Française,* ed. Comité d'études Historiques et Scientifiques de l'Afrique Occidentale Française. Bk. 1: *Senegal.* Paris: Librairie Larose, 1936.

Dupire, Margeurite. "Chasse rituelle, divination et réconduction de l'ordre socio-politique chez les Serer du Sine (Sénégal)." *L'Homme* 16, no. 1 (1976): 5–32.

———. "Classes et échelons d'âge dans une société dysharmonique (Sereer Ndut du Sénégal)." *Journal des africanistes* 61, no. 2 (1991): 5–42.

———. *Sagesse Sereer: Essais sur la pensee Sereer Ndut*. Paris: Editions Karthala, 1994.

Dupire, Marguerite, André Lericollais, Bernard Delpech, and Jean-Marc Gastellu. "Résidence, tenure foncière, alliance dans une société bilinèaire (Serer du Sine et du Baol, Sénégal)." *Cahiers d'études Africaines* 14 (1974): 417–52.

Eckstein, Harry. *Division and Cohesion in Democracy: A Study of Norway*. Princeton, N.J.: Princeton University Press, 1966.

Ekeh, Peter. "Colonialism and the Two Publics in Africa: A Theoretical Statement." *Comparative Studies in Society and History* 17, no. 1 (1975): 91–112.

Emmerson, Donald K. *Indonesia's Elite: Political Culture and Cultural Politics*. Ithaca: Cornell University Press, 1976.

Ensminger, Jean. "Changing Property Rights: Reconciling Formal and Informal Rights to Land in Africa." In *The Frontiers of the New Institutional Economics*, ed. John Nye and John Drobak. San Diego: Academic Press, 1997.

———. "The Political Economy of Religion: An Anthropologist's Perspective." *Journal of Institutional and Theoretical Economics* 150, no. 4 (1994).

Escobar, Arturo. *Encountering Development*. Princeton: Princeton University Press, 1995.

Etzioni, Amitai. *The Spirit of Community*. New York: Simon and Schuster, 1994.

Evans, Peter. *Embedded Autonomy: States and Industrial Transformation*. Princeton, N.J.: Princeton University Press, 1995.

———. "Government Action, Social Capital, and Development: Reviewing the Evidence on Synergy." *World Development* 24, no. 6 (June 1996): 1119–32.

Evans, Peter, Theda Skocpol, and Dietrich Reuschemeyer. *Bringing the State Back In*. Cambridge: Cambridge University Press, 1985.

Falk Moore, Sally. *Social Facts and Fabrications*. Cambridge: Cambridge University Press, 1986.

Fall, Babacar. "Labor under Structural Adjustment Program in Senegal." Working paper, Center for Afroamerican African Studies, University of Michigan, 1993.

Fallers, Lloyd. *Law without Precedent: Legal Ideas in Action in the Courts of Colonial Busoga*. Chicago: University of Chicago Press, 1969.

Fatton, Robert. "Clientelism and Politics in Senegal." *African Studies Review* 29, no. 1 (1986): 61–78.

Faye, Louis Diène. *Mort et naissance: Le monde Sereer*. Dakar: Nouvelles Editions Africaines, 1983.

Ferguson, James. *The Anti-politics Machine*. New York: Cambridge University Press, 1990.

Foster, George M. "Peasant Society and the Image of Limited Good." In *Peasant Society: A Reader*, ed. Jack M. Potter, May N. Diaz, and George M. Foster. Boston: Little, Brown, 1967.

Frank, Barbara E. "Caste versus Craft: Transformations in Identity and Artistry among the Mande-Speaking Peoples of West Africa." In *Redefining the "Artisan": Traditional Technicians in Changing Societies*, ed. Paul Greenough, 169–88. Iowa City: Center for International and Comparative Studies, University of Iowa, 1992.

Freedman, Jim. "Joking, Affinity, and the Exchange of Ritual Services among the Kiga of Northern Rwanda: An Essay on Joking Relationship Theory." *Man* 12 (April 1977): 154–65.

Gamble, David P. "The Wolof of Senegambia (Together with Notes on the Lebu and the Serer." In *Ethnographic Survey of Africa*, ed. Daryll Forde. London: International Africa Institute, 1957.

Garenne, Michel, and Pierre Cantrell. "Three Decades of Research on Population and Health: The ORSTOM Experience in Rural Senegal, 1962–1991." Paper presented at the IUSSP Seminar on Longitudinal Studies, Saly Portudal, Senegal, 1991.

Gastellu, Jean-Marc. *L'égalitarianisme économique des Serer du Sénégal*. Travaux et Documents de l'ORSTOM. Paris: ORSTOM, 1981.

_____. "Une séance de Mbayar: 'La terre appartient à ceux qui la cultivent' (pays Serer, Sénégal)." *Maitrise de l'espace agraire et développement en Afrique tropicale: Logique paysanne et rationalité technique*. Paris: Editions de l'ORSTOM, 1978.

Geertz, Clifford. *The Interpretation of Cultures*. New York: Basic Books, 1973.

_____. *Local Knowledge: Further Essays in Interpretive Anthropology*. New York: Basic Books, 1983.

_____. *Negara: The Theatre State in Nineteenth-Century Bali*. Princeton: Princeton University Press, 1980.

Geismar, L. *Recueil des coutumes civiles de races du Sénégal*. Saint-Louis: Imprimerie du Gouvernement, 1933.

Gellar, Sheldon, Robert Charlick, and Yvonne Jones. *Animation Rurale and Rural Development: The Experience of Senegal*. Ithaca: Rural Development Committee, Center for International Studies, Cornell University, 1980.

Gerskovitz, Mark, and John Waterbury, eds. *The Political Economy of Risk and Choice in Senegal*. London: Frank Cass, 1987.

Giddens, Anthony. *Central Problems in Social Theory: Action, Structure, and Contradiction in Social Analysis*. Berkeley: University of California Press, 1979.

Glazer, Nathan, and Daniel Patrick Moynihan. *Ethnicity: Theory and Experience*. Cambridge: Harvard University Press, 1975.

Gordon, Robert, and David Killick. "Adaptation of Technology to Culture and Environment: Bloomery Iron Smelting in America and Africa." *Technology and Culture* 34, no. 2 (April 1993).

Gouvernement du Sénégal. "Loi no. 64–46 du 17 juin 1964 rélative au domain national." *Journal Officiel du République du Sénégal*, no. 3692 (17 July 1964).

Gravrand, Henri. *Civilisation Serer: Cosaan (les origines)*. Paris: Les Nouvelles Editions Africains, 1983.

_____. *Civilisation Serer: Pangool (La genie religieux Sereer)*. Paris: Les Nouvelles Editions Africains, 1990.

_____. "Les Sereres." *Afrique Occidentale Française Magazine*, no. 15 (August 1956): 78–84.

Griaule, Marcel. "L'alliance cathartique." *Africa* 18, no. 4 (1948): 242–58.

Griaule, Marcel, and Germaine Dieterlen. "The Dogon." In *African Worlds: Studies in the Cosmological Ideas and Social Values of African Peoples*, ed. Daryll Forde. 1954. Reprint, London: Oxford University Press, 1965.

Guigou, Brigitte. "Les changements du système familial et matrimonial: Les Serere du Sine (Sénégal) (La souplesse du système patrimonial lignager)." Thèse de Doctorat, École des Hautes Études en Sciences Sociales, Paris, 1992.

Habermas, Jurgen. *Legitimation Crisis*. Boston: Beacon Press, 1975.

Hall, Peter. "Policy Paradigms, Social Learning, and the State." *Comparative Politics* (April 1993): 275–96.

Hart, H. L. A. *The Concept of Law*. Oxford: Clarendon Press, 1961.

Hegel, George Friedrich. *Philosophy of Right*, ed. T. M. Knox. London: Oxford University Press, 1967.

Held, David. *Models of Democracy*. Stanford: Stanford University Press, 1987.

Herskovits, M. J. *Continuity and Change in African Cultures*. Chicago: University of Chicago Press, 1959.

_____. *The Myth of the Negro Past*. Boston: Beacon Press, 1941.

Hesseling, Gerti. *Histoire politique du Sénégal*. Paris: Editions Karthala, 1985.

Hirschman, Albert. *Exit, Voice, and Loyalty*. Cambridge: Harvard University Press, 1970.

Hiskett, Mervyn. *The Sword of Truth: The Life and Times of the Shehu Usuman dan Fodio*. Evanston, Ill.: Northwestern University Press, 1994.

Hoare, Quintin, and Geoffrey Nowell-Smith, eds. *Selections from the Prison Notebooks*. London: Laurence and Wishart, 1971.

Hobsbawm, Eric, and Terence Ranger, eds. *The Invention of Tradition*. Cambridge: Cambridge University Press, 1983.

Huntington, Samuel. *The Clash of Civilizations and the Remaking of World Order*. New York: Simon and Schuster, 1996.

_____. *Political Order in Changing Societies*. New Haven: Yale University Press, 1968.

Hyden, Goran. "Governance and the Study of Politics." In *Governance and Politics in Africa,* ed. Goran Hyden and Michael Bratton. Boulder: Lynne Rienner, 1992.

———. *No Shortcuts to Progress: African Development Management in Perspective.* Berkeley: University of California Press, 1983.

Hymans, Jacques Louis. *Léopold Sédar Senghor: An Intellectual Biography.* Edinburgh: Edinburgh University Press, 1971.

Isaacs, Harold. "Basic Group Identity: The Idols of the Tribe." In *Ethnicity: Theory and Experience,* ed. Nathan Glazer and Daniel Patrick Moynihan, 29–52. Cambridge: Harvard University Press, 1975.

Jameson, Fredric. *The Ideologies of Theory: Essays 1971–1986.* Vol. 2. Minneapolis: University of Minnesota Press, 1988.

Johnstone, Sir Harry H. *History of the Colonization of Africa by Alien Races.* Cambridge: Cambridge University Press, 1899.

Joire, J. "Decouvertes archeologiques dans la region de Rao (bas Sénégal)" *Bulletin de l'Institut Fondamental d'Afrique Noire,* ser. B (July–October 1955): 249–333.

Jolls, Christine, Cass R. Sunstein, and Richard Thaler, "A Behavioral Approach to Law and Economics." *Stanford Law Review* 50, no. 5 (1998): 1471–550.

Joseph, Richard. "Class, State, and Prebendal Politics." *Journal of Commonwealth and Comparative Politics* 21 (1983): 21–38.

Kane, Moustapha, and David Robinson. *The Islamic Regime of Fuuta Tooro: An Anthology of Oral Tradition.* East Lansing, Mich.: African Studies Center, Michigan State University, 1984.

Kaplan, Robert D. *Balkan Ghosts: A Journey through History.* New York: St. Martin's Press, 1993.

———. "The Coming Anarchy: How Scarcity, Crime, Overpopulation, Tribalism, and Disease Are Rapidly Destroying the Social Fabric of Our Planet." *Atlantic Monthly* 273, no. 2 (February 1994).

Keane, John. *Democracy and Civil Society.* New York: Verso Press, 1988.

Keeton, Claire. "Mbeki to Promote African Recovery Plan at G8 Summit." *Agence France Presse International News,* 18 July 2001.

Kennedy, John G. "Bonds of Laughter among the Tarahumara Indians: Toward a Rethinking of Joking Relationship Theory." In *The Social Anthropology of Latin America: Essays in Honor of Ralph Leon Beals,* ed. Walter Goldschmidt and Harry Hoijer. Berkeley: University of California Press, 1970.

Klein, Martin. *Islam and Imperialism in Senegal.* Stanford: Stanford University Press, 1968.

———. "Slavery among the Wolof and Serer of Senegambia." In *Slavery in Africa,* ed. Suzanne Myers and Igor Kopytoff. Madison: University of Wisconsin Press, 1977.

Krishna, Anirudh, Norman Uphoff, and Milton Esman, eds. *Reasons for Hope: Instructive Experiences in Rural Development.* West Hartford, Conn.: Kumarian Press, 1997.

Laitin, David. *Hegemony and Culture*. Chicago: University of Chicago Press, 1986.

Lakoff, George. *Women, Fire, and Dangerous Things: What Categories Reveal about the Mind*. Chicago: University of Chicago Press, 1987.

Lapidus, Ira M. *A History of Islamic Societies*. Cambridge: Cambridge University Press, 1988.

Law, Robin. *From Slave Trade to "Legitimate" Commerce: The Commercial Transition in Nineteenth-Century West Africa*. Cambridge: Cambridge University Press, 1995.

Lemarchand, Rene. "Genocide in Comparative Perspective: Rwanda, Cambodia and Bosnia." Manuscript, 2000.

Leonard, David K. *African Successes: Four Public Managers of Kenyan Rural Development*. Berkeley: University of California Press, 1991.

Lericollais, André. "La mort des arbres à Sob, en pays Sereer (Sénégal)." *Tropiques, lieux et liens*. Paris: Editions ORSTOM, 1989.

_____. *Sob: Étude geographique d'un terroir Sérèr (Sénégal)*. ORSTOM Atlas des structures agraires au sud du Sahara, no. 7. Paris: Mouton and Company, 1972.

Lerner, David. *The Passing of Traditional Society*. Glencoe, Ill.: Free Press, 1958.

LeRoy, Etienne. "L'émergence d'un droit foncier locale au Sénégal." *Dynamiques et finalités des droits africaines*, ed. Gerard Conac. Paris: Economica, 1980.

_____. "La loi sur le domaine national à vingt ans: Joyeaux anniversaire?" *Mondes et Développement* 13, no. 52 (1985): 667–85.

Lévi-Strauss, Claude. *The Savage Mind*. Chicago: University of Chicago Press, 1966.

Linton, Ralph. *The Cultural Background of Personality*. New York: Appleton-Century-Crofts, 1945.

Lipset, Seymour Martin, ed. *The Encyclopedia of Democracy*. Washington, D.C.: Congressional Quarterly, 1995.

Locke, John. *Second Treatise of Government*. New York: Barnes and Noble, 1966.

Love, Chris. "Talking about 'Tribe': Moving from Stereotypes to Analysis." Africa Policy Information Center Background Paper, November 1997. Available on-line at http://www.africaaction.org/bp/ethall.htm, 18 April 2002.

Malkki, Liisa. *Purity and Exile*. Chicago: University of Chicago Press, 1995.

Mann, Kristin, and Richard Roberts. Introduction to *Law in Colonial Africa*, ed. Mann and Roberts. Portsmouth, N.H.: Heinemann, 1991.

March, James, and Johan Olsen. *Rediscovering Institutions: The Organizational Basis of Politics*. New York: Free Press, 1989.

Markovitz, Irving. *Leopold Sedar Senghor and the Politics of Negritude*. New York: Atheneum, 1969.

Martin, Joel W. *Sacred Revolt: The Muskogee's Struggle for a New World Order*. Boston: Beacon Press, 1991.

Martin, Victor, and Charles Becker. "Vestiges protohistoriques et occupations humaine au Sénégal." *Annales de Démographie Historique* (1974): 402–29.

Marx, Karl. "Preface to the First German Edition of *Capital*." In *The Marx-Engels Reader*, ed. Robert C. Tucker. New York: W. W. Norton, 1978.

Mbembe, Achille. *On the Postcolony*. Berkeley: University of California Press, 2001.

———. "Prosaics of Servitude and Authoritarian Civilities." *Public Culture* 5, no. 1 (fall 1992): 123–45.

———. "Provisional Notes on the Postcolony." *Africa* 62, no. 1 (1992): 3–37.

Mbodj, Mohammed. "Un exemple de l'économie coloniale: Le Sine-Saloum (Sénégal de 1887 à 1940: Cultures arachidières et mutations sociales)." Thèse de 3éme cycle, Université de Paris VII, 1978.

Mead, Margaret. *And Keep Your Powder Dry*. New York: William Morrow and Company, 1942.

———. *Coming of Age in Samoa*, 1–13. New York: William Morrow and Company, 1928.

Meillassoux, Claude. "The Economy in Agricultural Self-Sustaining Societies: A Preliminary Analysis." In *Relations of Productions*, ed. David Seddon. London: Cass, 1978.

Metraux, Rhoda, and Margaret Mead. *Themes in French Culture*. Stanford: Stanford University Press, 1954.

Miers, Suzanne, and Igor Kopytoff. *Slavery in Africa*. Madison: University of Wisconsin Press, 1977.

Migdal, Joel. "Studying the Politics of Development and Change: The State of the Art." In *Political Science: The State of the Discipline*, ed. Ada W. Finifter. Washington, D.C.: American Political Science Review, 1983.

Mitchell, Timothy. "The Invention and Reinvention of the Egyptian Peasant." *International Journal of Middle East Studies* 22 (1990): 129–46.

Moitt, Bernard. "Peanut Production, Market Integration, and Peasant Strategies in Kajoor and Bawol before World War II." Paper presented at Colloque "L'Afrique Occidentale Française: Esquisse d'une intégration africaine?" Dakar, 16–23 June 1995.

Moleur, Bernard. "Le droit de proprieté sur le sol Sénégalais: Analyse historique du XVIIème siècle à l'independance." Thèse pour le Doctorat d'état, Faculté des Sciences Juridiques et Politiques de l'Université de Dijon, 1978.

———. "Genèse de la loi relative au domaine nationale." *Annales Africaines* (1983–1985): 11–55.

Mooney, James. *Ghost Dance Religion and the Sioux Outbreak of 1890*. Lincoln: University of Nebraska Press, 1991.

Moore, Sally Falk. *Social Facts and Fabrications: "Customary" Law on Kilimanjaro, 1880–1980*. New York: Cambridge University Press, 1986.

Morgenthau, Ruth. *Political Parties in French-Speaking West Africa*. Oxford: Clarendon Press, 1964.

Mudimbe, V. Y. *The Invention of Africa*. Bloomington: Indiana University Press, 1988.

Nagel, Joane. "Constructing Ethnicity: Creating and Recreating Ethnic Identity and Culture." Special Issue on Immigration, Race, and Ethnicity in America. *Social Problems* 41, no. 1 (February 1994): 152–76.

Nagel, Joane, and Michael Snipp. "Ethnic Reorganization: American Indian Social, Economic, Political, and Cultural Strategies for Survival." *Ethnic and Racial Studies* 16. no. 2 (April 1993): 202–35.

Ndiaye, Birame. "La participation à la gestion des affaires publiques: Les communautés rurales sénégalaises." *Revue Française d'Administration Publique* 11 (1979): 79–112.

Ndiaye, Raphaël. "Correspondances ethno-patronymiques et parenté plaisantante: Une problématique d'integration à large echelle." *Environnement Africain* 8, no. 31–32 (1992): 97–128.

Netting, Robert McC., M. Pricilla Stone, and Glenn D. Stone. "Kofyar Cash-Cropping: Choice and Change in Indigenous Agricultural Development." *Human Ecology: An Interdisciplinary Journal* 17, no. 3 (September 1989): 299–19.

Niang, Mamadou. "Réflexions sur la réforme foncière sénégalaise de 1964." In *Enjeux fonciers en Afrique Noir*, ed. E. Le Bris, E. LeRoy, and F. Leimdorfer, 219–27. Paris: Editions Karthala, 1982.

———. "Le reforme de l'administration territoriale et locale au Sénégal." *Notes Africaines* 172 (1981): 103–9.

Noirot, Ernest. "Notice sur le Sine-Saloum, pays de Sine." *Journal Officel du Sénégal et Dependances*, 16 April 1892.

North, Douglass C. *Institutions, Institutional Change, and Economic Performance*. Cambridge: Cambridge University Press, 1990.

———. *Structure and Change in Economic History*. New York: Norton, 1981.

O'Donnell, Guillermo, Philippe Schmitter, and Lawrence Whitehead. *Transitions from Authoritarian Rule*. Baltimore: Johns Hopkins University Press, 1986.

O'Donoghue, T., and M. Rabin. "The Economics of Immediate Gratification." *Journal of Behavioral Decision Making* 13, no. 2 (April–June 2000): 233–50.

Olson, Mancur. *The Logic of Collective Action*. Cambridge: Harvard University Press, 1965.

Olukoshi, Adebayo O., R. Omotayo Olaniyan, and Femi Aribisala. *Structural Adjustment in West Africa*. Lagos, Nigeria: Nigeria Institute of International Affairs, 1994.

ORSTOM. *Projet Niakhar: Population et santé à Niakhar*. Dakar: ORSTOM, 1992.

Ostrom, Elinor. *Governing the Commons*. Cambridge: Cambridge University Press, 1990.

Parsons, Talcott. *The Structure of Social Action*. New York: Free Press, 1968.

Pasquier, R. "En marge de la guerre de succession: Les essais de culture du coton au Sénégal." *Travaux du Département d'Histoire de l'Institut des Hautes Études de Dakar*, no. 1 (1955).

Pateman, Carole. "Political Culture, Political Structure, and Political Change." *British Journal of Political Science* 1, no. 3 (July 1971).

Patrick, Glenda M. "Political Culture." In *Social Science Concepts*, ed. Giovanni Sartor. London: Sage, 1984.

Patterson, Orlando. *Ethnic Chauvinism: The Reactionary Impulse*. New York: Stein and Day, 1977.

Peires, J. B. "Paradigm Deleted: The Materialist Interpretation of the Mfecane." *Journal of Southern African Studies* 19, no. 2 (June 1993): 295–313.

Pelissier, Paul. *Les paysans du Sénégal: Les civilisations agraires du Cayor à la Casamance*. Paris: Imprimerie Fabrègue, 1966.

Pichl, W. J. *The Cangin Group: A Language Group in Northern Senegal*. Pittsburgh: Duquesne University Press, 1966.

Podro, Michael. *Critical Historians of Art*. New Haven: Yale University Press, 1982.

Poggi, Gianfranco. *The Development of the Modern State*. Stanford: Stanford University Press, 1978.

Polanyi, Karl. *The Great Transformation: The Political and Economic Origins of Our Time*. 1944. Reprint Boston: Beacon Press, 1957.

Price, Robert M. "Race and Reconciliation in the New South Africa." *Politics and Society* 25, no 2 (June 1997): 149–78.

———. *Society and Bureaucracy in Contemporary Ghana*. Berkeley: University of California Press, 1975.

Putnam, Robert. *Bowling Alone: The Collapse and Revival of American Community*. New York: Simon and Schuster, 2000.

———. "Institutional Performance and Political Culture: Some Puzzles about the Power of the Past." *Governance: An International Journal of Policy and Administration* 1, no. 3 (July 1988).

Putnam, Robert D., et al. *Making Democracy Work: Civic Traditions in Modern Italy*. Princeton: Princeton University Press, 1993.

Pye, Lucian W. "Political Culture." In *International Encyclopedia of Social Sciences*, ed. David Sills. New York: Macmillan, 1968.

Pye, Lucian W., and Sidney Verba, eds. *Political Culture and Political Development*. Princeton: Princeton University Press, 1965.

Radcliffe-Brown, A. R. "On Joking Relationships." *Africa* 13, no. 3 (July 1940): 195–210.

Reverdy, Jean-Claude. *Une société rurale au Sénégal: Les structures foncières, familiales et villageoises des Serer*. Aix-en-Provence: Centre Africaines des Sciences Appliquées, 1963.

Richter, Dolores. "Further Considerations of Caste in West Africa: The Senufo." *Africa* 50, no. 1 (1980): 37–54.

Riggs, Fred. *Administration in Developing Countries.* Boston: Houghton Mifflin, 1964.

Rivlin, Helen Anne B. *The Agricultural Policy of Muhammad 'Ali in Egypt.* Cambridge: Harvard University Press, 1961.

Roberts, Richard. "Text and Testimony in the Tribunal de Premiere Instance, Dakar, during the Early Twentieth Century." *Journal of African History* 31 (1990): 447–63.

Robertson, A. F. *The Dynamics of Productive Relationships: African Share Contracts in Comparative Perspective.* Cambridge: Cambridge University Press, 1987.

Roediger, David. *The Wages of Whiteness: Race and the Making of the American Working Class.* New York: Verso, 1991.

Röling, Niels G., et al. *Facilitating Sustainable Agriculture: Participatory Learning and Adaptive Management in Times of Uncertainty.* Cambridge: Cambridge University Press, 1998.

Rogin, Michael. *Fathers and Children: Andrew Jackson and the Subjugation of the American Indian.* New York: Alfred A. Knopf, 1975. Reprint, New Brunswick, N.J.: Transaction, 1991.

Rosen, Lawrence. *The Anthropology of Justice: Law as Culture in Islamic Society.* Cambridge: Cambridge University Press, 1989.

Rosenbaum, W. A. *Political Culture.* New York: Praeger, 1975.

Rothchild, Donald, and Naomi Chazan, eds. *The Precarious Balance: State and Society in Africa.* Boulder, Colo.: Westview, 1987.

Rousseau, Jean-Jacques. *The Social Contract.* Trans. from the French by Charles M. Sherover. New York: Harper and Row, 1984.

Rudolph, Lloyd, and Susanne Hoeber Rudolph. *The Modernity of Tradition: Political Development in India.* Chicago: University of Chicago Press, 1967.

Sahlins, Marshall. *Historical Metaphors and Mythical Realities: Structure in the Early History of the Sandwich Islands Kingdom.* Ann Arbor: University of Michigan Press, 1985.

Sarr, Alioune. "Histoire du Sine-Saloum." *Bulletin de l'Institut Fondamental d'Afrique Noire,* ser. B, 46, no. 3–4 (1986–87): 225–81.

Schaffner, Bertram. *Fatherland: A Study of Authoritarianism in the German Family.* New York: Columbia University Press, 1948.

Schmitter, Philippe C. "Idealism, Regime Change, and Regional Cooperation: Lessons from the Southern Cone of Latin America." Americas Program Working Paper no. 89–8, Americas Program, Stanford University, 1989.

Schumacher, Edward. *Politics, Bureaucracy, and Rural Development in Senegal.* Berkeley: University of California Press, 1985.

Schuster, Leslie Ann. "Workers and Community: The Case of the Peat-Cutters and the Shipbuilding Industry in Saint-Nazaire, 1881–1910." *Journal of Social History* 27, no. 4 (summer 1994): 777–97.

Scott, James. *Seeing Like a State: How Certain Schemes to Improve the Human Condition Have Failed.* New Haven: Yale University Press, 2000.

_____. *Weapons of the Weak: Everyday Forms of Peasant Resistance*. New Haven: Yale University Press, 1985.

Senghor, Léopold Sédar. *Liberté I: Négritude et humanisme*. Paris: Éditions du Seuil, 1964.

Sikkink, Kathryn. *Ideas and Institutions: Developmentalism in Brazil and Argentina*. Ithaca: Cornell University Press, 1991.

Sklar, Richard. "Democracy in Africa." *African Studies Review* 26, no. 3–4 (September–December 1983): 11–24.

_____. "The Nature of Class Domination in Africa." *Journal of Modern African Studies* 17, no. 4 (1979): 531–52.

Snyder, Francis. *Capitalism and Legal Change in Senegal*. New York: Academic Press, 1981.

Sollors, Werner, ed. *The Invention of Ethnicity*. New York: Oxford, 1988.

Special Issue: Access, Control, and Use of Resources in African Agriculture. *Africa* 59, no. 1 (1989).

Stevens, Philip, Jr. "Bachama Joking Categories: Toward New Perspectives in the Study of Joking Relationships." *Journal of Anthropological Research* 34 (1978): 47–71.

Stewart, Charles, and Rosalind Shaw. *Syncretism/Anti-Syncretism: The Politics of Religious Synthesis*. London: Routledge, 1994.

Suret-Canale, Jean. *French Colonialism in Tropical Africa, 1900–1945*. Paris: Éditions Sociales, 1964. Reprint, London: C. Hurst and Company, 1971.

Tamari, Tal. "Les castes au Soudan occidental: Étude anthropologique et historique." Thèse de Doctorat, Université de Paris X, 1987.

_____. "The Development of Caste Systems in West Africa." *Journal of African History* 32, no. 2 (1991): 221–50.

Tilly, Charles. "Reflection on the History of European State-Making." In *The Formation of National States in Western Europe*, ed. Charles Tilly. Princeton: Princeton University Press, 1975.

Tomlinson, John. *Globalization and Culture*. Chicago: University of Chicago Press, 1999.

Unger, Roberto. *Law in Modern Society*. New York: Free Press, 1978.

Vaillant, Janet G. *Black, French, and African: A Life of Leopold Sedar Senghor*. Cambridge: Harvard University Press, 1990.

_____. "The Problem of Culture in French West Africa: 'S'assimiler pas être assimilés.' " Paper presented at Colloque "L'Afrique Occidentale Française: Esquisse d'une intégration africaine?" Dakar, 16–23 June 1995.

Van Beek, Walter E. A. "Dogon Restudied: A Field Evaluation of the Work of Marcel Griaule." *Current Anthropology* 32, no. 2 (1992).

Van de Walle, Nicolas. *African Economics and the Politics of Permanent Crisis*. New York: Cambridge University Press, 2001.

Vengroff, Richard, and Alan Johnston. *Decentralization and the Implementation of Rural Development in Senegal*. Lewiston, N.Y.: Edwin Mellen Press, 1989.

Verba, Sidney. "Conclusion: Comparative Political Culture." In *Political Culture and Political Development,* ed. Lucian W. Pye and Sidney Verba. Princeton: Princeton University Press, 1965.

Villalón, Leonardo. *Islamic Society and State Power in Senegal: Disciples and Citizens in Fatick.* New York: Cambridge University Press, 1995.

Watts, Michael. "Capitalisms, Crises, and Cultures I: Toward a Totality of Fragments." In *Reworking Modernity: Capitalisms and Symbolic Discontent,* ed. Michael Watts and Alan Pred. New Brunswick: Rutgers, 1992.

——. "The Shock of Modernity: Petroleum, Protest, and Fast Capitalism in an Industrializing Society." In *Reworking Modernity: Capitalisms and Symbolic Discontent,* ed. Michael Watts and Alan Pred. New Brunswick: Rutgers, 1992.

Watts, Michael, and Alan Pred. *Reworking Modernity: Capitalisms and Symbolic Discontent.* New Brunswick: Rutgers, 1992.

Weber, Max. *The Protestant Ethic and the Spirit of Capitalism.* Trans. from the German by Talcott Parsons. New York: Scribner's, 1958.

Whitaker, C. Sylvester. "A Dysrhythmic Process of Political Change." *World Politics* 19, no. 2 (January 1967): 190–217.

White, Louise K. *Speaking with Vampires: Rumor and History in Colonial Africa.* Berkeley: University of California Press, 2000.

World Bank. *Accelerated Development in Sub-Saharan Africa: An Agenda for Action ("Berg Report").* Washington, D.C.: World Bank, 1981.

Yeostros, Janine. "The Bread from Dakar Is Better." Dakar: ENDA, 1990.

Young, Crawford. *The African Colonial State in Comparative Perspective.* New Haven: Yale University Press, 1994.

Young, Crawford, ed. *The Rising Tide of Cultural Pluralism: The Nation-State at Bay?* Madison: University of Wisconsin Press, 1994.

Index